Improving Quality and Productivity in the Logistics Process

Achieving Customer Satisfaction Breakthroughs

COUNCIL OF LOGISTICS MANAGEMENT

 **Printed on Recycled Paper**

Improving Quality and Productivity in the Logistics Process

Achieving Customer Satisfaction Breakthroughs

by
Patrick M. Byrne
William J. Markham
of
A.T. Kearney, Inc.
222 S. Riverside Plaza
Chicago, Illinois 60606
(312) 648-0111

for the COUNCIL OF LOGISTICS MANAGEMENT

TABLE OF CONTENTS

continued on next page

Table of Contents, continued

INTRODUCTION

Improving Quality and Productivity in the Logistics Process — Achieving Customer Satisfaction Breakthroughs is the third in a series of research studies sponsored by the Council of Logistics Management (CLM) and conducted by A.T. Kearney, Inc., a global management consulting firm.

The first research effort, undertaken in 1978, surveyed various approaches U.S. industry used to measure productivity in physical distribution. It was sponsored by the National Council of Physical Distribution Management, or NCPDM, the former name of the Council of Logistics Management. That research produced a book entitled *Measuring Productivity in Physical Distribution: The $40 Billion Gold Mine.* It offered distribution managers a framework for thinking about productivity measurement and a "how-to" reference guide to developing and implementing such measures.

The years immediately following 1978 brought major changes in the business environment, notably transportation deregulation, oil shortages, recession, and a technological revolution. These developments affected the way in which companies managed physical distribution thereby altering its role in business.

Transportation deregulation offered an array of new freedoms and challenges. Uncertainty about oil prices and availability sent shock waves through the economy. Interest rates peaked at the highest level in recent history. A worldwide recession brought about basic structural changes in various industries. And emerging computer technology made data capture and analysis available and affordable to users — including distribution management.

These changes opened a window of opportunity for companies to make major improvements in physical distribution productivity. As a result, NCPDM in 1983 commissioned A.T. Kearney to update and expand the earlier research with the focus on improving productivity. The 1983 project had three goals: to measure U.S. industry's progress in improving distribution productivity against the 1978 findings, to assess the impact such environmental changes had on productivity improvement since 1978, and to map out paths for further improvement.

That research produced a second book, released in 1984, entitled *Measuring and Improving Productivity in Physical Distribution: The Successful Companies.* In brief, the second study found that those companies that successfully bolstered productivity did so by using an improvement process containing seven common characteristics. These "successful companies":

- **Managed the process of change** with the same attention they used in managing day to day operations

- **Employed a project orientation** to implement change

- **Achieved early success** and built more ambitious programs as they gained experience and support

- **Focused on real productivity improvement** rather than cost reduction

- **Communicated upward,** laterally, and downward in order to publicize success and share credit

- **Spearheaded the program with a leader** who acted as its motivating force

- **Capitalized on "triggers"** — major changes that affected the corporation and created a fertile environment for improvement

Both the 1978 and 1983 study books have become standard references for logistics executives worldwide.

THE SHIFT IN EMPHASIS

The years since 1983 brought even more change, further focusing attention on logistics as a *process* rather than a series of individual activities such as warehousing, transportation, and inventory management. Heightened global competition forced companies to consider worldwide alternatives for sourcing, manufacturing, distributing, and selling their products. Foreign competitors raised customer expectations for quality, causing many firms to adopt a "Total Quality" focus. Cycle times collapsed for product manufacture and distribution as well as for new product introduction. Information technology in the areas of data capture, communications, processing, and analysis continued to explode.

In the tougher competitive environment, relying solely on product attributes as a means of attracting and retaining customers was insufficient. Customer service, therefore, assumed greater importance for many firms, becoming a weapon for gaining competitive advantage. Companies developed strategic alliances with customers and suppliers in order to align resources and harmonize operations more effectively. Third-party logistics service providers emerged as alternatives for in-house transportation, warehousing, and inventory management functions.

Company merger and acquisition activity accelerated through the 1980s, remaining strong even after the stock market crash of 1987. In many cases, integrating the logistics processes of two merged companies was a key factor for the ultimate success of the deal.

Management attitudes toward employees changed during these years. Many companies found that employee empowerment or, more appropriately, employee "ownership" of an improvement process was the key to ongoing improvement.

Finally, during the 1980s, the logistics concept — managing sourcing/purchasing, materials management, and physical distribution as a single business process — gained broader acceptance throughout industry. To reflect this attitude, NCPDM changed its name to the Council of Logistics Management.

THE 1991 UPDATE

In 1990, the Council of Logistics Management commissioned A.T. Kearney to update the 1978 and 1983 productivity studies. The emphasis of this third report reflects an expanded scope that includes not just productivity but the quality dimension of logistics as well. The update aims to:

• Understand the changes that have taken place since 1983 and how they will affect business in the 1990s

• Anticipate the effect of current issues and trends on logistics management

• Identify the best and most successful practices in quality and productivity improvement in the logistics process

• Articulate the role of the logistics process in successful companies in the 1990s

The 1991 study looks at the entire logistics process — all activities involved in movement and storage of goods from source to final consumer, the information flows supporting these operations, and the management process involved in achieving the required levels of customer service. Figure 1 depicts the logistics process.

Because the 1978 and 1983 studies emphasized productivity improvement, they focused primarily on cost reduction opportunities in logistics. The 1991 research investigates the quality dimension as well. In so doing, it points out the impact improved service quality has on customer satisfaction, revenue, and market share.

Figure 1

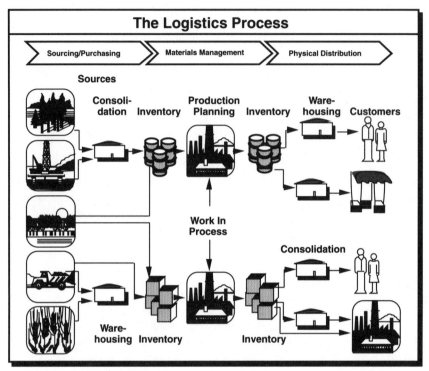

The 1991 study differs from its predecessors in another way. Quality improvement, unlike productivity improvement, requires a business process focus. It transcends functional, and often company, boundaries. The essence of quality improvement is understanding and satisfying customers' needs. Thus, this study explores how companies work with customers to carry out quality improvement.

By focusing on the logistics process, we expand the traditional physical distribution view of a company looking downstream at its customers to include upstream interfaces as well. To an outside supplier, for example, a company's purchasing function is the customer. Reviewing how leading-edge purchasing functions deal with suppliers on quality issues, therefore, offers valuable insights on quality.

We also study the supplier-customer relationships between corporate functions. Purchasing is a supplier to its customer — the manufacturing department. Sales is a supplier to its customers — the demand forecasting and order management departments. And manufacturing is a supplier to its customer — the distribution department. To meet the needs of the external customer (the one that generates revenue), each internal supplier must satisfy its downstream customer.

APPROACH TO THE RESEARCH

We conducted the research for this project over a nine-month period. Initially, a focus group of approximately 25 logistics executives helped define what quality and productivity mean in today's logistics environment. In early 1991, we distributed three survey questionnaires designed to gather statistical data on quality and productivity-improvement processes. We sent the first of these surveys (the Logistics Management Survey) to manufacturers, distributors, and retailers asking them questions about both internal and external quality and productivity-improvement initiatives.

With the second survey (the Customer Expectations Survey), we targeted key customers of these manufacturers and distributors inquiring about their service requirements and expectations. We used these responses to evaluate the match between the supplier's perception of customer requirements and the true customer expectations. Lastly, we directed the third (Logistics Service Provider) survey at companies such as transportation firms, public warehouses, and others who provide third-party logistics services. We focused this service provider survey on both internal quality and productivity-improvement initiatives as well as on joint initiatives with customers.

While the statistical data from these surveys provided a wealth of information about quality and productivity improvement, data alone do not paint a complete picture. To get the "story behind the story," we conducted personal interviews with 57 companies recognized as leaders in logistics quality and productivity improvement. These interviews explored:

• Background and major elements of their improvement processes

• Approaches to customer service goal setting

• Success stories in quality and productivity improvement

• Prerequisites for success

• Advice for others

We supported our primary research by extensive secondary research into quality, productivity improvement, and customer service. Finally, we documented the results of our research in this book.

THE SCOPE OF QUALITY IN THIS BOOK

Our secondary research found dozens of books and hundreds of articles on the subject of quality improvement. Much of this material addresses product quality. Certainly, product quality is a major component of overall customer satisfaction, but it is just part of the picture. Customer service quality is emerging as an equally popular topic in the consumer and business press as well as in research communities. Companies such as American Express, L. L. Bean, Nordstrom's, Disney, and McDonald's receive regular accolades as leaders in customer service quality.

It is interesting to note that most of these service leaders do business directly with the consumer. Far fewer companies receive recognition as service leaders if their customer is another manufacturer, a distributor, or a retailer. Customer service research and reporting, therefore, deals largely with pleasing the consumer, the ultimate user of goods and services. It offers few examples of how to improve the quality of business to business service throughout the entire chain from raw materials source to final consumer. We hope our research and this book help begin to fill this gap.

Because the scope of this research is logistics, we focus primarily on improving customer satisfaction through the quality and productivity of the order-fulfillment process (order placement, delivery, order receipt, and follow-up). We explore this subject from the viewpoints of the supplier and customer, also looking at the internal processes required to support these activities (e.g., procurement, forecasting, production planning, inventory management, warehousing management, transportation management).

We recognize that the customer satisfaction process goes beyond order fulfillment to include product characteristics, price levels, salesforce and technical support, post-sales support, and even the quality-improvement process the supplier has in place. Thus, Section III of this book discusses both the broad area of overall service as well as the logistics-focused order-fulfillment process.

STRUCTURE OF THE BOOK

This book has two missions. First, it aims to help companies create value for their customers and stockholders through logistics excellence. Second, it tries to help logistics executives achieve excellence by improving quality and productivity throughout the logistics process.

This book is divided into six major sections, with chapters in each, as shown in Figure 2. It also includes several supporting appendixes.

Section I, "The Process of Creating Value," focuses on creating value for customers and stockholders. Chapter 1 discusses value creation and its role in sustaining competitive advantage. Chapter 2 explores how companies create value through formal improvement processes such as Total Quality Management (TQM) and Total Customer Satisfaction (TCS).

Section II, "Creating Value Through Logistics Excellence," describes the key role of the logistics process in creating customer and stockholder value. Chapter 3 explores the role of logistics as a key business process and explains how that process will evolve during the 1990s. Chapter 4 describes what logistics excellence means and discusses its benefits.

Figure 2

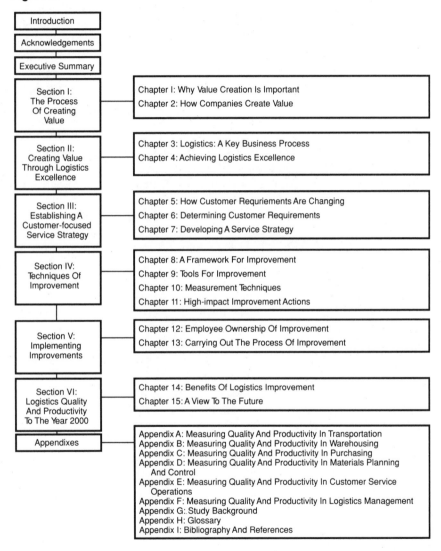

Section III, "Establishing a Customer-Focused Service Strategy," shifts the emphasis to the executional issue of *achieving* logistics excellence. Chapter 5 discusses the changing nature of customer requirements, addressing how customers evaluate suppliers. Chapter 6 analyzes various methods for determining what customers require and expect from suppliers. And Chapter 7 offers suggestions on structuring a service strategy, offerings, and goals to respond to these requirements. These form the service quality expectations against which logistics excellence is measured.

Section IV, "Techniques of Improvement," discusses the tools and techniques companies use to measure and improve logistics quality and productivity. Chapter 8 presents a general framework for improvement. Chapter 9 explores specific improvement tools, including process analysis, benchmarking, and statistical analysis. Chapter 10 discusses techniques for measuring logistics service quality and productivity and provides suggestions on measurement systems design. Chapter 11 addresses high-impact improvement actions identified during our research.

Section V, "Implementing Improvements," describes how companies manage the process of improvement. Chapter 12 discusses how to create employee ownership of the improvement process, including training, motivation, rewards, and recognition. Chapter 13 suggests a framework for selecting the right improvement actions. It also examines approaches for companies just starting out with an improvement process and approaches for those with existing processes that need help maintaining momentum.

Section VI, "Logistics Quality and Productivity to the Year 2000," summarizes the research and looks to the future. Chapter 14 discusses quality and productivity-improvement results to date and expectations for the next five years as reported by survey respondents. Chapter 15 looks ahead to the next five to ten years, offering views on how companies can expand quality and productivity improvement with their partners up and down the entire logistics channel to meet the needs of the ultimate customer — the consumer.

Appendixes A through F offer potential quality and productivity measures and potential improvement actions for key elements of the logistics process. Appendix G provides additional background information on the approach used in this research. Appendix H supplies a glossary of terms, while Appendix I provides a bibliography and references.

ACKNOWLEDGEMENTS

The authors would like to acknowledge the many significant contributions that made this study possible.

More than 400 executives took the time to complete the study's survey questionnaires describing their companies's logistics processes and their quality and productivity-improvement experiences. An additional 57 management teams shared with us, through personal interviews, their experiences and insights into the quality and productivity-improvement process. Many of the specific examples contained in this book came from their experiences.

Throughout the effort, the authors worked closely with the Council of Logistics Management Steering Committee chaired by Jim Keebler of Hill's Pet Products and including Bob Bowles of PPG Industries, Inc., Kathleen Strange of The Stride Rite Corporation, and Maria McIntyre of the Council's staff.

The Kearney project team for this study included Pat Byrne, Bill Markham, Sheila Dubin, Larry Kohn, Jim Krasner, Francine Levy, Mike Lipman, Pat Malloy, Meena Mansharamani, Knut Meyer, Rich Miskewicz, Mike Moriarty, Gary Plazyk, Ron Sanderson, Walter Strauss, and Chuck Wiza. A special thanks is due to those who took the time to review and provide input to this manuscript: Bob Camp of Xerox Corporation, Bob Delaney of Cass Logistics, Inc., Mike Frankenberger of Xerox Corporation, Bud LaLonde of Ohio State University, John Langley of the University of Tennessee, George Gecowets of the Council of Logistics Management, and Bram Bluestein, Mary Lynn Coyle, Jack Davoust, Brian Harrison, Paul Inglis, Jim Morehouse, Joe Romano, Ron Seger, and Manfred Tuerks of A.T. Kearney. Also, we are grateful for the editorial input of Lisa Harrington of Harrington Associates and Janice Brauer of A.T. Kearney.

A.T. Kearney and the Council of Logistics Management would like to thank the logistics executives from the 57 companies who gave so much of their time to explain the process of successful quality and productivity improvement in their companies. Although some companies that were interviewed have chosen to remain anonymous, the following have allowed A.T. Kearney and the Council to publicly acknowledge their contributions to the study.

Interview Participants	

• American Airlines, Inc.
• Apple Computer, Inc.
• Bausch & Lomb
• Baxter Healthcare Corporation –
  Distribution Division
• Burlington Motor Carriers
• CF Motor Freight
• Chesebrough-Pond's, Inc.
• Corn Products – A Unit of CPC
  International, Inc.
• The Dannon Company, Inc.
• Dow Chemical USA
• Dry Storage Corporation
• Eastman Kodak Company
• Esprit de Corp
• Exel Logistics – DCI
• Federal Express Corporation
• Ford Motor Company
• Fritz Companies Inc.
• W.W. Grainger, Inc.
• Hewlett-Packard Company
• Hill's Pet Products, Inc.
• J.B. Hunt Transport, Inc.
• Johnson & Johnson, Hospital
  Services Division
• Keebler Company
• Kraft General Foods U.S.A.
	• Maytag Corporation
	• The Mead Corporation
	• Menlo Logistics
	• Milliken and Company
	• Motorola, Inc.
	• Nabisco Brands, Inc.
	• Nalco Chemical Company
	• National Starch & Chemical Company
	• Pfizer, Inc.
	• PPG Industries, Inc.
	• Procter & Gamble Company
	• Preston Trucking Company, Inc.
	• The Quaker Oats Company
	• Rohm & Haas Company
	• Sandoz Chemical Corporation
	• Sara Lee Bakery – Sara Lee Corp.
	• Schneider National, Inc.
	• Scott Paper Company
	• The Stride Rite Corporation
	• Sylvania Lighting – GTE Products Corp.
	• Target Stores
	• Texas Instruments, Inc.
	• Trammell Crow Distribution Company
	• United Parcel Service of America, Inc.
	• Wang Laboratories, Inc.
	• Westinghouse Electric Corporation
	• Xerox Corporation
	• Yellow Freight System, Inc.

EXECUTIVE SUMMARY

STUDY OVERVIEW

We often hear of companies striving to be *customer focused.* They want to be known as *quality leaders.* They seek *world-class status.* They recognize that to accomplish these ends they must think *globally and empower employees.*

But because so many companies have adopted similar sounding statements of mission, goals, and values, mere words will not differentiate a company in the marketplace. Instead, the deciding factor will be the company's ability to **execute the key business processes** that deliver the customer value and quality that the words promise. One such business process is logistics.

An effective logistics process is essential to satisfy customers and to gain competitive advantage. Improving the **service quality** that the logistics process provides increases customer satisfaction and builds customer loyalty. These in turn lead to market share and margin increases. At the same time, focusing on **true customer needs** eliminates cost for services not valued. Improving the **productivity** of the logistics process also reduces cost. Together these actions help make products and services more attractive in the marketplace.

The Council of Logistics Management engaged A.T. Kearney to investigate and analyze how companies improve quality and productivity in logistics. The research resulted in this report, *Improving Quality and Productivity in the Logistics Process — Achieving Customer Satisfaction Breakthroughs.* This 1991 research study updates and expands two previous studies by A.T. Kearney for the Council in 1978 and 1983 dealing with productivity improvement.

Some companies have already had major successes in improving logistics quality and productivity. Others are early in the process but have some results to report. Still others have not yet begun. This study explores the reasons behind the successes and offers suggestions for beginning and sustaining a process of quality and productivity improvement in logistics.

DEFINITIONS

We define quality and productivity in the logistics process as follows:

Quality in logistics means meeting agreed-to customer requirements and expectations, including the following dimensions:

- Ease of inquiry, order placement, and order transmission
- Timely, reliable order delivery and communications
- Accurate, complete, undamaged orders and error-free paperwork
- Timely and responsive post-sales support
- Accurate, timely generation and transmission of information among the functions of the business and with external parties to support the planning, management, and execution of the above activities

Productivity in logistics means using the combined resources of all participants in the supply chain in the most efficient way to provide high quality, cost effective customer service.

These definitions reflect a customer satisfaction orientation. First, companies must ensure that they provide customers with required levels of service ("do the right things"). Then, they should seek ways to improve efficiency ("do things right").

MAJOR STUDY FINDINGS

1. **Companies that have had major successes in quality and productivity improvement share common characteristics.** Companies such as Motorola, Xerox, Hewlett-Packard, Milliken, Federal Express, Dow, Texas Instruments, and IBM have led the quality movement in the United States during the 1980s. To be successful, these leaders believe that quality improvement must be a companywide effort working with both customers and suppliers.

In most companies with successful quality-improvement processes, the Chief Executive Officer is the driving force. This commitment to quality improvement means a basic restructuring of how the business is run. It requires a culture change that shifts the focus *outward* towards the customer. It means a commitment to continuous improvement that transcends month to month budget performance. And it means a shift in management orientation. To realize full benefits, functional "silos" must give way to cross-functional business processes.

The CEO typically is the only executive properly positioned to challenge and overturn the deep-rooted traditions, assumptions, and measurement/reward systems that impede change. And CEOs often act at "trigger points" — events in the life of a company that let it suspend the traditional rules and support these kinds of breakthrough changes.

We found several common characteristics of the improvement processes used by successful companies:

- They focus strategically on increasing the value customers receive from doing business with them.

- They have adopted a Total Customer Satisfaction (TCS) marketing strategy and a Total Quality Management (TQM) philosophy.

- Their senior managements are totally committed to quality improvement and the corporate culture and style of management that it requires.

- They believe that quality improvement must encompass both product and service quality.

- Their product and service strategies are driven by a deep understanding of customer requirements.

- They use a structured approach towards improvement, including process analysis, statistical analysis, and multidiscipline improvement teams.

- Their employees take "ownership" for improvements (i.e., they take primary responsibility for identifying and acting on improvements).

- They support employees with major commitments to training and to rewards and recognition for tangible accomplishments.

- They actively involve suppliers and customers as partners in quality improvement initiatives.

- They have realistic expectations about the magnitude of the commitment and degree of change involved.

2. Within leading quality companies, logistics quality and productivity improvement is integral to overall improvement. Leading companies recognize the role of logistics in executing a customer-focused service strategy. They recognize that the logistics process weaves together all of the major operational functions of the business in order to meet customer requirements. They use the logistics process to integrate suppliers and service providers as partners in the effort. And they extend the logistics process to include customers as full partners in the process.

3. Despite the publicity that quality improvement has received, most

surveyed companies only recently began the process of improvement. Two-thirds of the companies in our survey indicate that they have a formal process in place to improve quality and productivity. However, of this two-thirds, 25 percent began since 1989, and an additional 50 percent began between 1987 and 1989. Most of these efforts began in the product quality area, often driven by their customers' own quality-improvement processes. Emphasis on service quality lags somewhat, with only 55 percent of the respondents extending the improvement process to logistics so far.

This means that 45 percent of the surveyed companies are already at a disadvantage if they compete on customer service. If they do not act soon, they may fall so far behind that they can never recover.

4. **Most companies have not yet established a foundation of logistics excellence to support a customer satisfaction strategy.** The logistics process is at the heart of executing a customer satisfaction strategy. Thus, we evaluated how ready the survey respondents were to support such a strategy. We defined eight dimensions of logistics excellence that measured:

- How thoroughly the company seeks to understand customer requirements and how effectively it translates the requirements into customer service goals

- How completely the long-range logistics planning effort considers the entire logistics process (including interfunctional planning and supplier-company-customer planning)

- How effectively the company carries out tactical (e.g., month to month) operations planning

- How committed the company is to ongoing improvement of the logistics process

- How effectively the company uses information technology to unite the participants in the logistics process and to support improvements

- How well employees and management work together as a team to carry out improvements

- How closely the company works with suppliers and service providers to improve the overall logistics process

- How effectively the company uses measures of progress and results to guide action

We found that only 10 percent of the respondents are "excellent" in logistics (what we term Stage III). These companies have the logistics infrastructure needed to support a customer satisfaction strategy. The majority (77 percent) were categorized as Stage II. These have one or more major weaknesses that may jeopardize such a service based strategy. Thirteen percent fell into Stage I. Weaknesses in logistics at these companies run so deep that they are fundamentally unable to support a customer-focused service strategy.

5. "Gaps" between suppliers and customers inhibit quality improvement in logistics for many companies. Our survey found that many suppliers don't understand the customer's service requirements well enough. Instead of asking the customer directly, they rely too heavily on salesforce input, competitors' service levels, or customer complaint levels. The customers we surveyed believe that this lack of understanding is a significant impediment to service quality improvement.

We also found that many suppliers rely on internally focused measures of service rather than measuring themselves from the customer's viewpoint. Rarely do they look for feedback from customers or provide feedback to customers on service performance.

Closing these gaps is critical to success. Customers continue to be more demanding of suppliers because their own downstream customers are increasing demands on them. Unless a company constantly updates its understanding of customer requirements and how well it is performing against those requirements, it will be left behind by global competition.

6. Future improvements in logistics will come from nontraditional areas. Traditionally, improvements to logistics performance have been measured in terms of cost reduction or productivity gains. The primary sources of these kinds of improvements were transportation and warehousing. We found that companies will be relying less on these traditional "gold mines" in the future.

Instead, they will look to purchasing, materials planning and control, and information systems as sources for future productivity gains from logistics. Benefits will come in the form of reduced inventories, more efficient production, more effective purchasing, fewer errors, more streamlined and accurate information flow, and less duplication and wasted effort.

Compared with transportation and warehousing, these emerging opportunities require even greater cross-functional and cross-company coordination and cooperation. Integration of the total logistics process will be the key to productivity gains in these areas.

More importantly, however, many companies are looking beyond costs and productivity levels to evaluate the performance of the entire logistics process. They are shifting emphasis to cycle time improvement and to service improvement. The results reported by the survey respondents so far are impressive.

For example, the average company surveyed reports order cycle time reductions of 30 percent over the past five years and expects to cut order cycles nearly in half from 1985 to 1995. Similar reductions were reported for inventory replenishment cycles.

On the service side, actual on-time delivery performance in 1985 averaged 81 percent across the companies we surveyed. Today, it averages 92 percent, and 97 percent is what respondents expect to achieve by 1995. In 1985, the percent of orders received damage-free averaged 92 percent. Today, it is 95 percent, and the average goal for 1995 is 97 percent. Similar improvements were reported for order completeness, line-item fill rate, and invoice accuracy.

These service gains are impressive. But when measured in terms of service failures, there is still much room for improvement. Even by 1995, the average service failure rate on the best of the five measures (invoice accuracy) will be 21,000 inaccurate invoices per million. By contrast, the "Six Sigma" quality requirement pioneered by Motorola would call for no more than 3.4 inaccurate invoices per million.

HOW THE REPORT CAN HELP

The study report provides guidance to executives on how to begin and sustain a quality and productivity-improvement process in their organizations. It provides a framework for developing an improvement process along with explanations about how to use various analytical techniques.

The study report also identifies a wide range of actions that companies can take to improve logistics quality and productivity. Among these are what we call "high-impact" actions, those that respondents believe provided them with the greatest bang for the buck.

The survey respondents identified 61 specific high-impact actions that produced major quality and/or productivity benefits for them covering:

• Customer service operations

• Order management

• Transportation strategy

• Transportation operations

• Transportation fleet management

• Warehousing methods and equipment

• Warehousing employee management

• Public warehousing

• Materials planning and control

- Sourcing

- Purchasing/buying

We found that selecting the "right" improvement actions for any one company depends on its capabilities, strengths, and weaknesses both internally and in the marketplace. The study report offers suggestions for determining what is right for specific situations.

To aid the more advanced companies, we explore how study participants are using logistics to gain competitive advantage. Through our interviews, we learned how leading companies were applying high-impact actions to support a customer-focused service strategy by fundamentally re-engineering the logistics process. The breakthrough initiatives that we examine in the report include:

- Developing flexible, tailored customer satisfaction strategies using the logistics process as a foundation

- "Failsafing" the logistics process (i.e., reducing the likelihood of a service quality failure)

- Reducing cycle times for orders and inventory replenishment by two-thirds or more

- Integrating the logistics process within their companies by

  — Coordinating strategies for marketing, sales, procurement, manufacturing, and distribution

  — Balancing demand with production and inventory plans to meet customer requirements

  — Using information to better plan and control day to day operations

- Developing shipper-carrier partnerships to help attain customer service goals and improve productivity

- Creating supplier-customer partnerships that produce major improvements in quality, productivity, and cycle time

THE BENEFITS OF AN IMPROVEMENT PROCESS

We asked respondents to report improvements to logistics service, cycle time, and productivity that they actually achieved from 1985 to 1990 and that they planned for 1991 to 1995. Table 1 and Table 2 present tangible results so far for these three dimensions and project the expected improvement over the ten-year timeframe.

Table 1

Logistics Service Level Improvements (Service Failures Per Million Occurrences)				
	Survey Average		Most Successful Companies	
Service Dimension	1990 Actual	1995 Goal	1990 Actual	1995 Goal
■ On-time delivery	84,000	30,000	10,000	1,000
■ Order completeness	104,000	50,000	41,000	10,000
■ Invoice accuracy	57,000	21,000	10,000	0

Table 2

Logistics Cycle Time And Productivity Improvements				
	Survey Average		Most Successful Companies	
Area	Five Year Actual [1]	Ten Year Expected [2]	Five Year Actual [1]	Ten Year Expected [2]
■ Order cycle time reduction	30%	49%	67%	90%
■ Logistics productivity improvement	10%	21%	22%	37%

Notes: (1) 1985-1990 actual
(2) 1985-1990 actual plus 1990-1995 projected

Clearly, the average company has realized significant results from improvements in logistics and expects similar gains in the future. But a company that just improves by the average amount doesn't differentiate itself and doesn't gain competitive advantage.

Some companies reported results that greatly exceed the average. These "most successful" companies use their logistics processes as competitive service weapons. As a result, they have achieved competitive advantages including:

• Improved service reliability that helps to increase long-term customer satisfaction, customer loyalty, revenues, and profit

• More responsive order fulfillment that helps them and their customers to:

— Bring the right quantities of the right products to market quicker

— Cut inventories dramatically

• A more efficient logistics process, which generates cost savings that can be used to support marketing and pricing strategies and to finance future process improvements

NOTES ON THE RESEARCH

The research included detailed survey questionnaire responses from over 400 U.S. based companies. Three survey documents were used:

- A Logistics Management Survey, directed at manufacturers, distributors, and retailers, covering quality and productivity-improvement approaches and results

- A Customer Expectations Survey, used to evaluate how well the customer's expectations for service matched with the supplier's perceptions of those requirements

- A Logistics Service Provider Survey, directed at carriers, public warehouse operators, and other third parties, focusing on their approaches to improvement

The statistical data were supported by a series of 57 personal interviews with leading companies in quality and productivity improvement. Topics included:

- Background and major elements of their improvement processes

- Approaches to service goal setting

- Success stories/high-impact actions

- Advice for others:

  — Prerequisites for success

  — How to get a process started

  — How to maintain momentum

THE PROCESS OF CREATING VALUE

Improvements to quality and productivity, whether in the logistics process or other areas of the business, are means to an end. Ultimately, the measure of a company's success is its ability to sustain a long-term competitive advantage by providing superior value to customers and shareholders.

In this section, we consider the process of value creation and how companies adopt and use processes for improvement to increase customer and shareholder value.

CHAPTER 1

WHY VALUE CREATION
IS IMPORTANT

In 1989, A.T. Kearney conducted a major research project exploring the competitiveness of U.S. manufacturing companies in a global economy.[1] The research report covered about 2,000 U.S. manufacturing companies, representing a broad range of industry perspectives. The survey highlighted perspectives from 200 Chief Executive Officers on key issues U.S. manufacturers would face in the 1990s and identified the directions these companies needed to pursue to gain and sustain competitive advantage.

According to these executives, their companies find it increasingly difficult to achieve competitive advantage through a product based strategy. Consequently, they expect management emphasis in the '90s to concentrate on creating customer value — integrating the mutual interests of customers and suppliers.

The survey asked the executives to rank the top factors that create value for customers in the 1990s. They rated customer service first followed by marketing, a focus on the quality processes by their total organizations, and finished product quality.

As Figure 1-1 shows, this emphasis on customer value is part of a continuing evolution of management focus over the last 50 years. In the 1950s, the emphasis was on production — converting war-time production capacity to meet the needs of a peace-time economy. In the 1960s, the emphasis shifted to marketing to take advantage of the production capacity made available in the previous decade. During the following decade, companies focused on business strategy as management struggled with choosing the right businesses and markets to pursue. By the 1980s, the emphasis shifted to product quality prompted by fierce international competition in industries previously untouched by foreign competition — steel, automobiles, consumer electronics, textiles, shoes, and computer technology.

As the 1990s get under way, management of leading-edge companies is rewriting the scope of quality improvement to cover the bundle of products and services that create value for the customer.

Figure 1-1

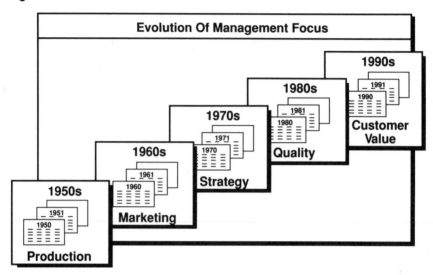

THE VALUE CREATION OBJECTIVE

Companies create value for customers in two ways: by meeting customer requirements and by exceeding customer expectations (often by providing better value for the price).

Creating superior value for customers is not enough, however. Companies have to create value for their shareholders as well. As Figure 1-2 illustrates, they have to create value for the customer in such a way that shareholders realize profits and returns on their investment. In other words, they must be productive while providing the quality customers require.

Still, creating value for customers is the key to generating value for shareholders. Customers are the major asset of a business, generating an ongoing stream of revenues and providing a source of new business through referrals and references. Dissatisfied customers cost businesses dearly. At the very least, the cost to replace the lost revenue from dissatisfied customers (that is, to find new customers) is very high, often consuming the first year's profits on this business. What is worse, dissatisfied customers tend to be vocal about their dissatisfaction, making it even more difficult to attract new customers to take their place.

If companies satisfy customers over the long term, however, they can enlarge share, widen margins, improve efficiency, and ultimately increase shareholder value.

Figure 1-2

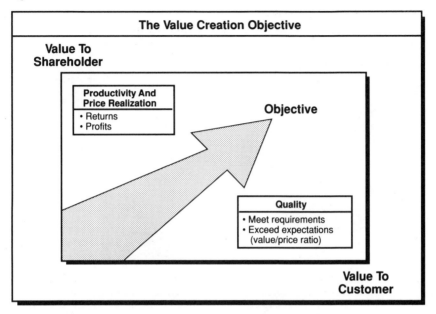

THE BURDEN OF POOR QUALITY

If quality creates value for the customer, the lack of quality reduces value for the customer — and for the shareholders. In his book *Quality Without Tears*,[2] Philip Crosby sets out four basic beliefs about quality:

• Quality is conformance to requirements, not goodness.

• Companies achieve quality by prevention, not appraisal.

• The performance standard for quality is zero defects, not acceptable quality levels.

• Quality is measured by the price of nonconformance, not by indexes.

Crosby's last point is key. It asserts the true measure of quality is the cost associated with failing to conform to requirements. This cost directly reduces customer and shareholder value.

Different authors estimate this cost of quality (or, more appropriately, the cost of not providing quality) at 20 to 25 percent of sales in a typical manufacturing setting. In a service company, the cost of quality can approach 40 percent of operating costs. When the *Fortune* 500 average pre-tax profit margin is only about 6 percent, it's easy to see how reducing the cost of quality by even a modest amount can improve value for shareholders and customers alike.

Figure 1-3 illustrates the elements comprising the cost of quality for a typical company. In this example, the company spends:

Figure 1-3

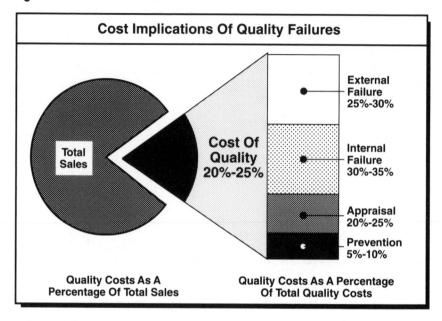

Cost Implications Of Quality Failures

Total Sales

Cost Of Quality 20%-25%

External Failure 25%-30%

Internal Failure 30%-35%

Appraisal 20%-25%

Prevention 5%-10%

Quality Costs As A Percentage Of Total Sales

Quality Costs As A Percentage Of Total Quality Costs

- $0.16 of every sales dollar correcting quality problems caused by external and internal failures (both before and after the customer experiences the problems)

- $0.06 determining if a mistake occurred by using some type of appraisal process (e.g., inspecting and/or tracking down the problem)

- $0.03 preventing mistakes (changing the process to remove recurring causes)

Of these expenditures, only the $0.03 spent averting errors adds value for either customers or shareholders. The remaining costs constitute waste.

THE CHALLENGE

Based on these figures, companies face a major challenge in the coming decade. They must learn how to create customer and shareholder value in the face of the drain on value creation that the cost of quality represents. Chapter II explores how some companies are meeting this challenge.

---

[1] A.T. Kearney, Inc., "U.S. Manufacturing Competitiveness"
[2] Crosby, Philip B., *Quality Without Tears, The Art of Hassle Free Management*

CHAPTER 2

HOW COMPANIES CREATE VALUE

Creating value is not a new concept. Since the early part of the 20th century, companies have increased shareholder value through productivity improvement. In logistics, this translated into increasing the number of orders picked per labor hour, miles traveled per gallon of fuel, or deliveries made per day.

PRODUCTIVITY: THE HISTORICAL FOCAL POINT

Historically, firms pursued productivity increases independently of quality improvement. Indeed, the 1978 and 1983 logistics productivity-improvement research studies found little evidence of quality improvement as an issue of concern. They also noted that customer service improvement received relatively less management attention than did productivity improvement.

In recent decades, U.S. companies made major strides in improving productivity in all parts of their operations. The two prior logistics productivity research studies found the best companies improved logistics productivity by more than 50 percent over a ten-year period.

This primary focus on productivity improvement, however, assumed that companies already knew what their customers wanted, were meeting their needs successfully, and simply needed to find a way to provide service more efficiently. In essence, by focusing on productivity improvement first, management assumes the company's output is of value to the customer. This may not be the case. In several cases, so-called productivity gains actually decreased the company's or product's value to the customer. For example, one company decided it could boost productivity by increasing the number of calls per hour that customer service representatives handled. The firm achieved this so-called productivity goal but in so doing compromised customer service and satisfaction. Customers couldn't get their questions answered or problems resolved.

Another firm — a distributor — overhauled its distribution center to improve productivity. By automating extensively and adopting wave-picking techniques, the company hiked productivity substantially. The wave-picking system allowed efficient picking and shipping by stockkeeping unit (SKU), and the conveyor and sortation systems minimized product handling. Staging and dock space were trimmed accordingly. Unfortunately, customers didn't want to receive by SKU. They preferred to receive goods packaged for designated user departments within their facilities to simplify the process of distributing goods internally. To overcome customer dissatisfaction, the distributor must rework its distribution center system ("productive" as it may be) to meet the real needs of the customers. It must bear the cost of this redesign — no small sum.

Perhaps these kinds of examples are best summarized by the anecdote about the rural bus company manager in Great Britain who commented that he could increase the productivity of his buses (measured in terms of stops-per-hour) if only the buses didn't have to wait for customers to get on and off.

The lesson of these stories is that before they can improve *real* productivity, companies must understand the customer's requirements and then design a productive system to meet those requirements.

THE SHIFT IN EMPHASIS TO QUALITY

Throughout the 1980s, company after company realized its primary job was to produce and deliver what the customers were willing to buy (provide quality) and then find ways to do that job more efficiently (improve productivity). Early in the '80s, most businesses defined quality as "conformance to requirements," "zero defects," "meeting specifications," and "reducing variation." These phrases, however, have a decided orientation toward products or manufacturing — an inward, product/production focus. Some authors refer to these views as the "little q" definition of quality.

Recently, emphasis is shifting toward a broader view of quality — called the "big Q" definition of quality — that incorporates both products and services. This approach links customers, suppliers, and employees as full partners in a Total Quality Management (TQM) process. Thus, it has an external, market/customer focus.

As described in Chapter 1, the 1980s was the decade in which business focused on quality. In the United States, this movement started with pioneers such as Milliken, Motorola, Texas Instruments, Hewlett-Packard,

Xerox, and Federal Express. Other companies picked up the ball as the pioneers shared their quality commitment with their suppliers and customers. Creation of the Malcolm Baldrige National Quality Award and the popularization of quality improvement in the media and in books by experts such as W. Edwards Deming, Genichi Taguchi, Joseph Juran, and Philip Crosby further stimulated interest in quality improvement.

Today, of the 308 companies that responded to our Logistics Management research study questionnaire, 67 percent have formal quality/productivity-improvement processes in place. However, three out of four began the process only within the past four years, and one out of four started less than two years ago.

PRIMARY EMPHASIS ON PRODUCT QUALITY

Even though 67 percent of respondents have a formal quality and productivity-improvement process at the business-unit level, only 55 percent have such a process in place for logistics. This is not surprising. Most quality-improvement initiatives began in the manufacturing area to improve product quality. Many of these firms have not extended their quality process to the service side of their business yet.

A closer look at who is leading today's quality initiatives in U.S. companies points out this manufacturing/production orientation. In 1989, The Conference Board surveyed 149 companies with quality-improvement processes.[1] In 82 percent of the cases, the initiatives were headed by individuals with backgrounds in manufacturing or related areas, finance, or planning. Executives with backgrounds in marketing, sales, customer service, or logistics did not even make the list (i.e., they were mentioned by fewer than four respondents each). This manufacturing orientation may be one reason service quality has received less attention than product quality to date.

MARKETING IS DRIVING SERVICE QUALITY

Service quality hasn't been ignored. Rather, it often exists under a different name and sponsor. At the same time that manufacturing and engineering were bringing quality "up from the shop floor" with the Total Quality Management (TQM) approach, marketing and sales were bringing the issue of customer satisfaction back from the marketplace — looking for ways to improve the quality of the products and services the customer wants to buy. Marketing and sales people refer to this as Total Customer Satisfaction (TCS).

Today, TQM and TCS approaches are converging on a single objective — to improve the value customers receive from doing business with their suppliers. As Figure 2-1 shows, the Total Quality Management road traces the evolution of quality improvement within a company from ignoring quality, to inspecting it in, then to designing it in, and finally to anticipating customer requirements. Similarly, Total Customer Satisfaction traces an evolutionary path beginning with promising whatever is required to make the sale and then providing what was promised. This is followed by differentiating what was promised based on what the customer requires and will pay for and ends with tailoring products and services to meet the unique needs of each customer. TQM and TCS converge at the point where the company anticipates needs and tailors product/service bundles to meet them.

Figure 2-1

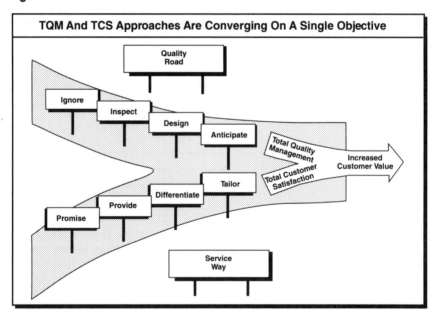

Improving service quality may present a bigger challenge than upgrading product quality, primarily because service and product quality differ in three key areas:

- Defining service quality is a far more subjective and imprecise task than defining product quality. Service quality, like beauty, is in the eye of the beholder (the customer) and thus may be as much perception as reality.

- Product quality is often defined as conformance to requirements. Companies have a long history of working with customers to understand their full set of product requirements. Blueprints, design specifications, tolerance limits, design committees are commonplace. Traditionally, companies have not used similar rigor in defining service requirements.

• Quality of service cannot easily be "inspected in" before it is provided. Product quality, on the other hand, can be inspected in, at least to some level of defects. Service quality must be designed in.

SUCCESS STORIES

Despite the challenges of service quality improvement and regardless of whether or not they adopt a TQM or TCS approach, leading-edge companies have realized major success by focusing on the customer. In more tangible terms, companies that adopted a customer focus during the 1980s substantially outperformed the Standard & Poor's 500 for those years. Figure 2-2 shows the stock price index for a portfolio of companies representative of customer-focused firms as compared to the Standard & Poor's 500. The customer-focused portfolio registered a compounded growth rate in stock price of 16.9 percent annually. This compares with a rate of 10.9 percent for the Standard & Poor's composite.

Figure 2-2

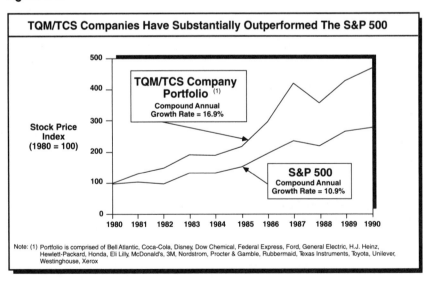

Data extracted from the Profit Impact of Market Strategy Database (PIMS) of Cambridge, MA[2] illustrate similar results. Figure 2-3 compares companies having customer-focused Total Quality Management processes with others in the PIMS database. TQM/TCS firms demonstrate superior performance in terms of product price, market share, sales growth, and return on sales.

Figure 2-3

Business Performance Implications Of TQM/TCS		
Performance Characteristic	Non-TQM/TCS Companies	TQM/TCS Companies
■ Relative price	98	107
■ Market share	2% Loss Per Year	6% Gain Per Year
■ Sales	8% Gain Per Year	17% Gain Per Year
■ Return on sales	1%	12%

Source: PIMS (Profit Impact of Market Strategy) Database, Cambridge, Massachusetts

Finally, a recent study by the U.S. General Accounting Office[3] analyzed the performance of 20 companies that were among the highest scoring applicants in 1988 and 1989 for the Malcolm Baldrige National Quality Award. Figure 2-4 summarizes data from the study. The figure shows average *annual* percent improvement on key measures of process performance and business performance.

As one example, these 20 companies reported cycle time reductions that averaged 12 percent *per year* beginning when they adopted a TQM/TCS approach. On the financial side, the companies reported *average annual increases* of 1.3 percent for return on assets over the same period.

CHARACTERISTICS OF SUCCESSFUL CUSTOMER-FOCUSED COMPANIES

A company can choose to compete on a number of dimensions including product innovation, technology, price, and customer service. Part of developing a business strategy is selecting the right combination based on the marketplace, competition, and the company's own strengths and capabilities. Not all companies choose a customer-focused strategy, but for those that do there are lessons to be learned from the successes of others.

Figure 2-4

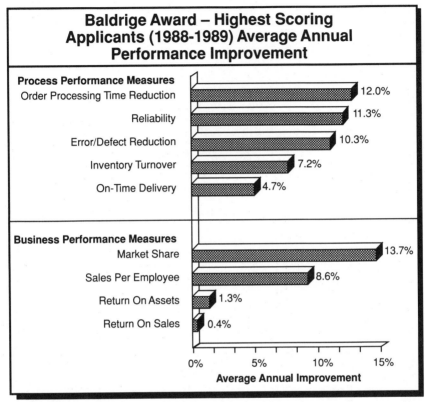

Baldrige Award – Highest Scoring Applicants (1988-1989) Average Annual Performance Improvement

Process Performance Measures

Order Processing Time Reduction — 12.0%

Reliability — 11.3%

Error/Defect Reduction — 10.3%

Inventory Turnover — 7.2%

On-Time Delivery — 4.7%

Business Performance Measures

Market Share — 13.7%

Sales Per Employee — 8.6%

Return On Assets — 1.3%

Return On Sales — 0.4%

0%   5%   10%   15%

Average Annual Improvement

Source: United States General Accounting Office

During our interviewing and secondary research process, we sought to identify what it takes to be successfully customer focused. Although each company interviewed tailored its improvement process to meet its own needs, successful firms shared striking similarities. The characteristics divide into four major categories as shown in Figure 2-5.

Companies create superior customer value by cultivating four main ingredients: a customer-driven service strategy, senior management commitment for improvement, a formal process for managing continuous improvement, and employees who assume ownership of the improvement process.

1. Customer-driven service strategy. For successful companies, developing a service strategy around the customer is key. These firms focus on customer needs and requirements using the customer's definition of quality. Customers are contacted regularly to determine and reconfirm requirements. The companies' goals are to meet requirements and expectations and thereby expand value to the customer. They individually tailor their approaches for each customer and find ways to exceed expectations on a customer by customer basis.

Figure 2-5

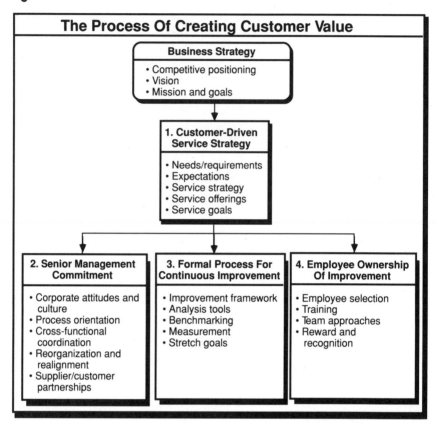

The Process Of Creating Customer Value

Business Strategy

- Competitive positioning
- Vision
- Mission and goals

1. Customer-Driven Service Strategy

- Needs/requirements
- Expectations
- Service strategy
- Service offerings
- Service goals

2. Senior Management Commitment

- Corporate attitudes and culture
- Process orientation
- Cross-functional coordination
- Reorganization and realignment
- Supplier/customer partnerships

3. Formal Process For Continuous Improvement

- Improvement framework
- Analysis tools
- Benchmarking
- Measurement
- Stretch goals

4. Employee Ownership Of Improvement

- Employee selection
- Training
- Team approaches
- Reward and recognition

2. Senior management commitment. Senior management at successful companies recognizes the need to drive the improvement process from its level. Positioning the company to meet, and even anticipate, customer needs often requires a fundamental shift in culture and management style as well as radical changes in operating methods. In many cases, this shift is triggered by a major competitive threat.

Such shifts in culture and style can only be driven by an *absolute* commitment on the part of top management. As part of this commitment, top management must develop a clear statement of the company's mission and goals — a statement that incorporates creating customer value. It must reshape corporate attitudes and culture to create a fertile environment for improvement. This may mean changing hiring practices, compensation, training, and rewards systems. Management must also commit to the process for the long term and refuse to allow poor quality products or services.

Only senior management can drive the kind of cross-functional coordination needed to improve business processes — to move beyond just improving activities within functions. Processes, not functions, create value and satisfy customers. In many cases, creating customer value requires realigning and reorganizing to move decisions closer to the customer (e.g., delegating authority to front-line employees). Finally, only senior management can commit the company to partnerships with key customers and suppliers needed to sustain a customer focus.

3. Formal process for continuous improvement. The third ingredient in creating customer value is a formal process for continuous improvement. This process includes an improvement framework that encompasses performance measures, analysis tools, and benchmarking systems. Most companies initiate their continuous improvement processes with pilot programs in which they achieve early successes. Top management rewards and publicizes these "wins" thereby setting the tone for future successes. Most also set aggressive "stretch" goals that drive the organization to break through traditional ways of operation.

4. Employee ownership of improvement. In the successful companies, employee ownership of improvement is the fuel that drives the engine of change. Employees are involved in the process at all levels. These firms institutionalize the improvement mindset by training their people in technical, leadership, and interpersonal skills. This training emphasizes a team approach and empowers employees to make improvements. Reward and recognition programs reinforce ongoing improvement efforts.

To ingrain the customer focus in their organizations, some companies use a technique called Policy Deployment to cascade senior management's vision, goals, and priorities down through all levels in the organization. For example, a policy objective might be to "improve service reliability" in support of the company's vision of being the "preferred supplier." To improve service reliability however, the company must "deploy" the objective throughout the organization by linking plans and expected results to it. Each part of the organization defines the tangible results (i.e., the type and amount of improvement) that it needs to achieve to improve service reliability along with the action plans to produce the results. For each level in the organization, its own tangible results and goals directly tie to the action plans of the next level up.

RESHAPING CULTURE

In Section I, we investigated why value creation for customers and shareholders is important to companies. We looked at how leading companies use customer-focused quality improvement to create value. And we noted the kind of commitment these improvement processes require of companies and their employees in terms of cultural change, managerial style and commitment, teamwork, and the like. Where does logistics fit into this discussion? In Section II, we explore this question, analyzing exactly what role the logistics process plays in a customer-focused company.

---

[1] Walsh, Jr., Francis, J., "Current Practices in Measuring Quality"

[2] Buzzall, Robert D. and Bradley T. Gale, The PIMS Principles, Linking Strategy to Performance

[3] United States General Accounting Office, Management Practices: U.S. Companies Improve Performance Through Quality Efforts

SECTION II

CREATING VALUE THROUGH LOGISTICS EXCELLENCE

Implementing a customer-focused strategy and creating value for customers and shareholders will depend on how well companies execute their key business processes. Excellence in these key business processes will be a prerequisite to achieving competitive advantage.

Chapter 3 discusses the concept of key business processes and describes why logistics is included among these. The chapter also explores several powerful forces that are redefining the way in which the logistics process must operate. Chapter 4 describes the characteristics of logistics excellence, reviews where companies stand today, and discusses the benefits to be gained from achieving excellence.

CHAPTER 3

LOGISTICS: A KEY BUSINESS PROCESS

Many companies, as Chapter 2 noted, have begun improvement processes aimed at becoming more "quality oriented" or "customer focused." In fact, most businesses today want to be recognized as customer-oriented, quality firms. They want to be viewed as leaders in their fields and world-class competitors. They see the need to operate on a global level to achieve these goals. They recognize that employee empowerment plays a key role in their success.

The net effect of this movement is that such business values and goals lose their power as differentiating factors. With many companies striving for quality and customer focus, the deciding factor between success and failure will be a company's ability to *execute* the processes that deliver quality and customer value. The logistics process is key to execution in most businesses and, thus, key to achieving these results.

LOGISTICS: A PROCESS, NOT A FUNCTION

Before discussing quality improvement and its relationship to logistics, we must emphasize that logistics is a process, not a function. This distinction is critical.

Most companies, at least at the business-unit level, are organized functionally around departments that "do something." The sales department sells. The manufacturing department makes product. The purchasing department provides raw materials and components. The distribution department distributes product. The accounting department accounts for revenues generated and costs incurred.

Each of these departments carries out a definable task. Individually, though, none creates value for customers or shareholders. Nor do they individually accomplish what the corporation has set out to do. Based on these traditional parameters, it's clear that functions perform tasks.

Processes, on the other hand, accomplish things and create value. This is where logistics comes in. The goal of the logistics process is to weave together and coordinate all activities involved in acquiring, converting, and distributing goods from raw material source to final consumer in order to accomplish the customer service objectives. This process includes the physical activities of moving and storing goods, providing information to support these operations, and managing the overall process. As Figure 3-1 illustrates, the logistics process, by definition, crosses traditional functional or departmental boundaries.

Figure 3-1

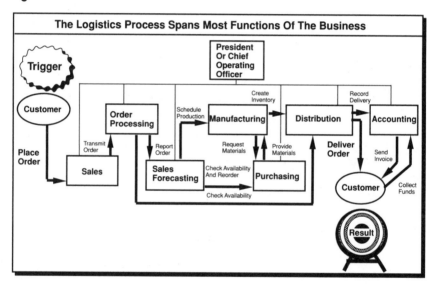

In the late 1970s and early 1980s, the solution to managing the logistics process seemed to lie in creating a logistics function and placing all activities involved in achieving required levels of customer service within this single organizational entity. Because the logistics process spans most of the operations side of a business, this meant that the head of a true logistics "function" would tie together virtually all operations — essentially playing the role of the Chief Operating Officer.

Today, opinion is shifting. Management realizes that managing logistics as a process does not require massive redrawing of organizational boxes and responsibilities. Instead, it demands cross-functional planning, coordination, and management.

VALUE CREATION THROUGH LOGISTICS

The goal of the logistics process is to deliver the required levels of customer service in an efficient, cost effective manner. Thus, the logistics process supports revenue growth by delivering the products the customers order on time, complete, and undamaged in a consistent, predictable way. When customers learn that suppliers can provide what they want when they want it, they perceive value and favor those suppliers with future business.

Pleasing customers is not the only goal of the logistics process, however. The costs of providing service quality must be in line with revenues generated. Thus, the logistics process must operate productively to generate profits for the company.

In addition to impacting the profit and loss statement, the logistics process can positively affect the balance sheet as well. On the asset side, reduction in order cycle time and stockouts may improve cash flow. Fewer billing errors — the result of more accurate order entry and selection/shipment — reduce accounts receivable financing costs. Lower inventory levels, coupled with more productive fixed assets and equipment, free up capital for other uses. On the liability side, reducing raw materials purchases through better materials requirement planning and procurement trims the amount of cash committed to in-process product. Thus, logistics process improvements can bolster operating earnings and improve the return on capital employed (ROCE).

LOGISTICS: A KEY BUSINESS PROCESS

Any business has dozens of processes that go on within it. Some are self-contained within functions, others span functions. The processes vary in importance — not all create equal value for customers or shareholders. Based on these realities, one of management's roles is to understand the relative value each process delivers and adjust the amount of emphasis, attention, and investment applied to each. Figure 3-2 offers a framework for thinking about the many processes in a business and how best to allocate management attention to each. The processes that fall in Quadrant I (upper left-hand corner) are *leveraging processes*, called that because they add value to shareholders but add little value to customers. An example of a *leveraging process* is cash management. Cash management does not create value for customers, so it doesn't deserve all-out management attention. On the other hand, by applying the right measure of attention to cash management, companies can boost cash flow and earnings and add to shareholder value.

Quadrant II (lower left-hand corner) represents *supporting processes*. These do not add value either to customers or shareholders. If a company could do without these processes, it probably would. Supporting processes are typically a requirement of doing business such as governmental reporting and general bookkeeping. With supporting processes, therefore, companies need to apply just enough attention and resources to meet minimum requirements.

Figure 3-2

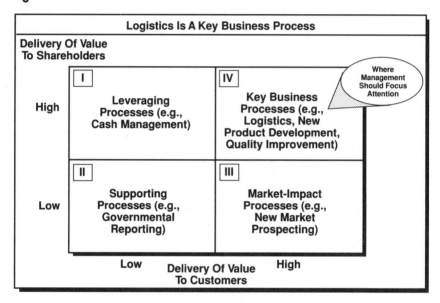

In Quadrant III (lower right-hand corner), we find *market-impact processes*. These add value to customers but produce little direct value to shareholders — at least in the short term. New market prospecting is an example of a market impact process. These processes typically involve investments in market growth or expansion. Because they don't generate much immediate value to shareholders, management should focus on making the right investment decisions in these areas.

Quadrant IV (upper right-hand corner) — *key business processes* — is where the action is. These processes add high value for customers and shareholders alike. Most companies have two kinds of key business processes: those related to managing today's business and those targeted at managing tomorrow's business. The logistics process exemplifies the first type of key business process. It is key to day to day customer satisfaction for companies that produce or distribute goods. New product development illustrates the "tomorrow-oriented" key business process. While the logistics process keeps customers satisfied today, new product development seeks to satisfy customers in the future.

For many, quality improvement is a key business process. It focuses both on today's business (improving quality against known customer requirements) and tomorrow's business (anticipating customer needs).

Regardless of their focus — today or tomorrow — most key business processes cross functional boundaries. Consequently, successfully managing these processes means involving a number of functional managers and positioning a senior general manager to coordinate efforts and resolve conflicts.

Successfully managing the logistics process is difficult today because it demands coordination across business functions and among customers and suppliers. Upcoming changes in business, however, will make this challenge even greater in coming years.

THE FORCES OF CHANGE

As a part of the research for this project, we investigated several major forces currently reshaping business in order to understand how these forces will alter the logistics process over the coming decade. One such force is the increased emphasis on quality and customer service that lies at the heart of this research effort. Seven other forces also will impact logistics significantly in the future. They are:

- Globalization of the world economy

- A renewed quest for productivity improvement

- Increasing demands from the marketplace

- Emerging strategic alliances

- Corporate restructuring

- Accelerating cycle times

- Environmental concerns

In the remainder of this section, we explore each of these forces and the effect they will have on logistics.

GLOBALIZATION

We asked our survey respondents the degree to which they already serve global markets and their plans for the future. Figure 3-3 displays their responses. Most companies surveyed already serve at least one market outside the United States with Canada being the most popular (58 percent). In the next five years, 30 percent of the respondents plan to enter at least one new market outside the United States. By far, eastern Europe will be the biggest growth market measured in terms of both absolute and relative increase in the number of companies entering that market. Other major growth areas include Mexico, western Europe, Africa, and the Pacific Rim.

Figure 3-3

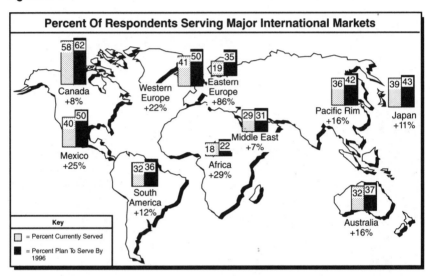

Survey respondents see their sales gradually drifting away from local or regional markets, and even North American markets, toward the rest of the world (see Figure 3-4).

Naturally, as companies evolve toward worldwide sourcing, supply chains lengthen. Transportation, handling, inventory, paperwork, and formalities all increase with distance. Additionally, longer supply chains involve more time and a greater number of players in the process. The potential for failure is greater and so are the risks. In short, the inbound side of logistics becomes much more complicated to manage. Procurement grows in importance as companies seek less expensive sources of materials and components worldwide. Domestic manufacturing lessens in importance.

Globalization doesn't only mean global sourcing — it means global marketing as well. As companies target the best markets worldwide, the distribution chain lengthens. Here too, more transportation, handling, inventory, damage, time, paperwork, and participants come into play. Even more significantly, however, each market has different requirements and expectations. These markets don't follow tidy national or social group definitions. In North America, Southern California is a different market than New England; Quebec is a different market than Ontario, which is different from British Columbia. Similar disparities exist within the European

Community (despite the impending creation of a single European market in 1992). Even within European countries such as Germany, the northern section is distinctly different from the southern section, Bavaria.

Figure 3-4

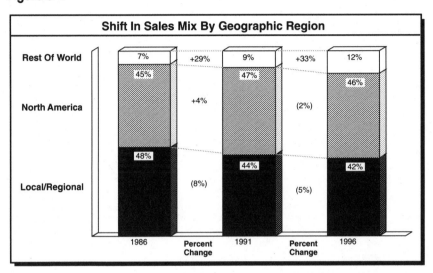

Competing in a world marketplace requires that companies understand the specific needs, requirements, and customs of as many as 200 to 300 regional markets. As companies seek foreign sources and pursue foreign markets, the logistics process becomes critically important to success.

RENEWED QUEST FOR PRODUCTIVITY

In the last twenty years, the rate of productivity growth in Japan has been five times that of the United States or Canada (see Figure 3-5). In virtually any industry where Japan has chosen to focus (e.g., electronics, computer chips, and automobiles), the absolute level of Japanese productivity has surpassed that of North America.

Productivity growth in western Europe, while proceeding at a slower rate than Japan, still exceeds that of North America. With Europe 1992, productivity growth in western Europe should accelerate as companies located in Europe gain economies of scale and cut their costs dramatically. Dissolution of the iron curtain adds momentum as well to European efforts. A well-educated work force and decades of pent up consumer demand in eastern Europe give western European companies an unprecedented opportunity to increase both their production capacity and sales.

Figure 3-5

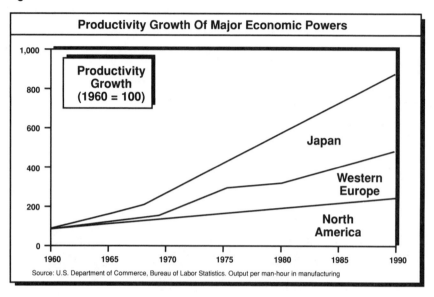

Productivity Growth Of Major Economic Powers

Productivity Growth (1960 = 100)

Japan

Western Europe

North America

Source: U.S. Department of Commerce, Bureau of Labor Statistics. Output per man-hour in manufacturing

Historically, productivity improvement efforts in North America have focused on direct labor. Although many firms realized major gains in this area in the past, direct labor accounts for only 5 to 10 percent of the cost of goods sold today. This means that any significant future productivity gains will come from areas beyond direct manufacturing labor — marketing, advertising, sales, information services, research and development, and, of course, logistics. Our two previous research studies identified opportunities to improve productivity in the logistics process by as much as 50 percent over a ten-year period — without compromising quality and customer service. While many companies have made significant gains since 1983, much opportunity still lies ahead. With the logistics process representing about 10 percent of the total delivered cost of goods, cutting expenditures by a third or more would have a profound effect on the competitiveness of North American companies.

INCREASING MARKETPLACE DEMANDS

In the early 1980s, a new, typical U.S.-produced automobile had three times the defects compared to a Japanese model[1]. Customers saw Japanese companies such as Toyota, Nissan, and Honda offering an attractive package of quality and price, so they bought their products. Japanese manufacturers, as a result, won a major share of the American market.

Today, U.S. automobile manufacturers can beat the Japanese manufacturer's performance levels of a decade ago. Unfortunately for U.S. car makers, however, the Japanese also reduced their defect rates. Japanese automobile manufacturers simply raised the industry standard another notch.

Higher consumer expectations aren't limited to automobiles. As consumers, we expect products to work right the first time. We expect quality. To get it, we're being more selective in choosing from whom we buy.

This is true not only in the consumer setting but also in the industrial environment. Companies are consolidating their supplier bases and building closer ties with remaining providers. They are requiring these suppliers to demonstrate their capabilities to support the company's own quality initiatives using ISO 9000 standards and the Baldrige criteria as models. Their objective is to create a mutually beneficial relationship that improves the effectiveness of the whole supply chain.

Overall, the trend toward a shrinking supplier base is clear. Fifty percent of the companies surveyed reported having a regular supplier base of 300 or fewer firms in 1986 (see Figure 3-6). By 1991, this figure grew to 55 percent of respondents. Projections indicate a further increase to 61 percent by 1996. Conversely, the percent of companies surveyed who regularly use more than 750 suppliers shrank from 30 percent in 1986 to 20 percent today.

Figure 3-6

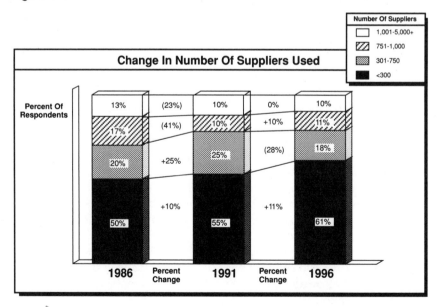

At the same time that customers are being more selective, suppliers are seeking "preferred" status with their customers. Suppliers base these relationships on long-term profitability rather than current revenue, recognizing that customers generating similar revenues may incur entirely different costs of service because of their varying requirements.

In response to the realities of customer demands and their effect on profitability, some firms develop differentiated service policies. As part of these policies, they try to balance the value provided to the customer by the product/service package (measured by how much the customer will pay for it) with the value to the company (resulting profits).

Unfortunately, many companies are not equipped to provide differentiated service because, historically, their service efforts have been oriented towards economy of scale, efficiency, or productivity. They target the average customer and serve that customer extremely well. In doing so, however, they invariably over-service some customers and under-service others. This creates particular problems for customers who want special services and are willing to pay for them. The company may not be able to accommodate these needs.

As customers become more selective and suppliers seek "preferred" status, individualized, value-added services will become the norm. Being able to adapt and tailor the logistics process to meet unique needs will be a key factor in bonding suppliers with customers.

EMERGING STRATEGIC ALLIANCES

Very few companies can do everything themselves. To get raw materials from the fields, mines, and forests into the hands of the final consumer in the form of products requires many partners along the supply chain. The most typical partnership relationships are between suppliers and customers and between shippers and carriers.

Suppliers, as partners, often can provide access to research and development as well as to new thinking in terms of designs, techniques, and technology. By going beyond an arms-length relationship, customers and suppliers can work together to improve the quality and productivity of their portions of the logistics process.

Most companies use some form of third-party logistics service provider. For-hire transportation carriers and public warehouse operators are the most common examples. However, these companies have greatly expanded and integrated their scope in recent years and now offer a wide range of services. The quality of service these companies give can make or break a customer relationship. Partnerships with quality oriented logistics service providers can yield substantial advantage through better information, control, speed, reliability, and productivity.

We asked the survey respondents to indicate if they have taken actions to develop closer relationships with suppliers and with carriers. Figure 3-7 summarizes their responses.

Figure 3-7

Actions That Link Suppliers With Customers And Shippers With Carriers	
	Percent Of Respondents
■ Reduce number of carriers	90%
■ Establish formal partnerships with suppliers	78%
■ Reduce number of regular suppliers	75%
■ Negotiate long-term contracts	68%
■ Develop strategic alliances with suppliers	66%
■ Establish formal partnerships with carriers	63%
■ Enter into more single-source supplier relationships	58%
■ Certify suppliers	55%
■ Develop strategic alliance with third-party logistics service providers	32%

As the table indicates, most survey respondents have taken some action to develop closer ties. Ninety percent have focused business with fewer transportation carriers. Over three-quarters of the companies have established formal partnerships with suppliers, while nearly as many have reduced their number of regular suppliers. Reductions of 10 to 15 percent are common, while some companies have made reductions of two-thirds or more.

In this same vein, a number of companies are opting for single sourcing for certain materials, concentrating their buying with one supplier. Increased vendor reliability and reduced variation in incoming materials drive this movement. Interestingly, the study found that 55 percent of respondents have formal supplier certification programs. These programs reduce or eliminate the need for incoming product inspection. Respondents report gaining major quality and productivity benefits through supplier certification programs.

Even though broad based third-party logistics service providers are relatively new, 32 percent of respondents already have developed strategic alliances with these types of firms.

Supplier-customer and shipper-logistics service provider partnerships are not the only types that exist, however. For example, wholesalers or distributors play a vital role in getting products to market for many firms. They make it possible to serve smaller or fragmented markets economically. The wholesalers or distributors a manufacturer uses to bring product to market are its representatives in the eyes of the customer. The way in which a distributor/wholesaler handles the manufacturer's product and provides service is critically important to the manufacturer's success.

Brokers are also partners. Acting as a company's salesforce, what a broker says, does, and promises on a company's behalf to customers is critical to success.

Contract manufacturers are partners as well. Traditionally, contract manufacturing was an arms-length relationship. Recently, however, managers began realizing the advantages to dealing with company-operated and contract plants in the same manner. Regardless of ownership, senior managers provide each plant with the same information and give plant managers identical responsibility and authority. In many cases, contract plants are actually more responsive to needs than are company plants.

Finally, third parties such as computer hardware and software vendors, equipment suppliers, and professional service firms can play a partnership role as well.

Companies cannot develop strategic alliances with every business associate. It's likely that only one or two dozen entities among the types of companies described above will make a difference in the competitiveness of a business. Identifying these partners and developing strategic alliances with them is a major challenge for the 1990s. In Chapter 11, "High-Impact Improvement Actions," we explore the partnership approach in detail.

CORPORATE RESTRUCTURING

The 1980s brought major upheaval to corporate society. Mergers and acquisitions occurred at an unprecedented rate. Figure 3-8 tracks U.S. merger and acquisition activity during the decade.

The 1980s divides into two distinct eras. From 1980 through 1987, we experienced an era of the Wall Street deal. It was a time of quick riches coming from heavily leveraged transactions and other financially clever maneuvering. Financing for such deals was relatively easy to obtain. Often, the prime measure of success was how quickly the acquired company could be broken apart and sold off in pieces to pay down the debt.

With the crash of the stock market in October 1987, this kind of merger/acquisition activity dropped sharply, and a new era began. The growth curve of merger and acquisition activity flattened and, in fact, declined significantly in 1990. The major difference was not so much the level of activity as the reason for the activity. The focus shifted to increasing shareholder value by bringing together businesses that are logical partners. This includes combining businesses to achieve economies of scale. It means buying into growing markets or merging complementary operations for the benefit of both parties. In fact, today's merger and acquisition activity is driven largely by strategic business reasons that produce a long-term payoff not by the desire for quick financial gain.

Figure 3-8

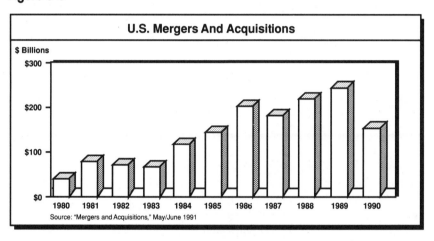

Among the companies surveyed in this study, 40 percent experienced a merger or acquisition during the past five years. Of this group, 55 percent considered the merger/acquisition a success, 27 percent a partial success, and 7 percent a failure with 11 percent saying it's "too early to tell."

Figure 3-9 shows the kinds of operational benefits respondents expected from the merger and indicates the degree to which their expectations have been met. More than half of the participants cited market share increase and/or cost reduction as the two most common reasons for the merger. Only 45 percent expected service improvement to result. And just one-third of the respondents believed the merger would create opportunities for plant/equipment asset reduction.

Actual performance following the merger either met or exceeded expectations for operational benefits in most cases. Still, a sizable minority of companies (from 26 percent in the case of market share increase to over 40 percent in the case of price stabilization) reported disappointment with actual benefits.

Figure 3-9

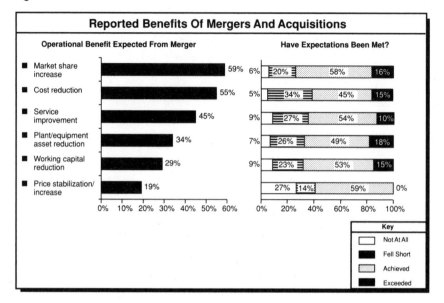

Reported Benefits Of Mergers And Acquisitions

The skill with which the logistics process is integrated in the merged operations affects most of the operational benefits. Figure 3-10 shows the extent of integration achieved as a part of the merger process. In 47 percent of the cases, customer service/order processing and outbound transportation to customers were completely integrated as a result of the merger. An additional 21 percent of respondents reported some integration among these areas.

Four of every ten participants reported integration of plant and warehouse networks, salesforces, and purchasing. In the case of plant/warehouse networks, however, 28 percent indicated that planned integration had not taken place. These companies have not yet realized expected savings in plant and equipment assets or in transportation or warehousing economies of scale.

In the case of salesforces, 31 percent of the respondents reported their salesforces were still separate. By failing to integrate salesforces as planned, companies may have missed market share, service, and cost reduction opportunities.

Successful integration is not easy. In fact, respondents reported encountering numerous barriers, which Figure 3-11 depicts. By far the biggest problem is information systems incompatibility. Over two-thirds of those participants involved in a merger/acquisition cited such incompatibility as a major stumbling block.

Figure 3-10

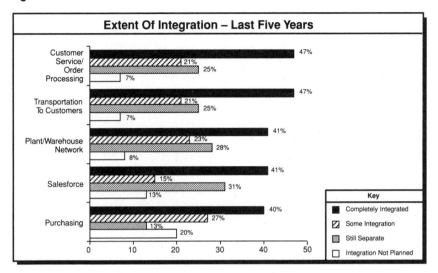

Extent Of Integration – Last Five Years

Customer Service/ Order Processing: 47% (Completely Integrated), 21% (Some Integration), 25% (Still Separate), 7% (Integration Not Planned)

Transportation To Customers: 47%, 21%, 25%, 7%

Plant/Warehouse Network: 41%, 23%, 28%, 8%

Salesforce: 41%, 15%, 31%, 13%

Purchasing: 40%, 27%, 13%, 20%

Key
- ■ Completely Integrated
- ▨ Some Integration
- ▨ Still Separate
- ☐ Integration Not Planned

Figure 3-11

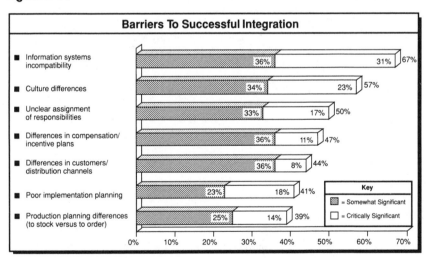

Barriers To Successful Integration

- ■ Information systems incompatibility: 36%, 31%, 67%
- ■ Culture differences: 34%, 23%, 57%
- ■ Unclear assignment of responsibilities: 33%, 17%, 50%
- ■ Differences in compensation/ incentive plans: 36%, 11%, 47%
- ■ Differences in customers/ distribution channels: 36%, 8%, 44%
- ■ Poor implementation planning: 23%, 18%, 41%
- ■ Production planning differences (to stock versus to order): 25%, 14%, 39%

Key
- ▨ = Somewhat Significant
- ☐ = Critically Significant

Second on the list is cultural differences, cited as a problem by more than half the respondents. Centralized versus decentralized management styles, union versus nonunion environments, North American versus European versus Japanese perspectives all are examples of cultural differences that can make mergers difficult.

This barrier also can surface when a manufacturer and distributor merge. In principle, these mergers make sense: the manufacturer gains access to a strong distribution network, while the distributor becomes the preferred (or sometimes exclusive) distribution channel for a major branded product. The attributes that make each firm strong in its own arena, however, can create conflict when the two merge. In many cases, the manufacturer excels in product capability (either its technical features or consumer franchise) and looks to the distributor for the ability to gain broader distribution at a lower cost. Because of the strength of the brand/product, the manufacturer may view value-added customer service as a secondary issue. For a distributor, on the other hand, value-added customer service is all it has to sell. Thus, the distributor may focus on servicing the customer with whatever the customer requires even though such services escalate costs. These differing priorities make mergers of manufacturers and distributors especially challenging.

Where mergers succeed involving manufacturers or distributors, they do so because the companies do a good job of blending the logistics processes. Where they fail, the reason often lies in a breakdown in merging the logistics processes.

ACCELERATING CYCLE TIMES

In the United States, if a consumer orders an automobile through a U.S. dealership, he can expect delivery in three to six weeks. A Japanese consumer placing a similar order in Tokyo, however, receives delivery of the new car in three days.

Twenty years ago, documents sent through the U.S. postal system took several days to get from one coast to the other. With the advent of overnight express delivery, that cycle time shrank from days to hours. Today, transmission of written documents occurs over facsimile machines, cutting the hours cycle to several minutes. With electronic mail, electronic data interchange, voice mail, and other such technologies, those minutes drop to seconds. The upshot of these developments is that in one management generation the speed of communication has moved from five days to five seconds — a cycle time reduction of over 99.9 percent.

Every day, more cycle time collapses occur. Television news used to be available three or four times during the day; now there are 24-hour news stations. Consumers needn't wait until stores open to shop; they can buy from home shopping television channels that operate 24 hours a day. Society is growing accustomed to getting faster access to what it needs.

The catalyst for this acceleration in cycle time is information technology. Mainframe computing power is virtually unlimited and widely available. Information systems can distribute data on a real-time basis to almost anywhere in the world. Using personal computers, users can access and analyze data in minutes. Just ten years ago, they would have had to wait days or weeks to get programming help from the systems department.

Not only do we have more and better access to existing data, but our ability to capture new data on a more timely basis has exploded. Ten years ago, for instance, a retailer was lucky to know what the total dollar sales were for each store in its chain at the close of the day. Today, using laser scanners at the checkout counter, retailers instantly know what was sold, at what price, and, in some cases, to whom.

With demands from the marketplace for instant gratification and access to technologies that enable that reality, many companies face a challenge. Should they continue their traditional approach to decision making and hope they don't drown in a flood of information? Or should they develop different ways to manage? So far, no one has fully resolved the issues of how to capitalize on the new technologies and meet the increasing demands of consumers. But companies need to consider at least three elements of response.

First, management must communicate more broadly its strategy and guidelines for decision making. Second, in order to accelerate the decision-making process, firms must delegate to front-line employees the authority to make decisions on a decentralized basis. Third, companies should capitalize on their information resources to monitor and improve the processes for decision making. Communicating and articulating strategy is a key ingredient in empowering people to make decentralized decisions. The receptionist in Des Moines, the sales person in Düsseldorf, and the delivery person in Dublin all should know the corporate strategy and mission well enough to make decisions.

When employees make decentralized decisions, they also make decentralized mistakes. Management, therefore, must not only invest in information systems that help people make better decisions but also monitor the decisions to improve the process.

Finally, companies need to find different ways to use information. Most information systems today are designed to support the financial accounting processes of a business. Financial accounting, however, looks only at history. To meet the demands of accelerating cycle times, companies need information systems that help people look into the future to plan and coordinate activities. In addition to looking ahead, this new generation of information systems must handle a flood of information, acting concurrently rather sequentially — with data updates and decision making taking place simultaneously across organizational and functional boundaries. They must shift from financial reporting and measurement to operations planning and coordination with the needs of the logistics process driving those requirements.

ENVIRONMENTAL CONCERNS

The by-products of 20th century life have caught up with society. Oil spills, acid rain, smog, congestion, overflowing landfills all appear on the nightly news with regularity. Governments have started acting in response to public outcry. New regulations abound, many directly affecting the logistics process.

Refuse must be recycled. Trucks are prohibited from city streets during ever-extending rush hours. Access to raw material sources such as forests and mine sites is restricted to preserve the ecology. Companies scramble to respond.

For some, the impacts are substantial. Newsprint mills traditionally have been located in forests, close to virgin fiber sources and remote from cities. When logistics in the paper industry was a one-way process, this made economic sense. However, newspapers must be recycled now, forcing a two-way logistics process. Mills located in the woods no longer make as much sense. Competitors are springing up closer to market, gaining advantages newly created by the two-way logistics flows.

In the chemical industry, the Responsible-Care initiative being led by the Chemical Manufacturers Association requires closer management of the movement and storage of chemicals. This means that chemical manufacturers, carriers, terminal operators, distributors, and users must join forces to implement safeguards against improper use or accidental discharge of chemicals, chemical packaging, and chemical waste.

In other industries, environmental concerns may not be as severe but cannot be ignored. A warehouse located on the wrong side of town for rush-hour traffic can add 5 to 10 percent to delivery fleet operating costs.

Key elements of the logistics process that were givens for decades — sources of supply, locations for manufacturing and distribution, and transportation linkages — suddenly become uncertain as a result of environmental factors.

WHY LOGISTICS EXCELLENCE IS A KEY TO SUCCESS IN THE FUTURE

Regardless of how well a company operates today or how well suited its business strategy is for the future, the seven forces discussed above will alter the way it operates in the future. Maintaining the status quo will not be good enough. Only through operational excellence — and particularly, for most industries, logistics excellence — can firms expect to meet these challenges and create value for customers and shareholders.

Achieving excellence in logistics provides several benefits:

• The capability for tailored service and higher service levels

- Improved service quality (consistency and reliability)
- Faster cycles
- Greater efficiencies and productivity across the supply chain
- Closer customer-company relations

From these benefits come increased market share, revenue, and profit. Logistics excellence, therefore, is a management imperative as the 21st century approaches.

---

[1] Woodruff, David, Karen Lowry Miller, Larry Armstrong, and Thane Peterson, "A New Era For Auto Quality"

CHAPTER 4

ACHIEVING LOGISTICS EXCELLENCE

Logistics excellence stems from achieving superior levels of logistics quality and productivity. Quality means doing the right things the first time, and productivity means doing things right, in an efficient manner.

DEFINING LOGISTICS EXCELLENCE

In our research, we discovered that companies define quality in logistics differently. They refer to it as "meeting customer requirements," "satisfying customer needs," "providing defect-free service," or "satisfying the customer the first time, every time." As no single definition garners widespread use, we propose the following:

Quality in logistics means meeting agreed-to customer requirements and expectations, including the following dimensions:

- Ease of inquiry, order placement, and order transmission

- Timely, reliable order delivery and communications

- Accurate, complete, undamaged orders and error-free paperwork

- Timely and responsive post-sales support

- Accurate, timely generation and transmission of information among the functions of the business and with external parties to support the planning, management, and execution of the above activities

The 1978 and 1983 research studies defined logistics *productivity* as the ratio of real output to real input consumed, where output is a measure of the amount of work accomplished and input is a measure of the resources used. Technically, this definition is accurate. Unfortunately, it does not capture the spirit of quality and productivity today.

Instead, we propose the following definition of productivity in logistics for the future:

Productivity in logistics means using the combined resources of all participants in the supply chain in the most efficient way to provide high quality, cost effective customer service.

The major conceptual differences between this definition and the earlier one are that true productivity improvement:

• Is customer focused. The output has value to the customer.

• Results from improving the overall logistics process not merely improving one part of it to the detriment of others (e.g., negotiating lower rates with carriers without commensurate productivity gains by the carrier to reduce costs).

There is no single test or measure of logistics excellence. Absolute service levels measure only what was achieved not what was required. Cost or productivity levels are hard to compare across firms because of differences in operations and product price (when using cost as a percent of sales as a measure).

Instead of evaluating logistics excellence on some scale of quantifiable performance, we believe the better way is to assess logistics excellence in terms of the approaches companies use to plan and manage the logistics process. Figure 4-1 depicts certain characteristics found in the three Stages of Logistics Excellence as measured by eight key factors. These factors are:

• Service goal setting

• Long-range planning

• Operations planning

• Ongoing improvement process

• Relationships between employees and management

• Information capabilities

• Measurement approach

• Vendor/supplier relationships

This framework builds on the one used in the 1978 and 1983 research to define stages of logistics productivity measurement and improvement. We discuss the major characteristics of each stage in the following paragraphs.

Stage I. A company whose logistics process exhibits Stage I characteristics has yet to pursue quality and productivity improvement in a

Figure 4-1

Characteristics Of The Stages Of Logistics Excellence

Dimension	Stage I	Stage II	Stage III
■ Service goal setting	• Handle each transaction as a separate situation • "Keep noise level down"	• All customers treated the same • Attain internally set goals	• Provide differentiated service • Meet/exceed customer requirements
■ Long-range planning	• Not formally carried out • Fragmented planning	• Narrow scope (e.g., distribution) • 1- to 3-year horizon	• Full logistics scope • 3- to 5-year horizon
■ Operations planning	• Today • Each transaction	• Period (e.g., monthly) • Budget-period based	• Period/annual • Rolling periods
■ Ongoing improvement process	• Quick-fix, "stop the bleeding"	• Cost reduction	• Continuous improvement toward goals • Quality and productivity
■ Relationships between employees and management	• Employees versus management	• Limited employee involvement	• Training • Empowerment • Shared goals/rewards
■ Information capabilities	• Process transaction • Little or no data • No analysis capabilities	• Report period's financial results • Fragmented data • Limited analysis capabilities	• Support planning with operational data • Easy-to-use shared data • Flexible analysis capabilities
■ Measurement approach	• Cost versus last year • Cost as percent of sales • Service "noise level"	• Cost versus budget • Productivity versus past levels • Service versus competition	• Service versus customer requirement • Productivity versus goal • Cost versus standard
■ Relationships with suppliers and service providers	• Unmanaged • Crisis-driven • Adversarial	• Cost-driven • Multiple sources • Competitive bid oriented	• Partnership • Results-driven • Joint improvement
■ Constraint to further improvement	• Lack of control	• Bureaucracy	• Parochialism

meaningful way. It approaches service goal setting by handling each transaction as a separate situation. The only goal is to "keep the noise level down," i.e., keep customer and salesforce complaints to a level that general management can tolerate.

Long-range planning for the logistics process does not exist. Individual activities (e.g., transportation) may have "plans," but the planning typically is short-term and fragmented. Operations planning — balancing supply and demand to meet service goals — takes place with a planning horizon of "today." Policies, priorities, and decisions change on a transaction by transaction basis.

In addition to their planning deficiencies, Stage I organizations lack ongoing improvement processes. As problems arise, managers find "quick fixes" that address the symptom not the problem.

In a Stage I logistics process, employee-management relationships are strained. Each views the other with suspicion and distrust. Additionally, the information capabilities of the Stage I operation do not extend much beyond the ability to process transactions. There is little or no analysis capability. Stage I operations measure performance in gross terms such as current versus past costs, cost as a percent of sales, or number of service complaints.

In a Stage I logistics operation, relationships with vendors or suppliers tend to be unmanaged. Improvement actions occur only in a crisis situation such as a product shortage or a carrier service failure.

Generally, the Stage I logistics process lacks fundamental control over its operation. This lack of control creates a major obstacle to improvement.

Stage II. In a Stage II operation, management sets service goals internally and directs them toward treating all customers the same (thereby over-servicing some and under-servicing others). Long-range planning occurs but typically only on a narrow scope within the logistics process. For example, the so-called long-range plan may deal only with outbound physical distribution with a planning horizon of one to three years.

A Stage II firm handles operations planning on a period by period basis (e.g., monthly) built around budget periods. The various functions comprising the logistics process tend to act in their own interests in order to meet their budget requirements for the period. This behavior causes the month-end and quarter-end spikes that are prevalent in many industries.

The ongoing improvement process in a Stage II company focuses on cost reduction. Budget performance is king. As a result, improvements that don't reduce costs frequently are not made, even though other benefits could be realized.

Stage II firms tend to limit employee freedom, responsibility, and decision making. In fact, these companies supervise employees closely in an effort to control costs.

In a Stage II operation, information resources are largely dedicated to generating reports tied to each period's financial results. Data exist but are fragmented throughout the organization. Additionally, analysis capabilities are limited. Measurement focuses on costs versus budget (with the budget typically developed by adding "X percent" to last year's budget). The firm does measure productivity and service quality but on an historical basis that compares current and past performance.

Stage II operations typically use competitive bidding techniques to select suppliers. By applying pressure to carriers and suppliers to drive down rates and purchase prices of materials at "any cost," these Stage II operations frequently sacrifice or overlook improvements to service and quality.

Stage II operations are control oriented by nature. While some control is necessary, if left unchecked a control approach eventually results in bureaucracy. And bureaucracy stifles improvement efforts.

Stage III. In Stage III, the various functions participating in the logistics process are functionally excellent. Each performs its part of the process as well as possible. Purchasing management works with suppliers to improve product quality, service reliability, and cost. Transportation management works with carriers to improve service quality and productivity. Materials planning and control teams up with manufacturing to improve reliability, shorten cycle times, and reduce costs. Order management works with sales to anticipate customer requirements better, improve forecasts, and make reliable promises to customers on product availability and delivery schedules as orders come in.

In a Stage III logistics process, management establishes service goals to meet or exceed customer requirements. Because of distinctions among customers, this means providing differentiated, specially tailored services. Long-range planning occurs across the full scope of the logistics process — from the customer through the company to suppliers. The planning horizon is relatively long, commonly three to five years.

Stage III firms execute operations planning both on a period and an annual basis without artificial boundaries at the end of accounting periods.

The approach to ongoing improvement is one of continuous quality and productivity improvement toward goals with breakthrough improvements at the appropriate time.

These firms base the relationships between employees and management on shared goals and rewards. Employees are trained in improvement techniques and empowered to make decisions and carry out improvements.

In a Stage III logistics process, sufficient information capabilities exist to support long-range and operational planning. Data are accessible and easy to use. The systems offer flexible analysis capabilities.

Measurement in a Stage III logistics process incorporates the three dimensions of service (quality), productivity, and cost. Each is measured against an appropriate target (e.g., service versus customer requirements, productivity versus goals, and cost versus standard).

In a Stage III logistics process, relationships with vendors and suppliers are based on the partnership approach. Each party works for mutual improvement and is results driven.

Although a Stage III operation represents functional excellence, parochialism may constrain further improvement.

CHARACTERISTICS OF LOGISTICS EXCELLENCE

Logistics excellence is characterized by eight primary attributes, as Figure 4-2 depicts. Combining these characteristics with related responses to key questions in our survey questionnaires, we developed a profile of logistics excellence among the companies surveyed.

Figure 4-2

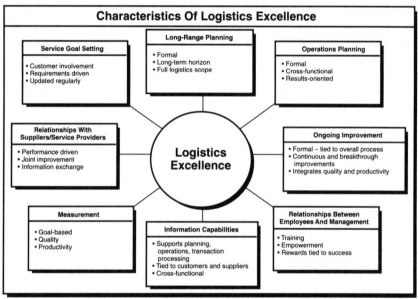

Characteristics Of Logistics Excellence

Service Goal Setting
- Customer involvement
- Requirements driven
- Updated regularly

Long-Range Planning
- Formal
- Long-term horizon
- Full logistics scope

Operations Planning
- Formal
- Cross-functional
- Results-oriented

Relationships With Suppliers/Service Providers
- Performance driven
- Joint improvement
- Information exchange

Logistics Excellence

Ongoing Improvement
- Formal – tied to overall process
- Continuous and breakthrough improvements
- Integrates quality and productivity

Measurement
- Goal-based
- Quality
- Productivity

Information Capabilities
- Supports planning, operations, transaction processing
- Tied to customers and suppliers
- Cross-functional

Relationships Between Employees And Management
- Training
- Empowerment
- Rewards tied to success

© Copyright A.T. Kearney, Inc., 1990

Figure 4-3 profiles respondents by Stage of Logistics Excellence for each of the eight dimensions and overall. As the graph shows, the percentage of respondents in each stage differs considerably across the eight dimensions. For example, the percent of respondents in Stage I ranges from a low of 10 percent on the service goal setting dimension to a high of 55 percent on long-range planning. For operations planning, 41 percent of the respondents exhibit Stage III characteristics, while only 7 percent do so for long-range planning.

Figure 4-3

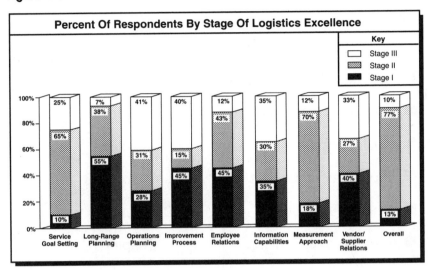

We also found that individual respondents may demonstrate characteristics of a number of stages across the eight dimensions. Thus, when we developed a composite stage for each respondent (based on the stage for each of the dimensions), we found that 13 percent tended to exhibit Stage I characteristics overall versus 77 percent for Stage II and 10 percent for Stage III.

We elaborate further on the specific techniques and approaches used by survey respondents for each of the eight dimensions of logistics excellence throughout this book. For reference, Figure 4-4 summarizes where each dimension is discussed.

LOGISTICS EXCELLENCE AND LOGISTICS PERFORMANCE

In principle, a logistics process exhibiting Stage III characteristics should perform better than one at a lower stage. We sought to test this theory by comparing the companies in our database on some key measures of performance.

1. Productivity improvement. Figure 4-5 breaks down the percent of productivity improvement in logistics overall by Stage of Logistics Excellence. Stage I companies clearly lag behind the others both in terms of cumulative improvement since 1986 and cumulative improvement expected between 1991 and 1995. Only minor differences separate Stage II and Stage III firms on actual productivity improvement over the past five years. Looking into the future, Stage II companies expect the greatest gains overall.

Figure 4-4

Reference Guide: Dimensions Of Logistics Excellence	
■ Service goal setting	Chapters 6, 7, 11
■ Long-range planning	Chapter 11
■ Operations planning	Chapter 11
■ Improvement process	Chapter 13
■ Employee relations	Chapters 11, 12
■ Information capabilities	Chapter 11
■ Measurement approach	Chapter 10, Appendixes A-F
■ Supplier relationships	Chapters 6, 11

Figure 4-5

Percent Cumulative Productivity Improvement In Logistics		
	Actual 1986-1990	Expected 1991-1995
Stage I	8.7%	8.7%
Stage II	10.6%	12.2%
Stage III	10.7%	10.1%
Overall	10.4%	11.7%

2. Cycle time and service improvement. We found that the distinctions between the Stage III excellent companies and the others were sharper for cycle time and service quality performance. We concluded that Stage III companies focus on these aspects of improvement to the logistics process and that gains don't show up using traditional productivity measures.

When comparing either absolute levels of cycle time and service level or changes in these measures across companies, we believe the only fair approach is to look at the data by industry. Because the number of Stage III companies in our database was small to begin with (10 percent), we found only two industries — chemicals/plastics and pharmaceuticals/drugs — that had enough in this group to make the analysis statistically meaningful.

Figure 4-6 displays actual order cycle time for the two industries in 1985 and 1990 as well as the respondents' goals for 1995. (Order cycle time is the elapsed time from order placement by the customer to delivery of the order to the customer.) The chart breaks down overall cycle times for each industry along with cycle times reported by Stage III companies.

Figure 4-6

Order Cycle Times				
		Cycle Days		
		1985	1990	1995 Goal
Chemicals And Plastics	Overall	8.9	6.1	5.0
	Stage III	6.0	3.7	3.3
Pharmaceuticals And Drugs	Overall	10.2	7.3	5.5
	Stage III	9.9	6.4	3.5

In 1985, the order cycle time of Stage III chemicals and plastics companies was 6.0 days — almost one-third less than the average. By 1990, the average chemicals/plastics company decreased its cycle days almost to the 1985 level of Stage III companies. During that time, the Stage III companies leapt ahead to a cycle time of 3.7 days. By 1995, the average chemicals/plastics company projects a five-day order cycle time, while the Stage III companies predict a further decrease to 3.3 days.

In the pharmaceuticals/drugs sector, differences among Stage III and average firms are not as dramatic for current performance. However, by 1995, Stage III companies expect to open a two-day gap between themselves and the average company in their industry. This represents a 36 percent acceleration of cycle time.

Figure 4-7 presents similar data for inventory replenishment cycle times. In the chemicals/plastics industry, Stage III companies boast inventory replenishment cycle times that are four days faster than the typical company in that industry. Further, they expect to retain that advantage through 1995.

Figure 4-7

Inventory Replenishment Cycle Times				
		Cycle Days		
		1985	1990	1995 Goal
Chemicals And Plastics	Overall	28.0	21.8	16.2
	Stage III	21.0	17.7	12.3
Pharmaceuticals And Drugs	Overall	55.1	41.0	26.2
	Stage III	42.0	31.4	21.8

In the pharmaceuticals industry, inventory replenishment cycle times have declined 25 percent overall since 1985 with another 25 percent decrease predicted by 1995. Even then, with anticipated inventory replenishment cycle times nearly five days shorter than those of average firms, Stage III companies will enjoy a significant advantage over the typical pharmaceutical and drug company.

Using another measure — order completeness — we see that Stage III companies outperform average ones in service improvements as well (see Figure 4-8). As the table shows, the pharmaceuticals/drugs sector excels in this area. Stage III companies in this business today have an order completeness rate 5 percent better than that of average companies. This gap will close somewhat by 1995, but the Stage III companies will retain their advantage.

Figure 4-8

Order Completeness Rates				
		Percent		
		1985	1990	1995 Goal
Chemicals And Plastics	Overall	84.5%	91.1%	97.0%
	Stage III	86.2%	91.7%	99.2%
Pharmaceuticals And Drugs	Overall	84.1%	90.3%	94.6%
	Stage III	90.6%	95.6%	97.4%

Although these analyses are limited only to the chemicals/plastics and pharmaceuticals/drugs industries, they support the argument that Stage III companies tend to be more service driven and process improvement driven than average firms. For Stage II companies, it appears that productivity improvement is a stronger driving force.

ACHIEVING LOGISTICS EXCELLENCE

Achieving logistics excellence creates value for customers through improved service quality. It creates value for shareholders through improved productivity and/or cost.

Achieving logistics excellence requires three things:

- A clear understanding of customer service requirements and a strategy for meeting those requirements (including service offerings and service goals)

- Tools and techniques for measuring quality and productivity, for identifying needed improvements, and for choosing among available improvement actions

- A framework and process for carrying out improvements across the various organizations involved

Sections III, IV, and V of this book offer materials to help you achieve excellence in your logistics process.

SECTION III

ESTABLISHING A CUSTOMER-FOCUSED SERVICE STRATEGY

Improving logistics quality begins by understanding customer requirements and expectations for service and developing a complete service strategy in response. This service strategy involves establishing specific goals and offerings.

In Section III, we highlight various approaches companies use to accomplish these ends. Within Section III, Chapter 5 expands on the theme discussed in Chapter 3 — that marketplace demands continue to increase and that today's *exceptional* service level will be tomorrow's *expected* service level. Chapter 6 offers suggestions on determining what customers require and expect. And Chapter 7 discusses how to translate customer requirements into service strategies, offerings, and goals.

CHAPTER 5

HOW CUSTOMER
REQUIREMENTS ARE CHANGING

Twenty years ago, one test of a company's ability to satisfy customers was its success in delivering the "right product to the right place at the right time at the right price." (Conceptually, this differs little from today's definition of providing quality customer service.) As long as a firm knew what the "right" components of this formula were, it had a clear picture of quality customer service toward which to work. The mission for the physical distribution process, as it was called then, was to "do things right," i.e., be as productive or efficient as possible.

In recent years, the ground rules changed. The "right things" are harder to identify. Uniformity has given way to customization both of products and services. Flexibility has supplanted economies of scale in manufacturing and distribution. A focus on responsiveness has replaced emphasis on volume and throughput. Providing acceptable levels of service — keeping the noise level down — is not good enough. Companies strive to supply superior service to gain competitive advantage.

Emerging demands for just-in-time and quick response inventory replenishment, electronic data interchange, scheduled deliveries, special packaging, marking and labeling, and other value-added services represent the wave of the future. These demands will continue to evolve. Companies, therefore, will need the means to identify requirements and refine offerings faster and more often than in the past.

Today's value-added service is tomorrow's necessity. Customers learn to expect what they have been receiving, and expectations spiral upward. Companies serving these customers must pursue a process of ongoing service refinement and improvement to stay with or ahead of competition.

THE PRODUCT/SERVICE BUNDLE

When customers buy a product from a supplier, they buy more than just physical goods. They purchase a complete bundle of product and service benefits. This bundle includes product characteristics, price levels, service, and, frequently, the supplier's commitment to a quality-improvement process (see Figure 5-1).

Figure 5-1

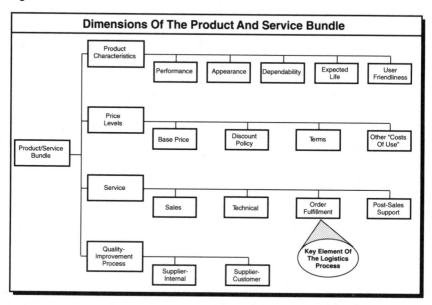

Customers look for certain characteristics when they buy a product, including performance (the product does what the specifications call for), appearance (it appears well made), dependability (it operates problem free), expected life cycle (it lasts a predictable amount of time), and user friendliness (it is comparatively easy to operate).

Pricing includes factors such as base price, discount policy, payment terms, and, increasingly, the "total cost of use" borne by the customer, including inspection, rework, inventory, and delays resulting from lack of quality in the supplier's product/service package.

Service includes sales (e.g., new account development, customer relationship management, new-product introduction), technical support, order fulfillment, and post-sales support in the form of repair and maintenance.

The quality-improvement process increasingly is becoming part of the overall product/service package. Customers want to buy from suppliers that demonstrate a commitment to quality improvement both in the supplier's internal operations as well as in the way the supplier works with customers.

Taken together, the elements comprising this new view of a total bundle of products and services expand the meaning of "right product, right place, right time, right price" considerably.

SERVICE AS THE DIFFERENTIATING FACTOR

The relative emphasis placed on each element of the product/service bundle (product, price, service, and quality) differs among industries, customers, and even product lines. For those industries having unique technologies, rapid product introduction, or brand loyalty, for example, product characteristics may be the preeminent concern for customers. This is more prevalent in one-time or infrequent purchase situations such as buying a mainframe computer, purchasing other capital equipment, or buying a new car. In these situations, the purchasing decision doesn't weigh as heavily on a supplier's on-time delivery performance or first-time invoice accuracy rate. Instead, the product's characteristics and, possibly, the vendor's post-sales support are often the deciding factors.

Where repetitive buying is the norm, service acquires greater importance. The supplier and customer share frequent, ongoing transactions. The quality of service provided during these interactions becomes noticeable and important. Even when product factors are critical to these repeat buying situations, improved service adds value by putting more of the product in more customer-facing locations sooner.

For many businesses, the product no longer is the sole source of competitive advantage. In fact, thanks to fierce competition, product quality is becoming a basic requirement — a given. In many cases, customers already know whether a particular supplier's product meets their needs. If several suppliers' products fit the need, service (and its impact on true product cost) becomes a differentiating factor. (In Chapter 11, we explore how some companies measure true product cost.)

To understand how service affects differentiation, we asked respondents to identify their deciding factors in product sourcing decisions (see Figure 5-2). Topping the list were basic product and service quality, including stability of supply. Interestingly, only 60 percent of respondents mentioned price as a critical factor in sourcing decisions. This response supports the belief held by many of our interviewees that price becomes a factor only after suppliers demonstrate they can meet product and service quality requirements. It also points out that low price alone is not sufficient if basic product and service thresholds are not met.

Value-added elements such as flexibility, technology, and manufacturing and design support received somewhat fewer but still a significant number of mentions by respondents. And lastly, participants noted that corporate policy directives on using or avoiding certain suppliers are minimally important elements in the sourcing decision.

Figure 5-2

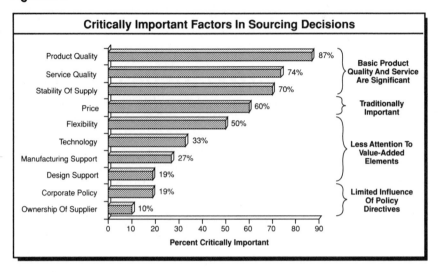

Critically Important Factors In Sourcing Decisions

Product Quality — 87% — Basic Product Quality And Service Are Significant
Service Quality — 74%
Stability Of Supply — 70%
Price — 60% — Traditionally Important
Flexibility — 50%
Technology — 33% — Less Attention To Value-Added Elements
Manufacturing Support — 27%
Design Support — 19%
Corporate Policy — 19% — Limited Influence Of Policy Directives
Ownership Of Supplier — 10%

Percent Critically Important

WHAT CUSTOMERS LOOK FOR

In the long run, customers evaluate suppliers based on their overall satisfaction with the business relationship. A key measure of this satisfaction is the value derived from doing business with a supplier. The so-called "buying experience" includes many dimensions both tangible and intangible. Tangible factors include product characteristics and quality, ease of order placement, order accuracy and completeness, timeliness of delivery, terms and conditions of the sale, and support in areas such as product design, training, maintenance, and repair.

Intangible factors relate to how the customer feels about doing business with the supplier. These intangibles include:

• Making customers feel they are important to the supplier

• Providing each person in the customer organization who influences the buying decision with a reason to feel good about doing business with the supplier

• Being easy to do business with

When customers seek out a supplier, they bring with them certain expectations. They want convenient, hassle-free transactions. They expect suppliers to handle the details involved in ensuring delivery of the right product at the right place, at the right time, and at the right price.

In addition, customers have basic requirements for handling exceptions. These exceptions might take the form of one-time or periodic special requests (emergency orders, expedited delivery, special packaging or handling, etc.). Exceptions also include specific transaction failures such as product damage, shipment delays, and invoicing errors. Exceptions may also encompass broader problems such as product recalls and hazardous-goods discharge. In every case, customers expect suppliers to manage the exceptions to a smooth resolution.

Often customers evaluate the essentials only in terms of minuses, giving the supplier no credit for getting them right but subtracting points when the supplier gets them wrong. Suppliers differentiate themselves and add value by consistently meeting and innovatively exceeding customer expectations. This means going beyond the customer's identified requirements to anticipate and satisfy other needs. Companies use points of differentiation to set themselves apart from their competition and position themselves competitively. Figure 5-3 shows the interrelationship between "essentials" and "points of differentiation." The bottom half of the diagram illustrates performance as it relates to essentials. When customers look to suppliers to meet requirements, they really are saying "do what I ask." In the worst case scenario, the supplier fails to meet the requirements and so fails the customer. More frequently, the supplier eventually manages to meet the customer's requirements.

Figure 5-3

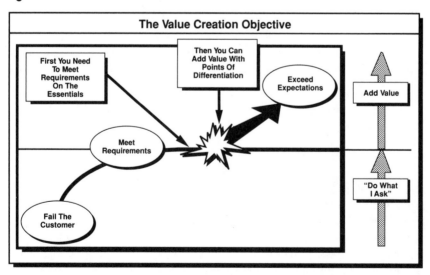

Unfortunately, just meeting requirements adds no value nor does it differentiate. Also, meeting requirements eventually leaves no room for improvement unless the requirements change. If the supplier already provides 100 percent on-time delivery, the supplier can't be *more* on time. If the vendor already meets the customer's cycle time needs, offering faster cycle time may add little value.

Instead, differentiation occurs when a supplier proactively exceeds expectations and provides value-added service in some area important to the customer. Value-added service takes two forms: either it helps customers reduce their costs and "hassle levels," or it helps customers service their downstream customers better and increase revenues.

The first benefit — reducing costs and "hassle levels" — takes several forms. For example, it might entail:

- Asking customers to order in pallet layer or full pallet quantities (e.g., 48 cases) instead of "round numbers" (e.g., 50 cases) to reduce unnecessary case picking and handlings

- Using EDI, standard formats, or other pre-refined formats for shipping documents (e.g., bills of lading, waybills, air bills) to avoid unnecessary paperwork and errors

- Performing services that are less expensive for the supplier to do than for the customer (e.g., rewinding paper at the mill so that the customer does not have to rewind it at its place of business or providing store-ready displays to retailers)

- Providing better information on product availability and order status to help the customer in inventory planning/deployment

- Streamlining communications with customers by installing proprietary data entry and communication terminals at the customer's premises (examples include McKesson Drug, Bergen Brunswig, and Baxter Hospital Supply Division)

Each of these actions goes beyond the essentials in adding value to the customer while reducing cost.

Several suppliers contribute value to customers by helping them serve their downstream customers better and increase total revenues. Achieving this task requires that the supplier understands the customer's operations and strategies. In manufacturing situations, for example, the vendor and manufacturer may team up on product design. Suppliers selling to the retail trade assist customers by helping with in-store merchandise design. Suppliers in the machinery and equipment business provide emergency replacement of equipment to keep the customer's operation going. In the grocery trade, suppliers of fresh meats, poultry, fruits, vegetables, and dairy products work with customers to reduce cycle time and increase product freshness, resulting in improved sales at retail.

The supplier and customer don't always agree about how much value a service adds. Several distributors in the healthcare industry, for instance, offer customers a "stockless" inventory program at a premium price. In these arrangements, the hospital supplier assumes inventory management and stock room responsibilities for the facility thereby freeing up space, capital, and manpower for other uses.

Although the program is popular with many hospitals, some show limited interest in this new service. From their perspective, the value received is insufficient to justify the higher price of the goods and services. In their view, it is true that inventory could be reduced. However, they believe that their store room space cannot easily be converted to other uses and is essentially a "sunk cost." And, in order to reduce head count, there must be substantial redesign of work duties and responsibilities that the hospital administrator may not be willing to undertake. Thus, in this case, at least some of the hospitals view the stockless program as not providing enough added value for the prices the suppliers wish to charge.

As this example illustrates, when suppliers promote value-added services they must make sure the customer truly believes in the value added.

SERVICE LEVELS VERSUS SERVICE QUALITY

One customer's requirements for service may differ significantly from another's. Each may want a different level of service based on needs and willingness to pay. It is important to distinguish, however, that a higher service level (e.g., faster delivery) is not the same as better service quality. As we defined in Chapter 4, logistics quality means meeting agreed-to customer requirements and expectations regardless of what those may be. Thus, furnishing 95 percent fill rates when the customer needs 97 percent results in worse quality than providing 92 percent fill rates when the customer expects 92 percent. Consequently, understanding what the customer requires and expects is the key to quality — in service and in logistics.

SERVICE LEVELS AND COMPETITIVE ADVANTAGE

Service requirements rarely are absolutes. Most customers accept a relatively wide range of performance on a service dimension. For example, if a customer expects on-time delivery service from suppliers to range between 96 and 98 percent, it is hard pressed to distinguish superior and poor performance as long as a supplier stays within that range.

For a supplier to gain a competitive advantage, it must provide superior service to the customer on critical service factors. Or, to avoid being at a competitive disadvantage, that supplier must improve performance into the acceptable range. Figure 5-4 illustrates these two points.

Not all service dimensions are critical. The key to creating competitive advantage for the supplier, therefore, is to focus attention on those few dimensions that swing the buying decision.

Figure 5-4

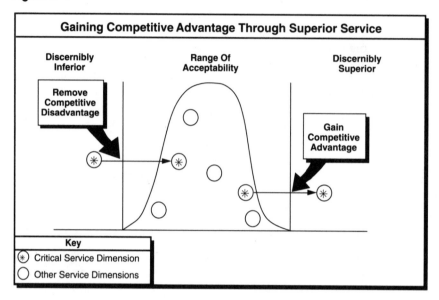

Gaining Competitive Advantage Through Superior Service

Discernibly Inferior

Range Of Acceptability

Discernibly Superior

Remove Competitive Disadvantage

Gain Competitive Advantage

Key

⊛ Critical Service Dimension

◯ Other Service Dimensions

SUMMARY OF EMERGING SERVICE ISSUES

In most industries, service is taking on new importance in the sourcing and buying decisions of customers. In this light, suppliers face two challenges. The first is identifying customer service requirements and developing service offerings that meet those requirements and add value. The second is to meet those requirements unerringly while exceeding customer expectations for those service dimensions on which it elects to seek competitive advantage. Taken together, these two challenges separate those suppliers that provide quality customer service from the rest of the competition.

As depicted in Figure 5-5, this is not a one-time process but an ongoing improvement cycle. It begins by defining customer requirements and evaluating how the company is positioned to meet those requirements. The cycle proceeds to identifying opportunities to correct significant deficiencies in service or to capitalize on inherent competitive advantages. These opportunities drive improvements that move the supplier into a preferred supplier position. They support an environment of performance measurement and continual improvement. And ultimately, they flow back into redefining customer requirements as the requirements change.

In the remainder of this section, we discuss this improvement cycle. Chapter 6 deals specifically with defining customer requirements, while Chapter 7 discusses how to turn those requirements into service goals and offerings and improvement actions.

Figure 5-5

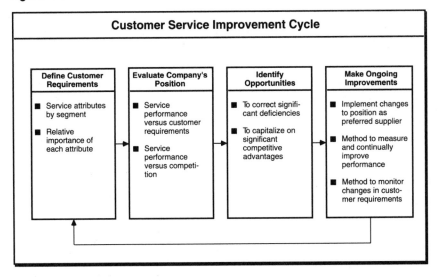

Customer Service Improvement Cycle

Define Customer Requirements	Evaluate Company's Position	Identify Opportunities	Make Ongoing Improvements
■ Service attributes by segment ■ Relative importance of each attribute	■ Service performance versus customer requirements ■ Service performance versus competition	■ To correct significant deficiencies ■ To capitalize on significant competitive advantages	■ Implement changes to position as preferred supplier ■ Method to measure and continually improve performance ■ Method to monitor changes in customer requirements

CHAPTER 6

DETERMINING CUSTOMER REQUIREMENTS

"What people in the business think they know about the customer and the market is more likely to be wrong than right. There is only one person who really knows: the customer."

Peter Drucker wrote these words nearly 30 years ago in his book, *Managing for Results.*[1] More recently, the brokerage firm of Paine Webber picked up on this theme in a series of television advertisements. In the series, a Paine Webber customer is discussing with a friend how his broker has helped him fund his retirement, a child's college education, and other major expenditures. The friend asks, "How did the broker know what you wanted?" The customer replies, "He asked."

SUPPLIER VERSUS CUSTOMER VIEWS

Ask the customer what is required and what is expected. As simple as this advice seems, a surprising number of companies fail to observe it effectively according to our research.

Most survey participants in our Logistics Management Survey (81 percent) rely on marketing and salesforce input to identify customer requirements as Figure 6-1 shows. They also depend heavily on customer complaints, reacting to the "noise level." Fewer than two-thirds of the suppliers actively solicit customer requirements through personal interviews, and only 53 percent conduct telephone or mail surveys. Over a quarter of the firms use competitors' goals to identify customer requirements.

Customers prefer proactive contact by suppliers according to the results of our Customer Expectations Survey. As Figure 6-2 illustrates, 85 percent of the customers believe suppliers should set service goals based on an in-depth understanding of customer operations. Fifty-nine percent think suppliers should use personal interviews as a primary means of establishing ser-vice requirements. A number of customer firms cited focus groups and phone/mail surveys as a good means of identifying requirements.

Figure 6-1

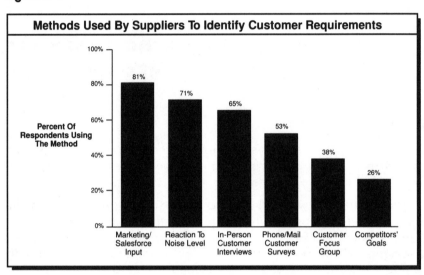

Methods Used By Suppliers To Identify Customer Requirements

Figure 6-2

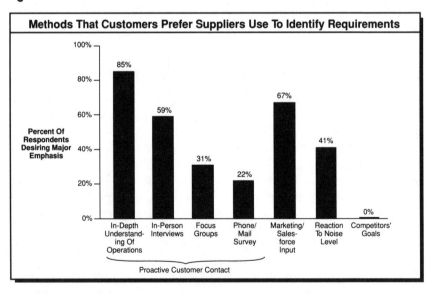

Methods That Customers Prefer Suppliers Use To Identify Requirements

And while many customers identified approaches such as marketing/salesforce input and "reaction to noise level" as important ways for suppliers to identify requirements, they recommend using them only as supplements to proactive customer contact. It is interesting to note that *none* of the respondents to the Customer Expectations Survey thought suppliers should use competitor's goals as a way to identify requirements. Clearly, customers would like to be able to say their suppliers knew what they wanted because "they asked." Only two-thirds of the suppliers in our survey appear to have gotten this message, however.

On a more positive note, suppliers and customers appear more in synch on the issue of how often suppliers should update their understanding of service requirements. Nearly 90 percent of the customers surveyed think suppliers should update their understanding of requirements at least once a year. Seventy-four percent of suppliers report doing so as Figure 6-3 shows. This represents a major shift from ten to 15 years ago when firms commonly updated requirements every two to three years. That slower cycle reflected the relative stability of customer requirements at the time.

Figure 6-3

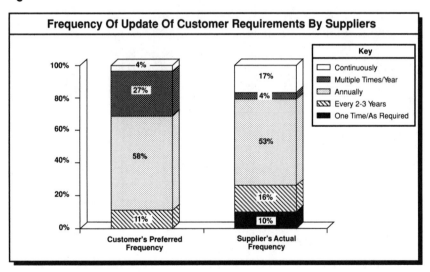

Next, we compared customer and supplier views on how well suppliers meet quantitative goals for several dimensions of customer service. Most suppliers think they're doing a good job of consistently meeting quantitative service goals (see Figure 6-4). Customers, however, don't share this opinion. On every service dimension, they give their suppliers' performance a lower score. The differences show up most dramatically in comparing responses related to the "goals consistently met" rating. For example, 39 percent of suppliers believe they consistently meet order cycle time goals, while only 4 percent of customers report such consistency. Similarly,

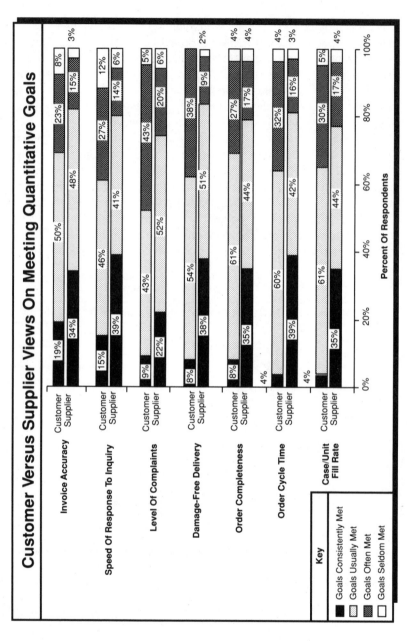

Figure 6-4

Customer Versus Supplier Views On Meeting Quantitative Goals

Key

■ Goals Consistently Met
▨ Goals Usually Met
▩ Goals Often Met
□ Goals Seldom Met

Invoice Accuracy	Customer	19% · 50% · 23% · 8%
	Supplier	34% · 48% · 15% · 3%
Speed Of Response To Inquiry	Customer	15% · 46% · 27% · 12%
	Supplier	39% · 41% · 14% · 6%
Level Of Complaints	Customer	9% · 43% · 43% · 5%
	Supplier	22% · 52% · 20% · 6%
Damage-Free Delivery	Customer	8% · 54% · 38% · 2%
	Supplier	38% · 51% · 9%
Order Completeness	Customer	8% · 61% · 27% · 4%
	Supplier	35% · 44% · 17% · 4%
Order Cycle Time	Customer	4% · 60% · 32% · 4%
	Supplier	39% · 42% · 16% · 3%
Case/Unit Fill Rate	Customer	4% · 61% · 30% · 5%
	Supplier	35% · 44% · 17% · 4%

Percent Of Respondents

0%   20%   40%   60%   80%   100%

35 percent of suppliers believe they consistently meet case or unit fill rate goals, while only 4 percent of customers share this perception.

These results point to a serious perception gap. In virtually every service area, suppliers believe they are doing a better job than their customers think they're doing. This perception gap may result, in part, from biases or differences in the measures used by customers and suppliers. Nevertheless, our research indicates that a very real gap exists between actual customer requirements and suppliers' perception of those requirements.

We asked suppliers that had proactively solicited customers' requirements to rate how well their perception of customer requirements matched the actual requirements determined by asking the customer (see Figure 6-5). For the three major elements of the order-fulfillment cycle — order processing, delivery cycle, and order receipt and follow-up — only one-third of these suppliers reported a match between perception and reality. The majority reported some differences, while a small but notable group (9 to 10 percent) reported major differences. This gap between perception and reality helps explain why suppliers believe they're doing better than the reality reported by customers.

Figure 6-5

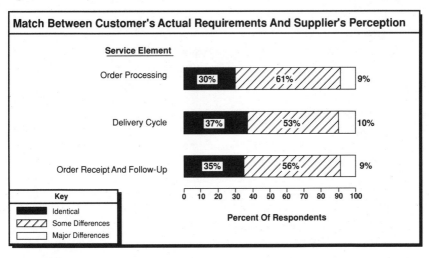

For a different view of the same problem, we asked customers to list the factors that impede their suppliers' ability to provide good service. As Figure 6-6 notes, at least 60 percent identified six key impediments. Heading this list is lack of understanding by suppliers of how their actions affect customers' quality and productivity. Some 90 percent of the customers cited this as a significant impediment with 41 percent calling it critically significant. A vendor may view shipment delays, incomplete orders, damaged goods, etc., as minor problems. To the customer supplying a production line or stocking retail shelves, they can cause major disruptions.

Figure 6-6

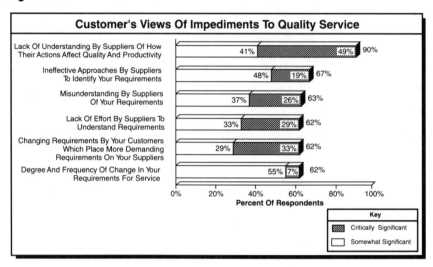

Customers reported three other impediments relating to lack of effort or understanding on the part of suppliers. These include ineffective approaches by suppliers to identify requirements, misunderstanding of requirements, or simply lack of effort to understand requirements. The response on these four areas indicates that customers think suppliers should do a better job soliciting their input on requirements.

Suppliers are not the only source of impediments to quality service as the figure indicates. Changing requirements by downstream customers, which cause companies to place more demanding requirements on their own suppliers, received a significant rating from 62 percent of the respondents. In fact, this impediment ranked second among those identified as critically significant, implying that suppliers should track the changing needs of both their immediate and downstream customers.

This kind of ripple effect occurs more and more frequently today. As customer requirements continue to change, the quality of the service provided by suppliers needs to be at least as high as that which the company gives to its own customers. Otherwise, the firm "in the middle" acts as a quality buffer and incurs additional cost. Take AT&T Computer Group's relationship with Intel, for example. Intel was an original equipment manufacturer for part of AT&T's personal computer line. AT&T placed a 99.8 percent incoming acceptance rate requirement on Intel's materials. To accommodate this, Intel had to push its quality standards up by 1,500 percent (from a 97 percent incoming acceptance rate). This, in turn, required Intel to demand better quality from its suppliers. To accomplish this, Intel began a supplier quality-improvement process working with its vendors to achieve a 99.8 percent acceptance rate on inbound materials.[2]

Thus far, judging from the research results, suppliers need to take a more proactive approach to identifying their customers' service requirements. The remainder of this chapter suggests a series of actions companies can take to better identify and understand requirements of current or potential customers and use these insights to formulate appropriate service offerings and goals.

PROCESS OVERVIEW

In general, the process of defining customer requirements comprises four steps:

- Understanding the customer's business

- Understanding who represents the customer in the buying decision

- Asking the representatives to express their requirements

- Interpreting what the customer wants and is willing to pay for

1. Understanding the customer's business. To offer value to a customer, the supplier must understand the customer's business — its missions, goals and strategies, competitive situation, key business processes, problems, issues, and, finally, the needs of its downstream customers. Historically, this task fell to the sales staff. As we discuss below, however, there is a growing trend toward involving other functions of the supplier's business in understanding the customer's business. This enlarged involvement makes it easier for the supplier to translate the service requirements into operational requirements.

2. Understanding who represents the customer. Understanding who the real customer is can be complicated. In most large organizations, the customer is not a single person. Rather, the tasks of selecting suppliers, placing orders, receiving goods, and paying invoices may fall to many different individuals. For example, the manufacturing manager in a factory, the nurse or physician in a hospital, and the store manager in a retail setting may be concerned primarily about product characteristics. The buying agent (e.g., the purchasing department in an industrial setting or the merchandising/buying department in a commercial setting) may be driven by price or time considerations. A third set of individuals may base supplier selection on convenience factors (e.g., the materials manager who prefers Supplier A because it always accommodates emergency orders or the receiving clerk who likes dealing with Supplier B because its goods are easy to unload and put away).

In addition to understanding who influences the purchasing decision, suppliers need to understand how each of these individuals track supplier performance. This means knowing the performance measurement process and the source of this information. As one executive we interviewed put it, "If you don't find out how the customers measure you and instead rely on your own internal measures, you're either egotistical, stupid, or both."

To understand all the requirements of a customer organization, a supplier needs to discern all the customer's buying influencers. Although these buying influencers vary among organizations, they typically include those elements shown in Figure 6-7.

Figure 6-7

Examples Of Buying Influencers	
Manufacturing Customers	**Wholesale And Retail Customers**
■ Product development	■ Marketing
■ Engineering	■ Sales
■ Production	■ Merchandising
■ Quality assurance	■ Logistics
■ Logistics	■ Finance
■ Finance	

3. Asking the representatives to express their requirements. The third step — finding out from the customer what its requirements are — is accomplished by asking each key decision maker or decision influencer questions such as:

• What's important to you?

   — Which service dimensions make a difference in your buying decision?

   — How do you prioritize those service dimensions?

- What constitutes discernibly superior and inferior performance?
  — What levels of performance on what dimensions will prompt increased purchases?
  — What levels of service problems reduce your purchases or cause you to disqualify a supplier?
- What is current performance? How do you measure it?
  — How well does our company meet the requirements?
  — How well do competitors meet the requirements?
- How can we be easier to do business with?
  — What things are we doing that we should not be doing?
  — What things aren't we doing that we should be doing?
- How can we create value?
  — What are we doing today that you like or value?
  — What are competitors doing that you like or value?
  — How can we do a better job of meeting your needs?

Understanding how customers measure suppliers is critical. Suppliers can never know for certain when they're providing quality service simply because they aren't the customer. The customer is the sole judge. A supplier, therefore, is wise to understand how the judging takes place.

In business, understanding your customers' needs and how they judge your service is akin to competing in Olympic figure skating. The compulsory figures portion of a skating competition is analogous to the essentials of customer service. By understanding the requirements of compulsory figures together with the judges' method of scoring, the skater can learn exactly what is expected. The scoring on compulsory figures is on a "points-off" basis. Perfection is the expectation; the judges deduct points for not meeting requirements.

The free-style portion of Olympic figure skating compares to the value-added portion of providing service. Measurement is based on whether the skater pleases the judge and crowd (except, of course, for major failures like a fall).

To win the competition, the skater must perform well in both the compulsory and free-style events. Sometimes, the skater with the best free-style program does not win the competition because of poor scores on the essential compulsory figures. Such is the case in business as well where companies must perform on the essentials as well as the value-added services in order to get and keep customers.

Depending on what the customer needs, the supplier can achieve superior performance by satisfying a broad range of value-added requirements. These may include:

- Training and educational support

- Technical/application support

- Maintenance, repair, and replacement support

- Assistance in disposition/sale of product at time of replacement

- Superior product quality and shelf life

- Special packaging and handling

- Inventory monitoring

- Order/usage history information

- Cost reduction advice for the client

- Flexible terms and conditions of sale

- Accessibility and responsiveness to questions and problems

As companies seek out customer requirements, they need to consider all of these factors.

4. Interpreting what the customer wants and is willing to pay for. This last step is the most difficult because it involves understanding the impacts and benefits that meeting requirements or providing discernibly superior service will have.

First, it requires analyzing the real value the customer places on each service dimension. This means determining such things as whether the customer will pay more for higher service levels in the short term and whether the service levels add to long-term customer satisfaction and retention.

Usually, there is no simple way to answer these questions. Test marketing doesn't always work. If the test finds customers like the improved service but are unwilling to pay for it, withdrawing the service can have repercussions. Market research can help, but customers tend to overestimate how much buying patterns will change and underestimate how much they will pay for new services. Lastly, expert opinion essentially is an informed guess. Despite the drawbacks of these methods, they are among the best tools available for predicting customer reaction to changes in service.

The task then becomes understanding the cost and profit impact of providing improved service. The supplier must analyze these factors based on current processes, including logistics, and on changes to the processes made to accommodate new service requirements. Profitability analysis, discussed in Chapter 11, is a starting point.

METHODS OF IDENTIFYING REQUIREMENTS

While the focus of this research is on the logistics process, the techniques for determining customer requirements and specifications are common across the entire product/service bundle. In fact, there are four basic approaches companies can use to identify customer requirements. They entail:

- Using the customer's own statements of expectations

- Soliciting customer input through a survey process

- Using current performance levels and "noise levels"

- Benchmarking against competition

1. **Using the customer's statements of expectations.** In some cases, customers are very explicit about their requirements and expectations from suppliers to the point of detailing the requirements in policy manuals and brochures. In a publication to vendors, Boise Cascade Office Products says a supplier should provide:

- At least 95 percent complete orders on the first receipt

- Consistent cycle times

- Vendor support for marketing and purchasing

Boise Cascade's manual also includes a 21-point instruction list on how to ship to Boise Cascade. This list covers carton labeling, palletization methods, requirements for paperwork consistency (e.g., manifest must match pallet/carton contents; invoices must be in purchase order item sequence; and purchase orders, bills of lading, freight bills, packing lists, and invoices must be cross-referenced), and freight bill and payment terms documentation.

Baxter's Hospital Supply Division has a ten-point supplier requirements program that sets out its expectations of suppliers. It includes:

- Assuming responsibility for product and service quality

- Delivering 100 percent of orders, filled complete, within established lead times

- Providing 100 percent accurate invoices 100 percent of the time

- Adhering to minimum notification requirements for any changes to products, service, or terms of doing business

- Becoming "EDI ready" in support of Baxter's efforts to operate in an EDI environment

While the customer's statement of expectations is a good starting point, suppliers should recognize that these may only represent the essentials. To understand the points of differentiation in value-added services, the supplier must consult the customer directly.

2. Soliciting customer input. Customers want suppliers to ask about requirements, and soliciting customer expectations through a survey process is the most effective way to gain understanding in this area. One of most effective techniques is the personal interview where a supplier representative interviews the various buyers and buying directors in the customer organization.

The interview approach offers several advantages. It necessitates direct contact with the customer, improving the quality of information gathered while demonstrating that the supplier cares. It enables the interviewer to ask follow-up questions and probe specific issues. And it gives the interviewer the opportunity to see and understand firsthand how the customer's facilities and processes work. Unfortunately, personal interviews take a lot of time and effort. Consequently, many companies reserve personal interviews for major customers and potential customers.

In some cases, the supplier may use outside research firms to conduct the interviews. Using an outside research firm can have several advantages over having company employees conduct the interviews. The research firm can protect the anonymity of the company that commissioned the survey if this is required. Tactical issues (such as responding to complaints about last week's late order) can be avoided. Customers are often more willing to discuss strengths and weaknesses of competing suppliers with a third party. Finally, such firms can provide specialized skills and experience in interpreting findings.

To gain broader customer input on a more affordable basis, companies use telephone and mail surveys. Telephone surveys offer the advantage of personal contact and the ability to probe responses. Mail surveys, on the other hand, do not facilitate follow-up questioning, lack the personal touch, and often have a low response rate. They are less expensive, however, and they can be very effective when the supplier seeks quantitative answers and can devise highly structured questions.

A fourth option — focus groups — may be useful in some settings. Focus groups are commonly used in consumer marketing research to pinpoint issues, explore concerns, and solicit opinions. With industrial- or commercial-customer focus groups, participants may be reluctant to discuss specific requirements while in the same room as their competitors. Nevertheless, focus groups can be useful in understanding general trends and requirements especially if customers come from a cross section of industries. Xerox, for example, uses focus groups to solicit input across its diverse customer base. Logistics service providers (carriers, public warehouse operators, third-party logistics services) may find focus groups useful given the breadth of their customer base.

3. Using current performance and "noise levels" to determine requirements. While this may be a useful supplement to direct customer contact, it represents a reactive approach. Responses from our Customer Expectations Survey indicate that customers prefer their suppliers not use this as a primary approach to identifying service requirements. However, "noise level" data in customer complaint records can offer useful insights about where improvements are needed.

4. Benchmarking. Benchmarking is a technique in which the supplier compares its service offerings and levels to those of the competition. Because it can provide feedback on current performance, it is a useful supplement to proactive customer contact. However, benchmarking does not define service requirements nor does it define what service should be. We discuss benchmarking in greater detail in Chapter 9.

In summary, direct customer contact is the best way to identify requirements. Personal interviews and focus groups are the most effective means of identifying opinions and future needs because of their capability for discussion and follow-up. Telephone and mail surveys are more appropriate for statistical fact gathering and for historical performance measurement (discussed in Chapter 10).

FREQUENCY OF CONTACT

As we noted earlier, customers want suppliers to conduct frequent updates of their understanding of requirements — at least once a year — according to a majority of firms surveyed. Reflecting this preference, several suppliers in this study manage a multi-tiered approach for maintaining customer contact and updating requirements. First, they conduct frequent "pulse" surveys of all customers using mail and telephone techniques. These pulse surveys measure customer perceptions of supplier performance on a variety of factors. Declining scores may indicate poor performance or changing requirements. Whatever the cause, the supplier can spot and respond to change quickly. Xerox uses pulse surveys to contact each customer at least twice per year. Federal Express conducts quarterly pulse surveys across various segments of its business base.

Burlington Motor Carriers (BMC) conducts a mail-in customer satisfaction survey twice per year. In each survey, the top 150 customers are polled along with 150 accounts chosen randomly. Information gathered includes:

- Overall satisfaction with BMC's services (both using a quantitative score on a one to seven scale and a "fill in the blank" opportunity for the customer to comment on the score)

- Relative importance to the customer of several service factors

- The customer's satisfaction with BMC on 16 service dimensions dealing with customer communications, operations, marketing, and administration

- The *single* thing BMC could do for that customer that would make it more satisfied with the company's trucking service

Additionally, Burlington Motor Carriers plans to begin making random follow-up phone calls on 50 loads per day to ensure that it met the customer's service expectations.

Customer pulse surveys often open the door to communicating with customers about their requirements. Preston Trucking uses a version of a pulse study to rate its service in different areas. The process asks customers to score Preston based on a ten-point rating scale. As the firm explains, the system works as follows. "If we score a six on a dimension, for example, we ask the customer what we have to do to go from a six to a seven. This forms the basis for a concrete short-term improvement plan to meet that customer's requirements. It has a lot more value than asking what we can do to leap from a six to a ten."

The second tier in maintaining contact includes periodic "vision surveys" using personal interviews, focus groups, and telephone/mail surveys. Vision surveys help identify requirements that grow out of a trigger point occurrence, when the assumptions for how a customer deals with its suppliers change. Such triggers take many forms:

- New processes, systems, or decision makers for existing or potential customers

- Specific customer concerns identified in pulse surveys

- Customer strategy shifts (e.g., overseas sourcing, JIT, supplier certification programs)

- New competitors entering existing markets or major competitor moves (e.g., major investments in markets, announced partnerships with customers, mergers and acquisitions of competitors)

- Emergence of new channels of distribution (e.g., warehouse clubs, mail order)

- Actions by suppliers to bypass intermediaries and distribute directly to customers

- New products and technologies that indicate customer requirements may be changing or that competing suppliers are changing their service offerings

Entry of new customers into a marketplace is a special kind of trigger.

Suppliers must understand the requirements of that specific customer as well as any changes in requirements by current customers in response to the new competition.

The third tier of customer contact involves maintaining continuous customer-specific communication with key accounts. By doing so, suppliers gain immediate feedback from customers and can anticipate and resolve problems before they occur. The real value of this approach, however, is that suppliers and customers learn one another's operations so intimately that they can design and execute process improvements that benefit both parties.

Several progressive companies now use this continuous communication approach. Procter & Gamble, for one, has assigned an account management team to work with Wal-Mart at the retailer's Arkansas headquarters to streamline and improve processes such as inventory replenishment. Similarly, key suppliers of Bose Corporation place representatives at Bose facilities to insure that requirements are constantly being met, reviewed, and updated.[3] Nalco Chemical Company assigns teams of sales engineers to work full time at customers' facilities to ensure that today's requirements are being met and tomorrow's are identified proactively.

OTHER TECHNIQUES FOR IDENTIFYING CUSTOMER REQUIREMENTS

Another good source for tracking customer requirements is the customer complaint. It is an unfortunate fact of business life that customers tend to broadcast their unhappiness about poor service far more often than they talk about great service. However, complaints can be turned to an advantage. Monitoring customer complaints is a good way to find out what the customer's "hot buttons" are about service failures and expectations. It's also a good source of information about the competition. Customer complaints can also provide information on where a supplier is at a competitive disadvantage and may be at risk of losing customers over time.

Companies can collect complaint information through a variety of means. They include:

• Offering 800 numbers for customer phone calls

• Training front-line employees to investigate and resolve complaints and to feed the complaint and the consequences to those responsible for defining and monitoring service requirements

• Using lost-business reports as a trigger to review requirements

Sandoz Chemicals has developed a method of entering complaints or inquiries from customers into a system and then automatically routing the system complaint to the correct functional manager (e.g., quality assurance, customer sales representatives, or field service) for a response. An additional feature of the system is that sales representatives can download data on recent complaints from a customer to their lap top computers so they do not get blind sided when they make a sales call. This allows them to improve their sales effectiveness.

Some companies have a formal "exit interview" with lost customers. Preston Trucking views these exit interviews as a major source of information. About these interviews, management comments, "Probably the best data we get is from the lost-business survey we conduct monthly. If we're failing one customer, we're failing others who aren't complaining or leaving."

UNDERSTANDING REQUIREMENTS OF THE ORDER-FULFILLMENT PROCESS

To this point, we've discussed understanding customer requirements on a broad based level. We turn now to logistics — specifically the order-fulfillment process. In the remainder of this chapter, we address specific issues related to defining the requirements of the order-fulfillment process (see Figure 6-8).

Figure 6-8

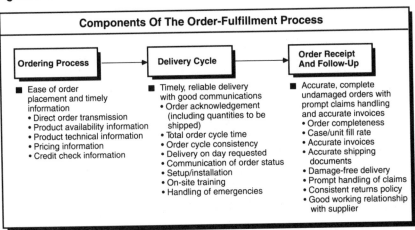

As the diagram notes, the order-fulfillment process is made up of three components:

• Ordering process (with requirements for ease of order placement and timely information)

- Delivery cycle (with demands for timely, reliable delivery with good communications)

- Order receipt and follow-up (requiring accurate, complete, undamaged orders with prompt claims handling and accurate invoices)

Imbedded in the order-fulfillment cycle are numerous requirements and expectations that customers have of suppliers. At a minimum, a supplier must understand customer requirements for each factor shown in Figure 6-9. Further, the supplier needs to understand how these requirements differ for the customer by order type (e.g., emergency, stock replenishment, custom, promotion, test/trial) and product type (e.g., core items, line extensions, custom items, critical versus noncritical items).

Figure 6-9

What Are The Requirements/Expectations?	
• Product line breadth and composition • Order cycle time and consistency • On-time delivery performance • Delivery frequency • Order completeness (order case, line fill) • Order accuracy • Product substitution • Backorder policies • Order status information • Order integrity (split shipments) • Product labeling requirements	• Product receiving requirements • Customer pickup requirements • Shipment routing preferences/ restrictions • Impact of minimums on ordering patterns • Returns processing expectations • Damage rate expectations • Freight allowance expectations • Claims processing expectations • Billing accuracy and timing expectations • Responsiveness to inquiries

To truly understand customer requirements, suppliers need to probe deeply. For example, when the customer talks about order completeness requirements, the supplier should know what measure the customer uses. Does the client measure by case- or line-fill rates or by orders filled complete? Does the customer measure on an overall basis or differently by type of item? Are there specific items for which the client expects 100 percent availability even though on average it will accept 95 percent for the total order?

Regarding delivery timeliness, the supplier should know what "on-time" means to the customer. Does it mean a time window plus or minus two days? Or does on-time mean delivery on a specific date and time? Are early deliveries acceptable or are they just as bad as late deliveries? How does the supplier learn a shipment's due date? Does the customer request a specific date or cycle time? Is each order negotiated individually?

The supplier should find out what role its sales representatives play in setting delivery commitments. Do they specify the due date by estimating when the customer needs the goods? Or do they set the date based on when they can safely promise delivery? In these two cases, sales staff opinion masks the true customer requirements.

As this list of questions indicates, the amount of information a supplier should collect can be overwhelming. To prevent this, suppliers can design the scope of the data gathering process to reflect the customer's importance. This means gathering extensive detail on major customers while collecting less detail for other customers. (In Chapter 11, we explore the kinds of information that a supplier might collect from a key account customer.) Then, by tracking potential triggers, suppliers can identify particular customers with whom requirements changes are likely and probe these in detail.

A PROACTIVE COURSE

As mentioned in the beginning of this chapter, fewer than two-thirds of the companies we surveyed proactively solicit their clients' service requirements. Clearly, suppliers need to address this situation. To judge how they're doing in this area, companies can take the quick self test in Figure 6-10. Being able to answer these questions for each key customer is the starting point for achieving quality customer service and producing value for customers.

---

[1] Drucker, Peter F., *Managing for Results, Economic Tasks and Risk-taking Decisions*
[2] Semick, J. William, "Tracking Quality Through The Supply Chain"
[3] McClenahan, John S., "So Long, Salespeople"

Figure 6-10

Self Test: Do You Understand What Each Key Customer's Requirements Are?

- ■ What are the customer's requirements?
  - • What are buyers and influencers expecting me to do
    - – What activities, how frequently
    - – Which ways/methods
  - • How does each person "win" by selecting one supplier over another

- ■ How is the customer measuring my performance?
  - • What are the standards (how many, how much, when, at what cost)
  - • How is performance being measured (data sources, scope of measure, formula)

- ■ How well am I meeting these requirements in the customer's eyes?

- ■ What am I already doing that adds real value? What should I be doing?

CHAPTER 7

DEVELOPING A
SERVICE STRATEGY

In days gone by, when suppliers asked customers what their requirements were, the answer came back "more, better, cheaper." Suppliers typically responded by saying, "You can have any two of the three."

Today, despite more sophisticated approaches to customer management, supplier-customer relations, and supplier-vendor management, the basic message in this exchange remains the same. Customer demands are increasing. However, not everything carries the same priority for the customer. For some, consistent delivery with a seven-day cycle time means more than a shorter but inconsistent cycle time. For some, service guarantees are important and worth an added cost; for others, service guarantees are nice to have but not worth any price increase. For a particular service dimension, a performance level ranging between 92 and 95 percent may have no influence over customer buying decisions. Performance above 95 percent, however, may add to revenues, while performance below 92 percent may prompt customers to seek another source.

From the supplier's perspective, it may be impossible to meet certain customer requirements. A manufacturer may not have access to certain technologies. A distributor may not have distribution rights for a certain vendor's products. A transportation carrier may be unable to provide next day service to certain less than truckload markets. Alternatively, suppliers may be able to meet customer requirements but not at the price the customer is willing to pay.

Finding a way to reconcile customer requirements with company capabilities is the essence of developing a service strategy. Figure 7-1 shows a generalized approach to this process.

Figure 7-1

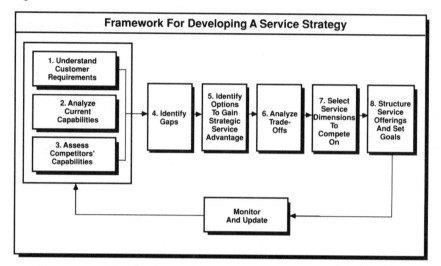

Chapter 6 described ways to determine customer requirements. To develop a service strategy, the supplier assesses these requirements in terms of its capabilities and those of its competitors to identify gaps. Gaps represent service dimensions that are most important to customers but where the supplier is at a competitive disadvantage.

Once the firm pinpoints its gaps, it identifies options to close or eliminate the gaps and so gain strategic service advantage. Companies create strategic service advantage by providing *required* levels of service in many areas and, at the same time, supplying *superior* service in areas that truly count in the eyes of customers.

Next, the firm must analyze tradeoffs, studying the benefits, costs, risks, and actions required to close the gaps. In some cases, the supplier decides not to close the gap. Dow Chemical, for instance, has a formal process for reviewing customer requirements and expectations. If a customer expects something that Dow can't deliver, whether for lack of expertise or too high a cost penalty, Dow notifies the customer that it cannot meet the requirement. The company goes one step further by incorporating that unmet expectation into its process for refining and developing future business and service strategies.

Once a company decides on a service strategy — identifying dimensions of service in which to excel or keep pace — its final task is to create service offerings based on that strategy and set goals against which performance can be measured. A complete discussion of how to develop a service strategy is beyond the scope of this book. Consequently, this chapter summarizes the major steps in the approach, specifically addressing how companies can structure service offerings and set goals.

STEP 1: UNDERSTAND SERVICE REQUIREMENTS

The first step in developing a service strategy is to understand the customers' service requirements. Numerous methods exist for accomplishing this task. As mentioned in Chapter 6, interviews and surveys can provide a wealth of information in this area. Figure 7-2 illustrates one approach for displaying the results of these efforts. A summary such as shown in Figure 7-2 can be prepared for each key customer or for groupings of other customers in logical segments. The format shows the relative importance of each dimension of customer service to the customer segment and what the customer or segment views as satisfactory or discernibly superior levels of service.

Figure 7-2

Developing An Understanding Of Customer Requirements			
Segment – XXXX		Performance Standards	
Customer Service Dimension	Relative Importance	Satisfactory	Discernibly Superior
■ On-time delivery	A	• 95% of shipments arrive on day requested	• 99% of shipments arrive on day requested
■ Repair service	B	• Response to service call in two hours	• Guaranteed recovery or loaner equipment in four hours

When addressing segmentation, vendors must go beyond traditional demographic or channel of distribution sectors and look at how the customer wants to buy from suppliers. When evaluating the service dimension of delivery cycle time, it is more meaningful to group customers by their service expectations (e.g., next day versus second day service) rather then by their types of business (e.g., supermarket versus wholesale club).

Differences within traditional segments take many forms. Some chain stores prefer to control distribution through their own distribution network, while others like goods delivered directly to stores. Some hospitals require patient-level labeling of product so it can be charged back to the patient upon use. Others operate their own storerooms and handle this function in-house. Some customers prefer to receive product on pallets, while others want to receive on slip sheets.

Identical products may have different service requirements depending on how the customers use them. In the paper industry, newspapers order newsprint based on relatively long lead times. Their delivery requirements are fairly flexible — generally on a "week of" or "month of" basis. Exact quantities are not required; newspapers allow a variance of as much as 10 percent on total tons ordered. Although commercial publishers use essentially the same newsprint, their requirements are much more stringent. Lead times seldom extend beyond 72 hours, and 24 hours is commonplace. At the very least, the delivery requirement is "day of" with specific timed deliveries often required. Because the commercial publishers order to specific press runs, they require exact quantities.

In the food/grocery industry, requirements for shelf replenishment differ from those for promotions. Likewise, for an assembly process, component parts going in to stock have a different set of requirements than those for a specific job.

Because of these differences, customers cannot be lumped together in terms of their service requirements. Further, traditional market segmentation approaches (size, location, type of business, etc.) often are unsuitable for developing service offerings and goals. What constitutes superior performance to one customer may be only satisfactory to another and a failure to a third. One customer's high priority service dimension may be of no value to another.

STEPS 2 AND 3: ANALYZE CURRENT CAPABILITIES AND ASSESS COMPETITORS' CAPABILITIES

Once the supplier understands the requirements of its key customers and market segments, the next step is to analyze its capabilities and those of competitors in meeting these conditions. Sober self assessment coupled with competitive benchmarking support these activities. Figure 7-3 illustrates this comparison process for a hypothetical consumer products firm, XYZ Co. For each customer service dimension listed, the chart compares XYZ with its competitors, noting whether its service is superior, satisfactory, or inferior.

STEP 4: IDENTIFY GAPS

Using the data derived from this comparison system, XYZ Co. then conducts a gap analysis. For the segment under scrutiny, quick response is a very important service dimension as the chart shows. Note that as far as quick response goes, Competitor B already performs at a service level that customers consider discernibly superior. XYZ's service, on the other hand, only rates a satisfactory score. In the area of emergency shipments, also a very important factor for this segment, XYZ provides superior performance, whereas the competition lags behind. For the on-time delivery dimension, XYZ not only lags behind competitors, but its service potentially jeopardizes business.

Summarizing the findings in this simple example, XYZ should be concerned about two gaps:

- In the quick response area, XYZ is stuck in the middle of the pack with Competitor B providing discernibly better service. Should XYZ try to break out of the pack and match Competitor B's service or should it find another dimension on which to compete?

- In the area of on-time delivery, the gap is more serious. At the very least, XYZ must find a way to provide satisfactory service in order to prevent customer defection. It also should decide whether superior service on this dimension will lead to overall service advantage.

Figure 7-3

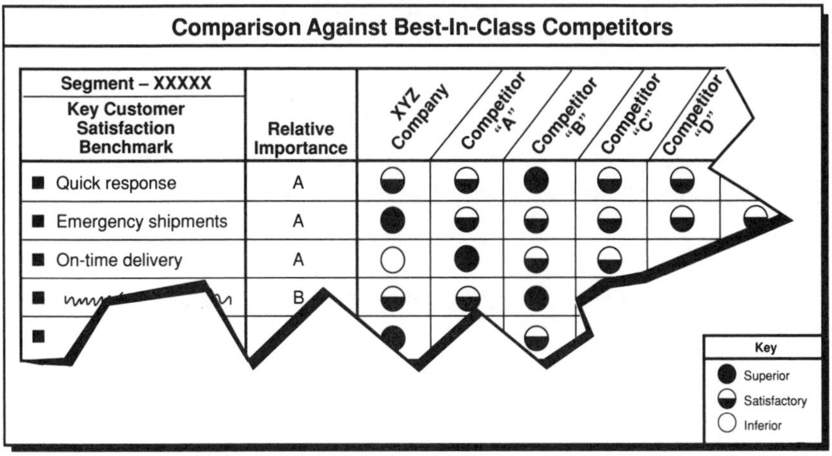

Comparison Against Best-In-Class Competitors

STEP 5: IDENTIFY OPTIONS TO GAIN STRATEGIC SERVICE ADVANTAGE

Once the firm identifies the gaps, its next task is to look at ways to close them and potentially outdo the competition. Several techniques are available. To close the quick response gap, XYZ could increase inventories and move them closer to the market. Alternatively, it could tie into customer usage data, establish a make-to-order system, and provide overnight delivery. For on-time delivery, XYZ could reduce total cycle time by getting better performance from carriers or by managing its delivery date promises so they are more realistic.

STEP 6: ANALYZE TRADEOFFS

Each option offers potential benefits. The customer benefits directly as the recipient of the improved service level. More difficult to gauge is the benefit to the company. What is the marketplace impact of moving performance out of the inferior category into the satisfactory category? How many service related lost sales does this action prevent and at what cost? Similarly, XYZ must assess the marketplace impact of providing superior service in a given category. Does this change really secure a competitive advantage? Naturally, XYZ Co. must weigh the costs associated with changing service levels against the benefits.

STEP 7: SELECT DIMENSIONS OF SERVICE ON WHICH TO COMPETE

Most companies can't afford to provide superior service on all service dimensions. Rather, they must pick the dimensions they believe will give them the greatest competitive advantage relative to cost. These dimensions may differ depending on market segments.

STEP 8: STRUCTURE SERVICE OFFERINGS AND SET GOALS

The eighth and final step is to flesh out the service strategy by creating service offerings for each key customer or segment and by setting quantitative goals for each service dimension. Figure 7-4 displays one such service offering for a grocery products manufacturer. The chart represents the service promise the firm makes to its three categories of customers — high- and medium-volume repeat clients and spot purchasers.

This offering reflects the firm's strategic decisions about customer service. Specifically, the company decided to meet customer service requirements on most service dimensions while exceeding requirements on three key dimensions that are especially important to its customers. These requirements are for:

• Truckload order cycle times of four days for volume repeat customers

- Fill rates on "A" items of 99 percent for both high- and medium-volume repeat customers and fill rates of 98 and 95 percent respectively on "B" and "C" items for high-volume repeat customers

- Status information within four working hours for high- and medium-volume repeat customers

Figure 7-4

Service Differentiation Example

Service Action	High-Volume Repeat Customers	Low-Volume Repeat Customers	Spot Business

• Order cycle time
  – Truckload
  – Fill in
  – Emergency
	4 Work Days
	3 Work Days
	ASAP
		5 Work Days
		3 Work Days
		ASAP
			7 Work Days
			–
			–

• Fill rates
  – A items
  – B items
  – C items
	99%
	98%
	95%
		99%
		95%
		90%
			95%
			93%
			If Available

• Order status information	Within 4 Working Hours	Within 4 Working Hours	Within 8 Working Hours
• Pricing/promotions	• MDF[1] support • Fill in at TL price once/month	• MDF[1] support • Fill in at TL price once/month	–
• Bill back processing	15 Days	15 Days	30 days

Note: [1] Market Development Funds

For other service dimensions listed on Figure 7-4, the grocery manufacturer chose not to try to achieve competitive advantage but merely to satisfy customer requirements. In the case of pricing and promotion support, the firm decided it could not afford to provide such service to spot business no matter how important that service dimension was to those buyers.

The profile depicted in Figure 7-4 illustrates the concept of differentiated service. In most cases, a single service offering to all customers is not the best strategy because not all customers want the same *level* of service. In fact, offering a single level of service tends to under-serve some customers and over-serve others.

The better plan is to create a multi-tiered service package that offers customers a choice. This helps clients manage their own expectations; they know what each tier of service means in terms of specific offerings and cost. Service offerings also need to be tied to pricing strategy. Superior levels of service should command premium prices, reflecting the additional value provided and cost incurred.

Based on responses to our survey, setting differentiated customer service goals is not a widespread practice. Only 51 percent of the respondents do so. Further, fewer than half the respondents set customer service goals based on meeting customer requirements as shown in Figure 7-5. Most set goals aimed at improving or maintaining last year's performance levels or meeting and exceeding competition.

Figure 7-5

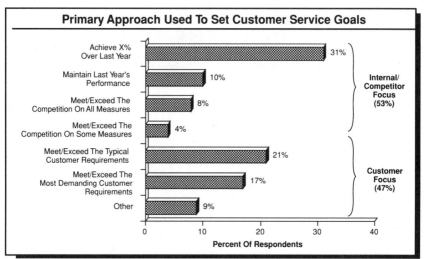

While service goals should reflect customer requirements, they also should be achievable. The intent of service goals is to make a promise and then deliver on that promise 100 percent of the time. Customers generally are more tolerant of suppliers who tell them up-front they can't meet service requirements for a particular order than those who make a commitment but later fail to honor it.

However, if the service strategy calls for performance improvements, the firm must set internal goals to help drive the process of improvement. These objectives should be designed as "stretch targets" that generate improvement over time. The goals that form the basis of a promise to customers aren't necessarily the same goals that drive the organization to improvement. Chapter 13 explores goal setting in detail.

At times, service guarantees play a role in a strategy. In certain cases, they contribute a powerful competitive advantage — not so much because of the penalty associated with the guarantee but because of the commitment to the customer the guarantee implies. Research shows that good guarantees share five characteristics.[1] They are:

- **Unconditional.** "We guarantee the order will arrive on time" *not* "We guarantee the order will arrive on time if the truck doesn't break down."

- **Easy to understand and communicate.** "If the package isn't there by 10:30 a.m., our service is free."

- **Meaningful.** The penalty is significant enough that a service failure gets noticed in the supplier organization.

- **Easy to invoke.** It requires no lengthy approval process or elaborate documentation.

- **Immediate.** The supplier makes good on the guarantee while the problem is still fresh.

QUALITY FUNCTION DEPLOYMENT — AN EMERGING APPROACH

Most service leaders establish their service strategies using an approach like the process just described. However, there's an approach used widely in Japan — called Quality Function Deployment (QFD) — that offers promise for the future.[2] It adds discipline and rigor to the strategy development process. Specifically, QFD is a structured approach that relates customer requirements to design characteristics of a product or a process. It has been used widely in product development but only recently adapted for analyzing service requirements and structuring offerings. In fact, the few U.S. companies we interviewed that use QFD in a service setting were reluctant to share their experiences. They consider the technique a major tool for gaining competitive advantage.

The QFD approach, depicted in Figure 7-6, is a framework for analysis that will be used widely in customer service strategy development in years to come. The framework often is called the "House of Quality" because of its shape. Although visually complex, the "House of Quality" follows a sound, logical approach for understanding and analyzing customer requirements and preparing a response.

Part 1 of the diagram lists customer requirements — what the customers say they want. Typically, these are listed in the customers' own words: "on-time delivery," "easy order placement," "undamaged product," etc. Part 2 of the diagram ranks the relative importance of the requirements to the customers, frequently on a ten-point scale. The information for parts 1 and 2 comes directly from the customer.

The third part of the diagram lists how the company translates the customers' requirements into product or process design characteristics. For example, if on-time delivery is a customer requirement, the process characteristics that drive "on-time" might include the level of inventory kept, carrier equipment availability, and order lead time.

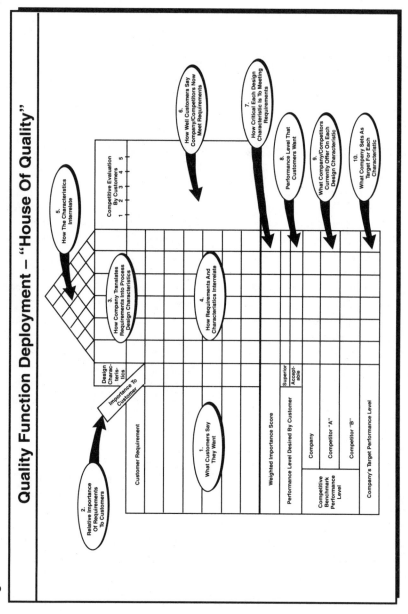

Figure 7-6

Quality Function Deployment – "House Of Quality"

1. What Customers Say They Want

2. Relative Importance Of Requirements To Customers

3. How Company Translates Requirements Into Process Design Characteristics

4. How Requirements And Characteristics Interrelate

5. How The Characteristics Interrelate

6. How Well Customers Say Company/Competitors Now Meet Requirements

7. How Critical Each Design Characteristic Is To Meeting Requirements

8. Performance Level That Customers Want

9. What Company/Competitors Currently Offer On Each Design Characteristic

10. What Company Sets As Target For Each Characteristic

Customer Requirement

Importance To Customer

Design Characteristics

Competitive Evaluation By Customers
1 2 3 4 5

Weighted Importance Score

Performance Level Desired By Customer — Superior / Acceptable

Competitive Benchmark Performance Level — Company / Competitor "A" / Competitor "B"

Company's Target Performance Level

Part 4 of the diagram is a simple relationship matrix that looks at how each process design characteristic relates to each customer requirement. Here, the typical approach involves using three levels of relationship — strong, moderate, and nonexistent — and places symbols in the cells of the matrix to indicate the nature of each relationship. Using these symbols helps people visually understand and interpret the relationships.

Part 5 of the diagram (the peak of the house) tracks the interrelationships between the various process design characteristics. Here, too, a symbolic scale helps show a strong positive correlation, a medium positive correlation, a medium negative correlation, and a strong negative correlation. Characteristics that have a positive correlation support one another while those with negative correlations work against one another (and indicate existence of a tradeoff decision). An example of logistics process characteristics that are negatively correlated are local inventory stocks in branch locations (to support same day delivery) and high product fill rates across a broad product line. Dispersing a broad product line of inventory to 50 or more local branches makes it difficult and expensive to achieve high fill rates on all items.

The first five parts of the "House of Quality" focus on customer requirements and how the company can respond to meet these requirements. Part 6 is an evaluation from the customer's perspective of how well the company and its competitors are doing in meeting each of the customer requirements. Typically, this is done on a five-point scale. This input comes from surveys of the kind described in Chapter 6.

Part 7 of the diagram estimates how critical each design characteristic is to meeting the requirements listed above. The score is calculated by weighting each requirement a characteristic meets against the importance to the customer of that requirement and the degree to which that characteristic relates to the requirement. Thus, if a requirement had an importance score of eight and the characteristic strongly addressed the requirement (i.e., had a weight of nine), the characteristic would get a score of eight times nine or 72 against that requirement. Adding the scores across all requirements yields the total weighted importance score.

Part 8 of the diagram represents the company's interpretation of performance levels that customers want. For example, if the customer survey process identifies 92 to 95 percent as the acceptable range for line-item fill rate and pinpoints 98 percent as discernibly superior, these would be the values used here for the process design characteristics related to order fill rates.

Part 9 benchmarks the company and its competitors on each of the design characteristics. This helps the firm decide if it is at a competitive advantage, at parity, or at a disadvantage. Using these data along with the performance levels the customers want (Part 8) and the weighted importance of each characteristic (Part 7) a company can decide what the target performance level should be for each of the design characteristics (Part 10).

QFD is an emerging tool for understanding customer requirements and establishing service responses. It is a structured way of planning, communicating, and documenting customer requirements as well as the company's planned responses. Based on widespread successes in manufacturing and the few service oriented examples seen in North America, it promises to be a major step forward in formalizing the service strategy development process.

TAILORING SERVICE TO NEEDS

As the chapters in Section III indicate, service has become a key competitive tool. To apply service in this manner, suppliers must understand true customer needs and requirements. They also must establish a service strategy that consistently meets those needs while also exceeding expectations on a few key service dimensions.

Achieving quality customer service and providing value to customers starts with understanding these requirements. Most companies don't have the financial resources or capability to meet every customer requirement. Instead, they must select those service dimensions on which to compete and set service goals to meet them. In many cases, this means differentiating their service — shifting service levels and resources to those markets and customers that improved service benefits most. It means striking a balance between service and profitability — increasing service to protect profitable customers, adjusting service for those in the middle, and increasing revenues or cutting costs for marginal or unprofitable customers.

In Section III, we've focused on current and future customer satisfaction as a key business strategy for creating customer and shareholder value (see Figure 7-7). We've discussed the means of achieving this approach: by defining and monitoring requirements, assessing capabilities, and taking strategic actions to respond to gaps and opportunities. Over time, this approach can lead to a sustainable position as a preferred supplier.

In summary, Section III provides a framework for identifying and understanding customer service requirements and defining a service strategy with which the company can meet these requirements and exceed expectations. This focus on customer requirements represents a company's first step toward providing quality customer service and the first step toward quality in logistics.

---

[1] Hart, Christopher W. L., "The Power of Unconditional Service Guarantees"

[2] Akao, Yoji, Translation by Glenn H. Mazur, *Quality Function Deployment, Integrating Customer Requirements Into Product Design*

Figure 7-7

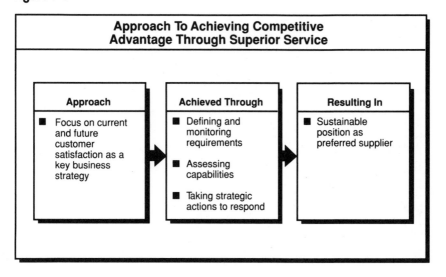

Approach To Achieving Competitive Advantage Through Superior Service		
Approach	**Achieved Through**	**Resulting In**
■ Focus on current and future customer satisfaction as a key business strategy	■ Defining and monitoring requirements ■ Assessing capabilities ■ Taking strategic actions to respond	■ Sustainable position as preferred supplier

SECTION IV

TECHNIQUES OF IMPROVEMENT

In Section III, we discussed approaches for developing a service strategy, offerings, and goals. These three elements form the basis for logistics service requirements.

In Section IV, we discuss the tools and techniques for measuring and improving quality and productivity in logistics in order to meet these requirements.

Chapter 8 discusses the framework that forms the foundation for most improvement processes. Chapter 9 explores the basic tools of process and statistical analysis. Chapter 10 discusses measurement approaches. And Chapter 11 examines high-impact improvement actions, i.e., actions that our survey respondents and interviewees said significantly improved the quality and productivity of their logistics processes.

CHAPTER 8

A FRAMEWORK
FOR IMPROVEMENT

Quality and productivity-improvement processes come in many shapes, sizes, variations, and combinations. Individual company approaches differ based on marketplace position, competitor strength, cost structures and leverage points in the business, management style, corporate attitudes and culture, and many other factors.

Despite these differences, improvement processes share several basic attributes. Most create a common framework for thinking about the process of improvement. They employ similar analytical tools and techniques and use similar quality and productivity measurement systems. Many share identical improvement actions. In this chapter, we discuss the first of these four shared characteristics, a framework for improvement.

THE PDCA IMPROVEMENT WHEEL

In the 1950s, W. Edwards Deming popularized an improvement process framework built around four simple steps. He advised companies to **plan** improvements, execute the plan (**do**), **check** whether the desired improvement was realized, and **act** by adjusting the plan if improvements fail to accrue or by institutionalizing the actions if improvements do materialize.

This approach is known as the Deming Wheel, the Deming Cycle, or simply the PDCA cycle. Figure 8-1 illustrates the PDCA cycle as a continuous process of challenging performance and developing plans to drive additional improvement. The PDCA cycle is key to a continuous improvement process the Japanese call *kaizen*.

Figure 8-1

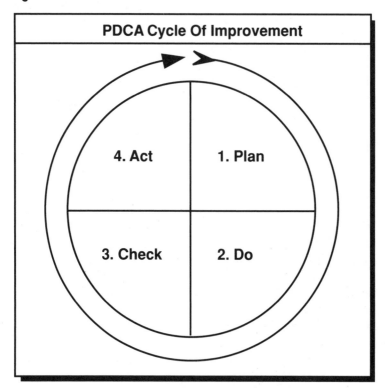

PDCA Cycle Of Improvement

4. Act　　1. Plan

3. Check　　2. Do

In the **plan** step, two activities occur: evaluation and action planning. Evaluation uncovers potential problems or opportunities and indicates the need for improvements. At this point, the firm assembles an improvement team to investigate the situation. The team's job is to understand the problem using process analysis techniques. The team then uses statistical analysis to pinpoint the reasons for the problem. (We explain both types of analysis in Chapter 9.)

The team's next mission is to identify alternatives for improvement. With improvement ideas in hand, the team begins planning action. This involves selecting and planning specific improvement actions, establishing measures, and setting goals for improvement.

Effecting improvement actions represents the **do** step. Implementation often involves making changes to processes, techniques, work flows, equipment, and methods. These changes frequently necessitate significant training for the people slated to carry out the changed activity.

The **check** step comes next. During this phase, the improvement team uses measures, on-site inspection, and employee input to answer three key questions:

- Was change implemented as planned?
- Were desired results achieved?
- What corrective actions are required?

The answers to these questions drive the fourth step in the process — **act**. If implementation does not go as planned or fails to achieve the desired results, this step gets the process back on track by recycling through PDCA. If implementation succeeds, the improvement team acts to standardize and institutionalize the improvements elsewhere.

Many companies successfully use the PDCA cycle to drive quality and productivity improvement in logistics. Continuous improvement is not the only way to move ahead, however. Under certain conditions, breakthrough improvements occur as well. These breakthroughs happen as a result of trigger points. As described in our earlier research study, a trigger point is an event that shakes a company to its foundation and forces management to fundamentally rethink its way of doing business. A trigger point may take the form of a new competitor, a merger, a major quality failure, or political change (e.g., Europe 1992). Alternatively, it might be a major customer demand. A customer, for example, might tell a supplier, "We want just-in-time (JIT) delivery from you, or we won't continue doing business with you." New corporate leadership frequently acts as a trigger point by creating an environment in which rapid change occurs.

Regardless of the cause, trigger points create unique windows of opportunity. Companies can realize major gains because the organization, and in some cases the suppliers and customers as well, sets aside traditional ways of doing business, discards incremental improvement, and looks for quantum advances.

COMPARING CONTINUOUS AND BREAKTHROUGH IMPROVEMENTS

Continuous improvements often come about from tweaking the existing process and generally occur within functions. Breakthroughs, on the other hand, involve major process changes that often are cross-functional or cross-organizational in nature.

Continuous and breakthrough improvements are not mutually exclusive approaches. Instead, each plays a role in an overall improvement process. Figure 8-2 characterizes these two types of improvements. Continuous improvement can be executed individually by functions and departments or collaboratively with other units that share common or compatible goals. Once established, the continuous improvement process demands no special action on the part of senior management except to nurture it and maintain momentum. Breakthroughs, on the other hand, are the product of challenging tradition and undertaking risk. With few exceptions, their success hinges on senior management involvement and cross-functional cooperation. As we discuss in Chapter 13, a successful improvement process incorporates a means to ensure continuous improvement and the ability to capitalize on trigger points to achieve breakthroughs.

Figure 8-2

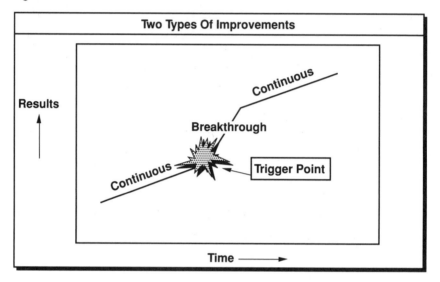

MAJOR IMPROVEMENTS COME FROM PROCESS CHANGES

In our earlier book, *Measuring and Improving Productivity in Physical Distribution,* we discussed how productivity improvement stems from changes in methods, improved utilization of resources, and increased performance against standards or goals. Improving the underlying methods or process produces most of the productivity improvement.

In quality improvement, the same relationship applies. The only way to effect major change in quality is to change the underlying process. Individual quality problems and service failures usually are symptoms of overall process problems. In the short term, the firm must correct the individual occurrences in order to keep customers happy. In the long term, however, management must address the underlying process flaws in order to eliminate the problems. On this subject, Deming comments that over 80 percent of quality problems are process oriented and are not related to the people operating the process. It is management's responsibility to ensure that the process functions properly and that individual employees aren't blamed for normal variations in quality performance that occur because of a process flaw.

The emphasis on process improvement is key because it has the greatest impact on the company. Its benefits include:

• Higher levels of service

• More reliable service

• Shorter cycle times

• Freed-up capacity and greater flexibility

• Streamlined and simplified processes

• Less waste

• Lower overall cost

Focusing on process improvement shifts management's attention away from just running the business by the numbers and managing the results. Instead, it focuses on managing the process that achieves those results. It is not enough simply to meet the numbers whether they be costs, productivity measures, or quality goals. Unless management understands why the process produced those numbers and acts to improve that process, there's no guarantee it will meet the numbers in the future.

In the next chapter, we discuss the techniques many companies use to analyze, understand, and improve the process and how firms apply these techniques to logistics.

CHAPTER 9

TOOLS FOR
IMPROVEMENT

Over the past several decades, a number of tools and techniques have been developed or adapted to help companies improve business processes. Most of the tools and techniques were first applied in manufacturing where approaches such as Statistical Process Control (SPC) were widely used.

In the late 1970s and early 1980s, use of these techniques moved off the shop floor as companies adapted them for use with suppliers. By teaching suppliers these tools and techniques, progressive manufacturers extended process improvement back upstream and, in so doing, made their suppliers partners in quality and productivity improvement.

More recently, application of these techniques has expanded beyond manufacturing and purchasing into areas such as transportation, warehousing, sales forecasting, and other elements of the logistics process. This chapter explores the tools and techniques used to improve business processes and explains how they are being applied to logistics.

TYPES OF TOOLS

In our secondary research, we identified a number of methods that help analyze and improve processes. Some authors refer to these methods as the "seven basic tools" or the "seven statistical tools." Unfortunately, the authors differ regarding what constitutes each group of seven. Rather than confuse the issue further, we choose simply to talk about basic and advanced tools. We also believe there is a distinction between tools used for process analysis and tools used for statistical analysis. Using these two dimensions — basic versus advanced and process versus statistical — Figure 9-1 summarizes the major tools now in use.

Figure 9-1

	Basic Tools	Examples Of Advanced Tools
Process Analysis	• Cause and effect diagram • Process flow chart • Brainstorming	• Interrelationship diagram • Affinity diagram • Systematic diagram • Process decision program chart • Force field analysis • Quality function deployment
Statistical Analysis	• Check sheet • Pareto chart • Histogram • Scatter diagram • Run chart • Control chart	• Design of experiments • Regression analysis • Multivariate analysis

For most of the companies we surveyed, the logistics improvement process relies on the basic tools shown in the first column of Figure 9-1. Several firms were using the more advanced tools in manufacturing improvement, however. As businesses implement the PDCA cycle, they often find that different tools are more useful at different points in the process. Figure 9-2 summarizes where each tool is of greatest benefit within the PDCA cycle.

Figure 9-2

Applying Basic Tools							
	◄——————— Plan/Do ———————►					◄—— Check/Act ——►	
	Identify Problem	Understand Problem	Collect Data	Analyze Causes	Plan Improvements	Measure Results	Institutionalize Results
Process Analysis							
■ Cause and effect diagram		●		●	●		
■ Process flow chart	●	●			●		●
■ Brainstorming	●	●			●		
Statistical Analysis							
■ Check sheets	●	●	●	●		●	
■ Pareto charts	●	●		●		●	
■ Histograms		●		●		●	
■ Scatter diagrams	●			●			
■ Run charts			●	●			
■ Control charts	●	●	●			●	●

In the remainder of Chapter 9, we discuss each basic tool and how it can be applied in the logistics process. For information on the advanced tools listed in Figure 9-1, readers should check the bibliography at the end of this book.

PROCESS ANALYSIS TOOLS

Process analysis tools allow people to understand how a process works so they can look for ways to improve it. The three basic process analysis tools are:

• Cause and effect diagrams

• Process flow charts

• Brainstorming

1. Cause and effect diagrams. Cause and effect diagrams illustrate the relationship of potential causes (reasons that a situation occurs) to an existing effect (the situation being analyzed). Input typically comes from brainstorming sessions (discussed later in this chapter). The cause and effect diagram sometimes is called the fishbone diagram because of its shape or the Ishikawa diagram, named after the Japanese quality expert who popularized it. Figure 9-3 depicts the general structure of a cause and effect diagram. The causes of the effect being examined are clustered together along a specific branch of the diagram (category of causes).

Figure 9-3

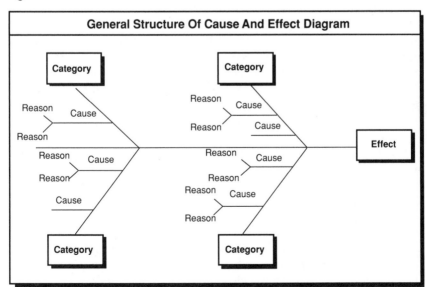

There are at least three general ways of categorizing the causes:

• Environment, machines, materials, measurement, methods, people

• Man, methods, machines, materials

• Equipment, policies, procedures, people

These categories offer a general starting point for developing a cause and effect diagram. Alternatively, companies may create custom tailored categories. Figure 9-4 illustrates how one company in the paper industry categorized and analyzed the causes that drove it to have inventory (the effect). This example carries four major categories of causes of inventory: customers, policy, process variability, and other objectives (which may conflict with the objective of keeping inventory levels down).

As Figure 9-4 shows, customer requirements in the form of short lead times and guaranteed availability motivate the company to carry inventory. Because certain customers can't accept barge/ship or rail deliveries, product must be trans-loaded. Some customers have insufficient storage space and expect suppliers to hold stocks for them. And certain customers don't receive product until they receive credit approval. All of these items result in the need for inventory.

Policy decisions also drive the need for inventory. The company wants to maintain a continuous supply to its customers and believes it has to build inventory to cover strikes, catastrophes, and planned mill down time. The company also has a policy of providing stable employment at the mill and seeks stable production to better regulate raw materials flow.

Process variability is the third major reason for needing inventory. Variability occurs in orders, mill operations, transit delays, and forecasts. Order errors cause products to be made that can't be sold. Order changes affect inventories in two ways: customers cancel orders for items already produced, or the company stocks additional inventory to cover last-minute increases by customers. Order damage means the firm must carry additional inventory to replace damaged items. Also, the damaged goods themselves become inventory until they are downgraded, rewound, or otherwise disposed of.

Process variability in mill operations also affects the need for inventory. Missed schedules mean the mill must carry buffer stock for certain items. Off-spec product sits in inventory until the mill finds a buyer. Producing too much inventory to fill out machine capacity for a particular run, for instance, also contributes.

Variability in transit times also contributes to the need for inventory. Unpredictable service from certain carriers prompts the company to carry additional safety stock. Customs clearance problems aggravate this situation, delaying shipments from a few hours to as much as a week, thereby tying up inventories unproductively.

Figure 9-4

Cause And Effect Diagram – Paper Mill Example

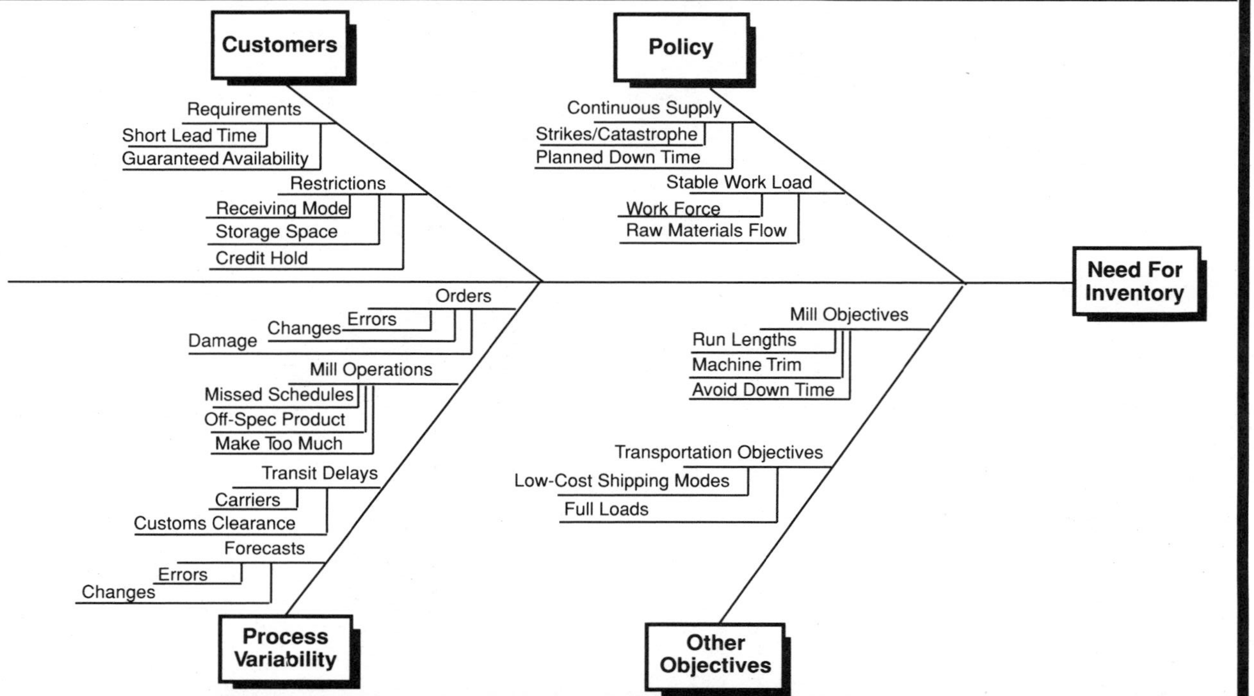

Need For Inventory

Policy

Continuous Supply
- Strikes/Catastrophe
- Planned Down Time

Stable Work Load
- Work Force
- Raw Materials Flow

Mill Objectives
- Run Lengths
- Machine Trim
- Avoid Down Time

Transportation Objectives
- Low-Cost Shipping Modes
- Full Loads

Other Objectives

Customers

Requirements
- Short Lead Time
- Guaranteed Availability

Restrictions
- Receiving Mode
- Storage Space
- Credit Hold

Orders
- Changes
- Errors
- Damage

Mill Operations
- Missed Schedules
- Off-Spec Product
- Make Too Much

Transit Delays
- Carriers
- Customs Clearance

Forecasts
- Errors
- Changes

Process Variability

Finally, variability in forecasts, due both to errors and changes in production planning, causes a need for additional safety stock and sometimes creates excess inventory.

The fourth major category causing inventory is other objectives. The paper mills want long production runs to keep their production rates high. They also sequence particular orders on the paper machine to maximize machine "trim" (utilize the machine width) instead of running orders in the scheduled sequence (which is planned to balance machine trim, inventory, shipping efficiencies, and service requirements). The mills also like to avoid down time, so they produce even though they don't necessarily have a specific customer for the product. All of these factors generate inventory.

Finally, the company's transportation objectives contribute to excess inventory. The mills prefer low cost shipping modes — ship and barge versus railcar and truck. They also like to ship in full-load quantities to get the lowest per unit cost. These policies contribute to inventory accumulation.

By using the cause and effect diagram, the paper firm understood why it had inventory in its system. This enabled the company to review each cause and find ways to reduce or eliminate the need for inventory. In doing so, the company found over $5 million in inventory reduction opportunities in the first few months after beginning the investigation.

As an aside, Figure 9-4 illustrates another point about cause and effect diagrams: they must use short, direct phrases in order not to confuse the diagram. The detail of longer phrases and descriptions is better suited to working papers that support the diagram.

2. Flow charts. Flow charts provide a pictorial display of the steps in a process. As an example of a flow chart, Figure 9-5 breaks out a simplified order-fulfillment process from order entry to delivery.

Flow charting has several uses. First, it helps define the processing steps and logic flow for carrying out an activity. Its pictorial nature encourages a common understanding of how the process works. Flow charting also helps identify weaknesses in a process such as bottlenecks, redundancies, gaps, and ambiguities. And lastly, flow charting assists in developing, describing, and documenting improvements to the process.

3. Brainstorming. The technique of brainstorming has many uses in quality and productivity improvement. It helps identify problems, pinpoint reasons for the problems, develop potential improvements, and plan improvement actions. Simply put, brainstorming is a technique for quickly generating ideas in a group setting.

Figure 9-5

Flow Chart Example – Order-Fulfillment Cycle

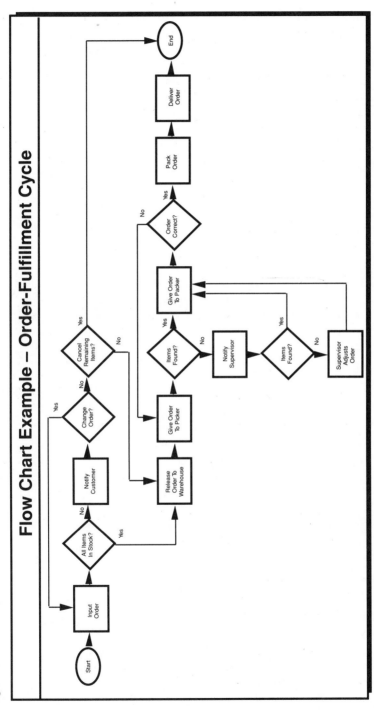

There are several techniques for carrying out brainstorming. Some involve flip charts, others use index cards. Some are highly structured (each participant takes a turn contributing an idea in sequence) while others are unstructured, and participants simply call out ideas as they occur. Figure 9-6 outlines a five-step brainstorming process we've seen used successfully in a number of companies.

Figure 9-6

Typical Steps In Brainstorming

1. Statement of the objective
   • Flipchart
   • Keep visible throughout

2. Idea generation
   • Anonymous and nondominant
   • 3" x 5" cards
   • Short phrases

3. Idea clustering
   • Common themes
   • Requires facilitator

4. Prioritization
   • 10 votes per person
   • Multiple votes per cluster OK

5. Concept development
   • Expand on ideas
   • Structure concept
   • Document results

First, a group facilitator or leader clearly defines the purpose of the brainstorming session. The objective often takes the form of a question such as "How can we reduce order pick errors in our Chicago distribution center?" The group usually has an opportunity to clarify and perhaps modify the objective. The modified objective then becomes the purpose for the list of ideas the brainstorming will generate. The objective usually gets written on a flip chart or overhead slide and remains visible throughout the session.

The next step in brainstorming is idea generation. Many companies get results by allowing people to contribute ideas anonymously. Each person receives several 3- by 5-inch index cards and a marking pen and jots down any ideas on these cards. The facilitator instructs participants to use short phrases rather than full sentences to describe their ideas. He then collects the cards and shuffles them to help protect anonymity. This approach allows all participants to present their ideas without fear of criticism. It also prevents the brainstorming session from being dominated by a few strong personalities.

The third step in the brainstorming approach is idea clustering. It requires the use of several large cork boards or a wall to which the 3- by 5-inch cards can be attached. The facilitator reads each card aloud and, following the instructions of the group, places it on the cork board or wall near ideas that are similar in concept or theme. When the clustering takes shape, the group commonly sees similarities among ideas and rearranges the cards to reflect those likenesses. The group may decide to merge two similar clusters or split a single cluster into two. This is all part of the process.

The first three steps of brainstorming generate ideas. With step four, participants begin exploring and discussing the ideas. Step four involves prioritizing the clusters, selecting which ideas to work on first. One prioritizing technique gives each participants ten votes (usually ten adhesive dots) and lets them place their votes/dots on the clusters they consider most important.

The last step in brainstorming (or arguably the first step in problem solving) is concept development. Beginning with the idea cluster that received the most votes, the group transforms the concept into a workable set of actions. Then the team documents the results and goes on to the next cluster.

Typically, brainstorming sessions take two to four hours. The first 60 to 90 minutes cover steps one through four with the remainder of the time devoted to concept development. The group often limits its concept development to the two or three top vote winners.

Brainstorming can be a very valuable process. With the right group of people — a mix of those knowledgeable about a process (especially those who actually operate the process) and one or two outsiders who can contribute fresh ideas — brainstorming can go a long way toward identifying problem causes and suggesting solutions.

STATISTICAL ANALYSIS TOOLS

The process analysis tools we've discussed are valuable in several ways. They help describe how a particular business process works, pinpoint possible causes of problems, and identify ways to improve the process. Statistical analysis tools supplement process analysis methods, increasing understanding of the business process by measuring what is going on, i.e., the levels of activity, frequency of problems, etc. Among those firms in our study that have formal improvement processes for logistics, 61 percent use statistical analysis tools to support problem identification and resolution.

Much has been written on the subject of statistical analysis tools. We do not intend, therefore, to provide a mathematical or technical discussion of statistical analysis. For that, we refer the reader to several excellent reference books on the subject listed in Appendix I. What we do offer is a summary of the fundamental concepts of each tool with examples of logistics process applications.

Statistical analysis is used with two basic kinds of data, attributes data and variables data. Attributes data refer to simple information that counts things, e.g., measurements such as yes/no, good/bad, pass/fail, complete/incomplete. Variables data represent broader measures of things, e.g., frequency, quantity, time, and money. Figure 9-7 portrays the difference between attributes and variables data for some sample dimensions of logistics service. As the chart shows, the attributes are measured in terms of yes or no. Either the shipment was on time or it wasn't; the order was complete or it wasn't; the invoice was accurate or it wasn't; the customer was satisfied or it wasn't. The variables data add dimension and depth to the attributes. They tell how many days the shipment was early or late, compare quantity ordered against amount delivered, report actual versus correct invoice amount, and the like. Lastly, variables data show how the customer ranks the company on a performance scale.

Figure 9-7

Examples Of Attributes Versus Variables Data	
Attributes	**Variables**
■ Was the shipment on time?	■ How many days early/late did the shipment arrive?
■ Was the order complete?	■ How many cases/lines/dollars were delivered versus ordered?
■ Was the invoice accurate?	■ What is the variation (in dollars or percent) between the invoiced amount and the correct amount?
■ Was the customer satisfied with our performance?	■ How does the customer rank us on a performance scale?

Figure 9-8 shows the difference using an example. In the figure, the attributes data tell only that 18 percent of the shipments were not on time. In this case, the variables data give a much better picture of logistics, showing that some shipments were three days early (and thus too *early* to be counted as on-time) and several shipments were late by as many as four days.

Figure 9-8

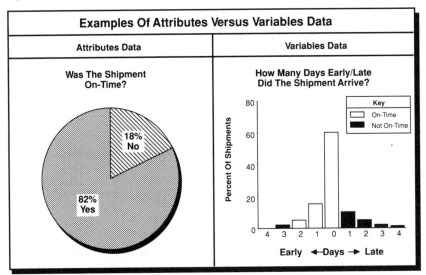

Attributes data generally are easier to obtain than variables data. However, they require clear definitions of what is acceptable (i.e., what gets a yes answer) and what is not acceptable. In quality terms, acceptable/unacceptable is usually termed conforming or nonconforming. Because these terms are common in statistically oriented texts, we use them as we explain the concepts. Figure 9-9 defines two key terms: nonconforming items and nonconformities.

A nonconforming item is a **single item** or unit that contains one or more nonconformities or defects. In manufacturing, this might mean a machine that does not function properly; in logistics, it might be an order with a service failure.

Nonconformities, on the other hand, are **single occurrences** of nonconformance to a requirement. In a manufacturing setting, this would be a single part that doesn't fit, is scratched or dented, or made of incorrect materials. In a logistics setting, nonconformities would be a service failure by type.

Figure 9-9

Nonconforming Items Versus Nonconformities	
Term/Definition	**Example**

■ Nonconforming item
  • Single item containing one or more
    nonconformities
  • A "defective unit"
	■ An order with a service failure

■ Nonconformities
  • Single occurrence of non-
    conformance to a requirement
  • A "defect"
	■ A service failure (by type); e.g.,
	  • Late
	  • Damaged goods
	  • Wrong merchandise
	  • Incomplete
	  • Faulty paperwork
	  • Wrong carrier/mode

Thus, an order with a service failure counts as a **nonconforming item** (it gets a no on the question of whether the order is acceptable or not), but the order might have been unacceptable (i.e., had more than one **nonconformity**) due to damaged goods *and* late delivery.

Keeping these definitions of attributes and variables data in mind, companies can use a number of basic statistical analysis tools to improve quality and productivity. These tools include check sheets, run charts, Pareto charts, histograms, scatter diagrams, and control charts.

Check sheets are a method of collecting attributes data. Figure 9-10 shows a check sheet used to track the type of calls received by a customer service representative during a week. In this example, Customer Service Representative Jones recorded the number of calls received each day by type using tick marks. He then totalled the calls for the week in the far right-hand column.

Check sheets are useful for tracking the nature and frequency of occurrences in a process. They also may be used to track incidence of damage by type, frequency of mis-picks by warehouse operator, number of shipments by order size, etc. Check sheets are a convenient way of counting the number of occurrences by category.

Run charts are designed to track the output of a process. Figure 9-11 shows how a run chart traces the number of daily late deliveries for a particular branch facility operation. Run charts are useful in spotting trends. In Figure 9-11, there is a clear upward trend in the number of late deliveries over a three-week period. This indicates a potential problem that should be investigated.

Figure 9-10

Example Of Check Sheet

Customer Service Calls Received

Person: _____Jones_____   Week Ending: ___4/3/9x___

Type Of Call	Monday	Tuesday	Wednesday	Thursday	Friday	Total
■ Order placement	‖‖‖ ////	‖‖‖ //	‖‖‖	‖‖‖ ///	‖‖‖ ‖‖‖	39
■ Order status	////	//	‖‖‖ //	//	///	18
■ Product availability	/		/	//		4
■ Pricing inquiry	//	///	/	‖‖‖	/	12
■ Product – technical	/					1
■ Late order	//	//		/		5
■ Invoice accuracy		/			//	3
■ Damaged order			/			1
■ Other	/				/	2

Figure 9-11

Example Of Run Chart

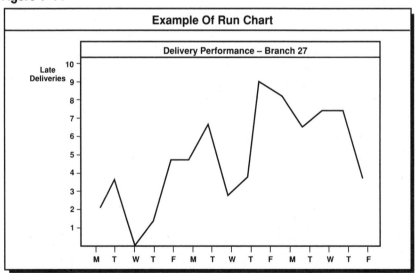

Delivery Performance – Branch 27

Pareto charts monitor the effect of Pareto's Law on an operation. Pareto's Law, otherwise known as the "80-20" rule, says that the greatest proportion of an effect comes from a small number of causes or factors. Applying Pareto's Law, we often see that about 80 percent of a company's business comes from about 20 percent of its customers; 80 percent of sales come from 20 percent of the SKUs; 80 percent of complaints come from 20 percent of customers, etc. Pareto charts graphically demonstrate this theory. The Pareto chart in Figure 9-12 depicts the reasons for premium freight shipments in one month at Division 5 in a company. These reasons, listed below the graph, include customer request, an out-of-stock situation at the local distribution center, a missed production schedule, incorrect due date entered on the order, and other less frequent causes. The scale along the left-hand side of the graph traces the number of occurrences of each reason. Cumulative percentages of occurrences are tracked with the scale on the right-hand side. Customer request, in this example, caused 125 shipments to incur premium freight in May. This figure constitutes 47 percent of the total number of shipments requiring premium freight handling. Stock outages at the local distribution center added 62 shipments to this volume, bringing the total to 71 percent. Missed production schedules added 34 more shipments to the premium freight volume, pushing the total to 84 percent. Clearly, these three areas — customer request, stock shortages, and production schedule problems — need to be brought under control if management hopes to lower the division's premium freight expenses.

Figure 9-12

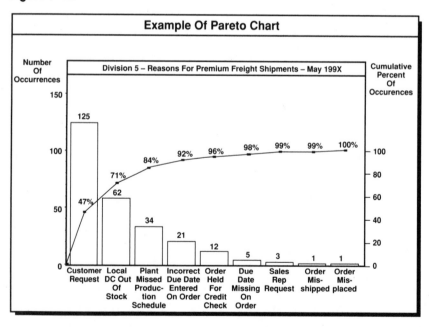

The technique for structuring a Pareto chart is important. The reasons for effect should be listed in descending order of frequency of occurrence, left to right, so when the cumulative percentage line is overlaid, the location of the 80-20 cutoff becomes apparent.

Histograms (or bar charts) are useful in analyzing the frequency distribution of data across a range. The histogram in Figure 9-13 summarizes a lead time analysis (order placement to delivery date) for a particular distribution center. Along the left side of the graph is a scale showing the number of orders; running along the bottom is a scale showing lead time measured in days. As the graph portrays, the most frequent lead time, with just over 400 orders, is five days. Lead times of six and seven days also occur frequently, while lead times of less than three days or more than eight days are relatively uncommon.

Figure 9-13

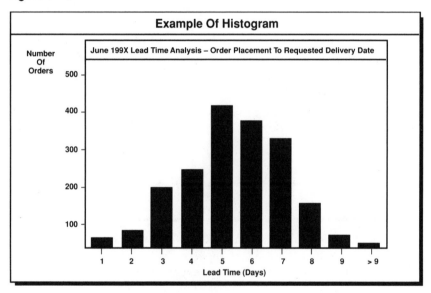

According to Figure 9-13, lead times vary significantly, running between three and eight days. Thus, if the internal process for order fulfillment assumes a five-day cycle, the histogram reveals that the more than 500 orders having lead times less than five days would require special handling.

Histograms have their limitations. They only show cumulative performance over a period of time and can mask trends or underlying patterns. For example, if Figure 9-13 tracked a one-year period rather than one month, seasonal differences might be overlooked. Lead times in summer months could exhibit a much different pattern than for winter months, and, if they were plotted together on a single histogram, a misleading graph could result. Care should also be taken not to mix two groups of data in the same histogram. For example, ship from stock and make-to-order items typically have different lead time requirements. As a result, they should not be plotted on the same histogram.

Scatter diagrams analyze the possible relationship between two variables. The scatter diagram in Figure 9-14 depicts the relationship between pick accuracy and weeks of service for new employees at a Memphis distribution center. Along the left-hand side of the graph is number of order pick errors per thousand lines picked. Along the bottom is employees' weeks of service.

Figure 9-14

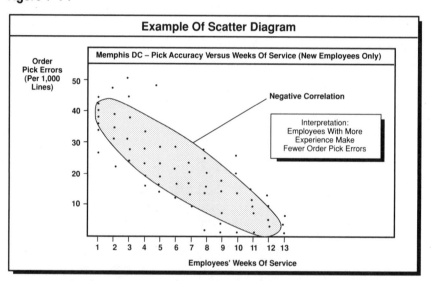

The scatter diagram shows a downward trend (negative correlation) between error rate and weeks of service. This information leads to the interpretation that employees with more experience make fewer order pick errors. If the data showed no drop in error rate with experience, there must be a reason. The company should then review the order picking process to see what the problem is.

The final and perhaps most widely used tool for statistical analysis is the control chart. Control charts measure variation of a process. They monitor the stability of a process and help identify trends that signal a change in the process. Figure 9-15 shows the general format of a process control chart. Along the left-hand side is the value of some key measure; the dimension of time is along the bottom. Through statistical formulas, upper control limits (UCLs) and lower control limits (LCLs) are calculated based on historical data about the process. The center line, or midway point between the UCL and LCL, also is calculated.

The process is in control as long as the measure stays within the upper and lower control limits and doesn't exhibit an abnormal pattern. The process is termed out of control if the measure falls outside the control limits. Control charts are used widely in manufacturing to control tolerances or defect rates.

Figure 9-15

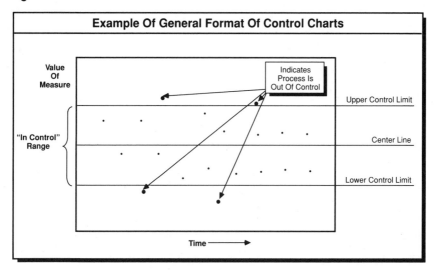

When a company first charts a process using this method, management often discovers the process initially is out of control. Its performance is not statistically predictable because of so-called special causes. Such causes might be poorly trained operators, bad materials, equipment breakdowns, or other abnormal occurrences. By using control charts, companies can systematically find and fix these special causes.

Once the firm eliminates its special causes, the remaining variation in the process results from common causes. The process is then in control and is operating as well as it is capable. **Any further variation reduction or performance improvement must come from a change in the process.**

People sometimes make the mistake of tampering with processes that are in control by making adjustments following each result intended to bring the next result closer to the center line. However, such adjustments just introduce a new form of variability to the process and do not result in any improvement. In fact, according to Deming, tampering can double the variation in a process and even cause it to go out of control.[1]

There are seven major types of control charts that can be used for this kind of analysis (see Figure 9-16). All use the concept of a center line (an average actual result) and upper and lower control limits. Selecting the most appropriate control chart depends on the type of factor being measured.

In our interviews, we found many companies use either the "p" control chart or the "c" control chart for logistics analysis. The following example, therefore, discusses uses of the "p" control chart. Applying the other types of control charts follows a similar pattern. For more detail on these, the reader should consult the reference books on statistical process control listed in Appendix I.

Figure 9-16

Types Of Control Charts			
Type Of Data	**Chart Type**	**Typical Factor Being Measured**	**Logistics Examples**
Attributes Data (Counts, Discrete Measurements – e.g., Yes/No, Good/Bad, Succeed/Fail)	pn or np	• Total number of defective units or nonconforming items in a sample (samples must be of equal size)	• Number of orders with service failures
	p	• Percent of defective units or nonconforming items	• Percent of invoices with errors • Percent of orders not delivered "on-time"
	c	• Total number of defects or nonconformities in a sample (all samples must be of the same size)	• Number of errors per invoice • Number of incorrect or missing data items per order
	u	• Total number of defects or noncomformities per unit	• (Not typically used in logistics. Example would be defects per square meter of material)
Variables Data (Measurements, Continuous Data – e.g., Weight, Time, Money)	X̄ and R X̄ = Mean Average R = Range	• Average of measured values for subgroups and range (high value minus low value) for each (e.g., subgroup = one day's occurrences)	• Number of days shipment varies from on-time delivery target • Dollar amount of invoice errors • Order cycle times
	X̄ and S X̄ = Mean Average S = Standard Deviation	• Average of measured values for subgroups and standard deviation of each (e.g., subgroup = one day's occurrences)	
	X and MR X = Observed Value MR = Moving Range	• Individual measured values and change from previous observation	

Constructing a control chart involves four basic steps:

• Calculating the center line

• Calculating the control limits

• Constructing the control chart

• Plotting live data on the chart

Each is discussed below.

1. Calculating the center line. In the following example, we want to build a control chart to track the percent of shipments *not* on time. Figure 9-17 displays daily shipment data for a four-week period in March. (Twenty days of data probably is the minimum number of data points to use in constructing a control chart.) It includes number of shipments not on time, total number of shipments per day, and the calculated percent of shipments not on time. In this case, the average for the four-week period is 2.7 percent of shipments not on time. This becomes the value of the center line shown in Figure 9-18.

Figure 9-17

Sample Shipment Data For Constructing "p" Chart

Date	Number Of Shipments Not On-Time	Total Number Of Shipments	Percent Of Shipments Not On-Time
3/5	35	1,126	3.1
3/6	41	1,612	2.5
3/7	33	1,815	1.8
3/8	55	1,403	3.9
3/9	58	1,602	2.6
3/12	44	1,119	4.0
3/13	85	2,314	3.7
3/14	27	1,672	1.6
3/15	40	1,302	3.1
3/16	56	1,477	3.8
3/19	25	1,191	2.1
3/20	39	2,161	1.8
3/21	13	1,381	1.0
3/22	43	1,663	2.6
3/23	26	1,190	2.2
3/26	32	1,771	1.9
3/27	76	2,106	3.6
3/28	62	2,380	2.6
3/29	42	1,400	3.0
3/30	52	1,690	3.1
Total	884	32,375	54.0
Average			2.7

Figure 9-18

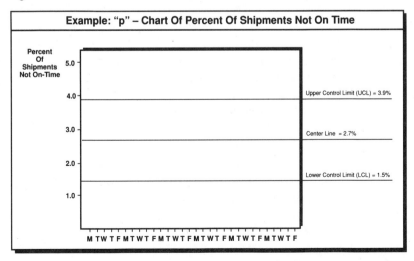

Example: "p" – Chart Of Percent Of Shipments Not On Time

2. Calculating the control limits. Typically, we set the UCL and LCL at plus or minus three standard deviations around the mean/center line. If the calculated LCL is negative, however, we can set it to zero.

In our example, the formula for calculating UCL and LCL for a "p" chart is:

$$UCL = \bar{p} + 3\sqrt{\bar{p}\,(1 - \bar{p})/\bar{n}}$$

$$LCL = \bar{p} - 3\sqrt{\bar{p}\,(1 - \bar{p})/\bar{n}}$$

Where:

$\bar{p}$ = Value of center line
884/32,375 = 0.027 or 2.7%

$\bar{n}$ = Average sample size
32,375/20 days = 1,619

$\sqrt{\bar{p}\,(1 - \bar{p})/\bar{n}}$ = Standard deviation of a binomial distribution (succeed/fail)

Note: The formula for the standard deviation varies depending on the type of control chart used

Based on this calculation, the UCL is 3.9 percent, and the LCL is 1.5 percent.

Note that the UCL and LCL are calculated based on the actual capability of process (based on statistical analysis) and are not based on specifications or requirements (what we would like the process to be capable of doing).

3. Constructing the control chart. As shown in Figure 9-18, the control chart should show the expected range of values for the process being measured along the left side with horizontal lines marking the upper and lower control limits and the center line. Along the bottom of the graph are indicators for the weekdays, above which each new day's data are plotted.

4. Plotting data. Figure 9-19 illustrates what the "p" control chart might look like for the months of April and May based on the March sample. The data plotting in Figure 9-19 indicates the process for achieving on-time shipments is not in control. On the third Thursday in April, the percent of shipments not on time exceeds the upper control limit. In statistical terms, this should not have occurred unless there was a special cause. Further, beginning in the last week in April and continuing into May, most of the data points plot above the center line — a disturbing pattern. Again, it's unlikely this could occur without a special cause.

Figure 9-19

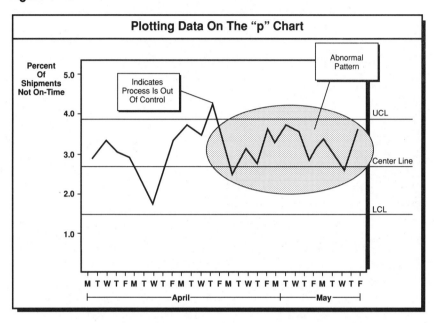

These two examples illustrate the two major warning signals for unstable or not-in-control processes. The first is a single point outside the control limits. The second is an abnormal pattern. This pattern may take several forms:

• Seven to nine consecutive points on one side of the center line

• Six to seven consecutive rising/falling points

• Two or three consecutive points beyond the warning limits (two standard deviations)

• Bias in a series of ten or more points where 80 percent or more of the points fall above or below the center line

• Cyclical patterns (e.g., where all data points fall below the center line early in the week and above the center line in the latter part of the week)

The process may still be in control if these patterns exist, but the process is varying abnormally.

The phrase "an out of control process" is an unfortunate choice of terms in some ways. The term simply means that something is going on in the process that causes statistically unpredictable behavior. By measuring when a process is out of control, a company can identify, investigate, and correct the special causes and so bring the process back into control.

Ultimately, the primary role of control charts is to help people understand what level of performance and degree of variability the process is capable of achieving. The control chart helps first by establishing whether the process is stable (in statistical control). Once a firm removes the special causes, the results of the process can be statistically predicted. **This is not to say that a stable process necessarily is capable of meeting customer requirements.** To determine whether a process is capable requires understanding the customer requirements (as described in Section III of this book) in terms of the target value, the upper specifications limit (USL), and the lower specification limit (LSL).

Figure 9-20 depicts how process capability and customer requirements don't always match. In this case, the customer wants a 96 percent line-item fill rate on average but a fill rate in the 94 to 98 percent range on any one order is acceptable — neither discernibly superior nor inferior. Thus, the supplier has set 98 and 94 percent as the upper and lower specification limits respectively. This range comprises the shaded part of the graph and is represented by the shaded bell-shaped curve to the right of the graph.

The *process* that currently delivers line-item fill rate, made up of forecasting, inventory management, production planning, etc., actually achieves 95.6 percent on average. However, the upper and lower control limits are 99.1 and 92.1 respectively. In this case, the process is stable but cannot reliably meet customer requirements. At times, customers receive discernibly superior service (above 98 percent), and, at other times, they experience inferior service (below 94 percent). Because this sample company has eliminated all the special causes of variation and the process is now in control, the next step is to change the process in order to improve the result.

Figure 9-21 shows the relationship between capability and fulfilling requirements in a slightly different way. Here the process being measured is order cycle time with a target of seven days and a tolerance of plus or minus one day (USL and LSL). In the top part of the chart, we see the process delivers an actual order cycle time averaging 7.5 days — just slightly worse than the target. The range is plus or minus 1.5 days at either end (three days total). In this case, the process is not capable of meeting the requirements as the range (three days) exceeds the target range (2 days). The company must get the variability of the process down to the two-day range and then find a way to reduce average cycle time from 7.5 to 7.0 days.

The center section of the chart shows a process that can meet the two-day range but has an average cycle time of 7.6 days. While the process is capable, it does not meet requirements. The task here is to find a way to change the process, to shave an average of 0.6 days off the order cycle time without losing the predictability that results in a two-day range.

The bottom part of the graph illustrates a process that is capable of meeting requirements and actually is doing so. The average cycle time is on target, while the range is the required plus or minus one day.

Figure 9-20

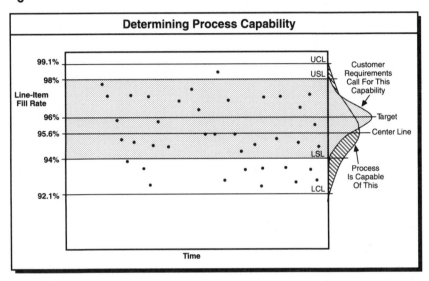

Figure 9-21

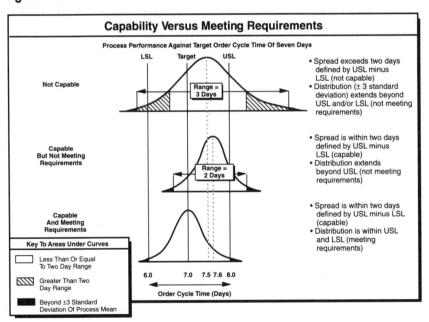

In summary, the *capability* of a process represents the best result that can be expected from the process. If the capability fails to meet requirements, the only way to improve results is to change the process.

Data Stratification

With each of the statistical analysis tools discussed above, an analysis technique known as data stratification may be useful in achieving better results. Simply put, data stratification means dividing the data into groups that share some common characteristic. Stratifying or "cutting" data helps identify underlying patterns in the data that are masked when the database is studied in its entirety.

One firm we interviewed used a data stratification approach to improve the freight bill payment process. The company thought its freight bill auditing costs were too high. The high freight bill error rate, however, meant they couldn't just discontinue auditing. So management decided to investigate the sources and reasons for freight bill errors. By stratifying the data by carrier, it discovered the vast majority of errors came from a handful of carriers' bills. Using this knowledge, the company eliminated auditing for other carriers and worked with the problem carriers to improve their billing accuracy. This allowed the firm to reassign its internal people from freight bill audit duties to more productive work in transportation analysis.

Stratifying data can be done along many dimensions, including by product, facility, customer, carrier, order size, order type, employee or work center, supplier, and time period.

BENCHMARKING

Benchmarking is the third kind of improvement tool that deserves mention in this book. Pioneered by Xerox and other companies, benchmarking has generated wide interest throughout American industry. Several books have been written on the subject, and it is not within the scope of this book to explore benchmarking in detail. However, we will provide a short description of the process and discuss how it relates to quality and productivity improvement.

Benchmarking is a process for identifying "best-of-the-best" practices by activity across industries and "best-of-the-best" performance levels as input to goal setting. Of the companies we surveyed that had formal quality and productivity-improvement processes for logistics, 39 percent use benchmarking.

Benchmarking consists of five major steps as illustrated in Figure 9-22. The first step is to plan the benchmarking process. This means selecting the areas to be benchmarked and identifying benchmark candidates and additional data sources. In a logistics setting, the areas to be benchmarked might be warehouse operations, order processing, forecasting, freight bill payment, packaging, and the like.

Figure 9-22

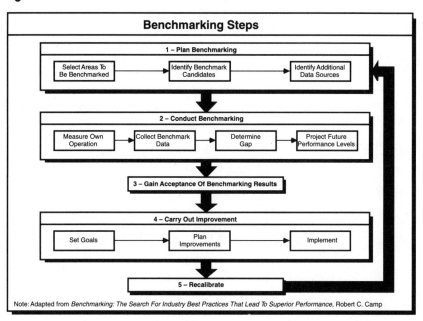

Benchmark candidates don't necessarily need to be members of a company's own industry. In fact, there are several advantages of going outside one's own industry to find new approaches to handling similar activities. As an example, Xerox benchmarks itself against catalog retailer L.L. Bean on warehousing and against American Express on collection processes.

To supplement benchmark data gained from "benchmark partners," companies often use other sources of data such as professional organizations, industry trade associations, literature searches, consultants, and academicians.

Once a benchmarking plan has been developed, the next step is to conduct the benchmark study. This begins by measuring the firm's own operation, gathering quantitative assessments, and analyzing processes. Next comes the collection of benchmark data through the use of surveys and on-site visits. With data in hand, the firm can "determine the gap" or identify how far the company is from the "best-of-the-best" practices and levels of performance. It uses this information to project what future performance levels should be and to set long-term goals and a vision for the future.

At first glance, many firms are inclined to carry out benchmarking as a staff function because line operations people "can't be bothered to take the time." In reality, though, many companies find it invaluable to include those responsible for implementing improvements — operations people — on the benchmarking team to show them what is possible based on others' experiences. Participation on the benchmarking team goes a long way toward building enthusiasm and gaining acceptance for the benchmark results.

The third major step in benchmarking is gaining acceptance of benchmark results. Benchmark studies often uncover new practices and levels of performance that stretch the imagination. In his book, *Benchmarking, The Search for Industry Best Practices that Lead to Superior Performance*, Robert C. Camp offers several suggestions for gaining acceptance of the validity and applicability of the results.[2] These include:

- Documenting both what best practices are and how they really operate

- Taking operational people on visits to see best practices first hand

- Validating results from multiple sources to add credibility

- Communicating methodology, results, and opportunities uncovered to all affected parties (e.g., functional management, employees, suppliers, customers, senior management)

Such actions help to "sell in" the findings and gain acceptance for the opportunities ahead.

The next major step in benchmarking is executing improvements. This means setting long-term stretch goals and achievable goals for the near term, planning improvements, and implementing the improvements.

Lastly, companies should review their processes after improvements have been made to make sure they incorporate the most current "best-of-the-best" thinking and results.

In looking at the benchmarking process, one might wonder why a company would allow itself to be benchmarked by another. Won't it lose competitive advantage by sharing its secrets? Most firms that benchmark extensively don't hold this view. Rather, they see it as an opportunity for two-way information exchange as well as an opportunity for improvement by learning from other leaders.

Additionally, several companies we interviewed said they don't worry about their competition finding out what they are doing through the benchmarking grapevine. By the time the competition catches up with their current level of performance, they say, their companies will have surpassed the original levels and reached new targets of performance.

This brings up a good point about benchmarking. Benchmarking against competitors only tells you where the competitor is today — not where it will be tomorrow. To gain competitive advantage, therefore, the company must aim ahead of the competition at the target the customer sets.

BENEFIT OF IMPROVEMENT TOOLS

Process improvement is at the center of quality and productivity improvement. Quantitative and qualitative tools and techniques exist to help people better understand how processes work, to define ways to improve them, and to receive input and ideas to the improvement process from outside the corporation.

The set of tools that rely on statistical analysis are based on measurement. In the next chapter, we explore measurement of logistics quality and productivity in detail.

---

[1] Deming, W. Edwards, *Out of the Crisis*

[2] Camp, Robert C., *Benchmarking, The Search for Industry Best Practices that Lead to Superior Performance*

CHAPTER 10

MEASUREMENT TECHNIQUES

Traditionally, measurement has been used as a means to keep score. A manager's success is often measured in terms of improvements in the operations for which the manager is responsible. These improvements may take many forms — increased market share, higher profits, lower head count, increased earnings per share, higher revenues, and lower cost — depending on the manager's particular responsibilities.

In our 1978 and 1983 studies, we described the generally accepted measure of improvement for logistics activities as cost reduction and, to a certain degree, service improvement. We went on to describe how cost reduction can be measured in a number of different ways, including changes to cost as a percent of sales, cost per case shipped, cost per delivery made, cost of carrying inventory per dollar of sales generated, and cost per unit purchased. We explained how these measures of cost improvement can be influenced by:

- Changes to the basis of measurement being used (a 10 percent price increase causes logistics costs as a percent of sales to drop without any real improvement)

- Changes to the per unit cost paid for resources (e.g., labor, fuel, equipment, outside transportation) without any fundamental change in the process for using the resources (but rather using clout in these instances to reduce rates and set up win/lose situations)

- Changes to the true productivity level (increasing the output for given level of input)

Among these three ways of reducing costs, true productivity improvement is the only one that is generally permanent. Lasting improvement in logistics costs results not from shifts in the base of measurement (which serve only to mask any true change) nor does it come from reducing the cost of resources by one-sided negotiation (which often results in confrontational catch-up situations later) nor because of prevailing economic conditions (e.g., fuel price changes). Instead, long-term cost reduction comes only from improving the basic underlying productivity of the logistics process.

If this were still our 1983 research, we might end our discussion about improvement here and continue by describing productivity measurement techniques. However, senior management increasingly is looking at the logistics process not only as a cost to be managed and reduced if possible but, more importantly, as one of the key business processes that drives customer satisfaction. As a result, keeping score of how well logistics managers do their jobs is rapidly expanding beyond cost/productivity (value to the shareholder) to incorporate customer service quality (value to customers) as well, as shown in Figure 10-1.

Figure 10-1

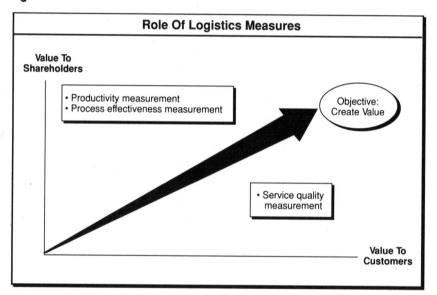

In this chapter, therefore, our discussion of measurement techniques covers both quality and productivity measurement in logistics. The major topics discussed include:

- Role of measurement in the improvement process

- Families of measures in logistics

- Service quality measurement

- Productivity measurement

- Process effectiveness measurement

- Measurement system design

THE ROLE OF MEASUREMENT IN THE IMPROVEMENT PROCESS

In Chapter 9, we saw how measures play a key role in the improvement process by supporting statistical analysis. In fact, measurement plays a much broader role in logistics. Companies use it to facilitate communications, identify areas needing improvement, gather data to help understand problems, evaluate alternatives, track progress toward goals, and quantify and report results. We discuss each of these six areas below.

1. Facilitate communications. Measurement helps establish an objective definition of "what is" so all parties can work off the same base of understanding. Selection and definition of measures, consequently, is very important. For example, it is meaningless to talk about a measure of on-time performance unless the company and its customer agree on what on-time means. For one party, it could mean day of; for the other, it could mean plus or minus three days. Clearly defining measures in a way that is meaningful to each party involved simplifies the task of communicating potential problems and identifying improvement opportunities.

2. Identify areas that need improvement. People love to compare their operations. They want to know: Are we doing better than last year? Are we meeting our quotas? Are we ahead of the competition? Are we on budget? Are our customers happy? Most professionals are not satisfied with simple yes/no answers to these questions. Instead, they want measures that will tell them **how well** they are doing versus last year, **how much** they are meeting or exceeding their quota, **how far ahead** of competition they are, **by how much** they are beating their budgets, and **how happy** customers are. If the answers to "how much, how many, how far" aren't what the manager expects, the measures have helped identify areas that potentially need improvement.

3. Gather data to help understand problems. Just knowing "how much, how many, how far" is of limited value in correcting a problem or making an improvement. As we discussed in Chapter 9, understanding problems often requires looking beyond what is going on to why it's occurring. Drawing on the example in Figure 9-12, to decrease the amount of premium freight, a company must know more than just how much is being spent. Management must also understand and quantify the reasons for the expenditure (the whys). In fact, an approach often used in Japan to determine root causes of problems is to ask "why" five times (the "five whys"). By the fifth answer, the root cause has usually been uncovered.

4. Evaluate alternatives. Measures help in evaluating alternatives for improvement by providing an objective means of comparison. For example, a company might be looking at ways to improve its on-time delivery performance. To do so, for example, it must compare measures of on-time performance, processing cycle times, and related costs/productivity for each alternative.

5. Track progress toward goals. Once a firm selects an alternative and implements improvements, measurement comes into play as a means of tracking progress toward a goal. In the example just mentioned, this might include tracking on-time deliveries — the result of the improvement — along with progress on other factors that influence the result (e.g., number of orders received with sufficient lead time to meet delivery requirements, production to schedule, carrier on-time pickups).

6. Quantify and report results of improvements. Measurement is an important factor in quantifying and reporting results of improvement. For most companies, the quality and productivity-improvement process is a major investment in terms of management time, commitment, training expense, and support. And improvement actions may require some level of investment. By having measures to quantify the results, management can identify the benefits of its investments and thereby secure continued support for further improvement.

A good measurement system offers another benefit to firms — it enables them to feed back performance data to customers. This information has two values to the supplier: It reminds the customer of the performance it receives from the company, and it differentiates the company as being capable of reporting results to customers and confident enough to do so.

For example, in its bimonthly newsletter for employees and customers — *Quality Driven* — Burlington Motor Carriers publishes actual control charts for measures such as on-time delivery, out-of-route miles, and driver turnover. This openness underscores the company's commitment to a formal, analytically based quality-improvement process. It also helps demonstrate and publicize progress and success.

FAMILIES OF MEASURES IN LOGISTICS

There are three major families of measures used to track quality and productivity in logistics. These are:

• Service quality

  — To customers

  — From vendors/suppliers

• Productivity (including cost)

• Process effectiveness

— Service to internal customers

— Other key benchmarks

Cycle time measures are not explicitly broken out as a separate family of measures because they are found in all three families in different forms. When cycle time is expressed as a service goal (e.g., order cycle time of "x" hours), performance against the goal is a measure of service quality. When cycle times of alternative processes are compared or when cycle time reduction is tracked, these become measures of productivity or process effectiveness.

This chapter describes each family of measures. Appendixes A through F provide a reference list of potential measures for use in the key functions and activities that constitute the logistics process.

SERVICE QUALITY MEASUREMENT

Productivity measurement in logistics is a much analyzed subject. Our two previous research reports explored the concepts in depth. Literally hundreds of articles have been written on the subject in terms of its concepts, framework, and application to logistics.

By contrast, service quality measurement in logistics is not nearly as well understood. We believe, therefore, that it is important to develop a framework, terminology, and way of thinking about service quality measurement in logistics in the same fashion that we structured these for productivity measurement 13 years ago.

How Quality and Productivity Measurement Differ

Service quality measurement is much more sensitive and demanding than productivity measurement. Service quality lies in the eye of the beholder/customer. As a result, from the supplier's standpoint, service measures are a surrogate for customer perceptions about the service the supplier provides. As we discussed in Chapter 6, suppliers aren't always adept at understanding customers' requirements and how customers measure performance against requirements. As a result, there are always several questions to consider. First, how well do the suppliers' and customers' measures match? Do they use the same definitions of measures and the same data? Second, how does a supplier know when a customer's criteria for and ways of measuring have changed?

More and more, customers are implementing their own service quality measurement systems for evaluating their suppliers. In the next chapter, we will discuss in detail an approach used by Motorola, Texas Instruments, Rockwell Aerospace, and a host of other companies to track both the product and service quality of their suppliers and **to directly use that information to make sourcing and purchasing decisions.** This approach brings into sharp focus the need for suppliers to understand how their customers are measuring them.

Productivity measurement, by comparison, is easy. It typically occurs within a single organizational unit and is inwardly focused. Quality measurement, on the other hand, is externally market and customer focused, occurs at the interface between organizational units, and involves parties that may have different understandings and conflicting objectives.

What Should "Service Quality" Measure?

As we discussed in Chapter 5, service measures should track performance against the essentials as well as performance on the value-added elements of service. The essentials — order completeness, on-time delivery, invoice accuracy, and damage rate — usually are internally generated measures derived from existing transaction systems (e.g., order entry, inventory management, invoicing). The value-added measures usually come from customer feedback. They represent the customers' views of how well the value-added services match their expectations.

In most companies, if service quality measurements exist, they focus only on the essentials. A few businesses, however, have begun to measure the value-added side as well. This kind of feedback is more commonly found with service companies that deal directly with the consuming public. Hotels and airlines ask consumers to rate them on a variety of service dimensions. However, some manufacturers have followed suit.

Motorola, for one, regularly surveys its customers to get feedback on a range of product and service related quality measures. These items include sales representation, delivery, billing and credit, installation, maintenance service, product, and Motorola's performance trend. The survey provides feedback on current performance and helps Motorola better understand what is important to its customers.

Xerox recently implemented a "Post Install Customer Satisfaction Survey" that is mailed to all customers six weeks after installation. It tests satisfaction with sales, delivery, and initial invoicing.

In her book, *The Man Who Discovered Quality*, Andrea Gabor notes that Ford Motor Company's customer satisfaction measures have shifted dramatically over the last 15 years from internally derived measures to direct customer query. In the 1970s, Ford's primary customer satisfaction measure was its warranty costs. In the early 1980s, the company started to measure "things gone wrong," i.e., what the customer didn't like about Ford products and services. Now, Ford tracks not only what the customer wants (a wish list) but also how well Ford is meeting customer requirements on both the essentials and the value-added dimensions.[1]

Another key concept of service measurement is that the measurement reflects the customer's viewpoint. This means the measure should track what the customer thinks it has purchased from its supplier. For example, if a customer is buying a computer system from a manufacturer, it is not just buying the equipment. It is buying delivery of an operational system. One computer company we interviewed used to have a service measurement system that overlooked that simple fact. The systems it sold to certain market segments drew components from several divisions. These divisions measured their service levels in terms of percent of orders shipped on time, recording performance levels ranging between 80 and 90 percent. The problem was that for certain customer orders as many as eight or nine divisions might be involved. With a 10 to 20 percent probability of not shipping on time for each division, the customers experienced a 50 percent on-time performance on the whole order — and a system that was not operational. Happily, the computer manufacturer recognized the problem and now measures service from the customer's viewpoint rather than from each division's.

There are other examples of this kind of myopia. On November 7, 1990, *The Wall Street Journal* reported a study by a public accounting firm of overnight service performance by the United States Postal Service (USPS). The accounting firm found that overnight mail was on time 81 percent of the time versus 94 percent as measured by the USPS. To the customer, on-time meant delivery using the measure of time elapsed from when the item was mailed to when it was delivered. The USPS, instead, measured from the time the item was postmarked (which could be several hours after it was mailed) until the time it was turned over to the postal carrier at the destination post office. The customer believed it was buying overnight delivery of the item from the mailbox to the addressee. The USPS chose a different, internally focused measure that did not reflect what the customer was buying. It thereby overlooked an additional 13 percent of the time that it fell short of the customer's expectations.[2]

In an article one week later, *The Wall Street Journal* told about Baxter Hospital Supply Division's service measurement problem. Customers of Baxter (hospitals) were measuring the company's service performance based on the completeness of an order on the first delivery after order placement. Baxter, on the other hand, measured its ability to ship on the first try out of the specified stocking location for each item. In most cases, that location was the local branch. For some products, however, the source was an area distribution center, a national distribution point, or even direct shipment from a vendor. In these cases, the items may have been available when ordered, picked and shipped as planned, and delivered as soon as possible. However, if they didn't arrive on the first delivery after the order was placed, some customers viewed the order as incomplete. As with the computer manufacturer, Baxter Hospital Supply Division is revising its internal measures of customer service to better reflect what the customer expects.[3]

For suppliers to the grocery trade, understanding what customers think they are buying also is key. For replenishment stock, many customers measure their suppliers against target fill rates on the different SKUs they order. The target fill rates are factored into the safety stock calculations that the customers build into their inventory replenishment logic. For promotional items, however, the customer is not simply buying cereal, canned vegetables, or paper towels to replenish shelf stock. Instead, it is buying a commitment from the supplier to provide the amount of promotional goods projected to sell during the promotional period plus the ability to reorder on a short lead time if the promotion goes exceptionally well. Although the items purchased may be identical, the grocery customer may measure service performance differently depending on what purpose the item serves. The supplier must recognize this and measure service differently as well.

, Another key to service quality measurement is measuring what the customer wants and not what it is coerced or persuaded into accepting. If the customer feels forced to accept a due date, a substituted product, or quantity other than what it expected, the supplier that measures performance against the coerced promise gets a very inaccurate picture of its service.

In his book, *Thriving on Chaos,* Tom Peters cites an example of this kind of situation. "A high tech firm boasted it was beating order due dates 98 percent of the time. But customers were not knocking down the doors with repeat business. It turned out that the 'due date' was actually a tortuously negotiated date; if the customer asked for the order by January 17th, a harried plant manager might insist that February 25th was the best he could do. So what's the big deal in beating that kind of 'due date' by even a week? When the firm switched to the 'customer request' (reasonable or not) as its measurement base, meeting or beating it slumped to a tawdry 32 percent. After a year of hard work, it has climbed back to 68 percent — and repeat business has grown."[4]

Peters makes a key point in this excerpt. Measures of service need to track performance against the *real* customer requirement (e.g., against the original request date before negotiations, against original item/quantity before substitutions). At the same time, suppliers must realize that not every customer request is a real customer requirement. In some situations, it is perfectly acceptable practice for the supplier and customer to negotiate a due date and agree on one that is mutually acceptable. This then becomes the requirement against which service should be measured.

Making Service Measures Robust

To some companies, achieving 95 percent on a service quality measure would be great news. For others, it might trigger concern and self analysis. Management might ask: What happened the other 5 percent of the time? Why did the 5 percent failure occur? How many failures did the 5 percent represent? How far off target were we — a few minutes or a few days? Were we short on all items or just some? Which customers were affected? What impact did our failure have on those customers and on our company?

The 95 percent figure measures results — it tracks what was accomplished. By itself, a results measure can only tell you that a change has occurred; it can't describe the reasons behind the change or its impact. Companies need more robust service measures than simple summaries such as 95 percent on-time or 98 percent fill rate. To this end, we believe three types of measures are needed to track and improve service quality. They include results, diagnostic, and impact measures.

• Results measures provide a snapshot of performance and answer the question "How are we doing?" Companies use them to measure trends and compare with goals. They compare results with service goals, for instance, to establish performance versus goal statistics for reporting purposes.

Diagnostic measures afford an in-depth look at the reasons and sources for performance below (or above) goal. They prompt actions aimed at correcting the problems and increasing performance. Additionally, they answer the query "Why?" that often follows the question "How are we doing?"

• The third type of measure — impact — tracks the direct and indirect costs of performance. It increases the visibility of problems in tangible terms and helps identify areas of opportunity for boosting performance.

All three kinds of measures are useful. Companies want to achieve results, but results can't be improved directly. Instead, firms must improve the processes that lead to results. To do this, measures must track both results and process performance.

Example of Service Measurement in a Paper Manufacturing Company

The following example illustrates how a major manufacturer of newsprint, pulp, and white paper developed a set of service quality measurements. The company, which we'll call ABC Paper Manufacturing Co., needed to improve customer service quality after a series of serious service failures occurred in the late 1980s. After identifying what dimensions of service were most important to customers (using a technique similar to that described in Section III), ABC pinpointed four key areas that required service quality measurement. These were:

• Accurate and complete orders

• On-time delivery

• Undamaged product

• Proper communication and documentation

For each area, the company decided that it needed results, diagnostic, and impact service quality measures. Using customer input from surveys and interviews, the company set out to define what each measure should cover for each of the four key service dimensions. This process began with a brainstorming session and went through a number of iterations internally and with customers.

The measures chosen for each service dimension are described in the following paragraphs.

1. Order accuracy and completeness. Because ABC served different types of markets, it had no common definition of order completeness. For its newsprint publisher customers, an order was considered complete if it had between 99 and 105 percent of the tons ordered. Commercial printers, on the other hand, required exact tonnages. These disparities made a simple overall measure impossible. Instead, ABC decided to track order accuracy and completeness by customer and then create a system to aggregate these findings based on customer type. Figure 10-2 lists the measures the firm selected for order accuracy and completeness.

Figure 10-2

Order Accuracy And Completeness Measures – Example

- ■ <u>Results</u>: percent of orders delivered "as ordered"
  - Exact product (before substitutions and upgrades)
  - Correct quantity within the agreed-to tolerance

- ■ <u>Diagnostic</u>: count and percent of orders incomplete upon delivery with associated reasons; e.g.:
  - Error in order entry
  - Product not produced
  - Product produced short
  - Shipped short/over/incorrect item
  - Could not locate product in storage
  - Not enough space in carrier equipment
  - Received short at customer
  - Mislabled/miscounted
  - Unathorized substitution
  - Damage
  - Loss
  - Incorrect product shipped

- ■ <u>Impact</u>: "cost" of inaccurate or incomplete orders; e.g.:
  - Value of order refused or canceled
  - Amount of customer credit allowance
  - Cost of returns handling
  - Excess distribution costs (for premium freight/handling to complete the order)
  - Excess inventory

2. On-time delivery. As with the order completeness measure, the definition of on-time delivery varied by type of customer. Also, the on-time promise date was often renegotiated after the order was placed to suit customer requirements or at ABC's request. Here too, the measures were tracked at the customer level and aggregate level by type. The measures ABC chose are shown in Table Figure 10-3.

Figure 10-3

On-Time Delivery Measures – Example

■ <u>Results</u>: percentage of orders delivered "on-time"
  • "On-time" window defined by product/customer segment, negotiable by order
  • On-time promise date based on "final promise" made

■ <u>Diagnostic</u>: count and percent of orders not delivered "on-time", with associated reasons; e.g.:
  • Misunderstanding between customer and customer service representative on date required
  • Miscommunications within company on date required
  • Order accepted too late to process for on-time delivery (i.e., a "bad promise" was made)
  • Late production (too late for vessel departure date) due to unplanned downtime, schedule break-ins, production below plan, other causes
  • Late shipment dispatch due to missed pickup time, equipment refused by mill, insufficient equipment, weather delay, material handling delay, other causes
  • Late transportation delivery due to environmental factors (e.g., snow, high seas), equipment failure, delays at customs, poor carrier performance, other causes

■ <u>Diagnostic</u>: count and percent of orders delivered on time, but via premium transportation

■ <u>Impact</u>: "cost" of late (or early) delivery
  • Value of orders refused/canceled
  • Value of customer credits/allowances
  • Cost of premium transportation versus preferred mode/carrier
  • Inventory costs for early shipments

---

3. Product damage. The measures chosen to track product damage are shown in Figure 10-4.

Figure 10-4

Product Damage Measures – Example

■ <u>Results</u>: count and percent of rolls/bales delivered undamaged

■ <u>Diagnostic</u>: count and percent of rolls/bales damaged, with associated reasons; e.g.:
• Nature of damage; e.g.:
– Cuts and edge damage, out-of-round and crushed roll cores, water
• Where damage was discovered; e.g.:
– At mill, in transit, at pier/warehouse, at customer
• Reason; e.g.:
– Operator error, equipment failure, accident/disaster (e.g., fire, derailment)

■ <u>Impact</u>: "cost" of damage
• Downgrading of product
• Credit/revenue loss
• Double handling
• Double transporting
• Value of canceled or refused orders

---

4. Proper communication and documentation. The measures that ABC selected for this dimension of service are shown in Figure 10-5.

The measurement system is still under development as of this writing. In most cases, the data for the results measures will come directly from ABC's order entry system. For the diagnostic measures, ABC will install a data capture process using techniques such as check sheets (described in Chapter 9) and service failure follow-up forms. For the impact measures, some data — such as credits and canceled orders — will come directly from the accounting system. Other data will come from tracking the cost of follow-up actions such as use of premium transportation to fill out an incomplete order. And ABC will collect any other impact costs on an as-needed basis.

Figure 10-5

Proper Communication And
Documentation Measures – Example

- Results: orders delivered without communication/ documentation failures

- Diagnostic: count and percent of orders requiring unplanned follow-up communication, with associated reasons; e.g.:
  - Contact customers to obtain information not captured by customer service representative at the time of order placement
  - Need to negotiate new "promise" due to problem (e.g.; "overbooking" of machine time, unexpected down time)
  - Notify customer in advance of service failure
  - Respond to customer after unanticipated service failure

- Diagnostic: elapsed time needed to respond to inquiries and communication/documentation failures

- Diagnostic: count and percent of orders requiring special attention or adjustments due to documentation problems, with associated reasons; e.g.:
  - Inaccurate and incomplete receiving documentation
  - Receiving documentation not available when product is delivered
  - Inaccurate/incomplete invoices; e.g., wrong product, wrong price, inaccurate calculations, incomplete information

- Impact: cost of communication/documentation failures
  - Value of canceled orders
  - Value of credits/allowances
  - Unproductive customer representative time
  - Communications cost

The results measures are the primary ones that ABC will track and use on a month to month basis. Where problems occur, ABC will tap into a database to create a set of diagnostic measures from the captured data. The impact measures will be an information source for analyzing the cost of service failures and possible savings accrued from upgrading the logistics process to increase order accuracy and completeness, improve on-time delivery, decrease damage, and improve the effectiveness of communication and documentation.

Before leaving the ABC company example, we should point out that its approach to service quality measurement represents just a first step. Companies often start out by measuring quality in terms of the percentage of time that they meet the customer's requirements (e.g., percent on-time delivery, percent case fill rate). Some look at the reverse of this (e.g., percent of orders late, percent of cases not shipped as ordered). But either measure can lead to complacency. While 99 percent on-time sounds good, it still means that 100 out of every 10,000 shipments are late.

Several progressive companies had moved beyond percents as the key quality measure and focus instead on the absolute number of defects or failures. (This is the concept behind Motorola's "Six Sigma" goal. Statistically speaking, "Six Sigma" translates to 3.4 defects per million opportunities.) Federal Express, Xerox, Texas Instruments, Baxter Healthcare, Hewlett-Packard, and Milliken are just a few of the other quality oriented companies that had adopted this approach.

As an example, Federal Express uses a "Service Quality Indicator" (SQI) to gauge overall service to customers. SQI is made up of a set of individual daily measures of service failures including the number of late deliveries-right day, late deliveries-wrong day, damaged packages, missing proofs of delivery, lost packages, abandoned telephone calls (where Federal Express exceeds its time standard in answering a call), and complaints reopened. Federal Express has assigned weighting factors to each type of service failure (e.g., a late delivery-wrong day is five times as serious as a late delivery-right day) and uses this weighting to calculate an overall SQI that is reported weekly. Since it began using this measurement approach in 1987, Federal Express cut the *absolute number* of service failures (as measured by the SQI) by 16 percent. Over the same period, total volume grew by over 80 percent.

Other Considerations in Establishing Service Quality Measures

ABC Paper Manufacturing Co. focused its service quality measures on those dimensions most valued by its customers — accuracy and completeness, on-time delivery, damage-free product, and good communication and documentation. These essentials exist in most companies that carry out a logistics process. For some firms, however, additional dimensions may fall into the essentials category and, therefore, need to be measured.

For companies with after-sales support and repair services, for instance, the key measures are how quickly the customer's machine can be serviced/repaired and brought back on-line. This means that measures such as elapsed time from customer notification to service response and time from notification to recovery/repair are the real measures of service quality performance. (Some companies measure parts fill rates even though anything less than 100 percent is of little value to the customer.)

Another consideration for service quality might be the effect the customer has on the supplier's ability to provide service. Suppliers should consider implementing service measurements that track customer performance. This may be a touchy subject area considering that it's the customer, not the supplier, that makes the buying decision. As companies evolve toward supplier-customer partnerships, however, this two-way measurement becomes important.

Depending on the type of industry and the specific situation, suppliers can use several kinds of measures to track how their customers affect overall service quality. These include:

- Delivery refusals or unloading delays

- Number of orders that violate specified lead times

- Inaccurate or incomplete ordering paperwork

- Inadequate or incomplete blueprints and specifications for make-to-order products

Summary of Service Quality Measurement

To summarize, service quality measurement starts by thinking about service from the customer's viewpoint. (What is it that the customer thinks he is buying? How is the customer evaluating the supplier?) Measures of percent performance are only the beginning. Progressive companies are looking beyond these to understand how frequently they fail to meet customer requirements, why the failures occur, and what impact the failures have. And companies are increasingly finding that service quality measurement is a two-way street. Customers measure supplier service quality, and some suppliers now measure the impacts that customers have on service quality.

PRODUCTIVITY MEASUREMENT

As we have described throughout this book, measuring service quality means assessing the *effectiveness* with which the logistics process meets customer requirements. Measuring logistics productivity means measuring the *efficiency* with which the logistics process meets the requirements. Said differently, service quality measurement tells how well the logistics process operates in support of the business's mission and goals. Productivity measurement tells how much effort (and cost) the logistics process expends to do so.

General Concepts

As we described in our two previous studies, productivity is the ratio of real output produced to real input consumed where:

- **Output** is a measure of the amount of work accomplished by an activity, e.g.,
    - Number of trucks unloaded
    - Number of line items picked
    - Number of orders taken
    - Number of pallets stored

- Input is a measure of the resource consumed to accomplish the work. Written in formula version, the formula for productivity looks like this.

$$Productivity = \frac{Real\ Output\ Produced}{Real\ Input\ Consumed}$$

It should be noted that productivity often is expressed in terms of the ratio of input to output, i.e., the unit cost. While this expression doesn't follow the strictest definition of productivity, it may be useful to think in terms of unit cost — adjusted for inflation — as a surrogate for productivity because of the prevalence of the measure "cost per unit."

Figure 10-6 displays the typically used productivity inputs and outputs for logistics.

In the context of productivity measurement, "real" means two things:

1. The output produced has value; it is not necessarily the amount of effort expended. For example:

- A truck can drive around an empty lot all day and produce a considerable amount of miles driven (effort expended), yet those miles have little or no value in terms of satisfying customer requirements.

- A customer service representative can increase the number of calls handled in a day by limiting each call to 20 seconds. This produces little value, however, if most customers' inquiries or problems cannot be handled in 20 seconds.

- In terms of tons moved per unit of cost, barge transportation is extremely productive. However, if a customer in New Orleans wants next day service from a supplier in Minneapolis, shipping by barge provides little value despite the high productivity.

- By applying piece-rate incentives in a warehouse, the number of orders picked per day might be increased. However, if this results in an increase in order pick errors or fewer complete orders (because the workers don't take the time to pick items that are in more remote parts of the warehouse), real output (complete and accurate orders to customers) hasn't improved.

Figure 10-6

Typical Productivity Inputs And Outputs For Logistics			
Inputs		Outputs	

• Human resources
  – Direct hourly
    labor
  – Indirect hourly
    labor
  – Salaried staff
  – Management
	• Technology
	  – Patents
	  – Techniques
	  – Systems
		• Sales units
		  – Orders
		  – Shipments
		  – Deliveries
		  – Invoices
		  – Line items
			• Units
			  – Pieces
			  – Dozens
			  – Cases
			  – Cartons
			  – Palletloads
			  – Carloads
			  – Miles

• Physical
  resources
  – Land, buildings
  – Facilities
  – Equipment
	• Energy
	  – Fuel
	  – Power
		• Weight
		  – Pounds
		  – CWT
		  – Tons
			• Value
			  – Cost
			  – Sales value of
			    goods sold
			  – Value-added

• Financial
  resources
  – Inventories
  – Receivables
	• Cycle time	• Volume
		  – Gallons
		  – Barrels
		  – Cubic feet
			• Value of goods
			  purchased

All output is not alike. Only output that adds value in the eyes of the customer can be considered truly productive.

2. "Real" also means that the value of the output produced or input consumed is unaffected by financial or monetary shifts. A company might measure productivity in terms of the dollar value of orders picked per employee hour. Under this measure, an increase in productivity doesn't result just because the selling price goes up. Similarly, an increase in labor pay rates doesn't mean that productivity goes down.

Three Ways to Improve Productivity

In Chapter 9, we talked about how quality can be improved in three ways: by identifying and eliminating special causes that produce process variations, by refining the process to reduce remaining variability that results from common causes, and by re-engineering the process to achieve breakthrough results. Like quality, productivity can be upgraded by three ways: re-engineer the basic process, improve resource utilization, and enhance performance against goals.

Re-engineering the process is where quality improvement and productivity intersect. Quality-improvement actions often spin off productivity improvement as well by virtue of eliminating bottlenecks, removing unnecessary steps, abolishing redundancies, and focusing resources on producing "real" output. This interrelationship between quality and productivity improvement is shown in Figure 10-7. Each of the three ways of improving productivity in logistics is discussed in more detail in the following paragraphs.

Figure 10-7

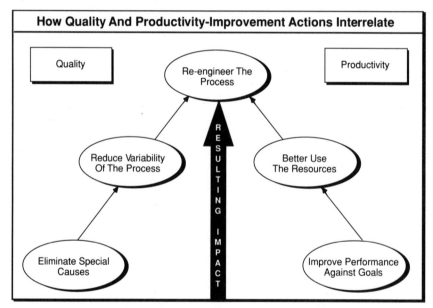

1. Re-engineering the process. Each logistics process has its own ways of accomplishing its job. The number/size/location of warehouses, inventory deployment strategies, use and size of a private fleet, type and sophistication of information systems employed — all are important elements in every logistics process.

Each part of the overall logistics process has its own inherent level of productivity. Productivity levels, therefore, are largely designed in when the process is chosen. For example, a company that designs its outbound physical distribution network to include master distribution centers and local service centers effectively locks in a certain productivity level (i.e., cost and cycle time to serve customers) related to operating that number of facilities. Thus, a logistics manager can improve the productivity of the logistics process by selecting and using more productive processes for satisfying customer requirements.

Process improvements range from major, structural changes such as reconfiguring the facilities network to updating specific operating methods used in a particular activity (e.g., vehicle specification). Productivity measures help evaluate the inherent level of productivity of one process versus another.

2. Making better use of resources. In addition to changing their processes, companies can boost productivity by matching the capacity for accomplishing work with the work to be done. For instance, if a warehouse is capable of storing 200,000 cases but has a peak need to store only 100,000 cases, the unused capacity places a cost penalty on every case passing through the warehouse. Similarly, if a firm usually needs 20 local delivery trucks each day, but on Thursdays only has enough orders to keep 16 vehicles busy all day, a decision to spread Thursday's work across 20 units results in lower capacity and labor utilization. The key to improving utilization is *planning* so that the actual capacity (of storage space, labor, vehicles, inventory, etc.) matches the true resource need. Once the firm commits to the capacity and its attendant costs, it may be too late to improve utilization. Utilization measures help management plan capacity requirements.

3. Improving performance against goals. The final way in which productivity can be improved is by increasing performance levels. By managing the performance of resources used, companies can achieve the designed-in productivity levels. Performance measures help point to specific improvement opportunities that can be corrected by various techniques, including training and closer supervision. The following examples illustrate this point.

- If operating technology (material handling equipment and layout) in a warehouse allows for an average productivity rate of 22 trucks unloaded per eight employee-hours yet the actual rate is 19 trucks per hour, performance is 86 percent (19 divided by 22).

- When an over-the-road truck driver requires 9.5 hours to complete a nine-hour trip, the driver's performance is 94.7 percent.

- When the data processing center requires three hours of computer time to process 30,000 orders versus a goal of 2.5 hours, its performance is 83.3 percent.

Note that productivity performance standards can be expressed either as a target productivity rate (22 trucks unloaded per eight hours) or a standard time allowed for accomplishing a given task (nine hours to complete a truck trip). Typically, firms employ target productivity rates when the work performed is uniform and predictable. When the work varies based on the mix of duties to be performed, work accomplished is usually translated into standard hours of work. Figure 10-8 displays the key productivity ratios (productivity, utilization, and performance) that relate to these three ways of improving productivity.

Figure 10-8

Key Productivity Ratios	
■ Productivity =	$\dfrac{\text{Output Produced}}{\text{Input Consumed}}$
■ Utilization =	$\dfrac{\text{Capacity (Resources) Used}}{\text{Capacity (Resources) Available}}$
■ Performance =	$\dfrac{\text{Actual Output Produced}}{\text{Standard Output Produced}}$ *Or* $\dfrac{\text{Standard Hours Of Work Performed}}{\text{Actual Hours Of Work Used}}$

Relationship of Inherent Process Productivity, Utilization, and Performance

The inherent productivity of a process, utilization, and performance is interrelated (see Figure 10-9). Each factor influences the actual level of productivity achieved.

Figure 10-10 offers an example of this relationship. Step 1 is the base case — current productivity is 12 lines per employee-hour. This figure is based on a defined process/method of picking to a hand cart — a process that has an inherent productivity rate of 20 lines per employee-hour. Sufficient work exists to keep each employee busy for 30 of 40 hours per week (75 percent utilization). When working, the labor force picks 16 lines per employee-hour (or 80 percent performance against standard).

By improving the process/method — instituting zone picking using electric carts (Step 2) — the facility increases the inherent productivity of the order picking function to 35 lines per employee-hour. But the firm did nothing to boost utilization or performance. As a result, actual productivity increased from 12 to 21 lines per employee-hour.

Figure 10-9

Relationship Of Inherent Process Productivity, Utilization And Performance	
■ Actual productivity =	Inherent Productivity Of The Process x Utilization x Performance ***Where***
■ Actual productivity =	$\dfrac{\text{Actual Level Of Output Produced}}{\text{Input Used}}$
■ Inherent productivity of the process =	$\dfrac{\text{Expected Level Of Output Produced}}{\text{Input Required}}$
■ Utilization =	$\dfrac{\text{Input Required}}{\text{Input Available}}$
■ Performance =	$\dfrac{\text{Actual Level Of Output Produced}}{\text{Expected Level Of Output Produced}}$

To improve utilization, the company could adjust staff levels to match the work available (Step 3). As utilization increases to 36 of the 40 hours available per week, productivity increases to 25.2 lines per employee.

Achieving higher performance adds further improvement (Step 4). The company increases its performance from 80 to 95 percent through improved training and a program of reporting performance against standards. The net effect on actual productivity is an increase to 29.9 lines per employee-hour.

In our previous research studies, we identified and catalogued hundreds of potential productivity, utilization, and performance measures. For reference, these are available in Appendixes A through F.

PROCESS EFFECTIVENESS MEASUREMENT

The third family of measures for use in logistics relates to process effectiveness. There are two main types of process effectiveness measures: measures of internal-customer service quality and key benchmarks of process effectiveness.

So far in this book, when we used the term "customer" we generally referred to external customers — those that generate revenue for the company. Embedded in the concepts of quality improvement, however, is the idea of the internal customer. Internal customers are people or departments that participate in a process and, in so doing, receive the output of others. Examples might include:

Figure 10-10

Example Of Process, Utilization And Performance In Warehouse Order Selection

Factor:	Inherent Productivity Of The Process	×	Utilization	×	Performance	=	Actual Productivity
Measure:	Standard Lines Per Picking Man-Hour	×	Picking Man-Hours Divided By Available Hours	×	Actual Lines/Picking Man-Hour Divided By Standard Lines/Picking Man-Hour	=	Lines Picked Per Available Man-Hour
1. Current productivity • Process: use hand cart – 20 lines/hour • Utilization: 30 hours per week per employee (75%) • Performance: 16 versus 20 lines (80%)	20	×	0.75	×	0.80	=	12.0
2. Improved process (use electric cart, zone picking) • Process: 35 lines/hour • Utilization: same as above (75%) • Performance: 28 versus 35 lines (80%)	35	×	0.75	×	0.80	=	21.0
3. Better utilization (adjusting staffing levels to provide 36 hours of picking work per employee) • Process: same as above (35) • Utilization: 7.2 of 8 hours (90%) • Performance: same as above	35	×	0.90	×	0.80	=	25.2
4. Higher performance (institute engineered standards and reporting, improve training) • Process: same as above (35) • Utilization: same as above (90%) • Performance: 33.2 versus 35 lines (95%)	35	×	0.90	×	0.95	=	29.9

- An order entry clerk who receives order data from a sales representative

- A production planner who receives demand information from the sales forecasting department and on-hand inventory information from the inventory management department

- A warehouse operator who receives a pick list from the order entry department

- A warehouse loading clerk who receives cases of goods to be loaded on a truck from an order picker

- The invoicing department that receives order shipment information from the warehouse

This list could go on and on. As it indicates, an internal customer exists any time physical product or information transfers from one person/department to another. Arguably, internal customers of the logistics process also include external customers (because they supply order information to the company), carriers, warehouse operators, and other third-party providers that act as agents of the supplier company.

The relative importance of providing quality service to internal versus external customers is an interesting topic for debate. Some argue that internal customers should be afforded the same degree of service quality as external customers regardless of the type of physical or informational exchange. Under this approach, the firm would place as much priority on a manager giving a secretary complete instructions on preparing a report as on having an order entry clerk relay specific shipping instructions for an order to the warehouse. Others prefer instead to emphasize in particular those *internal* supplier-customer relationships *that directly affect serving the external customer.* This means the internal activities that comprise the logistics process represent the key internal supplier-customer relationships in most companies.

The quality standards that a company builds into its internal supplier-customer relationships have a major impact on how well the company serves its customers. The reason for this is something that experts in product quality call tolerance stack-up. Essentially, tolerance stack-up means that the more places an internal service failure can occur and the more tolerance that exists for failure at these points, the greater the likelihood the customer will see a service failure.

Figure 10-11 portrays an example of how this happens. Listed in the table are ten transactions that make up a hypothetical order-fulfillment process. We list the probability of an error-free transaction next to each. Probabilities range from 95 to 99 percent with most at the high end of the range. The probability that the first step happens error free is 99 percent. However, the cumulative probability that the first two steps happen error-free is 98 percent (.99 x .99). After three steps, it is 97 percent (.99 x .99

x .99). The possibility of an error in each subsequent step further reduces the cumulative probability that the customer will view this as a perfect transaction (the customer got what was required). Individually, each step represents a transaction of its own between a supplier and a customer. By the time all ten steps are completed, the external (paying) customer has only an 85 percent chance of getting what was required despite the fact that each internal transaction has a high probability of succeeding.

Figure 10-11

The Compounding Effect Of Quality Failures		
Transaction Step	**Probability Of Error-Free Transaction (Example)**	**Cumulative Probability**
■ Customer correctly identifies requirements	99%	99%
■ Customer correctly communicates to supplier	99%	98%
■ Supplier accurately understands requirements	99%	97%
■ Supplier has product available	95%	92%
■ Supplier picks order and prepares documents correctly	99%	91%
■ Supplier ships order on time	99%	90%
■ Carrier delivers order on time	98%	89%
■ Customer receives undamaged goods	99%	88%
■ Customer accurately records and stores goods	99%	87%
■ Customer receives accurate invoice and pays it correctly	98%	85%
Probability Of A Perfect Transaction		**85%**

Admittedly, this is a fabricated example, although it is not far from the truth in many companies. Nevertheless, it illustrates that in order for the logistics process to satisfy the external customer a large percentage of the time, internal supplier-customer quality must be close to 100 percent at each transaction point. Quality improvement, therefore, should focus on internal processes as well as on those between suppliers and customers, and companies must have measures that support the improvement process. These measures should include accuracy and timeliness of information exchange as well as on-time delivery and damage-free handling of products — be they actual cases of product, order sheets and pick tickets, or transportation equipment.

Some examples of internal quality measures include:

- Timeliness of forecast updates from sales representatives

- Adherence to production plans

- Accuracy in recording inventory put-away locations

- Accuracy in inventory counts

- Achievement of required cycles times for order entry, picking, and shipment

- Close correlation between amount of inventory on hand and forecasted requirements

- Availability of all required information for an order in the order entry file

- Reduction in internal damage, waste, obsolescence, and spoilage rates

Additional measures of internal process effectiveness can be found in Appendixes A through F.

In addition to these measures of internal process effectiveness, a number of key benchmarks exist that provide useful insights into a logistics process. These benchmarks address how well or to what extent the logistics process is being managed or executed using progressive and innovative approaches. Examples might include:

- Percent of total purchases bought from certified suppliers

- Percent of freight hauled by carriers under contract

- Percent of revenue dollars generated by customers receiving value-added services

- Percent of orders received via EDI transmission

- Percent of logistics employees who are professionally certified (i.e., by The American Production and Inventory Control Society, The National Association of Purchasing Managers, The American Society of Transportation and Logistics)

- Percent of employees trained in quality and productivity-improvement techniques

These measures do not guarantee superior quality and productivity performance in logistics. They merely are good indicators that logistics management has taken the kinds of actions that lead to quality and productivity improvement and has the infrastructure in place to ensure that improvement continues.

MEASUREMENT SYSTEM DESIGN

Modern computer technology has made management data rich. Massive databases containing thousands of transactions and millions of data elements are available in most companies. Further, the data are more accessible than ever with distributed data processing capabilities now widespread and personal computers on the desks of people at all organizational levels. Even where data do not exist on a mainframe, companies develop local databases that are used to support quality and productivity measurement.

The main task in measurement system design, then, is to decide which data to use to develop key measures for managing logistics quality and productivity and how to present those measures in ways that people can understand and interpret. There are two major parts to designing a measurement system: selecting key measures and developing a reporting capability. The remainder of this chapter deals with these two topics.

Selecting Key Measures

Measurement for measurement's sake accomplishes nothing. After completing the 1978 productivity study, we had occasion to talk with a company that decided to adopt logistics productivity measurement — with a vengeance. Management decided it needed logistics productivity measures for everything and proceeded to measure every conceivable output and input. The first computer run of this measurement system produced a stack of paper four feet high. These pages contained a lot of data but little useful information. The company had answered the wrong question. Instead of asking "What *should* we measure?" it asked "What *can* we measure?"

The January 1990 issue of *Business Month Magazine* highlighted another example of misguided measurement. A manager at Motorola tells of a situation in which the company measured how efficiently brochure materials were delivered to its warehouse from the printers when supplies ran out. Later they realized that they "shouldn't even be measuring that, because we shouldn't run out of printed materials to begin with."[5]

To decide what to measure, a company should ask four key questions (see Figure 10-12). The first question addresses what the company is trying to accomplish. In the example in Figure 10-12, the company is trying to accomplish order completeness. In the case of Motorola, the company was trying to have brochure materials in stock when they were needed.

Figure 10-12

Steps In Developing A Measure	
Key Questions	**Example**
■ What are you trying to accomplish?	■ Order completeness
■ What is a good measure of this?	■ Total cases shipped versus cases requested
■ What is the formula for calculating this?	■ Cases shipped (as requested) on first delivery / Cases requested
■ What are data sources?	■ Cases shipped (as requested) first delivery • Shipment manifest system • Order entry system ■ Cases requested • Original quantity ordered before backorders and substitutions • Order entry system

The second key question is "What is a good measure of this goal?" If order completeness is the goal, total cases ordered versus cases shipped might be a reasonable measurement.

The third key question is "What is the formula for calculating this measure?" In our example, we chose the formula of cases shipped on the first scheduled delivery as a percent of total cases ordered. In this formula, cases shipped from a backorder don't count.

The final key question is "What are the data sources?" In our example, the information on cases shipped on the first scheduled delivery comes from the shipment manifest system. The cases ordered data comes from the original quantity ordered before backorders and substitutions.

These four key questions help guide managers in deciding what measures to include in their measurement system. They follow a simple logic flow based on the following questions:

• What are you trying to accomplish? (And if you aren't trying to accomplish something, why measure it?)

• If you want something accomplished, what is the right measure of accomplishment?

• How do you calculate this measure?

• Where can you get the pieces of data needed to make the calculation?

By following this logic flow, companies can avoid drowning in data. At the same time, they can ensure that their measures are on target.

Most quality and productivity measurement systems are made up of a set of measures. In our earlier research on productivity measurement, we found there are seven desirable characteristics of productivity measurement systems. These seven characteristics are easily adapted to quality measurement. The characteristics are described in the following paragraphs and summarized in Figure 10-13.

Figure 10-13

Seven Criteria For Effective Measures	
■ Validity	• Does the measure track true customer requirements or real productivity?
■ Coverage	• Does the measure (or group of measures) track all relevant factors?
■ Comparability	• Can the measure be compared across time or in different locations?
■ Completeness	• Are all important sources that yield an output tracked by the measures?
■ Usefulness	• Does the measure guide action?
■ Compatibility	• Is the measure compatible with existing data and information flow?
■ Cost effectiveness	• What are the tradeoffs between the cost of measurement and the potential benefits to be gained?

Validity. A valid service measure tracks true customer requirements in the customer's terms. For example, a service measure of on-time delivery should be based on how each customer defines on-time rather than on how the company defines it. A valid productivity measure accurately reflects changes in real productivity. Thus, if one of the functions of a warehouse's receiving area is to unload pallets of goods from trailers using a fork lift and then move them to the staging area, pallets loaded per hour is a valid measure of productivity. Cases per hour or pounds per hour would not be as valid a measure because it fails to reflect variations among pallets in number of cases and product density. These measures could change without impacting the real productivity of the operation, i.e., the number of pallets moved.

Coverage. The more completely a measure (or group of measures) covers all relevant factors the better the measurement system. To this end, service measures should track all dimensions of service that are important to the customer. Likewise, productivity measures should monitor all activities involved in a function. If a warehouse worker receives material and puts it away, the productivity measurement system should cover both activities.

Comparability. Differences in customer requirements, order profiles, product mix, work load, etc., can make it hard to measure quality and productivity across time or in different locations. For quality measurement, this means the company must establish a performance against goal measure by comparing actual levels of service with customer requirements. In productivity measurement, the firm must convert work load into standard units or hours of work. In a warehouse example, standard hours would comprise:

- Cases unloaded by hand multiplied by the time allowed for each
- Pallets unloaded multiplied by the time allowed for each
- Pallets put away multiplied by the time allowed for each

The combined times for these items become a measure of the standard work accomplished. The firm can compare this standard with the actual time spent on these tasks to determine performance. By establishing standard measures for quality and productivity, therefore, companies can compare performance from day to day and across all facilities.

Completeness. Completeness relates to the thoroughness with which all important resources are measured. In the case of the receiving operation, the resources include labor, energy for the fork lift, equipment depreciation, facility floor space, and vehicle demurrage. If all of these were important, the productivity computation could become quite complicated. In most operations, however, it is sufficient to measure and track only one of several resources (e.g., labor hours).

Usefulness. To be of greatest use, measures should guide action. Thus, in the service example cited earlier, knowing that the company met 95 percent of the customers' service requirements is of little use in resolving the service failures for the other 5 percent. In a productivity context, using a measure that tracks overall labor productivity (e.g., throughput cases per employee-hour) is of little value in identifying individual employees needing more training or closer supervision.

Compatibility. For ease of implementation, measures should be compatible with existing flows of data in the organization and with existing systems reporting.

Cost effectiveness. The final criterion for a meaningful measure is the tradeoff between the cost of the measurement and its potential benefits.

There is no perfect set of measures of logistics quality and productivity. Instead, one must select and blend various measures to create an overall system of measurement. Identifying individual measures using the four key questions described earlier is a first step. Choosing a set of measures that closely match the seven criteria listed above is a good second step. However, companies must recognize that other considerations come into play in selecting effective measures. They are as follows:

- For measures to endure, they must be on the senior executive's agenda. This is particularly true of service quality measures. While some service quality measures come directly from existing databases, others (such as customer attitude feedback and diagnostic measures) require some effort to collect. Unless senior management regularly reviews these measures, data collection efforts may grow lax.

- When designing measures, companies should make sure they include employee input. This is especially true in developing measures of internal customer service. Who knows better than the people doing the job what they need from their internal supplier and how to measure whether they get it?

- People tend to do what they are measured on. Companies, therefore, should make sure the measures selected relate to providing customer and shareholder value.

- The company needs to close the loop on measurement with rewards and recognition for accomplishments. Chapter 12 describes several types of rewards and recognition.

Developing a Reporting Capability

Even with a carefully selected set of measures, quality and productivity measurement in logistics involves a lot of data. This means the measurement system design must allow for flexible reporting capability. Such reporting might take one of three forms: summary, exception, and custom reports. Each is described below.

Summary reports take many forms. Figure 10-14 displays what one summary report might look like for service reporting. Moving from left to right, the key measures of service appear in the far left column. The next column lists the current score, covering the current month. Next to it appear three goals: minimum; short-term, covering the next three to six months; and long-term, covering one to two years. (Goal setting is discussed in Chapter 13.) The final column is an indicator of the four-month trend.

In this example, order completeness has a score of 95 percent. Although this figure exceeds the minimum of 94 percent, it falls short of the short-term goal. The four-month trend, however, indicates the order completeness score is rising. Similar interpretations can be made for the other measures. This report's snapshot look at overall performance indicates two areas that need further investigation — on-time delivery and damage-free shipment.

Standard exception reports provide the next level of detail. Figure 10-15 illustrates an example of a service exception report driven off the same database as Figure 10-14. Figure 10-15 incorporates both positive and negative figures. At the top of the chart, the Boston distribution center receives a high rating in on-time delivery with performance at 96 percent — 2 percent above the short-term goal. It is the second consecutive period in which performance exceeded the goals. Additionally, over the past four months, the on-time delivery performance has increased.

Figure 10-14

		Goals			
Measure	**Current Score**	**Minimum**	**Short Term**	**Long Term**	**Four-Month Trend**
■ Order completeness	95%	94%	96%	98%	Good
■ On-time delivery	91%	90%	94%	100%	Bad
■ Invoice accuracy	93%	92%	95%	100%	Good
⋮	⋮	⋮	⋮	⋮	⋮
■ Damage-free shipment	96%	90%	98%	99%	Bad

Example Of Summary Service Report

Note: Adapted from *Maximum Performance Management*, Joseph H. Boyett and Henry P. Conn

Figure 10-15

Example Of Service Exception Report

Positive Exceptions – Boston Distribution Center

Measure	**Current Score**	**Short-Term Goal**	**Consecutive Periods Over**	**Four-Month Trend**
■ On-time delivery	96%	94%	2	Good

Negative Exceptions – Denver Distribution Center

Measure	**Current Score**	**Minimum**	**Consecutive Periods Under**	**Four-Month Trend**
■ On-time delivery	86%	90%	3	Bad
■ Invoice accuracy	82%	90%	1	Bad

Note: Adapted from *Maximum Performance Management*, Joseph H. Boyett and Henry P. Conn

The bottom half of Figure 10-15 tells a more sobering story. The Denver distribution center has problems with on-time delivery and invoice accuracy. In both cases, current scores are below the minimum. Denver's on-time delivery failed to meet the minimum for three periods and has declined steadily over the past four months. Invoice accuracy also is under the minimum this month, although last month it met the minimum. Still, the four-month trend is negative.

Standard exception reports such as these are easy to generate using performance against goals as the base. These exception reports help highlight good and bad performance, thereby acknowledging the former while getting help for the latter.

The third type of reporting — custom — offers yet another level of detail in analyzing an operation. Using diagnostic measures, we could look into Denver's poor performance to understand its causes and potential remedies. In many cases, managers can create such reports easily using their personal computers.

The Corporate Transportation and Logistics Department at Westinghouse found this to be the case. When it first set up a quality measurement system for its carriers and other third-party suppliers, management installed a 4- by 6-feet cork board in the general office area. Newly available data on carrier service quality, coupled with enthusiasm for the quality improvement process, prompted people to develop all sorts of reports and graphs, quickly filling the cork board space.

After a few months, the department managers realized that they really needed to track only a handful of key measures every month. If these key measures indicated a problem, they could tap into their extensive database to develop custom reports and analyses. Now the cork board contains only the data the department needs to take the pulse of the operation. The rest of the data resides in the computer database where it can be called up on an as-needed basis.

A relatively new technology — Executive Information Systems (EIS) — offers interesting capabilities for the future. It allows an executive to sit at a personal computer or terminal and call up key reports and measures at the press of a key. When the executive sees a particular measure that triggers a question, the EIS automatically links into exception reports and additional detail to help the manager understand what drives the measure. Newer versions of EIS include artificial intelligence capabilities to aid in the analysis of the factors that drive the performance.

One of the keys to a successful measurement system is the ability to graphically display data. To paraphrase an old adage, a graph is worth a thousand numbers. In Chapter 9, we discussed techniques (many of which are graphically based) for statistically analyzing data. All through this book, we use pie charts, bar charts, trend lines, control charts, and other graphic devices to present data in an easily understandable format. Figure 10-16 offers yet another way of presenting data graphically. It represents the range of sales forecasts versus actual orders for a year's period in a consumer products company. For most of the product groups shown, high and low forecasts are relatively balanced, although the ranges in a few instances may indicate problems. For product groups 12000 and 28000, however, the graph demonstrates that actual orders were consistently above forecast for the entire year. Simply tracking month to month data would have overlooked this pattern as would analyzing columns of data. By displaying the data graphically, the pattern jumps out.

Figure 10-16

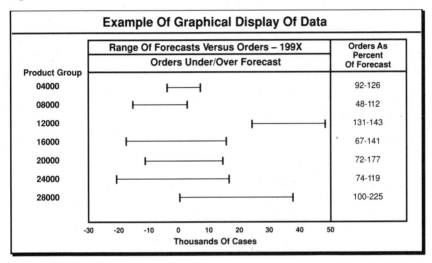

Example Of Graphical Display Of Data		
Range Of Forecasts Versus Orders – 199X		**Orders As Percent Of Forecast**
Orders Under/Over Forecast		
Product Group		
04000	⊢——⊣	92-126
08000	⊢———⊣	48-112
12000	⊢———⊣	131-143
16000	⊢————————⊣	67-141
20000	⊢————————⊣	72-177
24000	⊢—————————⊣	74-119
28000	⊢——————————⊣	100-225

-30   -20   -10   0   10   20   30   40   50
Thousands Of Cases

With powerful graphic display capabilities now on personal computers, there is little reason not to use the power of the picture.

Determining the Effectiveness of a Measurement and Reporting System

How do you know whether your measurement and reporting system is effective? The obvious answer is that it provides useful information, is easy to use, and leads to action. While these are all true, they sometimes are difficult to assess. A simple four-step test, however, can help determine whether you're on the right track. First, ask the person who regularly receives a report if you can see the most recent report. If the person can easily locate a copy of the report, it probably is a tool of some value to the person. Second, ask the individual to explain the report to you. If you get a clear, concise, and accurate explanation about the report's contents and meaning, that's another indication the report provides value. Third, ask the person what data are missing that he or she must find elsewhere. This could indicate the measures and reports aren't as complete as you may think. Finally, ask the user if you can take the report with you. If you are handed the *only* copy, the report isn't as valuable as you thought.

This quick test is not a sure fire way of determining the value of a measurement system, but it provides a start when looking for areas to improve the system.

A PLACE TO BEGIN

Measurement is part art, part science. The art comes from selecting the right measures and designing an effective measurement system. The science comes from the actual techniques of measurement — data collection and refinement, statistical analysis, and graphic display and reporting. There is no one right answer, but the comments and insights contained in this chapter, along with sample measures found in Appendixes A through F, offer a beginning for developing quality and productivity measures for your logistics process.

---

[1] Gabor, Andrea, *The Man Who Discovered Quality, How W. Edwards Deming Brought the Quality Revolution to America*

[2] Karr, Albert R., "Time is Elastic at Postal Service, Outside Test Finds"

[3] Bennett, Amanda, "Making The Grade With the Customer"

[4] Peters, Tom and Nancy Austin, *A Passion for Excellence, The Leadership Difference*

[5] Gill, Mark Stuart, "Stalking Six Sigma"

CHAPTER 11

HIGH-IMPACT
IMPROVEMENT ACTIONS

Thus far in Section IV, we've discussed a general framework for process improvement built around the PDCA cycle (Chapter 8), tools for evaluating processes and identifying opportunities for improvement (Chapter 9), and measurement techniques for tracking progress and results (Chapter 10). In Chapter 11, we complete our tools and techniques comments by describing high-impact actions for improving logistics quality and productivity. The actions discussed in this chapter are drawn from statistical analysis of our survey responses and from the interviewing process. We focus particularly on those actions that respondents said had the greatest impact on improving quality and productivity.

The chapter begins with a brief discussion of the kinds of approaches used to improve the logistics process. Following this, it reviews the actions the survey respondents identified as having the greatest impact on improving quality and productivity. Chapter 11 ends with a discussion of several groups of actions that respondents and interviewees found to be particularly good sources of improvement.

TYPES OF IMPROVEMENTS

Companies improve the logistics process for one of two basic reasons: to enhance the effectiveness with which the logistics process meets customer requirements or to upgrade the efficiency or productivity of the process as a means of driving down cost. Improving the effectiveness of the logistics process usually starts with defining the requirements and expectations of the customer. This forms the basis for developing a customer service strategy that sets priorities for attention. Section III discussed approaches used in these areas.

Businesses can also improve logistics effectiveness and efficiency through a variety of actions as shown in Figure 11-1. These actions are described below.

Figure 11-1

General Approaches To Improve The Effectiveness And Efficiency Of The Logistics Process

- Eliminate a process step

- Speed up a process

- Carry out steps in parallel

- Improve efficiency within a step

- Improve consistency and standardization

- Better coordinate activities of different parties

Eliminating a process step. This could mean combining steps as in the case of an order processing system where order entry, credit check, and inventory assignment are done in a single step. It also could mean eliminating a step such as providing store-ready displays to a retailer thereby ending the need to unpack cases and build displays in the store.

Speeding up a process. A company could accelerate a process by committing more resources — people, materials, data, machines — to eliminate delays in a processing step. A firm also could reduce the internal cycle time of a step.

Carrying out steps in parallel. A typical order placement and shipment process is a series of sequential steps. The order processing department receives and enters the order. It is transmitted to the warehouse, which picks the order. The warehouse, in turn, generates shipping documents and notifies the carrier that a load is ready for pickup. Some firms, however, conduct some of these steps in tandem. For example, as soon as the company receives an order, it informs the appropriate carrier that a load is being planned for pickup at a particular time and place. This allows the carrier to schedule its equipment better and provide quicker response when the warehouse calls for pickup.

Improving efficiency within a step. This approach represents mainstream productivity improvement discussed at length in the 1978 and 1983 research studies. It includes methods analysis, layout and work flow improvements, automation, training, etc.

Improving consistency and standardization. One of the basic tenets in quality improvement asserts that reducing variability improves quality.

Several firms have improved consistency and standardization by reducing the number of suppliers they use. Product quality and delivery become more reliable and predictable. An individual company might improve consistency and standardization by adopting "best practices" throughout the organization. For example, if a particular sales forecasting technique works well in one region of a company, management might adopt it in other regions as well. Not only can this action improve the sales forecasting process, but it supplies more consistent input to the internal customers that make use of the information. Another example would be adopting common coding schemes across systems and departments to eliminate mismatches, errors, and recoding.

Coordinating the activities of different parties better. Within a company, this means better cross-functional planning among sales, marketing, manufacturing, logistics, finance, research and development, and human resources. Across companies, it translates into better supplier-customer and shipper-carrier coordination.

Depending on the situation, a company may choose to implement some or all of these improvement actions. Naturally, each firm must tailor its actions to its situation, needs, and capabilities. Even so, much can be learned from the actions of others. With this in mind, we now discuss some of the specific improvement actions undertaken by our survey respondents.

HIGH-IMPACT ACTIONS BY SURVEY RESPONDENTS

In our Logistics Management Survey questionnaire, we identified 134 potential improvement actions. We asked respondents to indicate which of these actions they had implemented and then note the degree to which they had realized benefits/improvements to quality and productivity. The responses to all 134 actions are listed in Appendixes A through F, organized under the appropriate technical area.

From the aggregate response on the 134 actions, we extracted those actions that had the greatest impact on quality and productivity improvement for the respondents. These were actions that produced major benefits in terms of quality or productivity for at least 60 percent of the respondents implementing them. We call these high-impact improvement actions.

Some 61 actions qualified as high-impact. We grouped these into six categories:

• Customer service

• Order management

- Transportation
- Warehousing
- Materials planning and control
- Purchasing

We discuss the high-impact actions identified in our survey in the following paragraphs.

Customer service. Figure 11-2 displays the high-impact customer service actions identified in the survey. As the graph notes, the greatest quality benefits came from integrating quality processes with customers. Companies also realized substantial benefits from visiting customer facilities, meeting with clients to review perceptions of service, establishing joint teams with customers, and actively following-up on complaints/service breakdowns. The number of respondents that took these actions varied widely but, in each case, over two-thirds reported they realized major quality benefits.

The greatest productivity benefits derived from eliminating bottlenecks in dealing with customers. For those firms with programs in this area, 68 percent achieved major productivity benefits.

Figure 11-2

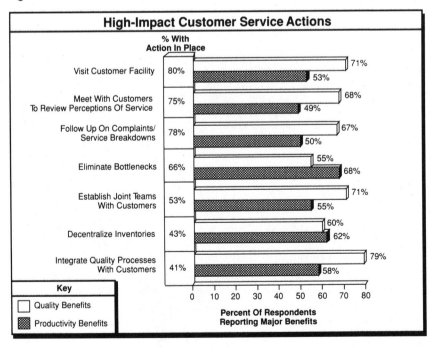

Order management. In the order management area, survey participants identified several high-impact improvement actions noted in Figure 11-3. Conversion from manual to computerized order entry, systems analysis of order processing systems, and design and implementation of new order processing systems each resulted in major productivity benefits for many of the respondents. For each of these actions, however, the percent of respondents reporting major quality benefits was 8 to 9 percent lower.

Figure 11-3

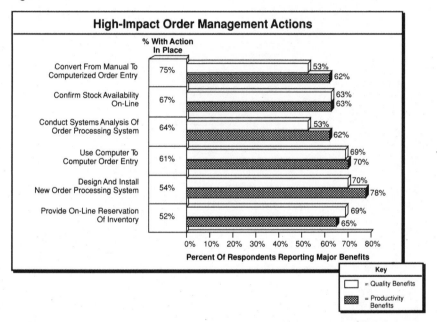

The ability to confirm stock availability on-line proved to have equally widespread quality and productivity benefits. The same is true with the use of computer to computer order entry. Lastly, on-line reservation of inventory offered major improvements to both quality and productivity.

Transportation. The transportation improvement actions were divided into three categories — strategy, operations, and fleet management. Our respondents identified high-impact improvement actions for each.

In the area of transportation strategy, the high-impact actions generally produced greater productivity benefits than quality improvements (see Figure 11-4). The exception was establishing transportation service standards with carriers.

The biggest spread between percent of respondents reporting productivity and quality benefits appears in the category of using a more cost effective transportation mode mix. More than 60 percent of respondents with such a program reported major productivity gains; only 46 percent noted a major quality boost. This response, in part, may reflect participants' concerns that a lower cost mode reduces flexibility or responsiveness and so hampers service quality. Among the six high-impact transportation actions shown in Figure 11-4, only the mode-mix action showed a significant drop in the number of users since our earlier survey. In 1983, 73 percent of participants took this action compared to 59 percent in this survey.

Figure 11-4

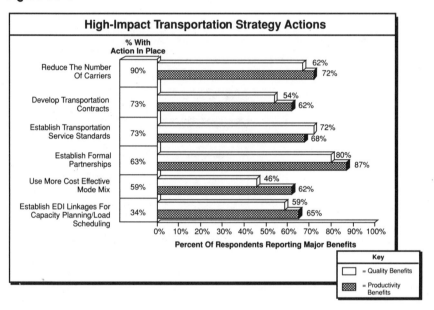

The five transportation operations actions shown in Figure 11-5 primarily are productivity-improvement oriented. In each case, the percent of respondents reporting major productivity benefits exceeded the percent reporting major quality benefits. These actions may illustrate situations where actions to improve productivity actually limit the company's ability to provide flexible service. For example, if customers are looking for next day delivery, using an outbound consolidation or pooling program can limit a firm's ability to meet that customer need. While unit cost declines, so too does real output measured in terms of next day delivery. Thus, real productivity (measured by customer satisfaction) does not improve.

In a similar fashion to the transportation operations actions, the high-impact fleet management items shown in Figure 11-6 also primarily affect productivity. Only in the case of using specialized equipment are reported quality and productivity benefits somewhat balanced. This balance reflects the nature of the specialized equipment market, i.e., equipment and service tailored to the customers' special needs.

Figure 11-5

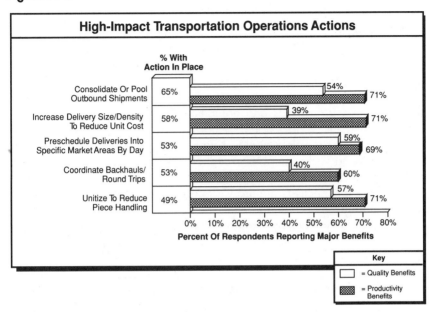

High-Impact Transportation Operations Actions

% With
Action In Place

Action	% With Action In Place
Consolidate Or Pool Outbound Shipments	65%
Increase Delivery Size/Density To Reduce Unit Cost	58%
Preschedule Deliveries Into Specific Market Areas By Day	53%
Coordinate Backhauls/ Round Trips	53%
Unitize To Reduce Piece Handling	49%

Percent Of Respondents Reporting Major Benefits

Key
☐ = Quality Benefits
▨ = Productivity Benefits

Figure 11-6

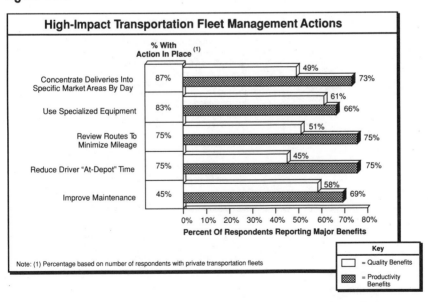

High-Impact Transportation Fleet Management Actions

% With
Action In Place (1)

Action	% With Action In Place
Concentrate Deliveries Into Specific Market Areas By Day	87%
Use Specialized Equipment	83%
Review Routes To Minimize Mileage	75%
Reduce Driver "At-Depot" Time	75%
Improve Maintenance	45%

Percent Of Respondents Reporting Major Benefits

Note: (1) Percentage based on number of respondents with private transportation fleets

Key
☐ = Quality Benefits
▨ = Productivity Benefits

In summary, high-impact transportation actions, whether strategic or operational, tend to be productivity oriented. Actions such as establishing formal carrier partnerships, reducing the number of carriers used, and setting transportation service standards are notable exceptions. We explore these in greater depth later in this chapter.

Warehousing. High-impact warehousing actions divide into two groups — those relating to company-operated warehousing and those affecting public warehousing. Regarding company-operated warehousing, two kinds of actions affect quality and productivity: methods and equipment improvements and employee management. Figure 11-7 lists seven actions related to methods and equipment improvement. In nearly every case, the percent of respondents reporting productivity benefits exceeds the percentage reporting quality gains. Improving package design to reduce damage is the notable exception. Nearly 70 percent of respondents reported major quality gains from this action, while 52 percent relate major productivity gains. Computerizing warehouse operations, while primarily viewed as an action leading to productivity improvement, also scored high in the quality-improvement area.

Figure 11-7

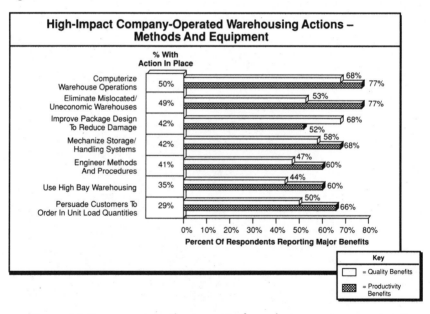

Figure 11-8 summarizes the impact of employee management actions on company-operated warehouses. Training workers in materials handling produced major quality and productivity benefits for a majority of respondents. Implementing performance goals for individuals and teams and using labor standards for work load and staff planning both offered major productivity gains for many respondents. The percent of respondents reporting quality gains from these actions, however, was comparatively less.

Figure 11-8

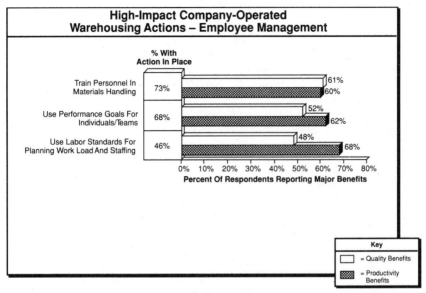

**High-Impact Company-Operated
Warehousing Actions – Employee Management**

% With
Action In Place

Train Personnel In
Materials Handling — 73% — 61% / 60%

Use Performance Goals For
Individuals/Teams — 68% — 52% / 62%

Use Labor Standards For
Planning Work Load And Staffing — 46% — 48% / 68%

0% 10% 20% 30% 40% 50% 60% 70% 80%
Percent Of Respondents Reporting Major Benefits

Key
☐ = Quality Benefits
▨ = Productivity Benefits

Two employee-management approaches that did not make this list were incentive schemes to encourage higher quality, productivity, or safety and self-directed employee teams for warehouse operations. Incentive plans are gaining popularity in logistics. Forty-three percent of the respondents in the current survey use them compared to 15 percent in our last study. This popularity growth comes even though only about half the respondents reported either major quality or productivity gains from this approach. In a similar vein, 42 percent of respondents use self-directed employee teams, but only half report major quality or productivity gains.

Shifting attention to the public warehousing sector, Figure 11-9 identifies five high-impact actions. Of those respondents using public warehousing, 62 percent report on-site audits contributed to major quality benefits because such audits encourage the customer and operator to communicate better regarding requirements and expectations. Over two-thirds of the respondents who share on-line computerized order/inventory management with their public warehouses report major quality and productivity gains.

In comparing the current study responses to those in 1983, we see a shift in the relationship between public warehouse operators and their customers. The earlier survey found that 64 percent of respondents used more aggressive rate negotiations with their public warehouses as a means of boosting productivity. In the current survey, only 44 percent noted using this technique. Related to this drop, 32 percent of the 1991 respondents said they had established strategic alliances with their third-party providers. Unfortunately, no such data are available from the 1983 study. These findings indicate that the relationship between the public warehouse and its customers is changing from an arms-length one to a partnership alliance.

Figure 11-9

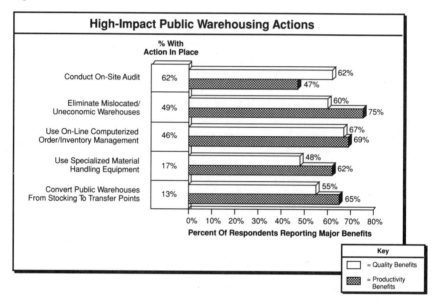

Materials planning and control. Figure 11-10 summarizes the high-impact improvement actions used in the materials planning and control area. Participants gained big productivity boosts by separating "A,B,C" items for inventory planning purposes and installing MRP (Materials Requirements Planning) systems. About two-thirds of the firms reported major benefits in productivity. Far fewer respondents noted significant effects on quality coming from these actions.

The big quality winners, on the other hand, included introducing zero-defects concepts in manufacturing, installing DRP (Distribution Requirements Planning) systems, and linking to customers' point-of-sale (POS) and electronic ordering systems (EOS) to improve forecasting accuracy. In the case of the POS/EOS systems linkages, two-thirds of the respondents realized major productivity benefits as well.

Purchasing. Product sourcing was another area of high-impact actions as detailed in Figure 11-11. Establishing formalized partnerships, developing strategic alliances, and certifying suppliers each proved to be a major source of quality improvement for 70 percent or more of the respondents taking these actions. Concentrating business with fewer suppliers, including single source relationships, also produced major quality benefits.

Figure 11-10

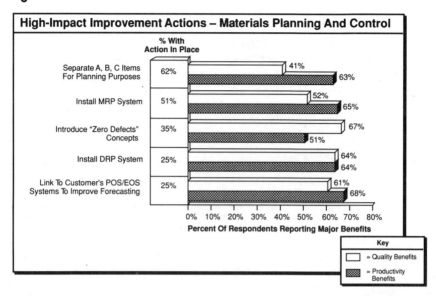

High-Impact Improvement Actions – Materials Planning And Control

% With
Action In Place

Action	% With Action In Place	Quality Benefits	Productivity Benefits
Separate A, B, C Items For Planning Purposes	62%	41%	63%
Install MRP System	51%	52%	65%
Introduce "Zero Defects" Concepts	35%	67%	51%
Install DRP System	25%	64%	64%
Link To Customer's POS/EOS Systems To Improve Forecasting	25%	61%	68%

0% 10% 20% 30% 40% 50% 60% 70% 80%

Percent Of Respondents Reporting Major Benefits

Key
☐ = Quality Benefits
▨ = Productivity Benefits

Figure 11-11

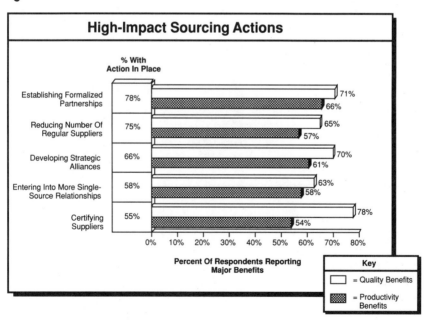

High-Impact Sourcing Actions

% With
Action In Place

Action	% With Action In Place	Quality Benefits	Productivity Benefits
Establishing Formalized Partnerships	78%	71%	66%
Reducing Number Of Regular Suppliers	75%	65%	57%
Developing Strategic Alliances	66%	70%	61%
Entering Into More Single-Source Relationships	58%	63%	58%
Certifying Suppliers	55%	78%	54%

0% 10% 20% 30% 40% 50% 60% 70% 80%

Percent Of Respondents Reporting Major Benefits

Key
☐ = Quality Benefits
▨ = Productivity Benefits

On the operational side of purchasing, Figure 11-12 lists the top seven high-impact purchasing/buying actions. Nearly 75 percent of respondents who met with suppliers to define service requirements said they realized major quality benefits as a result. Other quality-improvement actions include involving suppliers in the design and development process, implementing continuous improvement techniques, establishing joint improvement teams, creating a supplier performance monitoring and feedback process, and reviewing supplier performance and jointly agreeing on improvement actions. Providing suppliers with requirements planning information generated major productivity gains for 61 percent of the respondents using this approach.

Figure 11-12

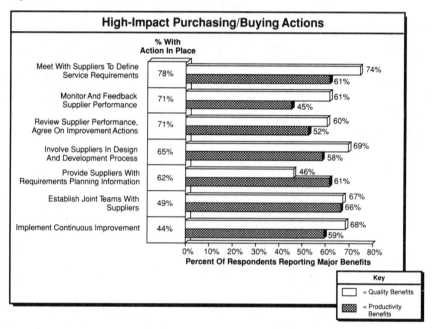

The improvement actions discussed thus far represent those that impacted a broad cross section of companies. Although this impact does not guarantee the actions are right for every company and application, the data indicate they certainly are worth considering.

Also, the data indicate some differences between sources of quality and productivity improvement. Most of the high-impact quality-improvement actions relate to close coordination and cooperation between a company and its customers, suppliers, or third-party logistics service providers. Actions that primarily affect productivity tend to be more inwardly focused within a specific logistics activity, e.g., transportation operations, warehousing, fleet management.

Therefore, as companies move ahead to improve quality, the actions involved in this process have a different scope and involve a different set of parties than those relating to productivity improvement. In fact, compared with the productivity focused approaches of the 1970s and 1980s, this represents a major change in how companies achieve improvement in the logistics process.

A CLOSER LOOK AT HIGH-IMPACT ACTIONS

During our interview process, we spoke with a number of leading companies about their efforts to improve quality and productivity. Many of the actions they took match the ones summarized above from the survey questionnaire; others go beyond. We have extracted five types of improvement actions to discuss in more detail, since we believe these represent major leverage opportunities for many companies into the 1990s. The five actions are:

- "Fail-safing" the logistics process
- Reducing cycle times
- Integrating operations management
- Implementing shipper-carrier partnerships
- Implementing customer-supplier partnerships

"FAIL-SAFING" THE LOGISTICS PROCESS

As mentioned in Section III of this book, there are two facets to providing quality customer service. The first is getting the essentials right — eliminating the service failures that irritate and frustrate customers. The second is adding value for the customers, exceeding customer expectations on the few key dimensions that matter most. Getting the basics right is not a value-adding function, but failing to get the basics right undermines value-adding services no matter how good they are.

Recognizing this reality, several companies we interviewed have implemented systems, procedures, and techniques that greatly reduce the likelihood of failures on essential services. This approach, which we call fail-safing a process, has been widely used in manufacturing, especially by the Japanese. In fact, the Japanese word *pokayoke* describes this technique exactly. In manufacturing, fail-safing might take the form of designing parts so they can only be assembled one way. Or it might mean using bins of a certain size to assure an exact item count. (Too few items are immediately noticeable, while too many items won't fit in the bin.)

In the logistics environment, we found a number of *pokayoke* approaches at work. These include:

- Providing separate labels for each box to be picked in a warehouse to ensure a correct total piece count

- Handling stock checking and reservation at the time of order entry so customers aren't promised items that don't exist

- Inspecting transportation equipment to screen out equipment that will cause damage

- Using exception reporting capabilities to flag unusual data for review thereby preventing errors (such as shipping five pallet loads of product where five dozen were ordered)

- Obtaining sales department input on statistically derived forecasts in order to factor in new/lost business and so forestall inventory surprises

- Weighing mixed-case picked items against a calculated order weight to help screen out mis-picks

- Making key data fields mandatory in the order processing system to ensure that the customer requirements are fully understood (e.g., requiring a specific delivery date rather than "ASAP")

- Implementing pallet loading standards with proper operator training to reduce damage from overhang, case crushing, and load toppling

- Implementing bar codes for check-in/tracking of case goods, rolls of paper, tote bins, etc.

- Taking special action on an order where available lead time is less than standard

- Using "kanban"/pull inventory techniques to ensure product is made on an as-needed basis and not simply stockpiled

These *pokayoke* actions are but a small sampling of practices that companies might implement in the logistics process. In each case, the objective is to reduce the likelihood of error, waste, or service failure. In achieving this goal, these actions play a key role in fail-safing a firm's ability to deliver on its service essentials.

REDUCING CYCLE TIMES

The second type of improvement action we will review in some detail is reducing cycle times. This technique offers major benefits for both quality and productivity.

In the manufacturing sector, faster cycle times cut the need for in-process inventory. This makes it easier to trace problem product lots and take quick corrective action. Cycle time reduction tends to squeeze out unproductive or low value activities thus streamlining operations and reducing cost. It also provides a closer link between the marketplace and the supplier, allowing the latter to adjust production levels and product mix to reflect current marketplace needs.

Our research identified several cases where companies had made major cycle time reductions. Motorola reduced the manufacturing cycle time for one of its paging devices from three weeks to two hours and still retained enough flexibility to produce the item in countless configurations.[1] Hewlett-Packard reduced its order-to-finished-goods cycle from four weeks to five days for electronic testing equipment.[2]

In the retail sector, cycle time reduction is a key objective of "Quick Response" initiatives. Quick Response began as a technology based system for suppliers to quickly replenish retailers' stocks based on current retail sales data. Now, suppliers and retailers are using Quick Response as a platform to develop partnerships, looking for ways to fundamentally re-engineer processes rather than just make incremental changes to traditional ways of doing things.

Perhaps the most widely publicized example of such an approach is the relationship between Procter and Gamble (P&G) and Wal-Mart. In its continuous replenishment system with Wal-Mart, P&G receives point-of-sale sales information and inventory data from the retailer via EDI. P&G then handles replenishment for Wal-Mart based on agreed-to inventory limits (minimums and maximums). In addition to this transaction level integration, a multifunctional team of about two dozen people from P&G are assigned to work full time with Wal-Mart counterparts at the retailer's headquarters. The joint customer-supplier team is continuously re-engineering and improving processes that link the two companies.

So far, the results have been impressive. Sales are up sharply, and, in the Paper Products sector, P&G has reduced the cycle time by half from when it places orders with its packaging materials suppliers until customers purchase their goods at retail.[3,4,5]

Target Stores now has "Quick Response Partnerships" with about 100 vendors. Taken together, these vendors have achieved goals of 40 percent reduction in lead time, 30 percent increase in inventory turnover, and 20 percent increase in sales.[6]

There are many other examples of cycle time reductions achieved within the apparel industry. Benetton, for instance, can replenish its U.S. stores in four weeks for make-to-order and a week from stock (versus several weeks for competitors) by electronically transmitting orders to a chain of pull-scheduled JIT factories. At these factories, fabric is cut and dyed to order thus minimizing roll goods inventory. Computer-aided design systems explode designs into a full range of sizes then transfer this information electronically to computer-controlled cutting machines.[7]

In 1989, the apparel/textile manufacturing industry began to cooperate in a "Quick Response" program intended to cut *total industry* cycle times from 66 to 21 weeks. Consultant Kurt Salmon Associates reports selected success so far from implementing Quick Response, including:

- J.C. Penney/Oxford/Burlington (tailored clothing) — inventory turns up 90 percent

- Wal-Mart/Seminole/Milliken (basic slacks) — inventory turns up 31 percent

- Dillard's/Cluett Peabody (blouses) — inventory turns up 31 percent

- Belk's/Haggar (business slacks and jackets) — inventory turns up 67 percent[8]

Applying this technique to the grocery industry offers an interesting opportunity for the future. Figure 11-13 displays typical cycle times for dry grocery products between the manufacturer and grocery retailer. Today, the total replenishment cycle takes 86 to 88 days. Already, manufacturers and retailers are using point-of-sale scanner data to help reduce this cycle. One of the limitations, however, is that scanner data are not generally available to manufacturers until a month after the sale. New technology is under development that will allow manufacturers to obtain scanner data directly from each store as frequently as once per day. This will allow manufacturers to better plan replenishment requirements and production based on current retail sales data. Equally as important, these systems will allow manufacturers to focus marketing and merchandising efforts immediately on specific markets if they find unexpected sales patterns.

The general approach to cycle time reduction is to look for ways to eliminate periods of inactivity in a process. As Figure 11-14 illustrates, the greatest portion of time in any process is wasted in waiting — doing nothing at all.

An especially useful technique for analyzing cycle time improvement opportunities is a flow diagram of a process. Such a diagram charts the flow of materials or information as well as the processing and waiting times. Figure 11-13 represents one version of such a flow diagram.

INTEGRATING OPERATIONS MANAGEMENT

One of the basic steps in enhancing the quality of the logistics process is to improve the way in which the functions of a company interact with one another to acquire raw materials, convert them into finished products, and distribute them to customers. Integrated operations management is an approach many firms are starting to use, drawing together the major operations functions of the business at the strategic, tactical, and transaction processing levels.

Figure 11-13

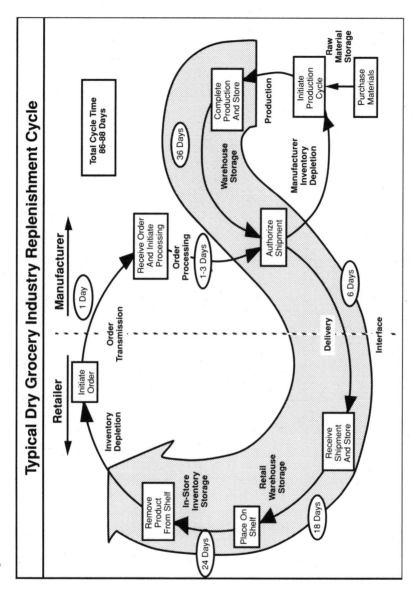

Typical Dry Grocery Industry Replenishment Cycle

Figure 11-14

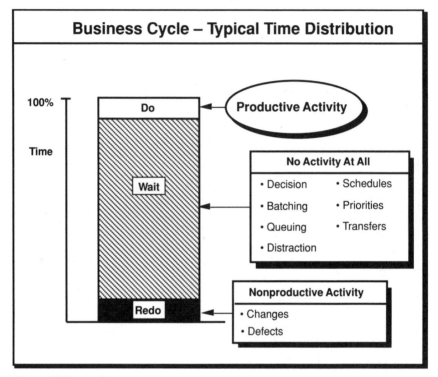

Source: A.T. Kearney, Inc.

At the strategic level, this means having strategies for marketing, sales, manufacturing, logistics, finance, information technology, and human resources that focus on meeting the needs of the customer, add value to customers, are compatible and support one another in the attainment of goals, and ultimately increase shareholder value. At the tactical level, it means having a process that brings together the major functions on a periodic basis to review supply and demand balance, special support plans for new customers, product introductions, and promotions and to develop an action plan for the future.

At the transaction level, integrated operations management requires all relevant functions to use the same order-stream and backlog data, inventory statistics, forecasts, production plans and schedules, and materials acquisition plans and schedules. Further, it means that when demand shifts or supply problems occur, all affected parties know about it immediately and mount a joint effort to address the problem.

This three-tiered integration effort has the interests of the corporation and its customers as its first priority and is not tied to meeting any one department's budget or quota for the month. Thus, it requires a logistics process that exhibits Stage III characteristics. In a Stage III company, this integration occurs within the company itself and even extends somewhat into relationships with suppliers and customers (see Figure 11-15).

Figure 11-15

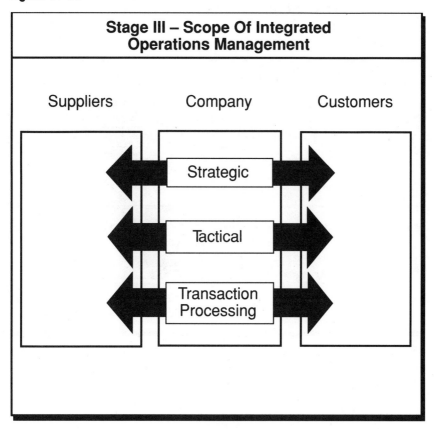

Stage III – Scope Of Integrated Operations Management

Suppliers   Company   Customers

Strategic

Tactical

Transaction Processing

In our Logistics Management Survey questionnaire, we asked respondents to indicate the degree to which they had integrated the management of the logistics process at the strategic, tactical, and transaction levels. The following paragraphs summarize the results.

Strategic Integration

Of the companies surveyed, 51 percent indicated they have a formal long-range plan for the logistics process. About half of these use a three- to five-year planning horizon with another 36 percent using a one- to three-year horizon. Most (78 percent) update their plans annually.

Figure 11-16 displays the objectives of these long-range logistics planning efforts. Most respondents sought profit improvement or cost reduction, while just under one-half viewed inventory reduction as an objective. On the service side, 63 percent of the respondents sought service improvement, while 58 percent sought quality improvement. It is interesting to note that fewer than one-third of the respondents expected lead time reduction as a result of their long-range logistics planning efforts.

Figure 11-16

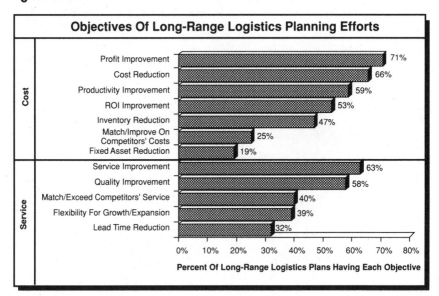

Figure 11-17 displays the kinds of alternatives that were considered in the long-range logistics plans of the respondents. We have divided the alternatives into four categories:

• Internal efficiency

• Marketing/customer service

• Partnerships

• Functional linkages

Each of these is discussed below.

1. Internal efficiency. By far, the most common alternatives considered in long-range logistics planning included warehouse location and number and inventory levels, mix, and locations. In both cases, three-fourths of the respondents looked at these strategic alternatives. Just over half of the respondents analyzed alternatives for warehouse service territories and transportation mode mix as part of their logistics plans.

Figure 11-17

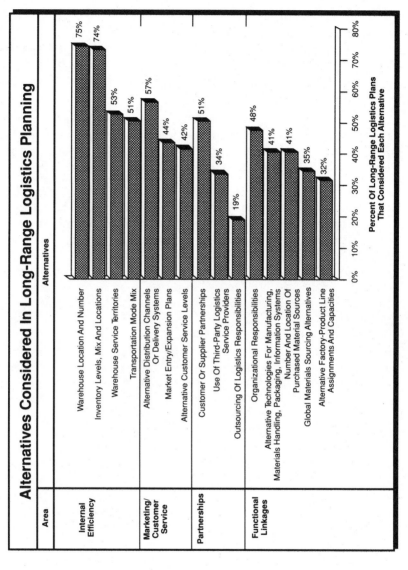

Alternatives Considered In Long-Range Logistics Planning

Area	Alternatives	Percent
Internal Efficiency	Warehouse Location And Number	75%
	Inventory Levels, Mix And Locations	74%
	Warehouse Service Territories	53%
	Transportation Mode Mix	51%
Marketing/ Customer Service	Alternative Distribution Channels Or Delivery Systems	57%
	Market Entry/Expansion Plans	44%
	Alternative Customer Service Levels	42%
Partnerships	Customer Or Supplier Partnerships	51%
	Use Of Third-Party Logistics Service Providers	34%
	Outsourcing Of Logistics Responsibilities	19%
Functional Linkages	Organizational Responsibilities	48%
	Alternative Technologies For Manufacturing, Materials Handling, Packaging, Information Systems	41%
	Number And Location Of Purchased Material Sources	41%
	Global Materials Sourcing Alternatives	35%
	Alternative Factory-Product Line Assignments And Capacities	32%

Percent Of Long-Range Logistics Plans That Considered Each Alternative

2. Marketing/customer service. Fifty-seven percent of respondents considered alternative distribution channels (e.g., via wholesalers) or alternative delivery systems (e.g., plant direct versus through a warehouse network). Fewer than half considered alternative market entry/expansion plans for the corporation or alternative customer service levels when designing their long-range logistics plans.

3. Partnerships. Just about half of the respondents considered customer or supplier partnerships in their logistics planning, while just over one-third considered the use of third-party logistics service providers. Nineteen percent looked at outsourcing of logistics responsibilities.

4. Functional linkages. Just under half of the respondents considered alternatives for organization structures and responsibilities to manage the logistics process. Only 41 percent of the respondents considered alternative technologies for manufacturing, materials handling, packaging, or information systems, while the same number looked at alternatives to the number and location of purchased material sources. Just over one-third of the respondents considered global materials sourcing alternatives, while 32 percent analyzed alternative factory-product line assignments and capacities as a part of the long-range logistics plan.

Based on the data in Figure 11-17, it seems that most of the long-range logistics plans in place today are fairly narrow in scope. Considerably fewer than half of the plans consider marketing, manufacturing, or purchasing alternatives. In other words, for many companies, the long-range logistics plan is essentially a physical distribution network plan.

This narrow scope of logistics planning in many companies is accounted for in part by the functions that participate in the logistics effort. Figure 11-18 summarizes the level of participation in the logistics planning effort by various functional departments in our survey respondents' organizations. In principle, the long-range logistics plan of a corporation should represent the best thinking of all functions that participate in or support the logistics process. Marketing and sales and MIS/EDP are usually involved in such efforts, but other key functions were excluded by a significant number of respondent companies. These functions include manufacturing, field sales management, field operations management, corporate planning, quality management, human resource management, and research and development. In at least 25 percent of the respondents' organizations, one or more of these key functions tied to the logistics process were not involved in the long-term logistics planning process.

Thus, while 51 percent of the respondents said they had formal long-range logistics plans in place, the data presented indicate that there are opportunities to improve strategic integration of the logistics process in most companies. These opportunities include a better balance between cost, service, and cycle time objectives; a more complete scope of analysis to include the entire logistics process and not just physical distribution; and better coordination and cross-functional participation in the planning effort.

Figure 11-18

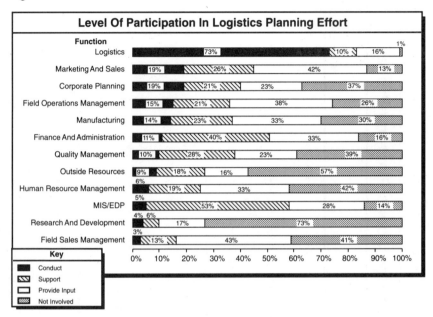

Level Of Participation In Logistics Planning Effort

Tactical Integration

We also asked respondents if they had a formal integrated planning process to balance supply and demand on a period (e.g., monthly) basis. We found that 69 percent had such a formal integrated operations planning process. For 62 percent of these, the planning cycle was monthly with an additional 16 percent using a weekly planning cycle and another 10 percent using quarterly cycles.

We next asked respondents to indicate the components that comprised their integrated operations planning processes. The responses are shown in Figure 11-19. Nearly all of the respondents have regularly scheduled meetings to agree upon an integrated sales, production, inventory, and service plan. However, only about three-quarters of the respondents with an integrated operations planning process use a common sales forecast by all operations oriented departments. Also, only about 75 percent measure performance against previous period's plans. Fewer than two-thirds of the companies incorporate special support plans into their planning processes to handle new customers, new product introductions, promotions, etc. Also, only 58 percent of the respondents translate the service plans (i.e., order fill rate, order cycle times, on-time delivery, etc.) into specific plans for transportation and warehousing.

Figure 11-19

Components Of Integrated Operations Planning Process

Component	Percent Of Respondents With IOP Element
■ Scheduled meetings, based on the planning period, to agree upon an integrated sales, production, inventory and service plan	91%
■ Use of a common sales forecast by sales, production planning, finance, distribution, and purchasing	76%
■ Measurement of performance against previous period's plans	75%
■ Incorporation of special support plans for new customers, new product introductions, promotion, etc., into the planning process	62%
■ Translation of the service plan into requirements and plans for transportation and warehousing	58%
■ Active participation in the planning meeting by all affected functional managers (i.e., marketing, R&D, sales, manufacturing, purchasing, distribution, finance, human resources)	50%
■ Leadership of the meeting by a senior general executive (e.g., COO, Division President, General Manager)	43%
■ Use of well-defined and well-understood policies and procedures to handle exceptions to the plan versus ad hoc case by case decisions	38%

Half of the respondents with integrated operations planning processes have planning meetings at which all affected functional managers actively participate. Only 43 percent of the respondents have planning meetings led by senior general executives who can act as mediators and tie breakers for cross-functional tradeoffs. Finally, 38 percent of the respondents have well documented policies and procedures to handle exceptions as they arise during the planning period (e.g., the month) to avoid ad hoc case by case decisions that may disrupt service, production, and inventory plans.

While most respondents have some room for improvement, they seem to be doing a better job of integrating the logistics process at the tactical (operations planning) level than at the strategic (long-range planning) level described earlier.

Transactional Integration

The third level of integration for the logistics process is the transactional level. Transactions include orders from customers, internal inventory replenishment orders, manufacturing orders, purchase orders to vendors, and shipping authorization and instructions to third-party logistics suppliers (e.g., carriers, warehouse operators).

To gauge the degree of integration at the transactional level, we asked respondents about the types of transaction related information systems they had in place or plan to implement by 1995. Figure 11-20 summarizes their responses, divided into three categories:

- External systems

- Cross-functional systems

- Data capture technology

1. External systems. External transaction systems are those that connect a company with its customers, suppliers, and logistics service providers. Most companies (91 percent) already have computerized order processing systems. By 1995, that number is expected to grow to 93 percent. Of this total, 19 percent plan implementation or major revision of a computerized order processing system during the period 1990 to 1995.

Just over two-thirds of the respondents have computer based purchasing systems, and the number should increase to just over three-quarters by 1995. Thirty-five percent of the respondents currently use computer to computer ordering to link with their suppliers at the transaction level, and the respondents indicate that number will rise to 74 percent by 1995. Further, 74 percent plan to integrate their order processing systems with customers (via computer to computer transmission) by 1995.

Finally, 4 percent of the respondents indicate they now use satellite tracking systems with carriers and with their private fleets to monitor shipments in transit. The respondents report that this will increase to 15 percent by 1995.

Figure 11-20

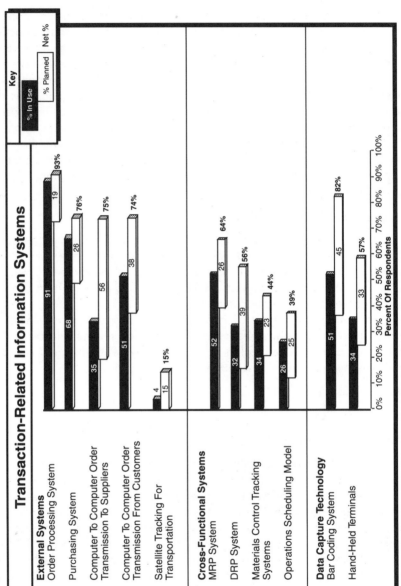

Transaction-Related Information Systems

Key
% In Use
% Planned
Net %

External Systems
Order Processing System — 91, 19, 93%
Purchasing System — 68, 26, 76%
Computer To Computer Order Transmission To Suppliers — 51, 56, 75%
Computer To Computer Order Transmission From Customers — 51, 38, 74%
Satellite Tracking For Transportation — 4, 15, 15%

Cross-Functional Systems
MRP System — 52, 26, 64%
DRP System — 32, 39, 56%
Materials Control Tracking Systems — 34, 23, 44%
Operations Scheduling Model — 26, 25, 39%

Data Capture Technology
Bar Coding System — 51, 45, 82%
Hand-Held Terminals — 34, 33, 57%

Percent Of Respondents
0% 10% 20% 30% 40% 50% 60% 70% 80% 90% 100%

2. Cross-functional systems. Cross-functional systems help integrate the functions involved in the logistics process by promoting the use of common data. Materials Requirements Planning (MRP) and Distribution Requirements Planning (DRP) systems are two good examples. Just over half of the companies use MRP systems with the number expected to grow to 64 percent in the next five years. About one-third currently use DRP systems, and this is projected to grow to 56 percent by 1995. These kinds of systems help to integrate customer orders, inventory replenishment and manufacturing orders, and parts and supplies replenishment orders.

Two other systems — materials control tracking systems and operations scheduling models — also play roles in helping integrate across functions. While not as popular as MRP or DRP systems, significant numbers of the respondents (44 percent and 39 percent respectively) plan to use these systems by 1995.

3. Data capture technology. Use of data capture technology such as bar coding and hand-held terminals supports transaction level integration with:

- More accurate and rapid data entry and transmission

- Reduced need for re-key entry of data at each processing step

- Ability to use a common database and upload/download data from it

- Ability to support customer and supplier programs to reduce/eliminate paperwork

Currently, 51 percent of the respondents use bar coding, and that number is expected to grow to 82 percent by 1995. About one-third of the respondents use hand-held data capture/entry terminals (e.g., for field sales order entry, inventory record keeping), and that number is expected to grow to 57 percent by 1995.

Integration of the logistics process at the transaction level is still in the early stages. Most companies already have or are working on having basic order processing and purchasing systems but relatively few use these systems to link with suppliers or customers. Similarly, only about one-half of the respondents have systems in place to support transaction integration within their companies across the various functions involved in the logistics process. Finally, only about half the respondents are using more advanced data capture technology to support integration. However, by 1995, our respondents indicate that they plan to make major advances in these areas.

Summary

Based on the survey responses, most companies still have major opportunities to improve the integration of the logistics process. At the strategic level, few companies have long-range logistics plans that encompass the full scope of logistics and address the range of issues that companies will face in the 1990s. At the tactical level, there is a greater degree of integration, but many of the surveyed companies are missing key components of an integrated operations planning process. Finally, a significant number of companies have not yet integrated the information flows at the transaction level with suppliers, customers, and within their own firms.

IMPLEMENTING SHIPPER-CARRIER PARTNERSHIPS

Once a company improves the quality and productivity of the logistics process in its own organization, the next step may be to form partnerships with carriers (and with other third-party logistics service providers). This is an example of a Stage III action.

Among the companies we interviewed, developing formal partnership relationships with carriers was the most frequently used improvement action. Several firms, including Hewlett-Packard, Texas Instruments, Westinghouse, Esprit de Corp, Rohm & Haas, Ford, GTE, PPG, and Xerox, have developed a formal cooperative approach toward improving quality and productivity with their carriers.

Basically, these corporations follow five general principles in their joint efforts with carriers:

- They concentrate their business with relatively few carriers.

- They carry out joint improvement efforts with their carriers.

- They have a formal system for measuring carrier performance.

- They employ a two-way feedback system on carrier performance and improvement plans.

- They use carrier performance as an objective basis for decisions on routing choices and rate levels.

Concentrate business with a few carriers. Most of the companies we interviewed began creating shipper-carrier partnerships in the early to mid-1980s. Because of transport deregulation, this was a major shakeout period in the transportation industry — particularly among the motor carriers. As shippers and carriers took advantage of the new freedoms to develop tailored services and long-term contracts, shippers naturally reduced their carrier base. The strong carriers, as a result, grew stronger and larger, while the weak ones fell by the wayside.

Today, shippers generally do business with fewer carriers than in the past. In fact, those shippers that aggressively sought out carrier partnerships during the 1980s have reduced their carrier base by as much as 90 percent over the past decade.

By focusing its business with fewer carriers, the shipper increases its negotiating leverage. More importantly, however, the shipper and carrier share an incentive to cooperate on improving service to the customer and increasing productivity.

Carry out joint improvement efforts. Many of the companies we interviewed view improvement as a joint shipper-carrier responsibility. Either side can take the lead in an effort to improve the *process* of which they both are a part. For example, Westinghouse, Yellow Freight System, and several other carriers have worked together to redesign the freight bill payment process. At some high volume locations, Westinghouse calculates the correct rate for a given shipment, generates a pre-rated bill of lading, and pays Yellow from this utilizing a full cycle EDI process. The freight invoice is eliminated altogether. Westinghouse reports that freight bill related processing costs have been reduced as a result.

Several companies we interviewed pointed to actions by their carriers to help improve loading practices (and reduce damage), to speed data exchange, and to improve service and productivity.

PPG Industries and truckload carrier Schneider National worked together to develop a system for planning, scheduling, tracking, and controlling truckload packaged shipments both inbound and outbound. The system, known as TOPS (Transportation Operations Planning System), helps PPG's central transportation operations staff plan schedules for the company's own private fleet and its dedicated carriers and assign loads to each carrier. Loads are entered electronically at PPG plants or other shipping locations. Carriers are notified of available loads through EDI. By accessing the central shipment database electronically, the carriers can update the scheduled and actual shipment status once the goods are in transit. PPG also uses the database to monitor service quality and identify improvement opportunities. PPG's system provides service measures such as:

- On-time performance

  — Pickup versus plant schedule

  — Delivery versus customer-specified time/date

  — Appointment versus scheduled time plus or minus ten minutes

- Elapsed time to confirm acceptance of a tendered load versus goal

- Percent of loads tendered that were rejected (target = zero)

Use a formal measurement system. Shippers such as PPG that have formal partnership programs with carriers do not award their business based solely on rates. While rates are important, service quality plays an increasing role in the decision-making process. As an example, at Rohm and Haas the sentiment is "We can't afford to use the low-cost carrier in many cases — our service requirements won't allow it."

The typical approach to measure and evaluate carriers includes:

• Using a range of measures

• Employing a weighting approach to develop an overall score

• Using thresholds on certain key measures to penalize carriers for poor performance

• Evaluating carriers against their peers, *and the individual carrier itself,* looking for continuous improvement

Figure 11-21 lists typical measures used by the companies we interviewed. They cover both quantitative and qualitative aspects. The quantitative measures include on-time performance, loss and damage rate, and a series of administrative measures. In some cases, the quantitative measures also include conformance with rate standards (i.e., does the carrier's rate match the shipper's calculation of what a fair rate should be?) and public safety record (accidents, D.O.T. adherence, etc.). Qualitative measures encompass carrier cooperativeness (ease of doing business) and a series of technical assistance and innovation dimensions, which represent the value-added service that the carrier can bring to the relationship.

Figure 11-21

Carrier Performance – Typical Measures

■ Quantitative
 • On-time delivery
 • Transit time consistency versus targets
 • Loss and damage rate
 • Billing accuracy
 • Customer complaint levels
 • Average claim amount
 • Settlement time on damage or overcharge
 • Cycle time for providing proof of delivery
 • Load accepted when tendered
 • Acceptable equipment
 • Conformance with rate standards
 • Public safety record

■ Qualitative
 • Carrier cooperativeness
  – Information
  – Inquiries
 • Technical assistance and innovation
  – Packaging
  – Loading
  – Scheduling
  – Information transfer

In many cases, the shipper has its own tracking system that supplies much of the quantitative data listed in Figure 11-21. In some cases, however, shippers ask carriers to measure themselves and report results back to the shipper. This often is tied in to the shipper's requirement that the carrier be actively involved in a quality-improvement process of its own and carry out statistical process control analysis on its operations.

For example, Burlington Motor Carriers uses control charts to track performance on a wide range of service and operating measures. These include:

- Percent on-time deliveries

- Cargo claims per load

- Percent of rebills

- Driver turnover

- Driver log violations

- Out-of-route miles

- Percent of linehaul loads pre-booked

- D.O.T. accidents per million miles

- Revenue per total mile

Employ two-way feedback. Typically, most shippers having a partnership relationship with carriers feed performance data back to carriers on a monthly or quarterly basis. Carriers, conversely, feed information to the shipper on factors that hinder their ability to provide quality service or inhibit their productivity. For example, this might include reports to the shipper on unproductive use of a trailer pool, delays experienced in scheduling pickups, delays at customer sites, incidents of inadequate lead time or unreasonable requests (e.g., the carrier commits to five loads per day out of a particular plant, but the facility repeatedly asks for 15 loads per day), and inadequate or illegible paperwork.

Using this formal two-way feedback, the carrier and shipper can agree on an action plan for the upcoming month or quarter aimed at addressing specific concerns and problems. At Rohm & Haas, for instance, carriers must report all service problems and identify the reason for them even though they fall outside of the carrier's responsibility. Using a Pareto chart analysis, Rohm & Haas transportation management and the carrier management can identify the major causes of service failures and assign the appropriate parties to develop a solution.

The Tennant Company uses an interesting approach to carrier measurement to encourage carriers to maintain performance levels throughout the life of a contract. The approach, described in an article written by Francis J. Quinn in the October 1990 issue of *Traffic Management*, recognizes that carriers may have a tendency to slack off after securing a freight contract with a company. To encourage carriers to maintain performance levels throughout the life of the contract, therefore, Tennant posts carrier rankings in its shipping facilities. These rankings are clearly visible to each Tennant employee and each carrier employee visiting the facility. The company also mails reports of carrier rankings monthly to the carrier's sales representatives. According to the article, Tennant finds this system goes a long way toward keeping carriers focused on continued high quality service.[9]

Use carrier performance to influence share of business and rate levels.
This last area is probably where the greatest differences appear from one
shipper to another. Some shippers directly link the amount of future business a carrier receives to its current performance. For example, a particular plant may have three carriers that are qualified to handle the freight.
Based on their performance, Carrier A might get 60 percent of the freight
for the next quarter or year with Carrier B and Carrier C receiving 20 percent each.

At the other extreme, other companies we interviewed do not formally
direct business toward carriers with the best performance. Rather, they
give carrier performance information to those people in their organizations who are responsible for making routing decisions and let them select
the carrier from the approved list.

Tying rate levels to performance is another area where approaches
differ greatly. In some cases, shippers develop standard rates for each
transportation lane and seek that rate from each carrier with whom they
negotiate. In other cases, shippers link rates and performance very closely.
For example, Xerox's "D/R carriers" (delivery and removal, the agents
who perform these services in the local district areas) are paid using a pay
for performance approach. Base rates were set several years ago based
on benchmarking. Except for adjustments for increases in fuel price,
increased service provided, or extreme economic situations, the only way
a carrier obtains an increase is to earn it through improved service performance. Xerox uses a number of quality criteria to assess performance,
including faultless installation and even driver appearance. Despite the
harsh sounding nature of this approach, both Xerox and its carriers report
being satisfied with this approach that has been nurtured through a close
partnership relationship.

Based on statistical data from the questionnaire survey and the results
of our interviews, supplier-carrier partnerships appear to be a major
source of quality and productivity improvement in the logistics process.
Shippers benefit from more affordable, consistent, reliable, and available
transportation services that are tailored to their needs. Carriers benefit
from having a more predictable business base on which to build and by
having the ability to work with shippers to improve the overall productivity
of the transportation process. Finally, the shipper's customers benefit from
improved service and, frequently, lower costs.

IMPLEMENTING CUSTOMER-SUPPLIER PARTNERSHIPS

Shipper-carrier partnerships are one manifestation of a broader phe-
nomenon: customer-supplier partnerships. Throughout all kinds of indus-

tries, customers are concentrating their business with a limited number of suppliers to improve quality and reduce costs for both parties. Whirlpool, for one, trimmed its vendor base in one year from 1,250 to 1,100 firms. Delta Faucet reported a 10 to 12 percent reduction in suppliers over a 24-month period.[10] Xerox reduced its number of suppliers by 92 percent over a several-year period, from 5,000 to 400 companies.[11] These are not isolated instances but rather exemplify the longer-term trend toward partnerships discussed in Chapter 3.

For many companies, shrinking the supplier base has become a formal part of the firm's procurement strategy. In her book, *The Man Who Discovered Quality*, Andrea Gabor talks about how Ford's procurement policies have shifted in recent years. Years ago, Ford required approval for situations where fewer than two suppliers were to be used for a particular component or part. Now, the policy calls for approvals if there is more than one supplier. Similarly, approvals were required for contracts that ran for more than one year. The new policy calls for approvals for contracts that run less than several years.

At Ford, suppliers strive to become a "Q-1" preferred quality supplier. This means commitment by the supplier to a never ending quality-improvement process and extensive use of statistical process control techniques. Through this approach, a supplier that achieves preferred status is exempt from many of the inspections that might otherwise be conducted on incoming material. Ford management says that eventually Q-1 preferred quality suppliers will be the only companies Ford will do business with.[12]

Motorola, the first total company winner of the Malcolm Baldrige National Quality Award, employs a similar approach. In 1989, Motorola management advised its suppliers that if they met the Baldrige Award eligibility criteria they were obliged to compete for the award in the future. Suppliers who declined or failed to respond were disqualified as Motorola suppliers. Additionally, Motorola has aggressively reduced the number of suppliers it uses for any one commodity or group of component parts.

Today, one of its pocket pagers contains components in 22 commodity groups. Each of these components is single sourced to a specific supplier — 22 commodities, 22 suppliers. For this approach to succeed, Motorola must have a close working relationship with each of its 22 suppliers. Winning the leading market share in Japan for its pager based on superior product quality is a testament to Motorola's success.

The ValueLink services program offered to hospitals by Baxter Healthcare Corporation is another example of a supplier-customer partnership. With ValueLink, Baxter assumes many of the responsibilities for storing and distributing supplies to and within the hospital. This lets the hospital focus on its primary mission — to provide healthcare. Both parties benefit — the hospital from reduced inventory investment and operating cost and Baxter from increased revenue and market share. One hospital administrator reported that the number of vendors and manufacturers the hospital had to deal with dropped from about 2,000 to essentially one general contractor — Baxter.

Purchasing decision based on "true costs." At the center of many of these supplier-customer relationships is a measurement system that helps focus both parties on the "true cost" of the supplier's goods and not simply the purchase price. In an article entitled "Can Supplier Rating Be Standardized?," published in the November 8, 1990 issue of *Purchasing Magazine,* author Tom Stundza describes a system developed at Rockwell International's Aerospace Division. The system, called "Supplier Rating and Incentive Program" (SRIP), was developed to help Rockwell award contracts based on best estimates of "true costs." Similar approaches are in use by several companies, including Honeywell, Ford, General Dynamics, Hughes Aircraft, Douglas Aircraft, Motorola, and Texas Instruments.[13]

This general approach works as follows. The company identifies a series of unproductive costs related to doing business with a supplier, develops estimates of those costs, and then adds the unproductive costs to the bid price of the item to develop its "true cost." Then, a "Supplier Performance Index" (SPI) is calculated for each supplier using the estimated "true cost" divided by the bid price to develop a multiplier factor. This multiplier is used to estimate the "true cost" of future bid items from that supplier. A simplified example of how this technique works is shown in Figure 11-22.

Figure 11-22

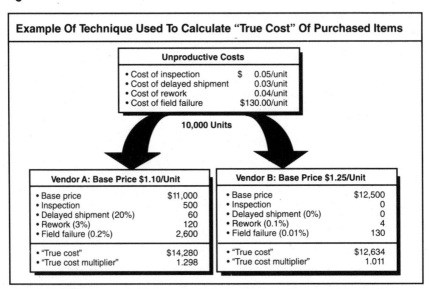

Example Of Technique Used To Calculate "True Cost" Of Purchased Items

Unproductive Costs

• Cost of inspection	$ 0.05/unit
• Cost of delayed shipment	0.03/unit
• Cost of rework	0.04/unit
• Cost of field failure	$130.00/unit

10,000 Units

Vendor A: Base Price $1.10/Unit

• Base price	$11,000
• Inspection	500
• Delayed shipment (20%)	60
• Rework (3%)	120
• Field failure (0.2%)	2,600
• "True cost"	$14,280
• "True cost multiplier"	1.298

Vendor B: Base Price $1.25/Unit

• Base price	$12,500
• Inspection	0
• Delayed shipment (0%)	0
• Rework (0.1%)	4
• Field failure (0.01%)	130
• "True cost"	$12,634
• "True cost multiplier"	1.011

In this example, a customer wants to buy 10,000 units of a particular component part. The customer has identified a series of unproductive costs related to inspecting supplier goods upon receipt, carrying additional inventory or disrupting production schedules because of delayed shipments, reworking an assembled product due to a failed component, and paying for a repair due to a failure in the field. Vendor A offers the component for a base price of $1.10 per unit, whereas Vendor B has a higher base price of $1.25 per unit.

A customer choosing suppliers strictly on base price would select Vendor A. However, there are significant unproductive costs hidden in Vendor A's product. Vendor A's component must be inspected upon receipt by the customer. For 10,000 units, this costs $500. Vendor A also has a history of being late on 20 percent of its shipments. This adds $.03 per unit to 20 percent of its units for a total delayed shipment cost of $60. The rework rate on products made with Vendor A's product is 3 percent, resulting in a cost of $120. The field failure rate for products containing Vendor A's component is 0.2 percent, but, at a cost of $130 per field failure, the total comes to a hefty $2,600. The calculated "true cost" for Vendor A is $14,280. When this is compared to the base price of $11,000, the "true cost multiplier" for Vendor A becomes 1.298.

In the case of Vendor B, the base price is $12,500 for the 10,000 units. Vendor B has received certification from the customer; its components do not require incoming inspection. Vendor B also has a record of no delayed shipments and so incurs no unproductive cost for either inspection or delayed shipment. Vendor B's rework rate is 0.1 percent or $4, and its field failure rate is 0.01 percent or $130 for 10,000 unit lot. Vendor B's "true cost" is $12,634, for a "true cost multiplier" ratio of 1.011. These two cases illustrate how the customer can use "true cost multipliers" to estimate the real cost of purchasing Vendor A's products versus Vendor B's.

In this example, we only used a few categories of unproductive costs. In an actual situation, the categories of unproductive costs vary from one company's application of this approach to another. However, some general components of unproductive costs include:

• Source inspection

• Receiving inspection

• Rework

• Returns

• Under-shipment

• Early receipt

• Over-shipment

- Late receipt

- In-process rejection

- Paperwork errors

- Failure in the field

The "true cost multiplier" indices play a key role in supplier selection. Also, due to suppliers' continuous improvement efforts, the multipliers constantly adjust — dropping as the suppliers reduce their unproductive costs. Rockwell's Aerospace Division offers a good illustration of this point. Rockwell uses a red line cutoff system. Suppliers whose SPI multiplier exceeds the red line cannot bid again until they can prove to Rockwell that they are in control of the factors that cause unproductive costs for Rockwell. In 1986, the red line was set at 2.0, i.e., the "true cost" could be no more than two times the bid price. By 1990, the red line had dropped to 1.4 — "true cost" could not exceed bid price by more than 40 percent.[14]

Texas Instruments uses a slightly different approach essentially setting statistical limits for its version of the multiplier. When it began using this approach, the upper limit was 1.4 or 40 percent above bid price. Currently, the upper limit is 1.18. To qualify for TI's Supplier Excellence Award, suppliers have to continually improve their multiplier year to year.

When Motorola adopted this approach, it too found that its unproductive costs added 40 percent to the bid price (i.e, a multiplier of 1.4). Over the past several years, Motorola has worked to tighten this requirement considerably. Now, to receive a Motorola Corporate Supplier of the Year Award, a company must have a multiplier of no more than 1.009 or 0.9 percent above bid. For some commodities, Motorola's "best in class" supplier performance is even tighter. Actual supplier performance in this supplier rating system has been the primary factor in determining which few suppliers won the major share of its business. This simple measurement tool enabled Motorola to establish mutually rewarding partnerships with the few suppliers that demonstrated world-class performance.

Our final example, Polaroid, shows a company using this technique. In the article "Managing Suppliers up to Speed," which appeared in the July-August 1989 edition of the Harvard Business Review, David N. Burt refers to Polaroid's "Zero-Based Pricing" approach. Rather than looking just at purchase price, Polaroid tracks acquisition prices plus all vendor- or part-specific costs incurred to convert the components into a finished product. Polaroid also includes field failure costs in the calculation.[15]

Field failure costs are an important factor to consider in calculating "true costs." There is a considerably higher cost to correct a field failure due to a defective item versus screening out the defective item earlier in the process. Some of the companies interviewed call this the "Rule of Ten" — costs to correct a defect increase by a factor of ten each time the defective item moves to the next step in the process. Figure 11-23 illustrates the concept. A defective item that could be eliminated for a few pennies at the supplier could cost several dollars to replace during product testing and several hundred dollars when it fails in the field.

Figure 11-23

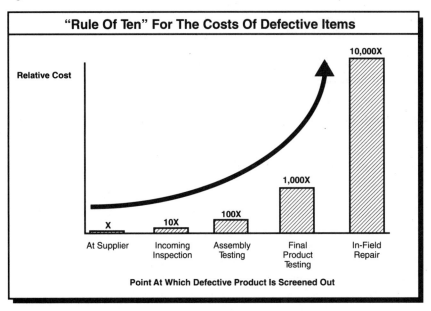

The "true cost" approach forces realistic commitments from suppliers on product quality, shipment due dates, invoice accuracy, etc. Equally as important, it requires realistic expectations from the customers who must provide good product specifications, blueprints, technical information, and delivery requirement information to the suppliers. Because suppliers are under the microscope to meet the multiplier goals, they certainly have an incentive to make sure their customer's expectations are achievable.

Other ways customers measure value. Customers work with their suppliers in a partnership relationship both in buying existing products and in designing new ones. In an industrial setting, this might mean creating joint design teams to study issues of design for manufacturability. For the retail customer, this might involve working with manufacturers on joint marketing and packaging efforts. While the techniques customers use to measure suppliers on these dimensions of value may not be as rigorous as "true cost" measurement, assistance in new product design is a key factor in selecting a vendor.

Analyzing the unproductive costs associated with a supplier's product is not the only technique customers use to test value. Many firms conduct value engineering and value analysis of the product or service being purchased to determine whether the price paid is appropriate given the value received. In an industrial setting, this often results in products being redesigned or modified to use a less expensive part with the same functionality. In the retail sector, companies evaluate the profitability of products sold not only on their gross margin but also in terms of their costs for handling, inventory financing, retail space, etc. The technique is called "Direct Product Profitability" (DPP) analysis. Where profitability is low, retailers work with suppliers to find ways to reduce cost. Alternatively, they may decide to drop the product in favor of a more profitable one.

Account Management: How Some Suppliers Respond

With customer demands for higher quality and improved performance on the rise, many suppliers are realizing that adequate response requires significant resources and effort. For most suppliers, this means they can only enter into a limited number of true partnerships with their most important customers — typically, just a handful.

To better accommodate the needs of this select group of customers, many suppliers adopt an account management approach. Account management — briefly discussed in Chapter 6 — begins by identifying who the handful of key customers are. For some suppliers, the answer may be obvious based on share of business, technological match, or need for access to certain retail channels. For others, it may not be as obvious; the supplier may have to analyze customer contribution and profitability.

Customer profitability analysis, as a technique, is several decades old. It is being rediscovered as part of a currently popular technique called "Activity Based Costing" (ABC). In fact, ABC principles are at the center of customer profitability analysis.

Customer profitability analysis looks at the cost of doing business with each customer on a transaction level basis recognizing differences in order mix and size, order frequency, distribution method, invoicing terms, payment history, and other customer-specific factors. Figure 11-24 is an example of a profitability analysis of a sample order for a store door delivery company. The analysis shows gross and net sales, variable production costs (based on product mix), and a host of transaction related costs specific to this particular customer's order. Finally, the table shows net contribution to overhead and profit, an allocation of overhead and general costs, and net profit from the transaction. A company can develop profitability profiles on its customers by aggregating such analyses over time.

The major benefit of customer profitability analysis is the ability to break customers into one of three groups. Group one consists of those customers that contribute the greatest amount of profitability. These are the customers the supplier needs to nurture and protect. The second group consists of customers that fall in the middle in terms of account profitability. The third group, which often is quite large, is made up of customers that do not contribute their fair share of profits and may, in fact, be unprofitable. The supplier must work with these companies to improve profitability.

Figure 11-24

Profitability Of A Sample Order		
Item	**Cost**	**Percent Of Gross Sales**
■ Gross sales	$ 1,575	
• Less discounts and allowances	– 126	8.0 %
■ Net sales	1,449	
• Less variable production cost	– 851	54.0 %
■ Gross contribution	598	
• Less transaction costs		
– Selling $29 – 1.8%		
– Order processing 12 – 0.8		
– Inventory carrying 10 – 0.6		
– Warehousing/shipping 75 – 4.8		
– Transportation 250 –15.8		
– Promotion/merchandising 7 – 0.4		
– Accounts receivable 45 – 2.9		
– Credits (returns/claims) 15 – 1.0		
	– 443	28.1 %
■ Net contribution to overhead and profit	155	
• Less general and administrative costs and overheads	– 86	5.5 %
Net Profit	$ 69	4.4 %

This is often done by examining transaction level costs versus averages to understand why there is a drain on profitability. Figure 11-25 shows such a comparison for the sample order in Figure 11-24. In this example, transportation costs and accounts receivable financing costs are both double the average. These are prime areas for attention to help improve this customer's profitability.

Regardless of what technique a company uses to identify its most important customers, its next step in account management is to establish a formal process for understanding customer requirements, knowing the factors on which customers base their buying decision, and agreeing on service requirements with customers. Typically, this step involves a three-pronged approach that includes top-to-bottom involvement, cross-functional teamwork, and formal contact/informal feedback.

Top-to-bottom involvement means establishing a system of contacts at senior management levels within the various functional areas and among the individuals who handle day to day transactions. Cross-functional involvement means involving a broad range of people and functions in the relationship, i.e., the functional counterparts in all major operational areas of the business, including manufacturing, sales, logistics, accounting, information resources, and even human resources. In effect, these teams become supplier-customer process design teams similar to joint product design teams. (One company we interviewed went so far as to start a formal employee exchange program with one of its customers.)

Figure 11-25

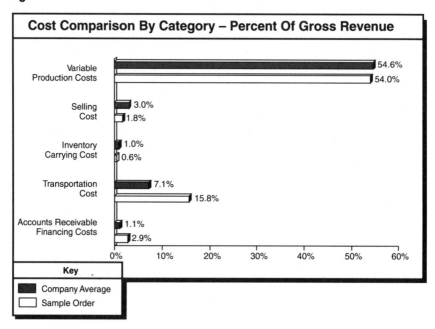

Formal contact includes regular periodic reviews of performance and formal tie-ins to each other's planning processes. Informal feedback involves two-way communication to identify and fix problems before they become big issues.

The account management approach entails a number of organizational interfaces beyond the traditional sales representative-buyer relationship. Figure 11-26 illustrates this point. It shows the typical organizational interfaces between a supplier's and customer's organization. In an account management approach, the requirements of each "customer" (in the left-hand column) must be understood by each "supplier" (along the top). The logistics process includes a number of those "suppliers." Consequently, those involved in the total logistics process are important players in any account management approach.

As a supplier shifts to an account management focus, it requires three key types of information about each account. These include general information about the account, operations data, and supplier performance evaluation criteria.

Figure 11-26

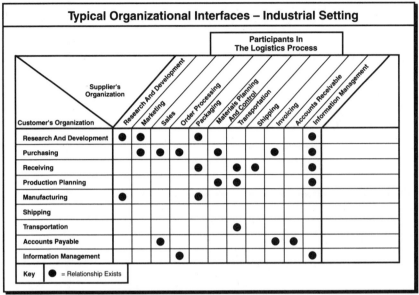

Typical Organizational Interfaces – Industrial Setting

General information about the account. This information describes how the customer's organization works, who the key players are, and how the company prefers to work with its suppliers to achieve its strategic objectives. Figure 11-27 illustrates the type of information needed.

Operations data. This includes knowing how the customer's operation works and how this affects the way in which it interacts with suppliers. The scope includes systems, procedures, physical capacities, and flows. It also encompasses understanding what the customer specifically requires of its suppliers. Figures 11-28 through 11-31 illustrate the depth of data required of a supplier doing business with the retail trade.

Supplier performance evaluation criteria. Not surprisingly, this segment of information includes understanding how the customer measures suppliers and what motivates the customer to increase, decrease, or discontinue its business with the supplier.

Much of this intelligence is similar in content to the information discussed in Chapter 6. The key differences in an account management focus are the depth of understanding required and the method of obtaining the information.

Although account management calls for a cross-functional team approach in dealing with the customer's organization, the process won't work without a team leader. Each team, therefore, usually has a quarterback (frequently the account manager and often a senior executive for a key account), but each person on the team (representative of the departments listed across the top of

Figure 11-27

Account Management Approach – General Information Required

- Organization
  - Structure and responsibilities
  - Backgrounds of key executives
  - Management style
  - Measurement and reward system

- Corporate and functional objectives and strategies

- Current situation
  - General trends
  - Financial performance (absolute, relative to competition)
  - Major initiatives
  - Strengths and weaknesses

- Positioning of your company
  - Ally, neutral, problem supplier, foe

Figure 11-28

Account Management Approach – Purchasing/ Merchandising Information Required

- Product management
  - Listing/delisting procedures
  - Notification requirements
    - Product changes
    - Price changes

- Promotions
  - What kinds are acceptable? Preferred?
  - What planning lead time is required?
  - Level of support required?
  - How are they implemented?

- Key contacts

Figure 11-29

Account Management Approach – Physical Operations Information Required

- Warehouse requirements
  - Special packaging requirements
  - Unitization methods/height requirements
  - Storage method
  - Pallet storage/exchange
  - Space availability

- Transportation
  - Receiving hours
  - Appointment requirements and lead times
  - Routing guides
  - Customer backhaul requirements
  - Trailer staging

- Order placement
  - Methods used/preferred
  - Confirmation required?
  - Policies on cuts, adds, substitutions, split shipments: e.g.;
    - Ship what is available and cancel remainder
    - Ship what is available and backorder
    - Hold until complete
  - Procedures for cuts, adds, etc.
    - New PO required?
    - Notification/authorization required?

- Key contacts

Figure 11-30

**Account Management Approach –
Accounting/Finance Information Required**

- ■ Policies and procedures
  - PO generation
  - Terms
  - Invoicing
  - Claims
  - Debits
  - Payment
  - Approvals/authorization limits

- ■ Requirements
  - Payment cycle times
  - Returns, refunds, credit processing cycles
  - Discounts on invoice by line item
  - Documentation

- ■ Key contacts

Figure 11-31

**Account Management Approach –
Information Systems Information Required**

- ■ Existing systems
  - Ordering
  - Payables
  - Promotion handling

- ■ Information exchange capabilities/supplier requirements
  - Orders
  - POS data
  - Billing

- ■ Specific formats

- ■ Key contacts

Figure 11-26) must work to maintain a relationship with his or her counterpart in the customer organization. Because the relationships tend to align by function, the supplier representative can talk to the counterpart at the customer in his or her own language, thus aiding communication.

Often, this communication entails on-site visits. Such visits are a good way to collect firsthand information about a customer's operation. In addition, visits tend to personalize the relationship between the people in the supplier and customer organizations. As one person we interviewed observed, "It's a way of getting our people to realize they're letting down their partner Joe or Sally in the customer organization rather than letting down some faceless business. That really drives home the idea of customer focus."

This personal touch approach is not limited to external accounts. Several retailers give their logistics functional personnel firsthand experience working in their own stores so they can better understand how order picking, packing, and shipping practices affect store operations.

Overcoming Barriers to Partnerships

Despite growing indications that supplier-customer partnerships are the coming trend, some customers are cautious. They are accustomed to spreading their business around and pitting supplier against supplier to keep prices down and retain a backup supplier.

In our interviews with companies, many of the managers commented on these traditional approaches. Regarding the idea of spreading the business around, these firms noted that the practice introduces additional possibilities for variations and problems. In the case of Motorola and its pager, if a component goes bad, Motorola immediately knows which supplier it needs to contact. With multiple suppliers, the company would have to trace back the bad lot. Further, it might have to adjust its assembly or testing procedures to accommodate the slight variations in components sourced from multiple suppliers.

Another drawback to spreading the business lies in reliability of supply. As the interviewees pointed out, "If the supplier is not your primary supplier, he probably is someone else's. In a shortage situation, who will get priority?" Probably the other customer.

When it comes to the practice of pitting suppliers against one another to get a better price, the interviewees had strong opinions. Negotiation on price alone, they said, gives the vendor no incentive to help the customer improve its own process or improve the processes for both firms simultaneously. In fact, if a supplier risks losing business based on the next bid, it is highly motivated to take a short-term view of things. A strong relationship with a customer, on the other hand, enables the supplier to invest in that relationship.

Finally, our interviewees cautioned against forcing suppliers to cut prices arbitrarily, noting that there may be hidden costs. One manager suggested customers take a good look at what the supplier may be giving up in order to meet the demand for low price. "The supplier has to cut somewhere," he observed. "I'd want to know how that cut will affect me."

THE PROMISE FROM PARTNERSHIPS

Among all the high-impact actions that emerged from the questionnaire surveys and interviews we conducted, supplier-customer partnerships clearly offer the greatest promise for the future. Suppliers and customers are steadily working toward fewer and closer relationships. This is especially noticeable in the industrial sectors, but, even in retail, evidence suggests the same type of trend. Through the vehicle of closer supplier-customer alliances, quality improvement becomes a shared responsibility. The customer bears the burden of clearly defining responsibilities and expectations. The supplier bears the responsibility of agreeing to and meeting those requirements. Together, they share the responsibility of improving the process for achieving quality and productivity.

As firms move into the 1990s, much will be written and spoken about supplier-customer partnerships particularly with respect to the intensity and formality of the relationships. Undoubtedly, the majority of companies will form partnerships with their suppliers and customers, but most companies will enter into only a few *strategic* partnerships. These will be situations where each party is so important to the other (e.g., they are on one another's "top 10" list) that they see *strategic advantage* from joining forces. The nature of these relationships will depend on the parties involved. However, we believe successful strategic partnerships will share six key characteristics as summarized in Figure 11-32. These include:

- Common values

- Intimate knowledge of each other's businesses

- An operating style conducive to partnership

- An operating mode that supports quality and productivity improvement

- Joint participation in value-added activities

- Free and open information exchange

By developing supplier-customer partnerships with these characteristics, companies will advance the evolution of logistics as a single process that ties together raw material sources and final consumers.

---

[1] Dumaine, Brian, "How Managers Can Succeed Through Speed"

[2] Dumaine, Brian, "How Managers Can Succeed Through Speed"

[3] Simmons, Ted, "Account Management; Food Manufacturers' Accounts with Supermarket Retailers"

[4] Martha, Joseph A., "Flexible Distribution Systems Needed; Logistics Technology for Manufacturer/Retail Partnerships"

[5] Council of Logistics Management, 1990 Annual Conference Program

[6] Longo, Don, "Quick Response: Quickly Shaping Retail Business"

[7] Dumaine, Brian, "How Managers Can Succeed Through Speed"

[8] Kurt Salmon Associates, "Quick Response Implementation, Action Steps for Retailers, Manufacturers and Suppliers"

[9] Quinn, Francis J., "Top 10 Logistics Ideas"

[10] Dowst, Somerby, "Made In The USA Can Still Be A Quality Label"

[11] Burt, David N., "Managing Suppliers up to Speed"

[12] Gabor, Andrea, *The Man Who Discovered Quality, How W. Edwards Deming Brought the Quality Revolution to America*

[13] Stundza, Tom, "Can Supplier Rating be Standardized?"

[14] Stundza, Tom, "Can Supplier Rating be Standardized?"

[15] Burt, David N., "Managing Suppliers Up to Speed"

Figure 11-32

Do You Really Have A Strategic Partnership?

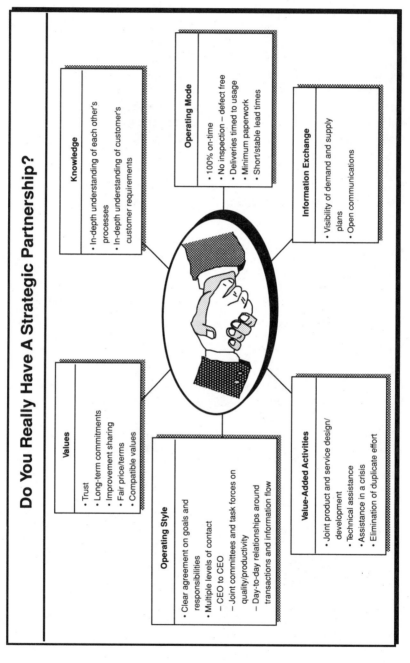

Knowledge
- In-depth understanding of each other's processes
- In-depth understanding of customer's customer requirements

Operating Mode
- 100% on-time
- No inspection – defect free
- Deliveries timed to usage
- Minimum paperwork
- Short/stable lead times

Information Exchange
- Visibility of demand and supply plans
- Open communications

Values
- Trust
- Long-term commitments
- Improvement sharing
- Fair price/terms
- Compatible values

Operating Style
- Clear agreement on goals and responsibilities
- Multiple levels of contact
  – CEO to CEO
  – Joint committees and task forces on quality/productivity
  – Day-to-day relationships around transactions and information flow

Value-Added Activities
- Joint product and service design/development
- Technical assistance
- Assistance in a crisis
- Elimination of duplicate effort

SECTION V

IMPLEMENTING IMPROVEMENTS

In Section IV, we discussed the tools and techniques of quality and productivity improvement. We presented a general framework for improving both built around the plan-do-check-act (PDCA) cycle. We discussed how continuous and breakthrough improvements fit into the overall improvement process.

We examined various techniques for analyzing problems and identifying improvements and explored the types of measures that can be used in logistics to track quality and productivity and support an improvement process. Finally, we looked at a number of high-impact improvement actions that the companies in our surveys/interviews identified as having major quality and productivity benefits.

In many ways, the material presented in Section IV and supported by Appendixes A through F is like a dictionary or a thesaurus. The tools are useful references on language (in our case, the language of quality and productivity in logistics) but alone do not help a person to use the language.

Section V provides insights on how to implement a quality and productivity-improvement process in your logistics operation. It describes how to apply the tools and techniques outlined in Section IV.

Beginning with Chapter 12, we discuss how to create the right environment for improvement and why employee ownership of the improvement process is a critical success factor. The chapter also examines how companies encourage employees to take the lead role in improvement. Chapter 13 addresses how firms are carrying out the process of improvement in logistics. It offers suggestions for companies that are just getting started and for companies that are looking for ways to maintain momentum.

CHAPTER 12

EMPLOYEE OWNERSHIP
OF IMPROVEMENT

W. Edwards Deming frequently is quoted as saying that most quality *problems* are systems or process related. In other words, once you remove special causes, variations in performance levels are built in to the design of the system or process. Deming suggests that it is the responsibility of management — not individual employees — to fix the system.

As we discussed in Chapter 10, changing the process is the greatest source of improvement for either quality or productivity. And, while it may be true that most quality problems are systems or process related, it also is true that most quality *solutions* only occur through the efforts of people. To improve the process or system, people must be involved in problem analysis, action planning, implementation, and operations.

THE WAY IT WAS

Ten years ago, the general approach toward making process improvements was to assemble a team of process improvement experts comprising industrial engineers, systems analysts, process engineers, consultants, internal auditors, and other objective third parties. This team analyzed the situation and recommended improvements. Line management then assumed the task of implementation.

In most cases, the employees charged with executing the process were involved in its design only on a limited basis if at all. As a result, the improved process frequently failed to realize its promise. The outside analysts blamed management for poor implementation. Management, in turn, blamed the employees for resisting the new, improved ways. Employees reacted by blaming both the analysts and managers for imposing a new process on them without understanding how things really operate.

"LET'S GET THE EMPLOYEES INVOLVED"

In the late 1970s and early 1980s, some U.S. companies looked to Japan for ideas about how to improve employee-management relations and how to increase employee involvement in planning and implementing improvements. One technique — quality circles — caught the attention of many American companies. In Japan, these were small groups of employees who voluntarily got together on a regular basis to explore ways of improving process quality and productivity. These quality circles operated with the support and encouragement of Japanese management and formed a key component of the continuous improvement process in many Japanese companies.

Managers in a number of U.S. companies liked what they saw in quality circles. The approach seemed like a cheap and easy way of making headway in quality improvement. It also demonstrated a more participatory management style.

Unfortunately, quality circles did not enjoy the success in the United States that they did in Japan for several reasons. First, quality circles in U.S. firms often were implemented on a mandatory basis. Employees felt coerced by management into participating and would not enthusiastically join in. In some companies, quality circles would generate improvement ideas, but their requests for implementation support fell on deaf ears. This lack of support prompted quality circle members to lose interest. And lastly, some American firms implemented quality circles in the hopes of making major improvements based on the ideas generated. They wanted results but did not want to invest in the resources, processes, and skills needed to achieve those results, i.e., training in problem solving, statistical process control, and team participation. Employees unfamiliar with working on a team could not live up to management's expectations. Frustration grew on both sides.

Although quality circles got a bad name in many companies in the 1980s as a result of these poor starts, some U.S. companies did succeed in making the concepts embedded in quality circles work in the American environment. In our interviews and secondary research, we found examples to this effect as well as a growing body of opinion that employee participation, involvement, and, ultimately, ownership for improvement is the key to a successful quality/productivity-improvement process.

THE CHANGING WORKPLACE

In their book, *Workplace 2000,* Joseph Boyett and Henry Conn argue that employee ownership of improvement will be a prerequisite for companies in the next century.[1] To meet the changing requirements of a more demanding marketplace, Boyett and Conn believe organizations of all types must be flatter, leaner, and more aggressive. The authors go on to say that with this streamlining will come greater employee self-management and control as the traditional supervisory layer in most organizations disappears and is replaced by trainers, coaches, and facilitators.

Because traditional management structures and chains of command will disappear, the authors believe business success will depend on finding new ways to communicate with, train, involve, and motivate employees. In the remainder of this chapter, we explore what companies are doing today in logistics to cultivate employee involvement and foster employee ownership for improvement.

COMMUNICATION

Among many of the companies we interviewed, one of the keys to bringing employees on board is clear communication from the top on why the company needs to improve quality and productivity. Generally, this begins with a statement from the CEO or President laying out the need for quality and productivity improvement — usually for competitive reasons. The communication doesn't stop there, however. Employees get regular updates on the improvement progress, competitive situation, and improvement targets for the future. Sometimes this communication takes the form of letters from the President, corporate quality newsletters, employee rallies, or even audio and video tapes available to the employees.

While this top-down communication is important for demonstrating leadership, vision, and commitment, it is just the tip of the iceberg. The successful companies we interviewed rely heavily on two-way communication between managers and employees in every area. The managers educate their employees in technical aspects of the job and in process improvement techniques. They keep employees informed on progress and results. Further, they coach and motivate. Employees, in turn, communicate with management about problems and concerns and solicit support for improvements.

Among the 55 percent of companies in our questionnaire survey who reported having formal quality and productivity-improvement processes in logistics, 77 percent said they had developed a communication and feedback process for their logistics employees about quality and customer service results. Despite this statistic, our interviews indicate that companies are not fully up to speed on communications with their employees. Communication often is left to the line management structure where the effectiveness of the communication depends largely on the individual. To assist managers and employees in communicating better with one another, therefore, several companies formally train people in communication techniques as part of their overall training processes.

TRAINING

Training plays a key role in establishing employee involvement, participation, and commitment in a quality and productivity-improvement process. Several of the companies we interviewed had established formal employee training programs that are worthy of note.

- Motorola believes so strongly in employee training that it has created Motorola University, a formal training institution at its corporate headquarters near Chicago. Motorola offers a full curriculum of training courses in quality and productivity improvement. These courses deal with such diverse topics as communication and leadership skills, problem solving techniques, group interaction, statistical process control, and participative management techniques. Through Motorola University and other formal training courses, each Motorola employee receives 40 hours of formal training annually — at a cost of $60 million in 1989. Motorola does not limit its commitment to training to its own employees. It makes Motorola University courses available to suppliers and customers as well. In 1991, over one-fourth of the students were nonMotorola employees.

- Texas Instruments' employees each go through a 40-hour training session that includes understanding customer requirements, the TI approach toward employee empowerment, and problem solving techniques.

- Procter & Gamble, in association with the University of Tennessee, has developed a series of training courses on quality improvement for its employees. In logistics, a large number of employees have received training in cycle time reduction techniques.

- Xerox requires all employees to go through a minimum of 28 hours of quality training. This includes TQM concepts, problem solving, and the quality-improvement process. Additionally, professionals and managers receive 20 hours of statistical training and 12 hours of group facilitation training.

Among the survey respondents with a formal quality and productivity-improvement process in logistics, two-thirds had quality and/or customer service training programs in place. As Figure 12-1 indicates, most of the respondents provide at least three days of training per employee per year, and 30 percent offer six or more days of training to their logistics employees.

In most firms, logistics employees were not heavily involved in training others (see Figure 12-2). This points to a potential opportunity to improve cross-functional coordination within a company. By using properly trained logistics employees as trainers in other functional areas — and vice versa — all functions involved in the logistics process could benefit.

Figure 12-1

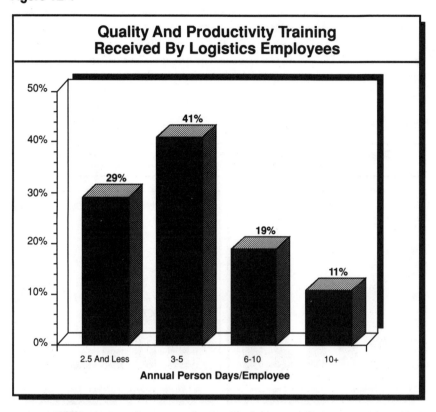

In the case of logistics employees training suppliers and customers, companies seem to fall into two camps. Either they provide minimal or no training (77 percent of the firms) or they furnish significant amounts of training (13 percent provide more than ten days of training). For those companies that allow logistics people to train customers and suppliers, the focus of this training usually is on basic statistical process control and measurement techniques. This is especially true in cases where the firm requires its suppliers and carriers to report these data.

The employee training that exists in the companies we interviewed typically covers a wide range of topics. There are general awareness courses on quality and productivity improvement, courses on interpersonal skills and basic problem solving (teaching simple data analysis and use of cause and effect diagrams), and even very sophisticated classes on statistical analysis. Companies offer on the job training programs for employees whose jobs changed after process improvements were made. And some companies offer remedial courses to bring employees up to speed on basic skills such as reading, writing, and mathematics. (In "The Education Crisis: What Business Can Do," published in the July 4, 1988 issue of *Fortune*, William Wiggenhorn, head of Motorola University, estimates that it costs $200 to train a worker in the United States in statistical process control versus $0.47 for a worker in Japan. The difference is this: Japanese workers are given a book to read and American workers must first learn to read.[2])

Figure 12-2

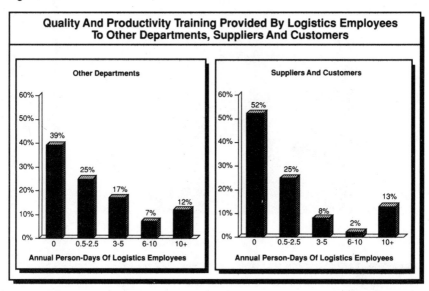

Specific training curricula differ by company, but certain themes, topics, and subject matter appear repeatedly. We have synthesized a typical set of training topics for a company's employees based on what Motorola, Xerox, Dow Chemical, Texas Instruments, and other firms offer. These training topics are tailored to three training audiences: all employees, team leaders, and managers.

Training for all employees. Employee training typically begins with general awareness training that includes sessions on the company's commitment to improvement as well as on what improvement process the company is using. Although most firms have the same basic structure for their improvement processes, as described in Chapter 2, each has its own unique aspects. This initial training typically takes one or two days.

The next kind of training for all employees addresses problem solving techniques. These courses introduce the concept of problem solving through employee involvement and discuss the tools and techniques used in these efforts. The fundamental details of data collection and interpretation are covered in these classes.

A third set of topics deals with identifying and understanding customer requirements. While not every employee has direct contact with the external customer, all employees have one or more internal customers with whom they must deal. This type of training focuses on how to work with the customer to understand requirements and reach agreement on how to meet them.

The fourth general set of training topics deals with interpersonal skills. This includes communication skills (e.g., speaking, writing, and listening) and teamwork.

Depending on a firm's training approach, this program of training could take place over a few months or over the course of a year or more.

Additional training for team leaders. As we discuss later in this chapter, several kinds of employee teams participate in implementing an improvement process. Each team needs a leader to guide and direct activities of the group. As a result, team leaders need additional skills and training beyond those required of every employee. These skills include team building, leadership, meeting facilitation, goal setting, opportunity identification and problem solving, application of statistical techniques, and project management.

The last item — project management — is an especially important skill for a team leader. Most employees chosen to be team leaders — whether they come from the ranks of supervisors or front-line employees — do not have much experience at implementing change. Therefore, training on both the technical aspects of project management (schedules, budgets, etc.) and the interpersonal side of project management (encouraging cooperation and overcoming roadblocks) becomes key for team leaders.

Additional training for managers. As companies encourage employee participation and ownership of improvement, the rules of management change. Traditional command and control must give way to leadership and coaching techniques. Thus, managers must learn the management essentials related to the new style of employee-management relationships. Managers also need to learn how to implement the improvement process in their organizations from a logistics standpoint — a topic we cover in the next chapter. Finally, managers must learn new approaches to personnel evaluation, recognition, and rewards. This includes learning how to provide meaningful feedback to employees that reinforces good performance and helps correct below-par performance.

Before leaving the topic of training, we'd like to share one key piece of advice that we heard from several companies we interviewed. By training employees, a company creates certain expectations in the employees' minds. Employees want to apply what they have learned (e.g., team problem solving or SPC). They grow frustrated if there is a long lag between learning these techniques and being allowed to apply them. Companies that support and encourage employees to apply training almost immediately have the greatest success.

EMPLOYEE INVOLVEMENT

There are many ways companies can involve employees in logistics quality and productivity improvements. They can offer training, include them in problem identification and solving, and empower them to take immediate action to ensure that customer needs are met.

Figure 12-3 lists the responses to our Logistics Management Survey regarding four specific employee involvement actions related to logistics improvement. Two-thirds of the companies with a formal logistics improvement process solicit employee suggestions for improvement. Nearly 50 percent use a "closed-loop feedback" process to make sure the employee knows management has reviewed the suggestion and decided on a course of action.

Figure 12-3

Employee Involvement Actions – Logistics Improvement Process	
	Percent Of Respondents
■ Formal employee suggestion process	66%
■ Empowerment of employees to "do what it takes" to satisfy customers	65%
■ Identification and implementation of improvements driven by employees who are responsible for execution	57%
■ Use of "closed-loop feedback" to ensure that all employees' suggestions are reviewed and responded to	46%

In 65 percent of the firms, employees are empowered to do what it takes to satisfy customers. This does not mean making unreasonable promises (e.g., accepting an order for an out-of-stock item and then trying to interrupt a production schedule to fill the order). Rather, it means doing whatever is necessary to deliver on a reasonable promise once that promise has been made. This might mean authorizing premium transportation to meet a scheduled delivery date or arranging for shipment from an out of town warehouse if an unexpected shortage occurs.

In 57 percent of the companies that have a formal logistics improvement process, those employees responsible for executing improvements — the front-line people — drive the task of identifying and implementing such activities. This means the employees take ownership or responsibility for the results of their activities by identifying and correcting problems and improving processes to eliminate problems. Usually, the employees perform these tasks in a team setting.

Most companies have several kinds of quality-improvement teams. These include quality management boards, cross-functional improvement teams, natural work unit teams, and quality-improvement task forces. Quality management boards typically comprise senior line and staff managers. Their mission is to oversee the quality and productivity-improvement effort for their part of the business (e.g., a division). Specifically, they:

- Decide what criteria the company will use to gauge progress in implementing a quality-improvement process (e.g., Baldrige award criteria, ISO 9000, tailored criteria)

- Make sure the other teams have sufficient resources to do their jobs (e.g., training, proper staffing levels, access to key individuals)

- Select specific areas that promise the highest impact on strategic goals on which to focus (e.g., waste reduction, cycle time reduction, customer service improvement)

- Authorize and guide major process changes

- Track improvement for their part of the business

- Create quality task forces to work on specific issues

Cross-functional quality-improvement teams include managers, supervisors, and employees from more than one functional area. Usually, they are permanent, ongoing teams. These teams select their own improvement opportunities and focus on problems that cross division/department lines.

Natural work unit teams consist of managers, supervisors, and employees from one functional or activity area. These teams also are permanent and ongoing and can select their own improvement opportunities. Their scope is generally limited, however, to their own area. They are called natural work unit teams because they align directly with the formal organizational structure.

Quality-improvement task forces are ad hoc teams assembled to address a specific issue. Team members come from wherever management can find the best skills and experience.

In every case except the quality management board, employees at all levels participate actively. As one of the interviewees pointed out, involving employees in problem identification and problem solving simplifies the process of implementing solutions. People generally are enthusiastic supporters of their own ideas.

MOTIVATION OF EMPLOYEES

The final element in building employees' commitment to improvement is motivation. To motivate employees, many of the companies we interviewed used techniques based on the concept of performance management popularized by Aubrey C. Daniels. Performance management is founded on the straight-forward principle that behavior (performance) is a function of its consequences. Daniels advocates positive reinforcement (i.e., providing a desirable consequence) as the primary means to encourage behavior and thus improve performance. Positive reinforcement helps sustain improved performance. Other approaches such as negative reinforcement create situations where people improve performance only enough to avoid an undesirable consequence.

At the heart of the concept is the principle of feedback — providing information about performance that allows the employee to confirm or adjust behavior. Daniels' book, *Performance Management, Improving Quality Productivity Through Positive Reinforcement,* offers several useful suggestions on implementing positive reinforcement and feedback.[3]

Most companies we surveyed use some combination of monetary reward and nonmonetary recognition to motivate employees. In our survey, we found 74 percent of the firms use a formal employee recognition process to support their quality-improvement process in logistics.

Recognition takes many different forms and reflects the individual company's culture. Many companies we interviewed have Employee of the Month or Team of the Month awards to recognize exceptional performance. However, some others we interviewed avoid employee/team of the month awards preferring instead to recognize performance of all who merit it and not limit recognition to just one individual or team per month.

During our interviews, we saw several examples of recognition approaches. Federal Express has a "Bravo Zulu" award (a term borrowed from the U.S. Navy, which means "well done") that line managers can give to employees on the spot to recognize outstanding service. Federal Express also provides its "Golden Falcon" award to employees who provide exceptional service. These employees are recognized in a formal awards program. "Golden Falcon" award recipients also receive Federal Express common stock in recognition of their contribution.

Texas Instruments has a formal employee recognition program in which it gives monthly and quarterly awards. In addition, the company has a "Hall of Fame" where employees are recognized for exceptional contribution to quality improvement.

At Xerox, equipment logistics employees can earn monetary rewards by completing pre-approved quality-improvement projects.

On a more operational level, Trammell Crow Distribution Co. recognizes its employees for the "Catch of the Day." This means that the employee took some action that prevented a service failure from occurring.

In addition to these recognition type rewards, companies increasingly incorporate improved performance into employee compensation systems. Among the companies with formal quality-improvement processes for logistics, our survey found that 43 percent had reward systems linked to quality/customer service for all employees. An additional 19 percent had reward systems that applied to managerial levels.

These kinds of pay for performance systems are the way of the future according to Boyett and Conn in *Workplace 2000*. As they see it, annual increases tied to the cost of living or seniority will give way to pay increases for merit. The authors see the emergence of group based incentives such as gainsharing, pay for knowledge, and eventual participation in the ownership of the business as major elements of the compensation system in many firms by the year 2000.

Group performance compensation systems pay employees a bonus based on exceeding certain goals. Sometimes these bonuses are tied to cost reduction initiatives; other times they relate to profit improvement. Pay for knowledge systems recognize the contribution of an individual. The employee's base pay grows as he learns more skills and is capable of performing more duties. Pay for knowledge often is tied to cross-training of employees. Cross-training fosters flexibility in the work force, provides job enrichment for employees, and helps employees understand how more of the company's processes work. Employee ownership of the corporation usually is tied to an employee stock options plan (ESOP). The concept behind ESOP is that if employees own a part of the company they will take a greater interest in its success. Boyett and Conn cite a study that shows that combining ESOP with a high level of employee participation in decision making helps companies achieve significantly higher than average growth.[4]

We were encouraged to see that 43 percent of the survey respondents have reward systems linked to quality/customer service performance. In the book *A Passion for Excellence*, Tom Peters and Nancy Austin cite two examples in which groups of company presidents were asked for their views on their companies' top priorities. In both cases, the executives unanimously said long-term customer satisfaction. When asked how many had incorporated impartial, quantitative measures of long-term customer satisfaction in their personnel evaluation/compensation systems, the answer was none.[5] The results of our survey indicate things are changing for the better.

OWNERSHIP FOR IMPROVEMENT IS KEY

Throughout all our interviews, survey data analysis, and secondary research, one message became clear. Employee participation, involvement, and ownership for improvement is key to a successful quality and productivity-improvement process. Without it, companies struggle in the traditional "we versus they," "labor versus management" conflict. With employee participation, businesses find they not only get the minds of the people who know the problem and can find solutions they get the hearts of the same people responsible for making the improvements happen.

---

[1] Boyett, Joseph H., Ph.D., and Henry P. Conn, *Workplace 2000*
[2] Perry, Nancy J., "The Education Crisis: What Business Can Do"
[3] Daniels, Aubrey, C., Ph.D., *Performance Management, Improving Quality Productivity Through Positive Reinforcement*
[4] Boyett, Joseph H., Ph.D., and Henry P. Conn, *Workplace 2000*
[5] Peters, Tom and Nancy Austin, *A Passion for Excellence, The Leadership Difference*

CHAPTER 13

CARRYING OUT THE PROCESS
OF IMPROVEMENT

Although two-thirds of the business units surveyed have a formal quality and productivity-improvement process and 55 percent have a process in place in logistics, most companies' efforts are relatively new (see Figure 13-1). Three-quarters of the business units started their processes after 1986, and 25 percent initiated their improvement processes after 1989. Within logistics, similar statistics apply. This indicates that the majority of the improvement initiatives are still in early development.

Figure 13-1

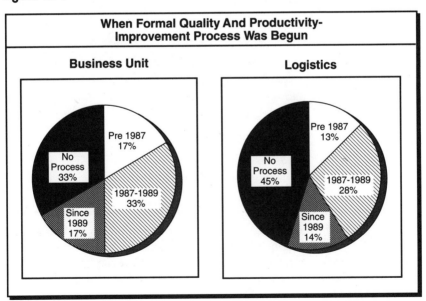

The purpose of Chapter 13 is to help companies without formal processes get started in quality and productivity improvement. It also aims to help those with new processes maintain momentum.

During our interviews, we asked those with successful processes to tell us what works and what doesn't, what made their processes successful, and what they would do differently next time. We summarize their advice in this chapter. We also offer guidelines for choosing potential improvement areas and review what our survey respondents said were the major hurdles in implementing quality and productivity improvement. First, though, we briefly discuss how survey participants approach the ongoing improvement process in logistics.

DRIVING FORCES FOR IMPROVEMENT

Figure 13-2 lists the major factors that prompted survey respondents to initiate an improvement process in logistics. For 72 percent of the firms, a major catalyst was their desire to gain advantage over competitors. In 66 percent of the cases, companies sought to reduce operating costs. Both of these reasons represent proactive decisions on the part of the companies.

Figure 13-2

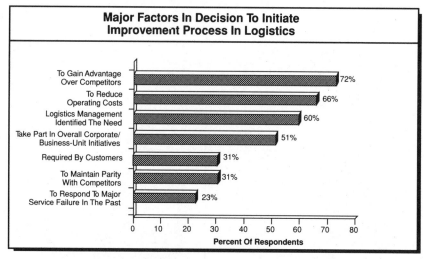

In 60 percent of the cases, a major factor contributing to the decision was logistics management identifying the need to do something about quality and productivity for logistics. In just over half the cases, the decision to act in the logistics area was at least partly driven by overall corporate/business-unit initiatives.

Another major factor for 31 percent of participants was a requirement by customers that the supplier initiate quality and productivity-improvement efforts. The need to maintain parity with competitors motivated another 31 percent. And responding to major service failures triggered 23 percent of the companies to act.

We also asked respondents to indicate the primary emphasis of the logistics improvement process and the extent to which it had changed between the 1980s and the 1990s (see Figure 13-3). In the 1980s, there was a clear emphasis on productivity improvement in logistics with 59 percent of respondents directing primary efforts there. For the 1990s, the emphasis has shifted dramatically. Forty-four percent of respondents indicate a quality-improvement emphasis, while the percent with a productivity-improvement emphasis dropped by half.

Figure 13-3

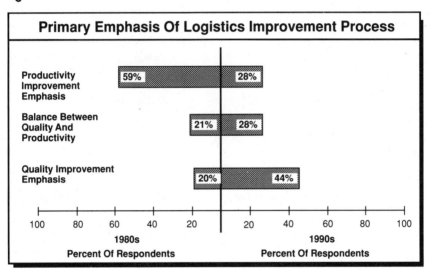

Figure 13-4 shows the interrelationship between quality and productivity-improvement processes for the surveyed companies. Two-thirds of the firms roll their quality and productivity efforts into a single process, while 13 percent say their quality process has replaced the productivity process of the past. In 21 percent of the companies, the two processes are separate and distinct. In such cases, companies must avoid any tendency to emphasize productivity improvement at the expense of quality.

Figure 13-4

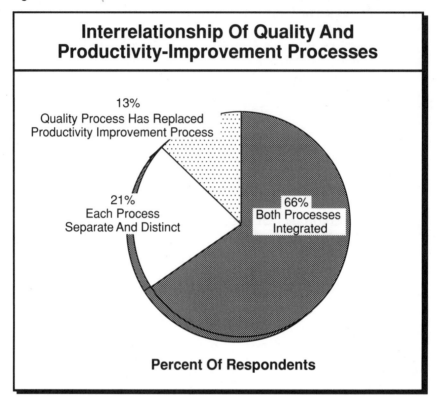

Interrelationship Of Quality And Productivity-Improvement Processes

13%
Quality Process Has Replaced
Productivity Improvement Process

21%
Each Process
Separate And Distinct

66%
Both Processes
Integrated

Percent Of Respondents

PREREQUISITES FOR SUCCESS

In our earlier research study that focused on productivity improvement in logistics, we found that companies with successful productivity-improvement processes shared seven common characteristics in their approaches. These companies:

• Managed the process of change with the same attention as they managed day to day operations

• Employed a project orientation for change

• Achieved early success and built more ambitious programs as they gained experience and support

• Focused on real productivity improvement rather than simply on cost reduction

- Communicated upward, laterally, and downward in order to publicize success and share the credit

- Spearheaded the program with a leader, a single key executive considered the motivating force by peers and the company

- Capitalized on triggers, major changes that created a fertile environment for substantial improvement

In our expanded 1991 research, we found these seven characteristics evident in successful quality-improvement processes as well. However, we discovered that these seven characteristics do not encompass all that is necessary for a firm to be successful in quality and productivity improvement.

Through our interviews and secondary research, we identified six other characteristics that are at least as important in determining a company's success in quality and productivity improvement. The six are:

- Absolute commitment and leadership by the CEO or equivalent

- Realistic expectations about the magnitude of the change involved

- Recognition that quality improvement requires the involvement of suppliers, service providers, and customers

- Major emphasis on employee involvement and ownership of improvement

- Tie-in between quality improvement and measurement and reward systems

- Strong information systems support for the improvement process

These six characteristics, along with the seven cited in the earlier research, create an environment for improvement and change in the company. We discuss each of the six characteristics identified in this year's research in the following paragraphs.

CEO commitment and leadership. In virtually every company we interviewed, the quality and productivity-improvement process was driven from the top of the organization. Most often this was the CEO but in some cases it was the divisional head of a major corporate unit. This individual sets the vision and agenda for quality and productivity improvement as well as the goals.

These top executives don't just pay lip service to quality. They demonstrate their commitment in decisions and actions by "walking the talk." In the successful companies, quality and productivity improvement is on the CEO's agenda every day.

Realistic expectations about the magnitude of change. For most companies, implementing a corporate-wide quality and productivity-improvement process requires a major culture change. For this reason, the CEO must drive the effort. Other executives generally lack the power base, perspective, and willingness to forgo short-term performance for long-term gains.

The degree of change required by a quality/productivity program surprises even those companies that go into the process with their eyes open. Xerox, for example, thought it could reach maturity in a corporate-wide quality-improvement process in four or five years. After spending three years making inroads, management concluded the process was in reality what the CEO called "a race without a finish line." For companies just beginning improvement processes, therefore, the experience of these trailblazers may help shorten the implementation time somewhat, but fundamental culture changes inevitably take time.

Recognition that improvement requires involvement of suppliers, service providers, and customers. Productivity improvement can occur within a company, a department, a factory, an office, or a warehouse. It is not necessarily dependent on the activities of people and processes outside a given unit. Quality improvement, on the other hand, is not so easy to achieve in isolation. At the very least, customers' requirements must be understood.

Without this understanding, the term "quality" is meaningless. Further, quality improvement usually involves third parties in meeting customer requirements. Few companies are fully vertically integrated; they must buy raw materials or component parts from someone. The quality of these materials or parts and the quality of service surrounding them directly affect the quality the company can provide its customers. Similarly, unless a firm handles all its distribution services, it must rely on service providers such as transportation companies and public warehouses to provide the final link between the company and its customer. Those businesses that succeed in improving quality make it a practice to involve their customers, suppliers, and service providers in the process.

Emphasis on employee involvement. As Chapter 12 points out, employees play a critical role in driving quality and productivity improvement. This is especially true in service oriented parts of the business such as the logistics process. Customer service representatives and delivery employees have direct contact with customers. Warehouse employees have the final responsibility to ensure product is shipped accurately, complete, undamaged, and properly labeled. Even on the purchasing side, a company's employees play a critical role in making sure the suppliers meet the needs of the company. Overall, successful companies realize employees are critical to providing quality service and improving quality.

Tie-in with rewards and recognition. As we noted earlier in Chapter 12, successful companies recognize that major benefits accrue from connecting quality and productivity performance to rewards and recognition. These rewards help focus attention on quality and productivity improvement and reinforce the culture change.

Systems support for the improvement process. Good measurement systems are basic to quality and productivity improvement. Successful companies make information support and technology available to aid measurement and analysis throughout the organization. They use these systems to measure quality of suppliers, logistics service providers, internal processes, and, most importantly, the ultimate service provided to customers.

GETTING STARTED IN LOGISTICS

Among the companies we surveyed, 45 percent had not yet instituted a formal process for logistics quality and productivity improvement. We address the following paragraphs to those firms. Our comments incorporate the advice gained from the 57 personal interviews conducted as a part of this research.

Building on an Existing Improvement Process

If your company already has a corporate quality and productivity-improvement process, our logistics interviewees recommend that you begin by taking advantage of that existing knowledge when starting a logistics program.

Learn from others. Seek out those people who already have experience with quality and productivity improvement and learn from them. Begin with those inside the company who have successful track records on improvement projects. From there, expand your research to include suppliers, customers, and logistics service providers who have experience in quality and productivity improvement. Often, these outside parties willingly share their experiences and insights. They realize they too will benefit from your improved quality.

Talking to others outside your immediate network of customers, suppliers, and service providers also can be of benefit. Logistics counterparts at companies that are recognized quality leaders can be a source of good ideas on technical matters as well as on more subjective matters like dealing with internal and external customers. As mentioned, some of these companies offer courses and formal education programs on quality improvement. If your firm offers no such training, these courses might be a good source of information on improvement issues and techniques.

Understand your company's customer service requirements. Because customer service requirements define logistics quality, the logistics manager must establish some understanding of what those requirements are. Section III of this book describes several techniques for determining customer requirements. If directly surveying customers is beyond the scope of your responsibilities, try to learn through your salesforce what customers expect and how they measure your performance.

Implement an improvement process. The process described in Section IV offers a starting point. It includes an improvement framework (the PDCA cycle), several tools and techniques for improvement (including process and statistical analysis), and ideas on quality and productivity measures. Chapter 11 also details an array of high-impact actions for consideration.

Work within your capabilities and management's comfort zone. If the quality and productivity process hasn't come to your part of the organization, it may be because senior management still is getting comfortable with the process. Some of the companies we interviewed experienced this kind of a situation. They recommend working within the senior manager's comfort zone. Until management is convinced that quality is here to stay, there's a natural tendency to emphasize traditional measures such as budget performance over quality and customer service oriented measures. This lack of conviction may constrain the logistics manager's efforts — at least temporarily.

At one company, the logistics manager encountered the comfort zone problem. He had to find nontraditional ways to improve traditional measures in order to stay within his manager's comfort zone. In other words, the logistics manager had to find a way to achieve quality and productivity improvement while still delivering the numbers for his boss. Naturally, this limited the kinds of improvements the logistics manager could undertake.

The second part of the comfort zone advice is a recommendation to work within your capabilities. In one sense, this means building a base in quality and productivity improvement within your own responsibilities before trying to expand. In another sense, it means recognizing your current strengths and weaknesses as you tailor a process to fit your capabilities.

Select the right kinds of actions. One way to think about this is to apply the Stages of Logistics Excellence framework discussed in Chapter 4. For parts of your logistics process that are in Stage I, efforts should focus on eliminating quality problems in everyday operations, i.e., making sure the essentials are done right. Efforts should also be directed at getting quick wins in productivity improvement. Good places to look for such opportunities are areas where inefficiencies or bottlenecks are readily apparent. These might include unnecessary handling of products in a warehouse, excessive waiting time by drivers for access to loading/unloading docks, and heavy use of emergency transportation services to make up for delays elsewhere in the logistics system.

Other places to look for obvious opportunities are areas where there are no controls. Examples here might include poor control over inventory shrinkage in a warehouse or lack of an auditing process for freight bill payments.

For areas of logistics in Stage II, actions might concentrate on providing superior service on the critical elements of customer service, handling exceptions in a hassle free manner, and supporting value-added efforts of others. On the productivity side, the focus of improvement actions for a Stage II operation is doing things *better*. Typically, data and analytical capability do not exist to support a thorough analysis for all alternatives to select the best for the operation. However, sufficient data, analytical capability, and practical experience exist to find an improved way to operate.

The types of improvements that are most effective for a Stage II operation take the form of better operational technology and reduction of underutilized capacity in warehouses, truck fleets, railcar fleets, staff levels, etc. Typically, improvements that focus within a single activity are carried out first. These would include:

- Concentrating shipments among a few qualified carriers and negotiating rate reductions

- Utilizing lane balancing to match round trip movements to reduce empty miles for carriers and/or private fleets

- Using better suited transportation equipment such as high-cube trailers and boxcars

- Purging obsolete inventory

- Consolidating warehouse locations (especially multiple public warehouses in the same area)

- Instituting inventory cycle counting to improve recordkeeping accuracy and spread out inventory taking work load across the year

In Stage III, the logistics process has a base of functional excellence upon which to build. Quality-improvement actions might center on providing differentiated, value-added service to customers. Productivity improvements come from fundamental changes to processes — doing things *differently* rather than just better. This includes integrating the logistics process across functional boundaries within the company and with customers, suppliers, and service providers.

The key point here is that what is right for one company's logistics process or for one part of the logistics process may not be right for another. Each logistics manager must make an honest appraisal of what the operation is capable of accomplishing and to what he is ready to commit.

The "VIP" approach to selecting actions may be a useful tool. This approach refers to a method used by several of the firms we interviewed of screening and prioritizing potential improvement actions. It looks at various problems or opportunities, examines the potential improvement actions, and compares the **visibility, impact,** and **probability of success** for each.

Visibility refers to a problem area or improvement opportunity that attracts a lot of attention. There is wide interest in solving the problem or seizing the opportunity. And success will produce measurable, tangible results.

Impact means the area is important enough to quality or productivity that improving it will build credibility, enthusiasm, and momentum.

Probability of success translates into tackling something that is not too complicated and is likely to produce results. It also means tackling something that people are willing to commit to and be a part of rather than something they shy away from for fear of failure.

By weighing the potential areas for improvement against these three criteria, you can improve the chances of success. As one of our interviewees put it, "Try to pick an area small enough to manage but large enough to matter. Get deep enough into the area to get yourself 'muddy.' Create goals that people can go after and put measures in place. Then document and publicize your results."

In selecting improvement projects, the interviewees offered one major word of caution: avoid making mistakes that will destroy credibility with employees. At the outset of a quality and productivity-improvement effort, employees tend to be cautious and wary. "Here comes the next program of the month," they say. Managers, therefore, should avoid actions such as:

- Implementing an employee suggestion system but then not using any of the suggestions

- Providing training to employees but then not letting them apply that training on the job

- De-emphasizing quality at the first sign that budget numbers won't come in as planned

- Creating a lot of hype without getting any quick wins

Create quick wins. Repeatedly, our interviewees stressed the need to achieve early or quick wins to establish credibility for the improvement process. Quick wins can come from something as simple as fixing a chronic problem that everyone knows about. Examples of such simple successes include:

- Fixing poor warehouse lighting that caused order pick errors and inaccurate inventory recordkeeping

- Staffing the customer service desk at lunch to avoid irritating customers and sales representatives trying to communicate with the department

- Working with chronic offenders whose late paperwork causes delays and subsequent rework by downstream internal customers

One person we interviewed tied together the concept of "VIP" and quick wins. "Make sure you get some quick wins," he said. "Find the pioneers in the organization who are willing to try something. Don't waste your time early on trying to overcome skepticism throughout the organization. There always will be skeptics, and the effort you use trying to convert them could have big payoffs if you use your energies working with the pioneers instead."

Another person we interviewed offered cautionary advice about the kind of results derived from some quick wins that employees may identify. "When we started out," he recalled, "our employees had all sorts of ideas for improvements — most of which had to do with improving the workplace rather than the process. The employees decided we needed new paint in the washrooms, new vending machines in the cafeteria, and a softball team. To maintain our credibility, we decided we had to support these ideas, although we also made it clear that what we really wanted were ideas on how to improve the operation itself."

At the beginning of any quality and productivity-improvement process there will be plenty of potential quick wins on which to work. This type of opportunity runs out after a while, our interviewees noted. At that point, managers need more sophisticated techniques — such as process and statistical analysis — to get at other opportunities.

Starting From Scratch

Nearly all of the companies we interviewed had formal improvement processes in place driven from top management levels. So when we asked them what an individual logistics manager could do on his or her own to get a quality and productivity-improvement process started, we got little firsthand advice. The few people we questioned who were on their own within their company as quality and productivity advocates offered some advice for starting a program in logistics. They said:

- Benchmark your logistics process (especially customer service) against others in your industry and communicate the results to management. Actions by competitors may impact management's views toward quality and productivity improvement.

- Supplement the benchmarking with case study material (e.g., articles, books, and this research report).

- Work within your own scope of responsibility to improve quality and productivity in your part of the logistics process.

- Obtain some training/education on structured approaches to problem solving and process improvement for yourself and your people. This gives you a common framework to begin quality improvement within your scope of responsibilities.

- If you have external interfaces (e.g., customers, service providers, or suppliers) within your scope of responsibilities, try to establish improvement processes with them.

- Try to improve internal customer service by enlisting allies who manage other parts of the logistics process.

- Finally, find a way to fund the effort emotionally by linking the quality and productivity-improvement efforts into something that is already on senior management's agenda.

Following this advice may help the logistics manager get an improvement process off the ground, but the task is not an easy one. In fact, trying to implement a logistics quality and productivity-improvement process inside a company that has no overall improvement initiative may be the greatest challenge a logistics manager faces in the 1990s.

MAINTAINING MOMENTUM

After a continuous improvement process has been in place for a while, it eventually begins to lose momentum. The initial enthusiasm and hype wears off; the "low hanging fruit" has all been picked; improvement teams are fatigued and some tough problems may have defied resolution. Or perhaps the window of opportunity created by a trigger has closed for one reason or another. Regardless of the cause, it is important to recognize that the continuous improvement process is not necessarily all that continuous. Most companies hit periodic plateaus.

According to our interviews, most firms hit their first plateau two to three years after they began their improvement process. They needed trigger points, rallying cries, and other ways of overcoming inertia to get the momentum going again.

Because such plateaus seem to be a natural part of any improvement process, we asked our interviewees how they maintain momentum. They suggested the following four basic steps. First, recognize you're at a plateau. Look for a slowing down of progress every 18 to 24 months. The trick is recognizing plateaus before they occur and having a plan in place to move through them quickly.

Next, look for breakthroughs as a way to rejuvenate the process. Try to avoid getting totally focused on continuous improvement. If you're losing momentum in an area, its probably because you have tapped all the readily identifiable opportunities for improvement. Further improvement will require some basic change in the process or activity.

Sometimes this requires another trigger point. Trigger points occur naturally in business (new competitors, new leadership, earnings shocks), but senior management can also create trigger points. Xerox's application for the Malcolm Baldrige award and its internal quality certification process acted as triggers to launch new breakthroughs. At Motorola, the CEO's call for a "Six Sigma" goal for 1992 was also a trigger. Once the company has a new mission and imperative for change, the breakthroughs can begin again. Of course, the reinvigorated process — like the start-up process — must produce early wins.

The third step in maintaining momentum involves switching to another area if progress in the current area is bogged down. Shifting from area to area keeps people from burning out on quality and productivity improvement. After an intensive effort in transportation, for example, a company might shift its attention to purchasing, inventory management, or warehousing.

To broach an area as yet untouched by quality and productivity improvement, one interviewee suggests the logistics manager arrange a meeting between the manager of that area and an improvement "guru" or expert who also can demonstrate real-world experience. Such a meeting could help get the manager involved and enthused.

Lastly, companies can sustain momentum by tying improvement to reward and recognition. This has become a recurring theme in this book. Several of the people we interviewed noted that improvement processes can bog down if the measurement and incentive systems don't support the commitment to improvement. Hype and excitement may keep a process going for the first year or two, but, over the long term, rewards and recognition are the elements that sustain a process.

ROLE OF THE CORPORATE LOGISTICS STAFF

Thus far in this chapter, we've directed our comments toward line logistics managers. A number of companies we interviewed also encouraged active participation in the logistics quality and productivity-improvement process on the part of the corporate logistics staff.

The corporate logistics staff can't drive quality improvement processes in individual divisions or operating units. Those processes must be engineered by the people responsible for delivering service to customers. Nevertheless, the corporate staff can help support a division's quality and productivity-improvement efforts in several ways. First, it can take the lead on cross-division initiatives such as working with the divisions to develop improvement processes with carriers and vendors. This is a common approach used by companies such as Westinghouse, PPG, Hewlett-Packard, Motorola, and Texas Instruments and usually takes the form of a corporate buying council (e.g., for logistics services or component parts). Each division, as well as the corporate staff, is represented. It is the corporate staff's job to establish policy and work with the vendors and carriers to set up quality-improvement processes. Since so many high-impact improvements require coordination or facilitation between operating units, the corporate staff is ideally positioned to drive corporate-wide improvements.

The corporate logistics staff can also support divisional initiatives with specialized training or analytical tools such as software that performs statistical analysis on vendor or carrier performance. Or it can act as an idea or "best practices" clearing house, disseminating the best thinking on a particular issue or improvement approach to all divisions. The corporate staff can also coordinate and support internal benchmarking efforts among the divisions. Overall, although it has only limited direct customer contact, the corporate logistics staff can play a valuable role in logistics quality and productivity-improvement processes.

GOAL SETTING

In talking with those interviewed companies that have the best improvement processes, we discovered a variety of reasons for their successes. All of them agreed, however, that aggressive goal setting was key to their programs. Why is aggressive goal setting important? In the words of Roger Milliken, CEO of Milliken and Company (*Fortune*, April 23, 1990), "You've got to shoot for objectives that stretch you, because then you force everyone to *find a better way* and not just do a little better."[1] (Emphasis added.)

Goals give meaning to measures; they help answer the question "How well am I doing?" Goals also help drive improved performance. Without goals, there is no way of knowing what is attainable and no way of knowing when you have gotten there.

There are two basic philosophies for setting goals. The first is incremental improvement, i.e., do better than last year. Several interviewees and secondary research authors caution against using incremental improvement goals. These kinds of goals only produce incremental results, they say. Incremental improvement does not challenge people to think differently about a problem. Rather, it asks them simply to find ways to push, poke, and adjust today's processes.

The second approach is setting a stretch goal based on best demonstrated practice or leadership goals (benchmarking is a good source for this information). Stretch goals act as magnets, drawing the company toward the goal. The only way to realize the stretch goal is to think differently about the process.[2] As an added benefit, customers tend to notice when you achieve a stretch goal. They rarely notice when you reach an incremental goal.

In their book, *Maximum Performance Management,* Henry Conn and Joseph Boyett describe three kinds of goals managers should use in their goal setting processes. The first is a long-term goal, i.e., a desired level of performance one or two years in the future. It usually represents a significant improvement over the current performance level. Also, it can be set by management dictate. "Six Sigma" at Motorola is a good example.

The second kind of goal is a short-term goal, attainable in a three- to 12-month time period. The short-term goal should be set at a level that exceeds recent average performance but doesn't surpass the current best. Rather than being imposed by management, the short-term goal should be negotiated between management and employees.

A third kind of goal is a minimum goal. This is a performance level that is less than or equal to the current average but not below the current worst. Minimum goals, like short-term goals, are negotiated. The short-term and minimum goals act as specification limits for the process or activity being measured.

Conn and Boyett believe that this three-tiered goal setting approach combines the best of incremental and stretch goals. It places an attainable goal in front of people over the short term yet keeps the stretch goal visible so opportunities for breakthroughs are not ignored.

Stretch goals can be abused. They should be used only if employees view them as attainable or so vital that failure to achieve them jeopardizes the company's well being. And finally, all goals, regardless of the type, should be specific (i.e., improve by 30 percent). A goal to "do better" is nearly as worthless as no goal at all.

IMPROVEMENT PROCESS PITFALLS

We conclude this chapter with a review of the major pitfalls and hurdles to quality and productivity improvement as revealed in our interviews and survey findings. Based on these findings, perhaps the greatest pitfall is focusing so intently on improving performance against a set of requirements that you fail to realize those requirements have changed. As one person put it, "Don't wind up shooting bull's eyes at where the target *was!*" To prevent such a mistake, the logistics quality and productivity-improvement process must tie in to ongoing updates on customer service strategy, service offerings, and service goals.

There are a number of other impediments to quality and productivity improvement in logistics as Figure 13-5 shows. Heading the list is inadequate information systems support. Almost two-thirds of the respondents cited this as a significant impediment, and nearly one-third said it is critically significant. Functional or organizational boundaries within a company were mentioned by 56 percent of the participants. It is interesting to note that in our last research study only 26 percent of respondents considered such boundaries a barrier to productivity improvement. This points out the difference between quality improvement in logistics (which requires multi-functional involvement) and *productivity* improvement (which can take place independently within individual parts of the logistics process).

Figure 13-5

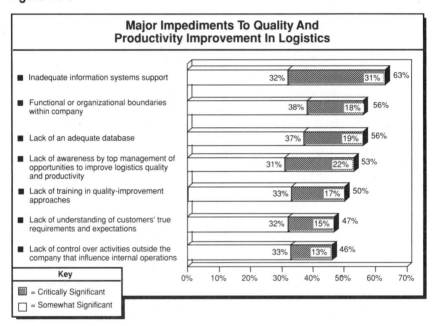

Another major difference exists between the 1983 and 1991 survey responses. In 1991, some 53 percent of respondents cited lack of aware-ness by top management of opportunities to improve logistics quality and productivity as a significant impediment. In the 1983 study, although the question dealt strictly with productivity improvement, only 28 percent of respondents ranked this as a major impediment.

Lack of understanding of customers' true requirements and expec-tations was a significant impediment for 47 percent of the respondents. This score contrasts sharply with responses to the Customer Expectations Survey (see Figure 6-6), which showed two things: over 60 percent of the customers view lack of understanding as a major impediment, and over 90 percent of customers thought suppliers' lack of understanding of how their actions affect customer quality and productivity was a major impediment.

LOOKING TO THE FUTURE

Managing the process of quality and productivity improvement in logistics is a complicated task. It requires new levels of employee involvement and ownership of the change process. It also involves being creative in setting up and running an improvement process. Chapters 12 and 13 covered these areas in detail and provided some hands-on advice for managers tackling the improvement challenge.

In the final section of this book, we summarize the results companies achieved in quality and productivity improvement in logistics and look at the future role the logistics process will play in creating value for customers and shareholders.

---

[1] Main, Jeremy, "How to Win the Baldrige Award"

[2] Boyett, Joseph H., Ph. D., and Henry P. Conn, *Maximum Performance Management, How to Manage and Compensate People to Meet World Competition*

SECTION VI

LOGISTICS QUALITY AND PRODUCTIVITY TO THE YEAR 2000

Since *Measuring Productivity in Physical Distribution* was released in 1978, hundreds of companies in the United States and throughout the world have made major gains in logistics productivity. During the 1980s, many of these firms also realized major gains in logistics service levels and cycle time performance.

In this final section, we summarize the successes of the past and look to the future. Chapter 14 presents statistical data on productivity, service levels, and cycle time improvements to date as well as expectations for the future. Chapter 15 looks ahead to the 21st century and draws conclusions about the role the logistics process will play in creating competitive advantage.

CHAPTER 14

BENEFITS OF
LOGISTICS IMPROVEMENT

Ultimately, the success of a quality and productivity-improvement process in logistics must be measured in terms of tangible results. We asked survey respondents to indicate the results they had achieved in the past five years in productivity improvement, service improvement, and cycle time reduction. We also asked for their expectations for further gains in the next five years. This chapter summarizes their responses.

PRODUCTIVITY IMPROVEMENT

For logistics overall, the companies in the 1991 survey reported a 10 percent productivity improvement from 1985 through 1990. They anticipate an additional 11 percent productivity improvement in the coming five years. Figure 14-1 displays these data along with improvement data by logistics activity — transportation, warehousing and materials handling, materials planning and control, purchasing, information systems, and management. When compared with the 1983 data, these results represent a decline in the rates of improvement. In that study, overall productivity improvement from 1978 through 1983 averaged 12.6 percent, and respondents projected an additional 12.5 percent over the subsequent five years for a total of 25.1 percent productivity improvement. The 1991 survey's total productivity improvement (achieved and expected) was 21 percent — 10 percent achieved and an additional 11 percent projected.

For those activities on which we have comparable data, we found that between the 1983 and 1991 studies transportation productivity improvements over a ten-year period dropped from 23 to 20 percent. Additionally, warehousing and materials handling improvements dipped slightly from 23.4 to 23 percent.

Figure 14-1

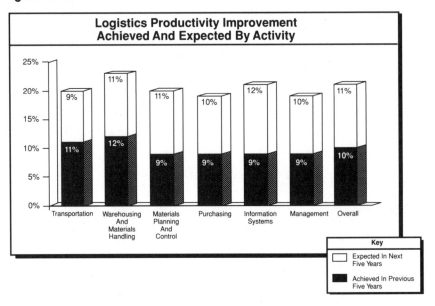

The dip in expectations uncovered by this study is due in part to the shift in emphasis in logistics from traditional productivity improvement to quality improvement and cycle time reduction. The data in Figure 14-2 support this shifting emphasis. In the traditional "gold mines" of logistics productivity improvement — transportation and warehousing — respondents' expectations decline for the coming five years. For transportation, 51 percent of respondents reported improvements greater than 10 percent from 1985 to 1990. During the next five years, however, only 32 percent expect improvements exceeding 10 percent. A similar, although less noticeable, decline appears in warehousing and materials handling.

In contrast to these declines, participants show increasing expectations regarding the nontraditional sources of productivity improvement in logistics. For example, in the case of materials planning and control, only 40 percent of the respondents reported earning productivity improvements in excess of 10 percent in the last five years. However, 48 percent project they will achieve at least 10 percent improvement in the next five years.

Despite the shift away from traditional sources of productivity improvement and a decline in overall expectation levels for the future, we still found a familiar pattern in the statistical distribution of improvement projections. As Figure 14-3 shows, companies that have made the greatest logistics productivity improvement gains in the past set goals to achieve similar improvements for the future. However, those that have not achieved any gains in the past set only incremental goals. This pattern was first identified in the 1978 study and has since been found in the 1983 update and in companion studies in Europe conducted during 1981 and 1986.

Figure 14-2

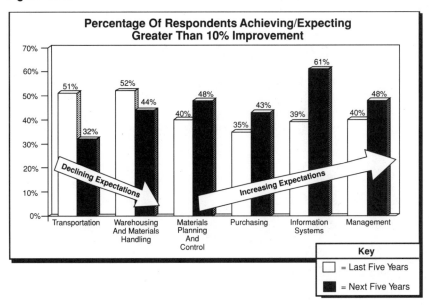

Figure 14-3

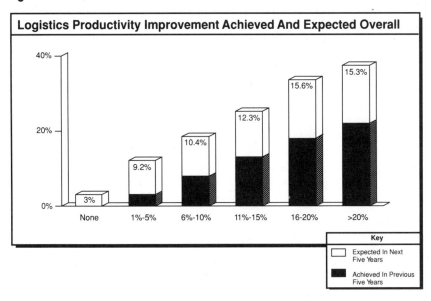

SERVICE IMPROVEMENT

Throughout this book, we've stressed that productivity improvements are only meaningful if they are compatible with providing ongoing customer satisfaction. For example, delaying shipments to build full truckloads and thereby missing delivery due dates is not a means to productivity improvement. In the logistics process, therefore, productivity improvement must be viewed as the secondary objective. The primary objective is to provide service that meets customer requirements.

Meeting customer requirements, i.e., service quality, should be measured on a customer by customer basis. This survey did not permit that depth of analysis with the firms we studied. Nevertheless, the research did reveal that businesses, in general, are improving the *levels* of customer service they provide on five key performance dimensions. These include:

- On-time performance

- Order completeness

- Line-item fill rate

- Invoice accuracy

- Damage-free receipt

Figure 14-4 summarizes actual service levels for 1985 and 1990 and expected service levels for 1995 for survey respondents. It also shows the improvement in these service levels as measured by reduction in errors/failure rate. A 96 percent on-time performance, for instance, represents a 4 percent failure rate. Boosting performance to 98 percent cuts the failure rate to 2 percent — a 50 percent improvement.

In all five dimensions listed in Figure 14-4, service levels improved significantly between 1985 and 1990. What is more notable, however, is that the respondents expect even greater improvements on each dimension over the next five years. By 1995, service levels ranging between 95 and 98 percent, depending on the service dimension, will be the *average* goals of suppliers. Individual industries and companies may be setting much higher goals, thus raising the stakes for the competition.

To gain further insights into goals for the future, we studied past performance and future expectations for each service dimension on an industry by industry basis.

Figure 14-5 presents on-time performance data by industry. Survey respondents reported sharp decreases in service failures between 1985 and 1990. The reductions range from a low of 41 percent for the food and beverage sector to a high of 73 percent for the automotive industry.

Participants anticipate similar improvements between 1990 and 1995. In most industries, the 1995 on-time performance goal is 96 percent or better.

Figure 14-4

Logistics Service Quality Improvements				
	Service Level			Reduction In Error Or Failure Rate	
Service Area	1985 Actual	1990 Actual	1995 Expected	Achieved 1985-1990	Expected 1990-1995
■ On-time performance	81.4%	91.6%	97.0%	55%	66%
■ Order completeness	83.1%	89.6%	95.0%	39%	52%
■ Line-item fill rate	87.0%	92.8%	96.4%	45%	50%
■ Invoice accuracy	90.3%	94.3%	97.9%	42%	64%
■ Damage-free receipt	92.2%	95.1%	97.2%	37%	43%

Figure 14-5

On-Time Performance By Industry				
	Service Level			Reduction In Error Or Failure Rate	
Industry Group	1985 Actual	1990 Actual	1995 Goal	1985-1990 Actual	1990-1995 Expected
Agricultural	84.6%	93.8%	96.6%	60%	45%
Automotive	82.3%	95.2%	98.6%	73%	71%
Chemicals And Plastics	84.3%	91.1%	97.1%	43%	67%
Clothing And Textiles	62.2%	82.6%	94.6%	54%	69%
Computer Hardware	73.1%	92.3%	98.0%	71%	74%
Electrical Machinery	63.3%	86.7%	94.8%	64%	61%
Electronics	76.5%	89.5%	97.5%	55%	76%
Food And Beverage	84.7%	91.0%	96.5%	41%	61%
General Merchandise	77.9%	93.0%	96.9%	68%	56%
Paper And Related	91.8%	95.8%	99.0%	49%	76%
Pharmaceuticals And Drugs	86.4%	95.1%	97.7%	64%	53%

In the area of order completeness, we surveyed past, present, and future service level performance by industry (see Figure 14-6). We found the 1995 goals range from about 85 percent in the automotive industry to 98 percent in the paper and electronics industries. Between 1985 and 1990, improvements ranged from 25 to 59 percent with most industries expecting bigger gains in the coming five years.

A third dimension — line-item fill rate — is shown in Figure 14-7. In general, the industries listed made major gains in reducing order fill rate failure between 1985 and 1990. They expect similar gains in the future. One exception is the paper industry. Its gains are not as large because the industry started out in 1985 at a fairly high service level (93.6 percent) and had less room for improvement.

Figure 14-6

Order Completeness By Industry					
		Service Level		Reduction In Error Or Failure Rate	
Industry Group	1985 Actual	1990 Actual	1995 Goal	1985-1990 Actual	1990-1995 Expected
Agricultural	85.0%	91.0%	95.3%	40%	48%
Automotive	81.4%	89.7%	97.0%	45%	71%
Chemicals And Plastics	84.5%	91.1%	97.0%	43%	66%
Clothing And Textiles	67.0%	81.6%	92.8%	44%	61%
Computer Hardware	87.2%	93.2%	97.0%	47%	56%
Electrical Machinery	61.3%	71.2%	87.3%	26%	56%
Electronics	91.7%	93.8%	98.7%	25%	79%
Food And Beverage	89.0%	92.1%	96.6%	28%	57%
General Merchandise	90.0%	95.9%	98.2%	59%	56%
Paper And Related	93.7%	95.8%	98.1%	33%	55%
Pharmaceuticals And Drugs	84.1%	90.3%	94.6%	39%	44%

Figure 14-7

Line-Item Fill Rate By Industry					
		Service Level		Reduction In Error Or Failure Rate	
Industry Group	1985 Actual	1990 Actual	1995 Goal	1985-1990 Actual	1990-1995 Expected
Agricultural	85.0%	93.0%	96.4%	53%	49%
Automotive	87.1%	92.8%	95.3%	44%	35%
Chemicals And Plastics	85.8%	91.2%	97.0%	38%	66%
Clothing And Textiles	62.0%	84.4%	94.5%	59%	65%
Computer Hardware	76.7%	90.0%	97.5%	57%	75%
Electrical Machinery	71.2%	83.7%	94.7%	43%	67%
Electronics	78.0%	88.5%	95.0%	48%	56%
Food And Beverage	94.3%	96.4%	98.4%	37%	56%
General Merchandise	89.3%	95.9%	98.1%	62%	54%
Paper And Related	93.6%	94.7%	96.0%	17%	24%
Pharmaceuticals And Drugs	90.1%	93.7%	96.6%	36%	46%

Figure 14-8 shows invoice accuracy rates by industry. In nearly every sector, the invoice accuracy goal for 1995 is at least 98 percent. In the computer hardware and electronics industries, respondents said they were targeting 100 percent invoice accuracy.

The final dimension measured is damage-free receipt by industry (see Figure 14-9). Companies currently do fairly well in this area, and the general goal for 1995 seems to be 98 percent or better.

Each of these comparisons demonstrates the strong commitment survey companies have to improving service levels in logistics.

Figure 14-8

Invoice Accuracy Rate by Industry					
	Service Level			Reduction In Error Or Failure Rate	
Industry Group	1985 Actual	1990 Actual	1995 Goal	1985-1990 Actual	1990-1995 Expected
Agricultural	85.8%	92.3%	96.7%	46%	57%
Automotive	93.9%	95.7%	99.3%	29%	84%
Chemicals And Plastics	85.6%	89.3%	93.0%	26%	35%
Clothing And Textiles	88.7%	97.0%	98.2%	73%	40%
Computer Hardware	98.0%	99.0%	100.0%	50%	100%
Electrical Machinery	87.5%	94.7%	98.0%	58%	62%
Electronics	95.0%	98.4%	100.0%	68%	100%
Food And Beverage	90.0%	93.7%	98.0%	37%	68%
General Merchandise	88.6%	94.4%	98.8%	51%	79%
Paper And Related	95.2%	96.5%	98.1%	27%	46%
Pharmaceuticals And Drugs	93.0%	96.5%	99.0%	50%	71%

Figure 14-9

Damage-Free Receipt By Industry					
	Service Level			Reduction In Error Or Failure Rate	
Industry Group	1985 Actual	1990 Actual	1995 Goal	1985-1990 Actual	1990-1995 Expected
Agricultural	90.2%	91.7%	97.3%	15%	67%
Automotive	93.6%	96.0%	99.4%	37%	85%
Chemicals And Plastics	94.7%	96.8%	98.9%	40%	66%
Clothing And Textiles	88.5%	95.5%	98.3%	61%	62%
Computer Hardware	97.4%	98.0%	99.2%	23%	60%
Electrical Machinery	89.9%	96.2%	99.0%	62%	74%
Electronics	96.0%	97.7%	99.7%	42%	87%
Food And Beverage	91.9%	95.7%	98.2%	47%	58%
General Merchandise	89.8%	94.8%	98.2%	49%	65%
Paper And Related	95.9%	96.8%	97.8%	22%	31%
Pharmaceuticals And Drugs	94.8%	97.2%	98.8%	46%	57%

SERVICE GOALS VERSUS REQUIREMENTS

As mentioned in our earlier discussions of benchmarking, data such as the statistics presented in this chapter should be used with caution. The service goals presented — even subdivided by industry — represent broad averages. The 1990 figures show what companies have achieved; they do not present what the customers actually required.

Judging from the data presented in Section III, some major gaps between service offerings and customer requirements currently exist. This means that while the 1995 goals may represent substantial improvements over today's performance, they do not necessarily reflect what customers will require in the future. Very high goals of 99 percent and above may not be good enough for some customers. Conversely, such high goals may constitute a level of service and cost that some customers don't need and are unwilling to pay for. In light of this variability, we encourage readers to seek customer input as they set future service goals.

CYCLE TIME REDUCTION

Beyond productivity and service quality improvement, there is a third measure of logistics process performance — cycle times. Figure 14-10 summarizes the logistics related cycle times for order processing and internal inventory replenishment among the companies in our database. In each case, the cycle times expected for 1995 are about half those achieved in 1985.

Figure 14-10

Logistics Cycle Time Reductions					
	Cycle Time			Improvement	
Service Area	1985 Actual	1990 Actual	1995 Expected	Achieved 1985-1990	Expected 1990-1995
■ Order cycle time	15.2 days	10.7 days	7.8 days	30%	28%
■ Internal inventory replenishment	35.2 days	26.5 days	18.4 days	25%	31%

Figure 14-11 and Figure 14-12 display cycle time data by industry. The order cycle times shown in Figure 14-11 for the agricultural, automotive, and paper industries indicate reductions of two-thirds or more from 1985 to 1995. The inventory replenishment statistics in Figure 14-12 show reductions of 60 percent in the automotive industry and 55 percent in the computer hardware sector. These cycle time reductions offer great potential for lower inventories and more responsive customer service.

IMPLICATIONS FOR THE FUTURE

The data presented in this section point to a clear trend in the decade ahead. The value created by logistics will not come primarily from productivity improvement and cost reduction. Instead, it will come from setting and meeting aggressive service and cycle time reduction goals to meet customer requirements. In the next and final chapter of this report, we explore what this means for the logistics process and for logistics management in the decade ahead.

Figure 14-11

	Order Cycle Times By Industry				
	Cycle Time (Days)			Improvement	
Industry Group	**1985 Actual**	**1990 Actual**	**1995 Goal**	**1985-1990 Achieved**	**1990-1995 Expected**
Agricultural	14.9	8.7	5.3	42%	39%
Automotive	20.4	9.7	4.8	52%	50%
Chemicals And Plastics	8.9	6.1	5.0	31%	18%
Clothing And Textiles	17.6	12.5	9.3	29%	25%
Computer Hardware	68.0	56.1	50.9	17%	9%
Electrical Machinery	12.9	7.9	5.3	39%	33%
Electronics	11.6	13.7	8.8	-18%	36%
Food And Beverage	7.1	6.2	4.9	13%	21%
General Merchandise	7.9	5.8	3.8	27%	34%
Paper And Related	8.1	4.3	3.0	47%	30%
Pharmaceuticals And Drugs	10.2	7.3	5.5	28%	25%

Figure 14-12

	Inventory Replenishment Cycle Times By Industry				
	Cycle Time (Days)			Improvement	
Industry Group	**1985 Actual**	**1990 Actual**	**1995 Goal**	**1985-1990 Actual**	**1990-1995 Expected**
Agricultural	45.0	34.3	32.5	24%	5%
Automotive	50.6	38.7	20.4	23%	47%
Chemicals And Plastics	28.0	21.8	16.2	22%	26%
Clothing And Textiles	22.7	15.2	11.0	33%	28%
Computer Hardware	48.5	36.7	22.0	24%	40%
Electrical Machinery	10.5	7.0	5.0	33%	29%
Electronics	71.0	55.5	37.0	22%	33%
Food And Beverage	16.2	12.0	8.9	26%	26%
General Merchandise	34.2	25.1	19.4	27%	23%
Paper And Related	24.7	19.3	15.5	22%	20%
Pharmaceuticals And Drugs	55.1	41.0	26.2	26%	36%

CHAPTER 1

A VIEW TO
THE FUTURE

Ten years ago, 99 percent service levels were practically unheard of in many industries. Now, many companies are striving for 99 percent and several are achieving it consistently. But 99 percent will not be good enough in the future. In our everyday lives, consider what a 99 percent quality standard would mean:

- 200,000 prescriptions filled incorrectly each day

- Water unsafe to drink four days per year

- 14 flat tires per car per year

- 180 aborted takeoffs or landings per day

- Five typographical errors per printed page

For today's pioneers, 99 percent already isn't good enough. Motorola's "Six Sigma" goal by 1992 is equivalent to meeting requirements 99.9999998 percent of the time (or an allowable failure rate of 3.4 times per million operations). Even that performance level will not be good enough for Motorola and, in turn, for its suppliers as the 21st century draws near.

This relentless pursuit of improvement will continue to raise customer expectations throughout industry. To compete, companies must expand and accelerate the improvement processes begun in the 1980s. To sustain such continuous improvement, businesses must recognize that individual customer requirements are evolving at an accelerating pace as these customers develop their own strategies to add value to their customers. Therefore, suppliers must develop flexible, tailored service offerings to accommodate each customer. To deliver a tailored customer response, companies must integrate key business processes internally, overcoming traditional organizational and functional boundaries as they mature into Stage III organizations. As they move toward Stage IV, they must operate as partners with customers *and* suppliers to remove redundancies and waste and to streamline the total logistics process. Each partner's role will be to add unique value to the joint goal of meeting and exceeding the ultimate consumer's expectations. Only by working together and extending their vision throughout the supply chain can firms find ways to make *their* total bundle of products and services the most attractive one in the eyes of the final consumer.

In this last chapter of our report, we summarize the lessons learned in our research. We also postulate how leading companies will use the logistics process to achieve competitive advantage in the coming decade. Finally, we offer suggestions for logistics executives and other senior executives on how to use the logistics process to position their companies for the 21st century.

DEVELOPING A CUSTOMER-FOCUSED SERVICE STRATEGY

We began this report by explaining how companies sustain long-term competitive advantage by providing superior value to customers and to shareholders. The definition of what constitutes customer value is a moving target. Customers are becoming more demanding in response to their own customers' requirements. Worldwide competitors seek to provide value to these customers through innovative product and service packages. As new markets such as eastern Europe, Latin America, and China open up, new customer demands emerge from markets extending around the globe. For many companies, action plans to provide superior customer value will be built upon a customer-focused service strategy.

As we explained in Section III, developing a customer-focused strategy begins by understanding customer requirements. This includes determining what factors will influence a customer to buy more or less from a particular vendor. It also includes understanding what the customer views as the essentials and what other components of service constitute value-added. Based on our survey, many companies can improve how they go about understanding customer requirements. For some companies, this means doing something as fundamental as asking the customer rather than relying on internal opinions or competitor actions. For leading companies, this means gaining an even more intimate knowledge of the customer's business. These companies will move beyond just understanding the current requirements and will begin to anticipate value-added requirements that may not even have been recognized by the customer.

Once a company understands customer requirements, the next step is to formulate a service strategy. As we discussed in Section III, not all things are equally valuable to customers. And for some service dimensions, customers only differentiate between suppliers based on discernibly inferior and discernibly superior service. Learning how to use this knowledge wisely and creatively will be key.

Companies simply cannot afford to provide every possible service to every possible customer. Instead, they will choose the dimensions of service upon which they want to compete — the ones that add value to customers. Also, they will integrate the service package with their pricing strategy (using approaches such as customer profitability analysis) to ensure that they are creating value for both shareholders and customers.

Companies will then develop and execute processes to deliver the basics of their customer service strategies flawlessly and to deliver a unique package of the value-added services to each customer profitably. Finally, companies will measure service performance in the customers' terms rather than using internally focused measures. There will be two-way feedback between customers and their suppliers on service performance. Each will measure service performance of the other and use this to drive ongoing improvement. Suppliers will actively seek customer input on a regular basis to help identify improvements and to anticipate changing needs. Customers will seek supplier input on better ways to accomplish their joint goals.

The companies in our Logistics Management Survey recognize the increasing demands for service improvement that are coming from the marketplace. Many have already acted. As Figure 15-1 shows, the respondents already report average reductions in service failures of 37 to 55 percent on five key service dimensions (on-time performance, order completeness, fill rate, invoice accuracy, and damage-free receipt) during the period 1985 to 1990. Over the ten-year period from 1985 to 1995, they expect to drive average service failures down by a total of between 65 and 84 percent on these measures. However, these improvements may not be good enough. Based on the 1990 statistics, only two of the measures of service failures (invoice accuracy and damage-free receipt) are at the three sigma (66,810 failures per million) level and, even by 1995, none will be at the four sigma (6,210 failures per million) level. With companies such as Motorola leading the charge toward "Six Sigma," will customers be content by 1995 to accept service failure rates that are orders of magnitude worse?

Reduced service failure is only one dimension of what customers expect from the logistics process. The other major component is accelerated cycle times. Between 1985 and 1990, the typical company in our Logistics Management Survey reduced its order cycle time by 30 percent and its inventory replenishment cycle time by 25 percent. For the decade between 1985 and 1995, the typical companies in our survey project a total reduction in cycle times approaching 50 percent (see Figure 15-2).

Figure 15-1

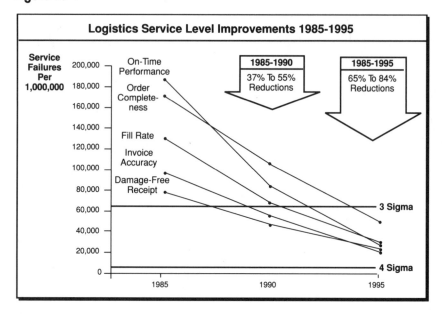

Figure 15-2

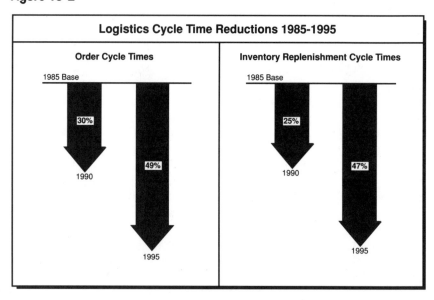

Several companies we interviewed have already reduced their order cycle times and inventory replenishment cycle times by two-thirds or more since 1985 and project significant increases into the future. To accomplish these major gains, the companies fundamentally re-engineered their processes and, just to keep up, their competitors will need to do likewise. By taking examples from other industries of what can be accomplished, leading firms will continue to look beyond refining today's processes and look instead at simplifying and ultimately eliminating whole steps. Benchmarking (a process of identifying improvements not just gathering competitive performance measures) will be a tool used by many companies to identify and explore new options for re-engineering their processes.

INTEGRATING KEY BUSINESS PROCESSES

During the 1990s, companies committed to continuous improvement will continue to make quality and productivity improvements within functions. Successful companies and successful managers within them will recognize that such improvement is driven by employee ownership of the improvement process. This means that logistics managers at the middle management ranks will find their roles continuing to evolve from the command and control responsibilities prevalent in the 1980s toward the role of enablers, coaches, and facilitators to help the work force and management improve operations.

Some companies have already been very successful in moving their improvement focuses beyond functional boundaries to include cross-functional teams and efforts. As the 1990s unfold, other companies will follow suit. However, cross-functional cooperation and coordination will not happen without effort. To succeed, it must become part of the overall change in corporate culture and values that accompanies quality and productivity-improvement initiatives.

Most companies still operate in a Stage III company culture with traditional functional objectives that are in conflict with one another. As Figure 15-3 shows, the marketing department is typically measured on share growth with little weight given to the effects on operations of actions to achieve that growth. Distribution is often measured on low transportation and warehousing cost with less emphasis on customer service attributes such as on-time delivery or damage-free goods. Research and development is often measured on the number of products it develops with less attention given to marketability, manufacturability, or cost of those products. Purchasing is often measured on low unit price but, as we discussed in Chapter 11, this can often lead to wrong decisions about selecting suppliers. The finance department wants to use capital productively so it applies pressure to keep inventories down even though this may result in shortages of critical items while warehouses burst with slow moving or discontinued inventory.

Figure 15-3

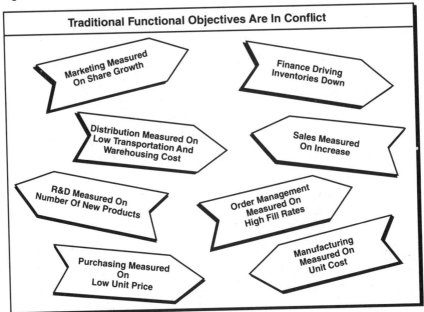

Traditional Functional Objectives Are In Conflict

Marketing Measured On Share Growth

Finance Driving Inventories Down

Distribution Measured On Low Transportation And Warehousing Cost

Sales Measured On Increase

R&D Measured On Number Of New Products

Order Management Measured On High Fill Rates

Purchasing Measured On Low Unit Price

Manufacturing Measured On Unit Cost

The sales department is measured on increased sales often without regard to cost or profitability. The order management function is measured on high fill rates, which often are measured differently than the customer views them. Manufacturing is often measured on low unit cost, driving them to economies of scale associated with long production runs.

None of these *functional* objectives directly addresses the business objectives of meeting customer requirements (the Stage III corporate goal) or creating customer value (the Stage IV goal).

For companies to successfully execute a customer-focused strategy in the 1990s, they will need to:

- Establish common (or at least compatible) objectives, supported by measurement and reward systems that encourage cooperation and not conflict, for each function involved in delivering customer satisfaction (see Figure 15-4)

- Achieve functional excellence (Stage III) for each function involved to establish a platform for interfunctional improvements

- Shift emphasis from functional excellence to business process excellence (Stage IV)

Figure 15-4

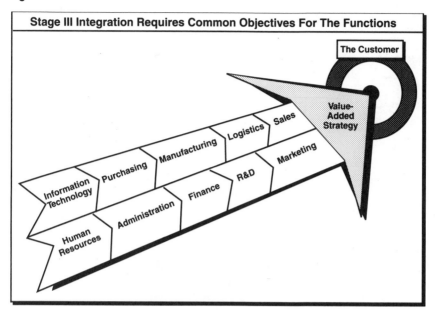

One basis for establishing common objectives is integrated planning as described in Chapter 11. This begins with integration of the strategies of the major functions of the business and extends to tactical planning (e.g., monthly supply/demand balancing). The integration even extends to the transaction level using computer technology as a way to support the re-engineering of processes instead of just automating the chaos in existing processes.

Functional excellence in logistics was described in Chapter 4. The major characteristics of Stage III are that the function is measured against standards and goals (as opposed to just against budget), the planning horizon extends beyond this week or this month, logistics integrates with other parts of the business, and the service goals and service focuses are differentiated to reflect a service strategy that meets the unique needs of each customer. The other major business functions such as manufacturing, marketing, sales, finance, research and development, and human resources will all need to be functionally excellent in their own right, with no laggard functions, before the company can successfully make the transition to a business process orientation. Without functional excellence of all of these key players, the chain will break at its weakest link.

Once goals and objectives are aligned and the company has achieved functional excellence in each major function, senior management can orchestrate the move to Stage IV where integration shifts the emphasis from functional excellence to business process excellence (see Figure 15-5). This shift to key business processes extends out to the customer and back to the suppliers, weaving together the functions of each of the three parties into a single process.

Figure 15-5

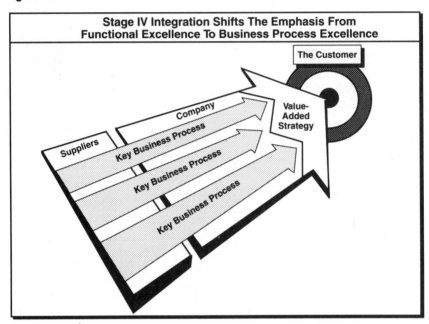

Stage IV Integration Shifts The Emphasis From Functional Excellence To Business Process Excellence

This move from Stage III to Stage IV, the integration breakthrough, offers challenges and opportunities for both logistics managers and senior executives. Once logistics has achieved functional excellence, the emphasis shifts to broader and broader business issues that cross functional and company boundaries. And just as all managers must adapt to a new style of managing employees (e.g., coaching and facilitating), both general and functional executives must adapt to a new style of cooperative management with counterparts up and down the supply chain and across the management hierarchy.

In many situations, the logistics manager will be "on the point," leading process improvement with both suppliers and customers. This should serve as valuable experience for the logistics executive to progress to a more general management role.

FOCUSING ON THE CONSUMER

To this point, our primary focus in this book has been on business to business logistics quality and productivity improvement. However, we recognize that nothing is really accomplished in the long term until the cash register rings and the ultimate *consumer* buys the product or service. Thus, the entire logistics process from raw material sources to the retail shelf (or to home delivery) will need to be better integrated as we enter the 21st century. This is a requirement if companies are to improve quality, speed up responsiveness, reduce cost, and add value in the eyes of the final consumer (see Figure 15-6). This means that *all* members of the logistics process need to work as a team — raw material suppliers, manufacturers, wholesalers, retailers, and a host of supporting partners all working to improve quality, eliminate waste, and add value.

Figure 15-6

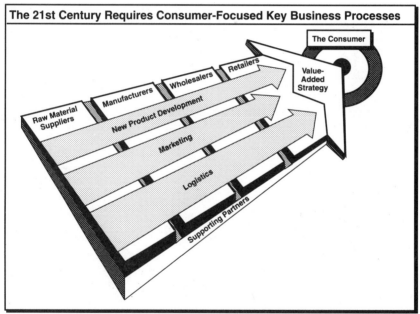

This re-engineering of the *entire* logistics process starts by understanding consumer requirements and rapidly feeding these back upstream to the various partners. It is supported by achieving Stage III functional excellence among *all* members of the supply chain so that there are no weak links and the productivity gains can be used to fund the cost of re-engineering. Finally, it means developing compatible goals and objectives for supply chain partners, which taken together will meet the needs and exceed the expectations of the final consumer. This is the ultimate Stage IV process that we believe will evolve into the dominant focus of successful enterprises in the 21st century.

CONCLUDING REMARKS

Companies are in business to create customer and shareholder value. We believe that integration across supply chain partners will be the key to achieving this goal for the 21st century. Excellence across the logistics process is a prerequisite to such integration. We hope that the concepts and examples presented in this book will help you and your company to improve logistics quality and productivity and thus achieve excellence in the decade ahead and competitive advantage in the 21st century.

TABLE OF CONTENTS: APPENDIXES

APPENDIX A: MEASURING QUALITY AND PRODUCTIVITY IN TRANSPORTATION

INTRODUCTION

The purpose of this appendix is to help companies develop or improve their transportation quality and productivity measurement systems and begin or expand their quality and productivity-improvement processes. It is divided into the following sections:

I.   Definition of Transportation Activities Included in this Appendix

II. Potential Measures for Transportation Management

- Quality
- Productivity
- Other key measures

III. Survey Respondents' Use of Actions to Improve Quality and Productivity in Transportation

Section I provides specific definitions of transportation activities used in this appendix to ensure clarity and understanding. Section II presents and discusses several measures that may be used to monitor quality and productivity. Section III presents the results of our Logistics Management Survey regarding quality and productivity-improvement actions that are currently in use to improve transportation.

This appendix is based on the concepts presented in the main report of this study. Thus, the reader is urged to carefully read and understand the contents of the main report before reading this appendix and to refer to the main report when using this appendix.

Although this appendix is not directed at those companies that are in the for-hire transportation business, many of the concepts of measurement and the improvement actions themselves may be of use and interest to carrier management.

I. DEFINITION OF TRANSPORTATION ACTIVITIES

Each company's transportation system is unique. Its traffic lanes and traffic volumes, the carriers used, the size and role of the private fleet, and the organization charged with managing transportation all differ in terms of the services provided and the costs incurred.

However, for purposes of measuring and improving transportation quality and productivity, transportation can be viewed as having the following components:

- Transportation strategy development
- Transportation management
  - Overall transportation management
  - Purchased transportation operations

— Private fleet over-the-road (OTR) trucking operations
— Private fleet pickup and delivery trucking operations
— Railcar/barge fleet management

As shown in Figure A-1, each of these components is related to the others. For example, developing a transportation strategy is a broad issue that drives the overall transportation management process. The four components of transportation management operate within the boundaries defined by the transportation strategy chosen and transportation management scope.

Figure A-1

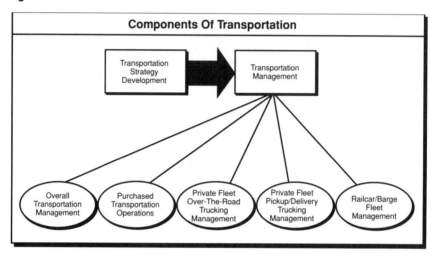

Following is a more detailed discussion about each of these components of transportation.

TRANSPORTATION STRATEGY DEVELOPMENT

A company's transportation strategy is designed to support its service strategy. The transportation strategy defines the inherent level of productivity that can be obtained in transportation. For example, if a service strategy calls for next day service and the logistics strategy calls for regionalized inventories, then the transportation strategy may require the use of premium transportation (e.g., air freight shipments). The transportation productivity of such a system (measured in terms of ton-miles per dollar of freight cost) is lower than a system built around truckload shipments.

Developing a transportation strategy is typically a major effort undertaken in response to significant changes in the company's marketing or manufacturing strategy or in response to external events such as changing customer requirements, competition, or a long-term energy crisis. As such, companies are usually able to thoroughly investigate a number of options and select from them the option that offers the right service level and best levels of productivity based on the strategies. Companies are also able to examine the service level options associated with each of the above issues. These options include:

- For the company:
  - — Role and size of the private fleet/railcar or barge fleet and related purchase/lease strategy for the equipment
  - — Carrier partnering/negotiating strategy
  - — Transportation systems support
  - — Transportation organization
- For each product and traffic lane:
  - — Mode mix
  - — Carrier selection
  - — Pooling and consolidation alternatives
  - — Contract rate provisions

Once these options have been analyzed and a strategy has been developed, responsibility for quality and productivity measurement and improvement in the transportation network falls to operational management.

TRANSPORTATION MANAGEMENT

Operational management must manage four areas of transportation:
- Purchased transportation operations
- Private fleet over-the-road (OTR) trucking
- Private fleet pickup and delivery (P&D) trucking
- Railcar/barge fleet transportation

(a) Purchased Transportation Operations

Those companies that use outside transportation services have relatively less influence over true transportation productivity than companies operating their own fleets. However, the users of outside transportation can affect the productivity of the transportation service in the following ways.

1. Loading. If a shipper has the responsibility for loading an outside carrier's vehicle, then the shipper is in a position to directly influence the utilization of transportation equipment and the productivity of loading labor, making it almost identical to the loading process for company-operated transportation. For example, if a pool of trailers is assigned to the shipper by the carrier, it is the responsibility of the shipper to manage the utilization of those trailers.

2. Linehaul. The user of outside transportation has relatively little influence over the productivity of the carrier's linehaul operation. One notable exception is the requirement on the part of the user for a particular type of vehicle (e.g., refrigerated car, flat bed truck, tank barge), which may introduce inefficiencies in the carrier's linehaul operation. Another exception is when the shipper can help the carrier find backhaul opportunities.

3. Unloading. Similar to the loading procedure, the user of outside transportation can influence the productivity of the unloading process in terms of the labor hours and elapsed time required.

(b) Private Fleet Over-the-Road Trucking

Over-the-road (OTR) trucking operations consist of three basic activities: loading, linehaul movement, and unloading. Each is discussed briefly below.

1. Loading consists of positioning the truck (trailer) at the loading location, physically moving the shipments from the dock to the truck, securing the load, preparing the proper documentation, and preparing the truck for travel. Depending on what operational and/or union constraints are in place, the private fleet transportation function's involvement may consist only of positioning the truck, handling documentation, and hauling the truck away or it may include all activities.

2. Linehaul movement is the point to point movement of the truck carrying shipments from origin to destination. (Certain stopoff arrangements may be made by which shipments are picked up/delivered on-route. This has similarities to P&D on-route activities described later in this section.)

3. Unloading consists of positioning the truck at the receiving location, physically removing the shipment(s) from the truck, preparing unloading documentation, and preparing the truck for travel (in the case of a stopoff). As with loading, certain unloading activities may be performed by transportation personnel while others may be performed by the warehousing or other destination facility personnel.

An additional activity that may be included in OTR transportation is the operation of shipment consolidation (or breakbulk) terminals. Relatively few company-operated transportation systems have such terminals since they are not required if most movements are single and multiple stopoff truckload lots (the most common use of private OTR fleets). The incidence of breakbulk terminals is much greater in for-hire carrier operations where less-than-truckload (LTL) shipments are predominant. The activities of a breakbulk terminal are quite similar to certain warehousing activities: receiving, staging and consolidating, and shipping. The reader is therefore directed to Appendix B — Measuring Quality and Productivity in Warehousing — for a discussion of measures for use in these activities.

(c) Private Fleet Pickup and Delivery Trucking

Pickup and delivery (P&D) transportation consists of the following activities: pretrip loading, stem driving, on-route driving, at-stop activities (loading/unloading), and end-of-trip activities.

1. Pretrip loading includes preparation of the truck and its load before the truck leaves the base of operations. In some companies, the driver may load the vehicle while in others the truck may be loaded before the driver begins work.

2. Stem driving is the driving between the base of operations and the first stop and between the last stop and the base of operations.

3. On-route driving is the driving among stops between the first and the last.

4. At-stop activities include the loading and/or unloading of shipments, customer contact, and the handling of shipment documents. Various sales or service related tasks such as stocking shelves or soliciting orders may also be included.

5. End-of-trip activities may include truck check-in, cash collection settlement, and the unloading.

(d) Railcar/Barge Fleet Transportation

For most companies that own railcar or barge fleets, the major activity of concern for productivity measurement is managing the location and utilization of the equipment. This includes:

- Tracking equipment location while it is in-transit (in the hands of the carrier) for tracing and expediting purposes
- Monitoring equipment time at plants, warehouses, and customer locations to ensure timely turnaround
- Managing or contracting for equipment maintenance and cleaning

(e) Transportation Management's Roles

Regardless of whether a company operates its own fleet, purchases transportation, or both, its transportation management is charged with providing the company with transportation services that are both cost effective and responsive to service needs within the established strategy.

It does so in a number of ways:

- Transportation departments can work with carriers to establish partnerships and implement joint quality and productivity-improvement processes, including ongoing measurement and reporting.
- Even within a transportation strategy, negotiation opportunities with carriers are substantial. Improvements in service can be reflected in greater volumes and performance based rates, while productivity can be reflected in rates whereby each party shares in the gain.
- Transportation departments can route specific shipments more effectively (via for-hire carriers or private fleet) to ensure that the freight is moving at the lowest rates applicable over the shortest distance.
- Transportation departments can monitor backhaul, pooling, and consolidation opportunities to gain even further economies.
- Transportation departments can audit freight bills to check that the carrier is correctly billing for services and to ensure that duplicate payment of freight bills does not occur.
- Transportation departments can work with other departments in their organizations to ensure that packaging and labeling of products for transportation is done in a manner to minimize loss and damage. This activity will not only reduce the carrier's cost (and the resultant rate level) but the company's internal cost for processing and settling carrier claims.
- Transportation departments can work within their companies to ensure that their facility locations and facility designs are not in conflict with transportation needs. Inefficient or inadequate loading or unloading facilities will result in productivity losses for both company-owned and purchased transportation.
- Transportation departments can work within industry circles toward the betterment of the transportation industry in both the private and government sectors. Efforts directed toward a viable and healthy for-hire transportation system will help to increase quality and real productivity in the long term.

- Transportation managers can continue to look for lower cost forms of transportation to meet service requirements. For example, consolidations, pooling, shipper co-ops, and shipper associations may offer very attractive ways to reduce total transportation costs.

A key to performing these activities is a meaningful planning and control system. Without the information supplied by such a system, it is very difficult to carry out any of the previously discussed activities on an ongoing basis.

The term "system" does not refer exclusively to extensive computerized programs. A good planning and control system may be as simple as a monthly manual recap of volumes, resources, cost, and service performance or as advanced as a state-of-the-art interactive transportation control system.

Regardless of the makeup of the system, good planning and control systems share certain characteristics:

- They are driven by a fairly detailed, up to date database of individual shipments.
- Summary information about service quality, productivity, utilization, and performance is generated regularly.
- Unusual variances are shown on exception reports.
- Significant variances are explained in some detail.
- Reporting is done at various levels of detail.

Section II of this appendix describes the various measures that can be used in quality and productivity measurement. Specific transportation input/output terms that are used in this appendix are defined in the Glossary in Appendix H.

II. POTENTIAL MEASURES FOR TRANSPORTATION MANAGEMENT

In this section, measures of transportation quality and productivity are discussed. Transportation quality measures can be used to evaluate how *effectively* the requirements of customers are being satisfied, i.e., shipments are on-time, damage free, and accurate. Transportation productivity measures can be used to determine how *efficiently* the transportation function is able to meet these requirements.

This appendix includes a wide range of potential measures — far more than any one company can and should use. We recommend that this appendix be used in conjunction with the discussion in Chapter 10 on "Measurement System Design" as you tailor a measurement to meet your company's specific needs.

TRANSPORTATION QUALITY MEASURES

This section discusses measures for managing the quality of the output of the transportation function, i.e., how effectively customer requirements are being met. The following potential measures can be used to evaluate the quality of the transportation function, including measures of results (what is required), diagnostics (why requirements are not satisfied), and impact (effect of not meeting requirements) for these areas:

- On-time delivery
- Complete and damage-free delivery
- Accurate freight bills
- Timely response to inquiries and claims

(a) On-Time Delivery

Results: Percent of orders delivered on-time, as defined by the customer's requirement, based upon the final promise made to the customer

Diagnostic: Number and percent of shipments not delivered on-time, including reasons for late deliveries, e.g.,
- Equipment failure
- Shipment dispatch delay
  — Insufficient equipment
  — Weather factors
  — Material handling delay
  — Production delays
- Miscommunication of date required
- Other transportation related delays
- Other causes not related to transportation

Diagnostic: Number and percent of shipments delivered on-time but using premium transportation

Impact: Cost of late delivery, e.g.,
- Value of lost orders (refused by customer)
- Value of customer credits/allowances
- Incremental cost of premium transportation
- Cost of management/clerical time

On-time delivery is one of the most important measures of transportation quality. Performance can be measured by customer segment, by account, by carrier, and by product category to analyze differences in performance levels. Deliveries that fail to meet delivery window requirements should be monitored to determine if the cause of the poor performance can be traced to transportation or nontransportation sources.

(b) Complete and Damage-Free Delivery

Results: Percent of shipments that are complete and have no damage when received by the customer

Diagnostic: Number and percent of deliveries that incur loss or damage, including reasons for damage:
- Type of shortage or damage, e.g.,
  — Missing case/carton
  — Missing goods within shipping container
  — Crushed product

- — Contamination
- — Packaging damage, leakage
- — Breakage
- — Water
- — Cuts
- Source of shortage or damage
  - — Loading
  - — In-transit
  - — Unloading
- Cause of damage
  - — Accident in-transit
  - — Theft
  - — Vandalism
  - — Lost astray
  - — Weather
  - — Operator error

Impact: Cost of loss or damage, e.g.,
- Lost revenue
- Additional handling or transportation
- Cost of rework/replacement

Loss and damage is an important measure of transportation quality, including long-term as well as short-term quality. Recurring problems in this area can be an indicator of equipment problems, poor packaging design, deficiencies in procedures and methods, or inadequate personnel training. It is a clear indicator of long-term performance quality for a private fleet or a for-hire carrier.

(c) Accurate Freight Bills

Results: Percent of freight bills with no errors

Diagnostic: Number and percent of freight bills that have errors, along with reasons for errors, e.g.,
- Incorrect rate
- Incorrect entry of data
- Incomplete information
- Communication problem between shipper and carrier

Impact: Cost of freight bill errors, e.g.,
- Clerical time
- Credits/allowances for incorrect charges to customers
- Credits/allowances

(d) Timely Response to Inquiries and Claims

Results: Percent of customer requests responded to in a timely manner, as defined by customer standards:

- Percent of inquiries answered within acceptable time standards and to customer satisfaction
- Percent of customer claims that are settled in a timely manner

Diagnostic: Number and percent of inquiries not answered to customer satisfaction, along with reasons, e.g.,

- Inquiry not responded to in time to meet customer requirements
- Customer inquiry not completely answered
- Inaccurate response

Diagnostic: Number and percent of claims not settled in a timely manner, along with reasons:

- Late response to customer claim
- Customer dissatisfaction with response

Impact: Cost of untimely response, e.g.,

- Lost revenue
  — Clerical and management time

TRANSPORTATION PRODUCTIVITY MEASURES

This section is divided into the following parts:
- Transportation strategy development
- Overall transportation management
- Purchased transportation operations
- Private fleet OTR trucking
- Private fleet P&D trucking
- Rail/barge fleet management

Each of the tables presented in this section corresponds with a cell in the matrix shown in Figure A-2. The applicable input for each activity (e.g., loading labor) is noted along with measures (in terms of productivity, utilization, and performance) for that activity/input. The measures listed for each activity/input pair are a composite of those used by a broad cross section of industry and are not intended to represent the best possible system.

(a) Transportation Strategy Development

A transportation strategy defines the constraints and options under which transportation management must function. These constraints can be internal (resulting from the corporate marketing strategy, for example) or external (resulting from competition). Designing a productive system that meets service requirements means considering factors such as:

- Service requirements
- Supply sources
- Facilities design
- Carrier relationships

- Establishment of assembly/pooling/consolidation programs
- Private fleet operational scope
- Equipment purchase/lease
- Rate negotiations
- Routing guides
- Methods changes

Figure A-2

Transportation Activity/Input Matrix				
	Inputs			
Activity	**Labor**	**Equipment**	**Energy**	**Overall Cost**
■ Transportation strategy development	–	–	–	X
■ Transportation management	–	–	–	X
■ Purchased transportation operations				
• Loading	–	–	–	X
• Linehaul	–	–	–	X
• Unloading	–	–	–	X
■ Private fleet over-the-road trucking				
• Loading	X	–	–	X
• Linehaul	X	–	–	X
• Unloading	X	–	–	X
• Overall	X	X	X	X
■ Private fleet pickup/delivery trucking				
• Pretrip	X	–	–	X
• Stem driving	X	–	–	X
• On-route driving	X	–	–	X
• At-stop	X	–	–	X
• End-of-trip	X	–	–	X
• Overall	X	X	X	X
■ Rail/barge fleet management	–	X	–	X

In evaluating options, managers must be able to compare the resources required and the results to be gained as well as to consider the quality implications for each alternative. To effectively accomplish this, information is required describing inputs and outputs as well as a measure of comparison. For example, common inputs to the decision process are labor, equipment, fuel, capital, and cost. Outputs include ton-miles transported and planned service time.

If, for example, one is evaluating routing guidelines for specific traffic lanes, information is needed on costs, volume moved, and the stated service standards of the carrier as well as its actual service. The standards of comparison are the planned service levels and the expected productivity of the option. Thus, in the case of routing analysis, ton-miles transported per unit of cost is evaluated based on assumed levels of utilization and performance.

For most companies, this measurement is done as a part of a specific project effort; it is not available from an ongoing measurement system. This is because no data would be available in the ongoing system to provide measures for the options not now in use (e.g., to determine the productivity of a shipment consolidation program, cost data would be required for the consolidation activity. Unless the company already operated a similar program, it is unlikely to have such data readily available.)

In measuring the productivity of different transportation options, it is often necessary to employ such techniques as lease versus buy analysis (including tax considerations), net present value calculations, and simulation/optimization of operations as the situation warrants. Thus, no single measure or set of measures is appropriate across every transportation strategy development situation.

(b) Overall Transportation Management

The chief responsibility of transportation management within a company is to provide transportation service that meets customer requirements to the users of transportation at low cost. In some companies, this may involve only the management of a private fleet. In other companies, it may involve only the interface with outside carriers. In still others, management may involve the control of both a private fleet and outside carriage (with attendant tradeoff decisions) plus the management of a fleet of railcars or barges. The following measures deal with gauging how well transportation management meets its *overall* responsibilities.

1. Private Fleet Transportation. Table A-1 shows key measures that can be used to gauge the effectiveness of the management of company-operated private fleet transportation.

Productivity of transportation management can be measured in terms of the amount of transportation provided for the cost incurred. Depending on whether the company-operated transportation is OTR, P&D, or both, the transportation provided can be measured in terms of ton-miles transported (OTR), stops served (P&D), volume of goods transported to destination, and shipments transported to destination.

A company may operate both OTR and P&D fleets or may have OTR fleets that have substantially different operating characteristics (e.g., long haul, short haul, shuttle). In these situations, the company should use separate sets of measures for each type of fleet.

Company-operated transportation's utilization can be measured best by various ratios that compare total transportation capacity used with the capacity that was available (paid for by the company). The ratios should include factors considering labor hours, vehicle hours or days, and vehicle capacity in terms of volume and miles per day.

Table A-1

TRANSPORTATION MANAGEMENT
PRIVATE FLEET TRANSPORTATION MANAGEMENT MEASURES

Productivity	Utilization	Performance
1. Total ton-miles transported/ total actual company-operated transportation cost	1. Total transportation used/transportation capacity paid for	1. Actual company-operated transportation cost/budgeted company-operated transportation cost
2. Total stops served/total actual company-operated transportation cost		2. Standard company-operated transportation cost/actual company-operated transportation cost
3. Total weight of goods transported to destination/total actual company-operated transportation cost		
4. Shipments transported to destination/total actual company-operated transportation cost		3. Actual transit times/standard transit times
5. Standard ton-miles/total actual cost incurred		

Performance can be measured by comparing either budgeted or standard cost with actual and by comparing service provided with service standards. An example of the latter is a measure of actual versus standard transit times.

2. Purchased Transportation. Table A-2 displays measures for gauging the effectiveness of management in using outside transportation. Management emphasis in controlling purchased transportation should focus on exceptions to normal operations. Controlling exceptions requires a budgeting and operational reporting system that reports financial results as a function of change in operating indicators.

For example, a transportation budget may be established to report on the cost of linehaul operations. The indicators that influence linehaul cost are tonnage and distance. A transportation budget for linehaul could be built up for each traffic lane based on estimates of both factors. Variances from the budget (e.g., beyond +5 percent to –5 percent) would then trigger investigation of the causes.

Among the exceptions that can be tracked are:

• Deficit weight
• Higher quantity/volume than budgeted
• Costlier mode
• Costlier carrier

Utilization of transportation is measured by comparing the amount of transportation used with the amount paid for. The best measure of this is the comparison of ton-miles used with ton-miles purchased.

Table A-2

TRANSPORTATION MANAGEMENT
PURCHASED TRANSPORTATION MANAGEMENT MEASURES

Productivity	Utilization	Performance
1. Total ton-miles transported/ total actual transportation cost	1. Total transportation used/total transportation capacity paid for	1. Actual transportation cost/budgeted transportation cost
2. Total stops served/total actual transportation cost		2. Standard transportation cost[1]/actual transportation cost
3. Total weight of goods transported to destination/total actual transportation cost		3. Actual transit times/standard transit times
4. Shipments transported to destination/total actual transportation cost		
5. Standard ton-miles/total actual transportation cost incurred		

Note: [1] Based on standard cost per hundredweight established by traffic lane and shipment size

Performance in managing transportation can be measured in terms of both cost and service. Budgeted transportation costs can be compared with actual costs. Service can be measured in terms of actual transit time versus standard.

3. Overall Transportation Management. Table A-3 shows the measures that can be used to track the overall effectiveness of the transportation department.

Productivity of overall transportation management is gauged by the amount of transportation provided for the amount of money spent. The amount of transportation provided can be measured in terms of ton-miles (or other unit-miles), stops served, or volume of goods transported to final destination.

Utilization is measured by comparing the amount of transportation capacity used with the amount of transportation capacity purchased. When considering tradeoffs between private fleet and purchased transportation, it is important to recognize the cost of any unused capacity that may occur in the private fleet if outside transportation is chosen in place of it.

Performance of overall transportation management can be measured in terms of budgeted versus actual costs. Also, standard costs (the lowest cost for each move compatible with service needs) can be tracked with actual cost.

(c) Purchased Transportation Operations

Outside transportation services can be divided into three activities: loading, linehaul movement, and unloading. In certain cases, these loading and unloading activities may be performed by the shipper or consignee personnel respectively.

When this occurs, the productivity of these activities (as it directly relates to the transportation user) is measurable by the same factors that can be used to track the productivity of company-owned transportation. These measures will be discussed in the subsection dealing with company-operated OTR trucking.

Table A-3

TRANSPORTATION MANAGEMENT
OVERALL MANAGEMENT MEASURES

Productivity	Utilization	Performance
1. Ton-miles transported/total actual transportation cost	1. Total transportation capacity used/total transportation capacity paid for	1. Actual transportation cost/budgeted transportation cost
2. Stops served/total actual transportation cost		2. Standard transportation cost[1]/actual transportation cost
3. Volume of goods transported to destination/total actual transportation cost		3. Actual transit times/standard transit times
4. Shipments transported to destination/total actual transportation cost		
5. Standard ton-miles/total actual transportation cost		

Note: [1] Standard based on cost if work performed by private fleet transportation or based on engineered standard costs

However, where the carrier provides the loading and/or unloading as well as the linehaul movement, a different set of measures should be used to gauge effectiveness in transportation. These measures are discussed below.

1. Loading Overall. Table A-4 displays measures of productivity, utilization, and performance against which loading outside transportation can be gauged.

Productivity measures are in terms of physical output compared with actual loading cost. The physical measures are vehicles loaded, equivalent vehicles loaded, pieces loaded, and weight loaded.

Utilization is measured in terms of weight and cube loaded compared with the weight and cube capacity paid for by the user. It should be noted, however, that these measures become meaningful only for volume (truckload, carload) shipments because at higher volumes (e.g., 25,000 pounds or above for a specific truck move) the user may find it less expensive to ship the load at a higher weight (e.g., 30,000 pounds) to take advantage of lower TL rates. If this type of situation occurs, then the utilization of the capacity paid for (in this case, the 30,000 pounds) can be measured in terms of how well the user "fills up" the 30,000 pounds capacity with freight.

2. Linehaul Overall. Table A-5 displays measures of outside carrier effectiveness in linehaul movement.

Table A-4

**PURCHASED TRANSPORTATION
OVERALL LOADING MEASURES**

Productivity	Utilization	Performance
1. Vehicles loaded/actual loading cost	1. Weight loaded/ weight capacity available[1]	1. Standard loading cost[2]/actual loading cost[3]
2. Equivalent vehicles loaded/actual loading cost	2. Cube loaded/cube capacity available	
3. Pieces loaded/actual loading cost		
4. Weight loaded/actual loading cost		

Notes:
[1] These utilization measures are meaningful only for volume shipments. Capacity available is described in the text.
[2] Cost if company employees loaded vehicle
[3] Based on published or contract rate

Table A-5

**PURCHASED TRANSPORTATION
OVERALL MOVEMENT MEASURES**

Productivity	Utilization	Performance
1. Ton-miles transported/ actual movement cost	1. Weight transported/ weight capacity available	1. Standard movement cost[1]/actual movement cost
2. Standard ton-miles/actual movement cost	2. Cube transported/ cube capacity available	2. Actual transit time/ target transit time
		3. Actual transit time/ standard transit time[1]

Note: [1] Standard as provided by a company-operated fleet or as determined by engineering the transit time and cost

Productivity of outside transportation's linehaul movement activity is best measured by comparing ton-miles transported with the cost of the movement. This can then be compared with various alternatives (such as other modes).

Utilization for linehaul can be measured using the same ratios as used for loading. The weight and cube actually moved are compared with the weight and cube that could have been moved at the same cost.

Performance for linehaul by outside carriers can be measured in three ways. The first is to compare standard cost (for a company-owned fleet, for instance) with the cost of outside transportation. The second is to compare actual transit time with the outside carrier's target for transit time for each shipment. Finally, the outside carrier's actual transit time can be compared with a standard time for the shipment (based on a company-operated fleet's time, for instance, or on "engineered" times).

3. Unloading Overall. Table A-6 shows measures for unloading by outside carriers.

Productivity of unloading by an outside carrier can be measured by comparing the amount of physical unloading performed to the cost of the unloading to the user. The amount of unloading done can be measured in terms of vehicles unloaded, equivalent vehicles unloaded, pieces unloaded, and weight unloaded.

Table A-6

PURCHASED TRANSPORTATION
OVERALL UNLOADING MEASURES

Productivity	Utilization	Performance
1. Vehicles unloaded/ actual unloading cost		1. Standard unloading cost[1]/actual unloading cost[2]
2. Equivalent vehicles unloaded/ actual unloading cost		
3. Pieces unloaded/actual unloading cost		
4. Weight unloaded/actual unloading cost		

Notes:
[1]Cost if company employees unloaded vehicle
[2]Based on published or contract rate

Utilization of outside transportation for unloading is not a meaningful measure; thus no ratio is presented.

Performance of outside transportation unloading can best be measured by comparing standard unloading costs based on the cost of company employees performing the work with the actual loading charge per a published or contract rate.

(d)   Private Fleet OTR Trucking

The following paragraphs and tables describe measures that can be applied to private fleet OTR trucking operations.

1. The first activity covered is the **Loading Activity.**

1.1 Loading Labor. Table A-7 displays various potential measures for this activity.

Productivity measures are all in terms of measurable output compared to labor hours devoted to the loading process (including paperwork and preparing the vehicle for travel). The outputs range from gross measures such as vehicles loaded to more finely defined measures such as number of pieces or weight loaded.

Table A-7

PRIVATE FLEET OTR TRUCKING: LOADING LABOR MEASURES

Productivity	Utilization	Performance
1. Vehicles loaded/loading labor hours	1. Labor hours of loading/labor available	1. Actual equivalent vehicles loaded per labor hour/standard equivalent vehicles loaded per labor hour
2. Equivalent vehicles loaded/ loading labor hours		
3. Weight loaded/loading labor hours		2. Actual weight loaded per labor hour/standard weight loaded per labor hour
4. Pieces loaded/loading labor hours		
5. Pallets (unitized loaded) loaded/loading labor hours		3. Standard hours of work accomplished/ actual labor hours used

Utilization of labor for loading is defined as the number of labor hours devoted to loading activities compared with the total labor that was available for use in loading activities. The difference between the two is primarily the amount of time the available labor was idle because there was no loading to be done or because someone else was doing the loading while OTR drivers were waiting.

Performance measures are suggested as a measure of actual productivity versus standard (goal) productivity. Although each actual productivity measure could be compared with its standard, it is suggested that performance measured in terms of equivalent vehicles, weight, or standard times is best for most companies since these outputs are more comparable over a period of time.

The measures presented in Table A-7 range from very simple (e.g., vehicles loaded/labor hours) to relatively sophisticated (e.g., standard hours of work accomplished). In choosing one or a group of measures for a transportation operation, one must carefully consider how well each proposed measure fits the desirable characteristics of a measurement system for the particular operation to be measured. For instance, if pieces handled are reasonably uniform in size and weight and handling procedures do not vary, pieces per labor hour might be a good measure of labor productivity. However, if the mix of products includes both large and small pieces, this measure probably would not be appropriate. If the mix of products loaded is not reasonably uniform, then it may be necessary to combine individual measures by converting each to a time value of equivalent work accomplished (i.e., standard hours) and using that as the basis for measurement.

Similar consideration should be given to choosing measures from those listed in the remainder of this appendix.

1.2 Overall Loading. Table A-8 displays overall measures for the loading operation of private fleet vehicles. The productivity measures displayed in this table represent total physical output (e.g., pieces loaded) as compared with total cost of loading. Performance measures are actual versus budgeted loading costs and standard costs earned versus actual costs incurred.

Table A-8

PRIVATE FLEET OTR TRUCKING
OVERALL LOADING MEASURES

Productivity	Utilization	Performance
1. Total vehicles loaded/ total loading cost	1. Vehicles loaded per day/loading capacity	1. Actual loading costs/budgeted loading costs
2. Total equivalent vehicles loaded/total loading cost		2. Standard costs earned/total cost incurred
3. Total weight loaded/ total loading cost		
4. Total pieces loaded/ total loading cost		
5. Total unitized loads loaded/total loading costs		

2. The next activity for private OTR trucking is the **Linehaul Movement Activity.** Measures for each key input follow.

2.1 Linehaul Movement Labor. Table A-9 displays measures for linehaul labor.

The productivity measures suggested for this activity are ton-miles transported compared with labor hours and miles driven compared with labor hours. (It should be noted that "hundredweight" is an acceptable substitute for "ton" in measuring weight in transportation. In some cases, cubic feet, barrels, containers, or standard units could be substituted for tons as well.) Comparison of ton-miles (rather than just miles driven) with labor hours is perhaps a more appropriate measure to use as it reflects loaded — or productive — miles driven.

Utilization of driver labor can be measured by relating employee-hours of driving to employee-hours available for driving.

Table A-9

PRIVATE FLEET OTR TRUCKING
LINEHAUL MOVEMENT LABOR MEASURES

Productivity	Utilization	Performance
1. Ton-miles transported/ linehaul labor hours	1. Labor hours of actual driving/labor hours available	1. Standard hours earned/actual hours
2. Miles driven/linehaul labor hours	2. Labor hours actual driving/D.O.T. regulatory hours	2. Actual miles driven/standard miles

Labor performance can be measured in two ways. First, standard time for linehaul driving can be compared with actual time, reflecting differences in driving speeds. Second, actual miles driven can be compared with standard miles driven to reflect off-route, unauthorized mileage. This measure is especially important in operations where linehaul labor wages are tied to actual miles driven.

2.2 Linehaul Energy. Table A-10 shows potential measures for linehaul energy consumption.

Table A-10

PRIVATE FLEET OTR TRUCKING
LINEHAUL MOVEMENT ENERGY MEASURES

Productivity	Utilization	Performance
1. Ton-miles transported/ linehaul fuel use (gallons)		1. Actual fuel use per ton-mile/standard fuel use per ton-mile
2. Miles driven/linehaul fuel use (gallons)		

In a manner similar to linehaul labor, the productivity of linehaul fuel consumption can be measured either in terms of ton-miles transported per gallon of fuel use or miles driven per gallon of fuel. The ton-mile measure is probably the more appropriate of the two. It may be appropriate when comparing fleet fuel productivity to separate data by type of vehicle, type of operating condition (winter versus summer, mountains versus highway driving, etc.), and type of operation (point to point truckload versus truckload with stopoff).

Energy consumption utilization is not a meaningful term, and, thus, no measure has been displayed for it.

Performance measures for energy consumption are based on ratios reflecting actual standard fuel used per ton-mile and per mile driven. Also useful to management is a measure of actual versus standard driving speeds monitored via on-board computers that can be used to measure fuel consumption performance variations.

2.3 Overall Linehaul. Table A-11 displays measures that can be used to gauge the overall linehaul activity.

The key measure of linehaul productivity is the number of ton-miles (or an appropriate unit-miles measure) transported related to the linehaul cost of transporting the goods. A more sophisticated version would divide standard (origin-destination) ton-miles by cost.

Overall linehaul utilization can be measured by comparing freight hauling miles driven as a percentage of total miles driven or total ton-miles transported as a percent of ton-miles of fleet capacity (actual mileage multiplied by available load capacity). This is a more sophisticated version of the traditional measure "percent empty miles," which, because of the lack of a single definition for empty miles (e.g., "the vehicle is totally empty," "the vehicle has under 500 pounds of freight on it," etc.), cannot easily be used to compare across time or across different operations.

Linehaul performance can be measured in terms of costs (actual versus budget) and service (actual elapsed hours in transit versus standard). Standard cost compared to actual cost incurred is also a useful performance measure for the overall linehaul activity.

Table A-11

PRIVATE FLEET OTR TRUCKING
OVERALL LINEHAUL MOVEMENT MEASURES

Productivity	Utilization	Performance
1. Actual ton-miles transported/ total linehaul movement cost	1. Loaded miles driven/ total miles driven	1. Actual cost per ton mile/budgeted cost per ton-mile
2. Standard ton-miles earned/ total linehaul cost	2. Ton-miles transported/ ton-miles of fleet capacity transit hours per trip	2. Actual transit hours per trip/standard transit hours per trip
	3. Standard cost earned/ actual cost incurred	

3. The third major activity for OTR Trucking is the **Unloading Activity.** Measures for each key input follow.

3.1 Unloading Labor. Table A-12 displays potential measures for unloading labor.
The productivity measures for unloading labor are essentially the same as those shown in Table A-5 for loading labor. Each represents a physical unit unloaded compared with labor hours to accomplish the unloading.

Table A-12

PRIVATE FLEET OTR TRUCKING
UNLOADING LABOR MEASURES

Productivity	Utilization	Performance
1. Vehicles unloaded/labor hours	1. Labor hours of unloading/labor hours available for unloading	1. Actual equivalent vehicles unloaded per labor hour/standard equivalent vehicles unloaded per labor hour
2. Equivalent vehicles unloaded/labor hours		
3. Weight unloaded/labor hours		2. Actual weight unloaded per labor hour/standard weight unloaded per labor hour
4. Pieces unloaded/labor hours		
5. Pallets (unitized loads) unloaded/labor hours		3. Standard hours of work accomplished/ actual labor hours used

Utilization of unloading labor is measured by comparing the number of labor hours used in this activity to the number of labor hours available for unloading.

Performance measures for labor unloading include actual versus standard measures of equivalent vehicles unloaded, weight unloaded, and standard times.

3.2 Overall Unloading. Table A-13 shows overall measures for the vehicle unloading process.

Table A-13

PRIVATE FLEET OTR TRUCKING
OVERALL UNLOADING MEASURES

Productivity	Utilization	Performance
1. Total vehicles unloaded/ total unloading cost		1. Actual unloading costs/budgeted unloading costs
2. Total equivalent vehicles unloaded/total unloading cost		2. Total standard cost of unloading/ total actual cost
3. Total weight unloaded/ total unloading cost		
4. Total pieces unloaded/ total unloading cost		
5. Total unitized loads unloaded/total unloading cost		

Productivity measures relate total physical output (e.g., weight unloaded) to total costs of transportation unloading. Performance measures are actual versus budgeted unloading costs and standard cost earned versus actual cost incurred.

4. The final set of measures deal with **Overall OTR Fleet Measures.** Measures for each key input are discussed below.

4.1 Overall Labor. Table A-14 shows overall labor measures for OTR trucking.

Productivity of OTR labor is best measured by comparing the amount of work done (ton-miles transported) with the associated labor hours or labor cost.

Table A-14

PRIVATE FLEET OTR TRUCKING
OVERALL LABOR MEASURES

Productivity	Utilization	Performance
1. Total ton-miles transported/ total OTR labor cost	1. Total OTR labor hours used/total OTR labor hours available	1. Total actual OTR labor cost/total budgeted OTR labor cost
2. Total ton-miles transported/ total OTR labor hours	2. Total labor hours driving/total labor hours worked	2. Standard hours of work accomplished/ actual OTR labor hours
3. Standard ton-miles/total OTR labor hours		

Utilization can be measured by comparing OTR labor hours used with OTR labor hours available and by relating labor hours of driving with total labor hours worked.

Performance measures are actual versus budgeted labor cost and standard hours of work accomplished versus actual labor hours worked.

4.2 Overall Equipment. Table A-15 shows overall measures of productivity, utilization, and performance for OTR equipment. Productivity measures for OTR equipment are in terms of ton-miles of output, which is compared with the number of vehicles used and the actual vehicle cost incurred.

Table A-15

**PRIVATE FLEET OTR TRUCKING
OVERALL EQUIPMENT MEASURES**

Productivity	Utilization	Performance
1. Total ton-miles transported/ actual vehicle cost	1. Total ton-miles transported/total ton-miles of fleet capacity	1. Total actual vehicle cost/total budgeted vehicle cost
2. Total ton-miles transported/number of vehicles used	2. Total vehicle-hours operated/total vehicle-hours available for operation	2. Total actual vehicle cost incurred/ total standard cost earned
3. Standard ton-miles/ number of vehicles used	3. Total freight hauling (loaded) miles/ total miles driven	3. Total actual vehicle miles driven/ total standard vehicle miles driven
4. Standard ton-miles/number of vehicles used		

Utilization of OTR equipment can be measured in a variety of ways. Ton-miles transported can be compared with the fleet capacity for ton-miles (over a period of time). Vehicle hours of operation can be compared with total available vehicle hours. Loaded miles can be compared with total miles driven.

Equipment performance can be measured either in terms of cost (actual versus standard, actual versus budget) or in terms of miles driven.

4.3 Overall Energy. Table A-16 displays overall energy measures for OTR trucking.

Productivity measures for energy use relate ton-miles and total miles driven to gallons of fuel consumed.

Performance measures include comparisons of actual versus standard fuel consumption per ton-mile and per mile as well as actual versus standard miles driven per gallon of fuel.

4.4 OTR Fleet Measures. Table A-17 shows overall measures for company-operated OTR trucking.

Productivity measures relate physical output with total OTR trucking costs. Physical outputs included are ton-miles transported, tons hauled, and miles traveled. Ton-miles is the most accurate of the three measures, although tons can be a meaningful measure if the length of haul is constant (e.g., a single lane) and miles can be meaningful if the weight of the load is constant (e.g., always full truckload).

Table A-16

**PRIVATE FLEET OTR TRUCKING
OVERALL ENERGY MEASURES**

Productivity	Utilization	Performance
1. Total ton-miles transported/ linehaul fuel used (gallons) 2. Total miles driven/ linehaul fuel used (gallons)		1. Total actual fuel used per ton-mile/total standard fuel used per ton-mile 2. Total actual fuel used per mile/total standard fuel used per mile 3. Actual vehicle miles driven per gallon/ standard vehicle miles driven per gallon

Table A-17

PRIVATE FLEET OTR TRUCKING: OVERALL MEASURES

Productivity	Utilization	Performance
1. Total ton-miles transported/ total OTR transportation cost 2. Standard ton-miles transported/total OTR transportation cost	1. Ton-miles carried/ ton-miles of fleet capacity 2. Standard ton-miles carried/ton-miles of fleet capacity	1. Total actual OTR transportation cost/ total budgeted OTR transportation cost 2. Total actual OTR transportation cost/ total standard OTR transportation cost 3. Total equivalent cost of outside transportation (as substitute for company-operated)/ total actual OTR transportation cost 4. Total equivalent cost of outside transportation (as substitute for company-operated)/ total budgeted OTR transportation cost

Performance measures relate actual OTR costs with budgets and standards. Another performance measure relates the cost of outside transportation services (e.g., motor carrier rates) with both actual and budgeted company-operated transportation costs.

(e) Private Fleet P&D Trucking

The following paragraphs and tables describe the suggested measures for private fleet P&D truck fleets.

1. The first area to be discussed is **Pretrip Activity.**

1.1 Pretrip Labor. Potential measures for pretrip labor are presented in Table A-18.

Table A-18

PRIVATE FLEET P&D TRUCKING: PRETRIP LABOR MEASURES

Productivity	Utilization	Performance
1. Vehicles loaded/labor hours	1. Labor hours of loading/labor hours available at start of trip	1. Actual equivalent vehicles loaded per labor hour/standard equivalent vehicles loaded per labor hour
2. Equivalent vehicles loaded/labor hours		
3. Orders loaded/labor hours		
4. Shipments loaded/labor hours		2. Actual weight loaded per labor hour/standard weight loaded per labor hour
5. Pieces loaded/labor hours		
6. Pallets (unitized loads) loaded/labor hours		3. Standard hours of work accomplished/ actual labor hours
7. Weight loaded/labor hours		

The measures presented in Table A-18 are for those operations in which P&D labor loads the vehicles. If warehousing (or other) labor performs this activity, suggested measures are presented in Appendix B — Measuring Quality and Productivity in Warehousing. Potential measures for equipment used in the loading activity are also presented in Appendix B.

1.2 Overall Pretrip. Table A-19 presents potential measures for the overall pretrip activity.

Productivity measures for the overall pretrip activity are in terms of a physical output against total pretrip costs. Performance is best measured by comparing actual pretrip costs to budgeted costs or standard cost earned.

Productivity measures for the overall pretrip activity are in terms of a physical output against total pretrip costs. Performance is best measured by comparing actual pretrip costs to budgeted costs or standard cost earned.

Table A-19

PRIVATE FLEET P&D TRUCKING: OVERALL PRETRIP MEASURES

Productivity	Utilization	Performance
1. Vehicles loaded/ total P&D pretrip costs		1. Actual P&D pretrip costs/budgeted P&D pretrip costs
2. Total equivalent vehicles loaded/total P&D pretrip costs		2. Standard costs earned/actual costs incurred
3. Total orders loaded/ total P&D pretrip costs		
4. Total shipments loaded/ total P&D pretrip costs		
5. Total pieces loaded/ total P&D pretrip costs		
6. Total pallets loaded/ total P&D pretrip costs		
7. Total weight loaded/ total P&D pretrip costs		

    2. The Stem Driving Activity is the next area of P&D fleet operations that will be discussed.

    2.1 Stem Driving Labor. Potential measures for stemdriving labor are displayed in Table A-20.

Table A-20

**PRIVATE FLEET P&D TRUCKING
STEM DRIVING LABOR MEASURES**

Productivity	Utilization	Performance
1. Stem miles driven/stem driving labor hours		1. Actual stem miles driven per stem driving labor hour/ standard stem miles per stem driving labor hour
		2. Standard hours of stem driving accomplished/actual stem driving hours

2.2 Stem Driving Energy. Table A-21 presents measures for stem driving energy.

2.3 Overall Stem Driving. Measures for the overall stem driving activity are presented in Table A-22.

Table A-21

**PRIVATE FLEET P&D TRUCKING
STEM DRIVING ENERGY MEASURES**

Productivity	Utilization	Performance
1. Stem miles driven/ stem mileage fuel cost		1. Actual fuel used per mile/standard fuel used per mile
2. Stem miles driven/ stem mileage fuel consumption (gallons)		2. Actual miles driven/standard miles

Table A-22

**PRIVATE FLEET P&D TRUCKING
OVERALL STEM DRIVING MEASURES**

Productivity	Utilization	Performance
1. Stops per route day/ total stem driving costs		1. Total stem driving costs/budgeted stem driving costs
2. Total stem driving mileage/ total stem driving costs		2. Standard costs earned/actual costs incurred

3. Measures for the On-Route Driving Activity will be the next topic discussed. Because of the relatively short trips between stops, on-route driving requires special measurement attention.

3.1 On-Route Driving Labor. Suggested measures for labor in the on-route driving activity are provided in Table A-23.

Productivity for on-route driving labor is frequently measured in terms of miles driven per hour or miles driven per stop. The more useful measure, however, is performance based on an engineered standard for driving considering the type of road and traffic conditions encountered (e.g., congested city, expressway, suburban).

3.2 On-Route Driving Energy. Table A-24 presents measures for fuel use in on-route driving.

Productivity for the energy input to on-route driving is measured in terms of miles driven per gallon or miles driven per dollar of fuel cost. These productivity measures compared with standard fuel consumption provide performance measures for energy. However, there is a real question whether assembling data to separate on-route from total P&D fuel consumption data is worth the incremental effort. For most companies, total fuel economy data by vehicle is usually sufficient.

Table A-23

**PRIVATE FLEET P&D TRUCKING
ON-ROUTE DRIVING LABOR MEASURES**

Productivity	Utilization	Performance
1. On-route miles driven/ P&D on-route driving hours 2. On-route miles driven/ P&D on-route driving miles		1. On-route miles driven per P&D on-route driving hour/ standard on-route miles driven per P&D on-route driving hour 2. Actual on-route miles driven/ standard on-route miles 3. Standard on-route driving hours/actual on-route driving hours

Table A-24

**PRIVATE FLEET P&D TRUCKING
ON-ROUTE DRIVING ENERGY MEASURES**

Productivity	Utilization	Performance
1. On-route miles driven/ on-route fuel cost 2. On-route miles driven/on-route fuel consumption (gallons)		1. Actual fuel used per mile/ standard fuel used per mile 2. Actual miles driven/ standard miles

3.3 Overall On-Route Driving Potential measures for overall on-route driving are presented in Table A-25.

Again, comparison with standards is the preferable measurement approach.

Table A-25

**PRIVATE FLEET P&D TRUCKING
ON-ROUTE DRIVING OVERALL MEASURES**

Productivity	Utilization	Performance
1. Stops per route day/total on-route driving cost 2. On-route miles driven/ total on-route driving cost		1. Total actual on-route miles driven/total standard on-route miles 2. Total standard on-route driving hours/total actual on-route driving hours 3. Total actual on-route driving cost/total standard on-route driving cost

4. The next area of measurement for P&D fleets is **At-Stop Activity.**

4.1 At-Stop Labor. Measures for at-stop P&D labor are provided in Table A-26.

Table A-26

**PRIVATE FLEET P&D TRUCKING
AT-STOP LABOR MEASURES**

Productivity	Utilization	Performance
1. Stops served/actual at-stop hours	1. At-stop hours/total route hours	1. Actual at-stop costs/standard at-stop costs
2. Weight picked up or delivered/actual at-stop hours		2. Standard hours of work accomplished/ actual at-stop hours
3. Pieces picked up or delivered/actual at-stop hours		
4. Shipments picked up or delivered/actual at-stop hours		

Productivity for at-stop labor is measured either in terms of the number of stops served compared to at-stop hours (which provides an average at-stop time) or by the number of pickups/deliveries (in terms of weight, pieces, shipments, etc.) made compared to at-stop hours.

4.2 Overall At-Stop. Potential measures for the overall at-stop activity are provided in Table A-27.

Table A-27

**PRIVATE FLEET P&D TRUCKING
OVERALL AT-STOP MEASURES**

Productivity	Utilization	Performance
1. Stops served/total at-stop cost		1. Total actual at-stop costs/total budgeted at-stop costs
2. Weight picked up or delivered/total at-stop cost		2. Total standard at-stop hours/total actual at-stop hours
3. Pieces picked up or delivered/total at-stop cost		3. Standard cost earned/actual at-stop costs
4. Shipments picked up or delivered/total at-stop cost incurred		

The productivity measures suggested for this activity all use total at-stop cost as the input. Although the use of dollars is generally discouraged because of fluctuations that are unrelated to underlying productivity, it is often the common denominator for measurement of an overall activity. Performance measures relate actual at-stop costs or hours to budgeted or standard costs or standard hours. Again, standards form the basis for measurement of the combination of factors that affect at-stop performance and productivity.

5. The last individual activity within P&D fleet operations is the **End-of-Trip Activity.** Potential measures or each input are provided below.

5.1 End-of-Trip Labor. Potential measures for a P&D driver's end-of-trip activity are presented in Table A-28.

Table A-28

**PRIVATE FLEET P&D TRUCKING
END-OF-TRIP LABOR MEASURES**

Productivity	Utilization	Performance
1. Vehicles unloaded/ labor hours	1. Labor hours of unloading/labor hours available at end-of-trip	1. Actual equivalent vehicles unloaded per labor hour/standard equivalent vehicles unloaded per labor hour
2. Orders unloaded/ labor hours		
3. Shipments unloaded/ labor hours		
4. Equivalent vehicles unloaded/labor hours		2. Actual weight unloaded per labor hour/standard weight unloaded per labor hour
5. Pieces unloaded/labor hours		
6. Pallets (unitized loads) unloaded/labor hours		3. Standard hours of work accomplished/ actual labor hours
7. Weight unloaded/labor hours		

The measures presented above are suggested for those operations where the P&D driver is responsible for unloading the vehicle. If warehouse labor performs this activity, suggested measures are presented in Appendix B — Measuring Quality and Productivity in Warehousing. Suggested measures for unloading equipment are also provided in Appendix B.

5.2 Overall-End-of-Trip. Measures for the overall end-of trip activity are provided in Table A-29.

6. The final set of P&D fleet measures discussed in this appendix deals with **Overall P&D Operations.** Measures for each key input follow.

6.1 Overall P&D Labor. Potential measures for overall P&D labor are presented in Table A-30.

6.2 Overall P&D Equipment. Suggested measures for P&D equipment (i.e., vehicles) are presented in Table A-31.

Measures of utilization for P&D vehicles that relate actual load to capacity are not especially meaningful for regular use because the prime objective in P&D operations is often not to fill each vehicle each day but rather to fill each driver's day with a full day's work. Because of variations in route mileages and number of stops to be served, this may result in less than full trucks being dispatched on some days, although driver labor is fully utilized.

Such vehicle utilization measures do have value, however, when making decisions regarding fleet specification and sizing. By having a history of actual loads, management is in a position to select a vehicle better suited for future needs.

Table A-29

**PRIVATE FLEET P&D TRUCKING
OVERALL END-OF-TRIP MEASURES**

Productivity	Utilization	Performance
1. Vehicles unloaded/ total P&D end-of-trip costs		1. Actual P&D end-of-trip costs/budgeted P&D end-of-trip costs
2. Total equivalent vehicles unloaded/total P&D end-of-trip costs		2. Standard cost earned/actual costs incurred
3. Total orders unloaded/ total P&D end-of-trip costs		
4. Total shipments unloaded/ total P&D end-of-trip costs		
5. Total pieces unloaded/ total P&D end-of-trip costs		
6. Total pallets unloaded/ total P&D end-of-trip costs		
7. Total weight unloaded/ total P&D end-of-trip costs		

Table A-30

**PRIVATE FLEET P&D TRUCKING
OVERALL LABOR MEASURES**

Productivity	Utilization	Performance
1. Stops served/labor hours	1. Labor hours worked/ labor hours available for work	1. Actual stops per labor hour/standard stops per labor hour
2. Weight picked up or delivered/labor hours	2. Labor hours worked/ labor hours paid	2. Actual labor cost/ standard labor cost
3. Pieces picked up or delivered/labor hours		3. Standard hours of work accomplished/ actual labor hours
4. Shipments picked up or delivered/labor hours		

Table A-31

PRIVATE FLEET P&D TRUCKING
OVERALL EQUIPMENT MEASURES

Productivity	Utilization	Performance
1. Total stops served/ number of vehicles used 2. Total weight transported/ number of vehicles used	1. Total vehicle-hours operated/total vehicle-hours available for operation 2. Cubic load per vehicle/cubic capacity per vehicle 3. Weight load per vehicle/weight capacity per vehicle	1. Total actual equipment cost/ total budgeted equipment cost 2. Total actual equipment cost/ total standard equipment cost 3. Total actual miles driven/total budgeted miles driven 4. Total actual miles driven/total standard miles driven

6.3 Overall P&D Energy. Measures of overall P&D energy are presented in Table A-32.

Productivity measures for P&D energy are expressed in terms of gallons of fuel used or the cost of fuel used. Caution should be exercised if the cost of fuel is used as an input to the productivity equation due to the potential for wide swings in fuel costs.

Table A-32

PRIVATE FLEET P&D TRUCKING
OVERALL ENERGY MEASURES

Productivity	Utilization	Performance
1. Total stops served/ total fuel used (gallons) 2. Total miles driven/ total fuel used (gallons) 3. Total stops served/ total fuel cost 4. Total miles driven/ total fuel cost		1. Total actual fuel used per stop/ total standard fuel used per stop 2. Total actual fuel used per mile/ total standard fuel used per mile

6.4 Overall P&D. Potential measures for overall P&D are presented in Table A-33. Total P&D cost is the common denominator for productivity measures and is compared to budgeted or standard costs for overall P&D performance.

Table A-33

PRIVATE FLEET P&D TRUCKING
OVERALL MEASURES

Productivity	Utilization	Performance
1. Total stops served/ P&D cost		1. Total actual P&D cost/total budgeted P&D cost
2. Total weight picked up or delivered/total P&D cost		2. Total actual P&D cost per stop/ total standard P&D cost per stop
3. Total pieces picked up or delivered/total P&D cost		
4. Total shipments picked up or delivered/total P&D cost		3. Standard P&D cost earned/actual P&D cost incurred
5. Total value of shipments/ total P&D cost		

(f) Rail/Barge Fleet Management

Many companies, particularly in the bulk industries (e.g., chemicals, petroleum, coal, etc.), own or lease railcar or barge fleets. These fleets are used to transport their product instead of using the carrier's (railroad's or barge company's) equipment or where carrier-owned equipment is not available.

Where a shipper does have a choice, the desirability of owning such a fleet is determined by management. Ideally, this would be done by measuring the inherent productivity of the owned fleet approach against that of using the carrier's equipment during the development of a transportation strategy. This approach was discussed in Section I of this appendix and would include a thorough tradeoff analysis of costs and investments to measure each alternative's productivity.

However, once the fleet is in place, it is necessary to ensure that the inherent levels of productivity assumed during the tradeoff analysis are being achieved as planned. Here, measurement is applied for control purposes.

The productivity of a railcar or barge fleet can be measured during the activities of loading, unloading, and linehaul movement as well as in terms of overall productivity of the equipment.

1. Measuring the Loading Activity. Table A-34 displays the various measures of loading. (The term "barge" may be substituted for "railcar" as appropriate.)

2. Measuring the Linehaul Activity. Table A-35 displays measures used to track fleet productivity for linehaul activities.

3. Measuring the Unloading Activity. Measures used to track equipment productivity during unloading are shown in Table A-36.

4. Measuring Overall Activity. Measures of overall railcar/barge fleet productivity are shown in Table A-37.

Table A-34

RAIL/BARGE FLEET: LOADING MEASURES

Productivity	Utilization	Performance
1. Railcars loaded per year/ total railcar ownership or lease cost per year	1. Number of times loaded per year/railcar 2. Volume of product loaded/carrying capacity of railcar	1. Standard loading time per railcar/ actual loading time per railcar

Table A-35

RAIL/BARGE FLEET: LINEHAUL MEASURES

Productivity	Utilization	Performance
1. Railcar days in linehaul service/total railcar ownership cost per year 2. Ton-miles transported/ railcar ownership cost per year	1. Number of days per month in linehaul service/ railcar 2. Number of days per month in linehaul service/ number of days per month up time[1]	1. Standard transit time per trip/actual transit time per trip

Note: [1]Total days in the month less planned down time for maintenance, repair

Table A-36

RAIL/BARGE FLEET UNLOADING MEASURES

Productivity	Utilization	Performance
1. Railcars unloaded per year/total railcar ownership cost per year	1. Number of times unloaded per year/ railcar	1. Standard unloading time per railcar/actual unloading per railcar

Table A-37

RAIL/BARGE FLEET: OVERALL MEASURES

Productivity	Utilization	Performance
1. Annual ton-miles transported by railcar fleet/total ownership cost of railcar fleet 2. Number of trips[1] per month/railcar	1. Number of railcar-days in use[2]/number of railcar-days available[3]	1. Standard ton-miles transported per railcar/ actual ton-miles transported per railcar 2. Standard trip cycle days[4]/ actual trip cycle days

Notes:
[1]Origin to destination movements
[2]"In-Use" = loading, unloading, in linehaul service
[3]Total days in period (e.g., month) less down time for planned maintenance and repair
[4]Standard developed for each origin-destination trip, to include loading, in-transit, and unloading days

OTHER TRANSPORTATION EFFECTIVENESS MEASURES

Several other key measures of the effectiveness of the transportation function can be tracked. These measures generally indicate how well various components of the transportation system are performing. They are indicators of good or poor practices and can be used as benchmarks.

(a) Transportation Management

- Dollars of freight expense recovered (charged-out) versus dollars of freight expense incurred that should be recovered per pricing policy. This measure gauges how well transportation related pricing policies are being followed.
- Dollars of freight bill adjustments/dollars of freight bill charges. This gauges how accurate the carrier's freight bills are and how well the freight audit function is able to monitor errors in carrier freight billing.
- Dollars of freight claims charges (losses and damage) filed with carriers/dollars of freight bill charges incurred. This measure gauges how well transportation management selects carriers who will minimize damage or loss.
- Number of freight claims filed with carriers/total number of shipments tendered to carriers. This measure gauges the percent of freight transactions that involve a loss or damage.

(b) Private Fleet OTR Trucking

- Number of shipments transported within standard service times/total number of shipments transported
- Number of accidents/number of miles driven
- Dollar value of accident losses/number of miles driven
- Dollar value of accident losses/cost of transportation services provided
- Dollar value of OS&D claims incurred/dollar value of freight handled

(c) Private Fleet P&D Trucking

- Labor hours at-stop/total labor hours
- Total at-stop P&D cost/total P&D cost
- Total sales per driver (caution: this measure may have little to do with the amount of work performed)
- Number of deliveries returned or pickups not made/total number of deliveries or pickups scheduled

CONCLUDING REMARKS ON MEASUREMENT

The measures presented in this appendix represent a broad cross section of potential measures. As stated earlier, no company can or should use all these measures. Instead, we recommend developing a tailored measurement system using these potential measures as a starting point.

III. SURVEY RESPONDENTS' USE OF ACTIONS TO IMPROVE QUALITY AND PRODUCTIVITY IN TRANSPORTATION

In this last section of Appendix A, we present the responses to our Logistics Management Survey that deal with transportation.

Figure A-3 presents responses to transportation strategy actions, while Figure A-4 presents responses to transportation operations actions.

Figure A-3

Transportation Strategy Improvement Actions		
	Percent Of Respondents With Action In Place	
Action	1983	1991
■ Increase leverage in negotiation through reduction in number of carriers used	79%	90%
■ Capitalize on aggregate tender and volume rates, backhaul rates, and other discounts	68	73
■ Develop contracts for truck or rail carriage	55	73
■ Establish transportation service standards for private fleet and for-hire carriers	–	73
■ Establish formal partnership relations with a select group of carriers to achieve improved customer service and productivity	–	63
■ Use more cost effective transportation mode mix	73	59
■ Centralize fleet operations (e.g., transportation subsidiary)	43	47
■ Establish cost-based rates with carriers	–	40
■ Use fast-service carriers to reduce inventory in-transit time	–	36
■ Increase use of freight forwarder, shipping agents, and shipping associations	36	35
■ Establish electronic data linkages with carriers for capacity planning/load scheduling	–	34
■ Use company-operated or third-party consolidation/ breakbulk centers	42	32
■ Develop a transportation-flow database and analysis model	–	31
■ Establish dedicated for-hire fleet	–	25
■ Outsource fleet operations to a third-party provider	–	12
■ Outsource transportation management to a third-party provider	–	6

Figure A-3 shows significant increases since 1983 in the percent of respondents that have truck and/or rail transportation and the percent that have reduced the number of carriers they use. The percent that use a more cost effective mode mix dropped significantly, perhaps indicating a greater importance being placed on speed and reliability versus cost.

For transportation operations (see Figure A-4), there were significant increases in several actions related to operating private truck fleets.

The improvement actions presented in these tables may not be appropriate for every company. However, they provide a good starting point for developing a list of potential improvements to consider.

Figure A-4

Transportation Operations Improvement Actions

Action	Percent Of Respondents With Action In Place	
	1983	1991
• Concentrate deliveries into specific market areas on selected days to reduce inter-stop distances (1)	64%	87%
• Review routes regularly to minimize distance traveled (1)	58	75
• Reduce drivers' time "at depot" to maximize time spent on route and delivering (1)	58	75
• Consolidate or pool outbound shipments (to customers)	63	65
• Apply standard times to plan routes better (1)	25	60
• Increase delivery size, weight or density to reduce unit transport costs	56	58
• Coordinate carrier backhauls (inbound/outbound) and round-trip scheduling	54	53
• Preschedule deliveries into specific market areas on selected days with scheduled dispatch dates	61	53
• Change customer delivery hours to allow more deliveries per vehicle day (e.g., night deliveries) (1)	28	52
• Use computer-based vehicle routing and scheduling (1)	–	52
• Use incentive programs to encourage higher service/productivity/safety	19	50
• Measure fleet and carrier service performance	–	50
• Improve equipment procurement and retirement methods	–	50
• Unitize to reduce individual piece handling	38	49
• Improve maintenance effectiveness	–	45
• Consolidate inbound LTL shipments (from single or multiple vendor sources)	43	44
• Use specialized equipment that complements the type and size of loads to be transported	42	33
• Conduct methods analysis of drivers' activities at stops	27	32
• Help carriers reduce driver turnover (e.g., schedules that allow more frequent driver visits home)	–	15

Note: (1) Percentages based on number of respondents with private truck fleets

APPENDIX B:
MEASURING QUALITY AND
PRODUCTIVITY IN WAREHOUSING

INTRODUCTION

The purpose of this appendix is to help companies develop and refine their ware-housing quality and productivity measurement systems and begin or expand their quality and productivity-improvement programs. This appendix is a continuation of the main report. Thus, the concepts presented in the main report should also be considered in the design of a warehouse productivity measurement system.

Appendix B is organized into the following sections:

I. Definition of Warehousing Activities Included in this Appendix

II. Potential Measures for Warehouse Management

- Quality

- Productivity

- Other key measures

III. Survey Respondents' Use of Actions to Improve Quality and Productivity in Warehousing Management

I. DEFINITION OF WAREHOUSING ACTIVITIES

To facilitate communication, this section provides definitions of warehouse activities used in this appendix, including activities performed by company-operated and public warehouses and definitions of specific input/output. Terms used in this appendix are presented in the Glossary (Appendix H).

In this appendix, warehousing has been divided into company-operated ware-housing and public warehousing. Each of these functions has been defined to include the following activities:

1. Company-Operated Warehousing:

- Receiving
- Put-away
- Storage
- Replenishment
- Order selection
- Checking
- Packing and marking
- Staging and order consolidation
- Shipping
- Clerical/administration

2. Public Warehousing:

- Storage
- Handling
- Consolidation
- Administration

(a) Company-Operated Warehousing

Figure B-1 displays the relationship of each defined activity for a company-operated warehouse. This diagram is in no way intended to portray an ideal warehouse layout but is provided only to present pictorially the activities defined in this section.

Figure B-1

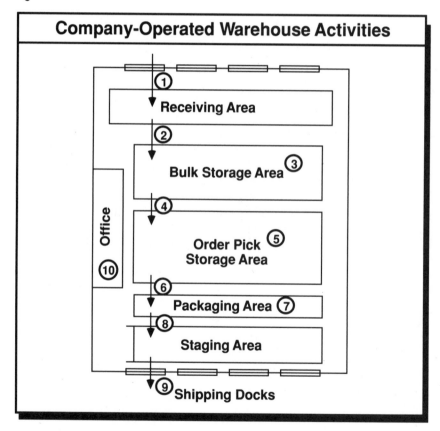

Company-Operated Warehouse Activities

- ① Receiving Area
- ② Bulk Storage Area ③
- ④ Order Pick ⑤ Storage Area
- ⑩ Office
- ⑥ Packaging Area ⑦
- ⑧ Staging Area
- ⑨ Shipping Docks

The following activities are numbered in accordance with Figure B-1:

1. Receiving. Physically accepting material, unloading that material from the inbound transportation mode, staging, verifying quantity and condition of the material, and documenting this information as required.

2. Put-Away. Removing the material from the receiving dock (or other location of receipt), transporting the material to a storage area, placing that material in a staging area, moving it to a specific location and recording this movement, and identifying where the material has been placed.

3. Storage. The retention of products for future use or shipment. Other than occasional inventory verification or physical transfers within the storage area along with documentation of the transfer, there is usually no labor involved in this activity.

4. Replenishment. Relocating material from a bulk storage area to an order pick storage area and documenting this relocation.

5. Order Selection. Selecting or picking the required quantity of specific products for movement to a packing area (usually in response to one or more shipping orders) and documenting that the material was moved.

6. Checking. Verifying and documenting order selection in terms of product number and quantity. In some cases, this activity includes the verification of product condition or quality.

7. Packing and Marking. Packing or unitizing one or more items of an order into an appropriate container and marking and labeling the container with customer shipping destination data as well as other information that may be required.

8. Staging and Consolidation. Physically moving material (usually on an order by order basis) from the packing area to a staging area based on a prescribed set of instructions related to a particular outbound vehicle or delivery route often for shipment consolidation purposes.

9. Shipping. Loading an outbound vehicle with material from the staging area and completing the documentation associated with the movement.

10. Clerical/Administration. Several related activities necessary for the warehousing operation, generally including, but not limited to, the following:

- Updating inventory files based upon receipts, shipments, and adjustments
- Maintaining labor and equipment records
- Performing stock location, order consolidation, and other similar functions
- Verifying inventory on a continuous or periodic basis

It is possible that one or more of these activities do not exist in a given facility or are combined with other activities. For example, bulk storage and order pick storage may be combined in one area. In this case, the replenishment activity (number 4) would not exist. Or, once the order selection activity has taken place, the product could be moved directly to an outbound transportation vehicle. In this case, order selection, checking, packing and marking, staging and consolidation, and shipping (numbers 5 through 9) would all be combined into one physical operation thereby requiring the measurement system to be redefined according to this particular situation.

It should also be noted that while this appendix is primarily oriented toward a finished packaged goods warehousing operation, the concepts can be applied to other storage and warehousing operations as well. These would include:

- Raw materials/work in process warehouses or storerooms

- Repair parts storerooms
- Retail store receiving docks and stockrooms
- Bulk product storage facilities

(b) Public Warehousing

The purchaser of outside (public) warehousing does not have control over the specific inputs associated with the services provided. For purposes of this study, the activities of public warehousing are defined according to the services typically provided to customers.

1. Storage. Holding or maintaining inventory material received from a company for subsequent reshipment to the company's customers or a company-operated facility

2. Handling. The combined activities of receiving, put-away, order selection, checking, packing and marking, and shipping

3. Consolidation. Combining several shipments or orders for a given geographic area on an outbound transportation vehicle

4. Administration. The activity associated with daily operation of the warehouse that includes, but may not be limited to, the following:

- Updating inventory files based upon receipts, shipments, and adjustments
- Maintaining labor, equipment, and facility records
- Performing stock location, order consolidation, and other similar functions
- Supervising the work force
- Additional services as required by the company utilizing the public warehouses

II. POTENTIAL MEASURES FOR WAREHOUSE MANAGEMENT

In this section, measures of warehouse quality and productivity are discussed. Warehouse quality measures can be used to evaluate how *effectively* the warehouse function meets the requirements of its customers, i.e., destinations for order shipments. These destinations can include customer warehouses, customer plant receiving, distributor warehouses, or other warehouses within the supplier distribution network.

They may also include internal destinations such as replenishing distribution centers from a plant warehouse or supplying a manufacturing line from a raw materials warehouse. Warehouse productivity measures can be used to determine how *efficiently* the warehousing function is able to meet these requirements.

This appendix includes a wide range of potential measures — far more than any one company can and should use. We recommend that this appendix be used in conjunction with the discussion in Chapter 10 on "Measurement System Design" as you tailor a measurement to meet your company's specific needs.

WAREHOUSING QUALITY MEASURES

This section discusses measures for managing the quality of the output of the warehouse management process, i.e., how effectively the warehousing function is satisfying requirements. Requirements that must be satisfied typically relate to the quality of order selection, processing, and shipping, which results in correct products shipped in the right quantities in a timely manner with no damage.

The following suggested measures can be used to evaluate the quality of the warehouse management process, including measures of results (what is required), diagnostics (why requirements are not satisfied), and impact (effect of not meeting requirements):

- Order selection measures
- Order administration measures
- Order shipping measures

(a) Order Selection Measures

Results: Percent of orders picked with no errors:

- Percent of orders
- Percent of lines
- Percent of units or weight

Diagnostic: Number and percent of orders with errors, along with reasons for errors, e.g.,

- Selection error (tracked by individual)
- Unclear/ambiguous labeling
- Mislabeled product
- Product in wrong location
- Order entry errors
- Product not located
- Damaged product

Impact: Cost of order selection errors, e.g.,

- Additional labor cost to correct the order
- Administrative costs to correct database
- Potential lost revenue when error is detected by customer

When the order selection activity is performed at a high quality level, the cost for checking and correcting errors will decrease, resulting in a more productive warehousing function. At the same time, the likelihood of an error existing in the shipment when received by the customer will decrease, resulting in improved quality.

(b) Order Administration Measures

This activity covers receiving the order from the order entry function or system and administering it through the warehouse. It includes preparing picking and shipping documentation and updating inventory records.

Results: Percent of orders processed in the warehouse with no errors or delays:

- Percent of orders
- Percent of lines
- Percent of units

Diagnostic: Number and percent of orders processed with errors or delays, along with reasons for errors, e.g.,

- Data entry errors by type
- Error rate by individual order clerk
- Delay in processing and source of delay

Impact: Cost of order processing errors, e.g.,

- Additional clerical time
- Cost of errors in order picking
- Customer dissatisfaction if error in shipment
- Inventory cost increase

Although order administration in the warehouse may be viewed as simply one component of the total warehousing process, it is in fact a fundamental measure of the overall quality of the process. In addition to having an impact on warehousing productivity, undetected errors in order administration can have a negative impact on customer satisfaction, resulting in lower warehousing effectiveness.

(c) Order Shipping Measures

Results: Percent of orders shipped with no errors or delays:

- Percent of orders
- Percent of lines
- Percent of units

Diagnostic: Number and percent of orders shipped late, with reasons for delays, e.g.,

- Delays due to order picking problems
- Delays due to order administration problems
- Consolidated order with one part of the order received late

Diagnostic: Number and percent of orders shipped with errors, along with reasons, e.g.,

- Errors in order picking
- Errors in order processing
- Insufficient stock
- Unauthorized substitution
- Product damage, mislabeling, etc.

Impact: Cost of errors or delays in shipments, e.g.,

- Customer dissatisfaction, resulting in lost revenue
- Cost of management or clerical time
- Cost of additional handling, including returns

WAREHOUSE PRODUCTIVITY MEASURES

Each of the tables presented in this section coincides with a cell in the matrix

shown in Figure B-2. The warehouse resource inputs in this matrix are:
- Labor
- Facilities
- Equipment
- Energy
- Financial investment
- Overall cost

Figure B-2

Warehouse Activity/Input Matrix						
	Inputs					
Functions/Activities	Labor	Facilities	Equipment	Energy	Financial	Overall Cost
■ Company-operated warehousing					–	X
• Receiving	X	X	X	–	–	X
• Put-away	X	–	X	–	–	X
• Storage	–	X	–	X	–	X
• Replenishment	X	–	X	–	–	X
• Order selection	X	–	X	–	–	X
• Checking	X	–	X	–	–	X
• Packing and marking	X	X	X	–	–	X
• Staging and consolidation	X	X	X	–	–	X
• Shipping	X	X	X	–	–	X
• Clerical and administration	X	–	X	–	–	X
• Overall	X	X	X	X	X	X
■ Public warehousing						
• Storage	–	–	–	–	–	X
• Handling	–	–	–	–	–	X
• Consolidation	–	–	–	–	–	X
• Administration	–	–	–	–	–	X
• Overall	–	–	–	–	–	X

The relationship between these inputs and the warehouse activities described earlier leads to specific activity/input measures of warehouse productivity as indicated by the cells in which an "X" appears. For each activity/input that can be measured, potential measures of productivity, utilization, and performance are discussed in the following sections. This discussion reflects good current practice in industry. It is not intended to describe the most sophisticated measurement system possible.

Chapter 10 presented the desirable characteristics of measurement systems. There are some unique features of warehousing that underscore the importance of considering these characteristics when designing productivity measures. Some of these features are:

- **Product Handling Characteristics.** Most warehouses handle multiple products with different sizes, weights, packaging, etc. These variations should be reflected in the measurement system.

- **Throughput Volume.** A warehousing operation is subject to external forces that dictate day to day throughput volume. The warehouse must respond to these forces. The measurement system must be sensitive to *both* utilization and performance, since these are factors that affect productivity.
- **Order Size (shipment size).** Every order (shipment) has a fixed (setup, paperwork) and variable (piece handling) component. Order and shipment mix should be considered in the design of the measurement system.
- **Inbound/Outbound Transportation Mode.** Differences in loading and unloading procedures for trucks, barges, railcars, etc., affect the comparability of receiving and shipping productivity measures across these modes.
- **Physical Facility Design.** Layout, procedures, and levels of automation will vary between facilities thus impacting the comparability of productivity measures.
- **Differences in Quality of Information.** Both the kind of information available in a facility and the accuracy of that information can affect productivity levels.

These unique aspects of warehousing point to the need to reduce warehousing activities to a common denominator. The most effective way to provide for trackability and comparability of productivity measures is to state them in terms of standard times (or output) that properly reflect differences in procedures, methods, and equipment. This provides the basis for consistent productivity measurement.

PRODUCTIVITY MEASURES FOR COMPANY-MANAGED WAREHOUSING

The following measures deal with activities typically found in a company-managed warehouse.

(a) Measuring the Receiving Activity

1. Receiving Labor. Table B-1 depicts various measures used for this activity/input.

Productivity measures are generally expressed in terms of a measurable output compared to labor hours. These outputs range from dollar value received, on a gross basis, to the number of cartons or units received. The input is usually labor hours actually devoted to receiving.

Utilization is best measured in terms of labor hours used in receiving compared to total hours worked in the receiving area. The difference here is the time used for other nonreceiving activities such as area cleanup.

Performance is generally a measure of actual productivity against a standard or specific goal for that productivity with the exception of a measure based on standard hours versus actual hours. Performance measured in terms of equivalent vehicles, weight, lines, or standard times is generally the best measure for most companies since these outputs are generally the least variable over time.

The measures presented in Table B-1 range from very unsophisticated (e.g., dollars received/labor hour) to relatively sophisticated (e.g., standard hours of work accomplished). In choosing one or a group of measures for an individual warehouse, one must carefully consider how well each proposed measure fits the "Desirable Characteristics of Measurement Systems" presented in Chapter 10 as well as the particular features of the warehouse. For instance, if cases handled are reasonably uniform in size and weight and handling procedures do not vary, cases per labor hour might be a good measure of labor productivity. However, if the mix of products includes both large and small cases, this measure might not be appropriate.

Table B-1

RECEIVING LABOR MEASURES

Productivity	Utilization	Performance
1. Dollar value received/ labor hours	1. Labor hours receiving/labor hours worked	1. Actual equivalent vehicles unloaded per labor hour/standard equivalent vehicles unloaded per labor hour
2. Vehicles unloaded/ labor hours		
3. Equivalent vehicles unloaded/ labor hours		2. Actual weight received per labor hour/standard weight received per labor hour
4. Weight received/labor hours		
5. Cartons received/labor hours		
6. Pallets received/labor hours		3. Actual lines received per labor hour/standard lines received per labor hour
7. Lines received/labor hours		
8. Units received/labor hours		
		4. Standard hours of work accomplished/ actual labor hours

If the mix of products in the warehouse is *not* reasonably uniform, then it may be necessary to combine individual measures by converting each to a time value of equivalent work accomplished (i.e., standard hours) and using that as the basis for measurement. These factors should be considered in choosing measures from those presented in the remainder of this appendix.

2. Receiving Facilities. Receiving facilities for most warehouses can be adequately measured in terms of the number of dock doors or vehicle slots available, although they could also be measured in terms of square feet of space devoted to receiving. Marine slips and rail sidings could also be included as facility inputs. Potential measures of productivity, utilization, and performance are shown in Table B-2.

3. Receiving Equipment. Table B-3 presents representative measures of receiving equipment.

Productivity in this case is measured in terms of dollar value, weight received, or units received compared to equipment hours used in receiving. Depending upon the variability of such output, pallets or lines could, of course, be substituted. In addition, a useful measure of the equipment itself is equipment operating cost per operating hour. This measure not only permits comparison and evaluation between different pieces of equipment in the receiving area but also across other areas in the warehousing function where similar material handling equipment is utilized.

Table B-2

RECEIVING FACILITIES MEASURES

Productivity	Utilization	Performance
1. Vehicles unloaded per dock door/day 2. Weight unloaded per dock door/day	1. Dock doors used per day/dock doors available 2. Hours dock doors used/available hours	1. Actual vehicles unloaded per dock door per day/ standard vehicles unloaded per dock door per day 2. Actual weight unloaded per dock door per day/ standard weight unloaded per dock door per day

Note: "Dock door" is used generically in these examples. Other measures such as rail sidings and marine slips can be substituted.

Table B-3

RECEIVING EQUIPMENT MEASURES

Productivity	Utilization	Performance
1. Dollar value received/ equipment hours 2. Weight received/ equipment hours 3. Units received/ equipment hours	1. Equipment hours used in receiving/equipment hours available 2. Actual weight per movement/maximum weight capacity	1. Actual equipment down time/standard equipment down time 2. Actual equipment cost/budgeted equipment cost

The two utilization measures in the table cover the most important aspects of equipment utilization — time and weight capacity usage.

Performance measures of importance are equipment down time and actual annual costs compared to budgeted costs.

4. Overall Receiving. Table B-4 presents measures for receiving that are of particular value when specific nonlabor inputs (facilities and equipment) are not tracked independently.

In addition, when viewed as overall indicators of the receiving activity, these measures complement the more specific measures of the individual inputs.

Table B-4

OVERALL RECEIVING MEASURES

Productivity	Utilization	Performance
1. Total dollar value received/ total receiving costs	1. Total volume received per day/ total receiving capacity per day	1. Actual receiving costs/budgeted receiving costs
2. Total equivalent vehicles received/total receiving costs		2. Standard cost allowances earned/ total cost incurred
3. Total weight received/ total receiving costs		
4. Total pallets received/ total receiving costs		
5. Total cartons received/ total receiving costs		
6. Total lines received/ total receiving costs		
7. Total units received/ total receiving costs		

Of the productivity measures indicated, the most useful measures over time will be those that measure physical output such as weight, lines, or units.

The utilization of the receiving activity is determined by comparing the total volume received (in terms of weight or units) with the total receiving capacity. The receiving capacity is usually based on labor, equipment, and/or facility availability on a daily basis.

One of the performance measures indicated in the table is that of actual cost to budgeted cost. While dollars are one of the least desirable forms of productivity measurement, budget performance is an extremely important aspect of management. It can be effective if based on a variable budget, which is calculated on the actual volume experienced during that period. The standard costs associated with the receiving activity compared to actual costs incurred can be a valuable management tool if standards have been established for the receiving activity.

(b) Measuring the Put-Away Activity

1. Put-Away Labor Measures

The productivity measures are expressed in physical units of weight, units, and lines, all compared to hours of put-away labor. Labor utilization is based on hours actually involved in put-away versus the total hours assigned to the activity. Labor performance is generally based directly upon the productivity measures compared to a standard for each. If the put-away activity involves products with different handling characteristics (or for comparison between facilities with different physical layouts), standard hours earned compared to actual hours worked will be the most accurate indicator of labor performance. (See Figure B-5.)

Table B-5

PUT-AWAY LABOR MEASURES

Productivity	Utilization	Performance
1. Weight put-away/ labor hours 2. Lines put-away/labor hours 3. Units put-away/labor hours	1. Labor hours put-away/labor hours worked	1. Actual weight put-away per labor hour/ standard weight put-away per labor hour 2. Actual lines put-away per labor hour/ standard lines put-away per labor hour 3. Actual units put-away per labor hour/ standard units put-away per labor hour 4. Standard hours earned/actual hours

2. Put-Away Equipment. Table B-6 presents potential measures for put-away equipment. Another common measure for put-away equipment is operating costs per operating hour.

Productivity is meaningfully measured in weight or units put-away per equipment hour. Equipment utilization is measured in terms of hours and weight capacity. Performance measures are based on down time and actual versus budgeted cost.

Table B-6

PUT-AWAY EQUIPMENT MEASURES

Productivity	Utilization	Performance
1. Weight put-away/ equipment hours 2. Units put-away/ equipment hours	1. Equipment hours used in put-away/ equipment hours available 2. Actual weight per movement/maximum weight capacity.	1. Actual equipment down time/standard equipment down time 2. Actual equipment cost/budgeted equipment cost

3. Overall Put-Away. Potential measures for the overall put-away activity are presented in Table B-7.

Table B-7

OVERALL PUT-AWAY MEASURES

Productivity	Utilization	Performance
1. Total weight put-away/ total put-away cost	1. Total volume put-away per day/ total put-away capacity per day	1. Actual put-away cost/budgeted put-away cost
2. Total lines put-away/ total put-away cost		2. Standard put-away cost allowance earned/actual cost incurred
3. Total units put-away/ total put-away cost		

(c) Measuring the Storage Activity

1. Storage Facilities. Potential measures of the storage facility are based on area or volume. These measures are listed in Table B-8.

Table B-8

STORAGE FACILITY MEASURES

Productivity	Utilization	Performance
1. Dollar value inventory/ square foot	1. Square feet of storage used/ square feet of storage available	1. Actual storage used (occupancy)/ standard occupancy goal
2. Dollar value inventory/ cubic foot		
3. Weight of inventory/ square foot	2. Cubic feet of storage used/cubic feet of storage available	
4. Weight of inventory/ cubic foot		
5. Units/square foot	3. Storage locations used/storage locations available	
6. Units/cubic foot		

Facility measures can be in terms of dollar value, weight, or unit storage per square foot or cubic foot. Caution should be exercised when dollar value is used because of changing dollar values across even short increments of time.

Utilization measures must be viewed carefully due to the difficulty in actually measuring capacity. Improperly designed storage facilities, in terms of rack layout and working aisles, can limit the relative capacity of the facility. Thus, high utilization of a poorly conceived facility is not truly productive even though the measures would so indicate.

Performance, as measured by standard occupancy, can also be misleading if the standard is based on existing constraints of poor layout.

These problems are typically not associated with the storage of bulk liquid or gas, since bulk storage tanks are generally of a standardized design with a maximum safe capacity specified for given operating conditions such as temperature.

2. Storage Energy. Measurement of energy consumed in the storage activity has only recently become important in many companies. Relatively few companies measure energy in terms of anything other than dollar cost. However, energy consumption in a warehouse/storage activity becomes increasingly important as the cost of energy escalates. This is particularly true for companies whose products require environmentally controlled facilities.

The productivity measurements listed in Table B-9 are in terms of energy units. These units could be BTUs, kilowatt hours, or other meaningful measures depending upon the type of energy used.

Table B-9

STORAGE ENERGY MEASURES

Productivity	Utilization	Performance
1. Dollar value of inventory stored/units of energy used		1. Actual energy cost/budgeted energy cost

In temperature controlled facilities (e.g., coolers or freezers), some companies track cube utilization as a means of improving energy productivity. They find that the greater the percentage of cubic space occupied by product the lower the cost for energy. This is because the product retains its temperature better than air does.

3. Overall Storage. Table B-10 indicates that the primary measure for overall storage is in terms of *dollar cost*. While, as mentioned before, this is a poor measure, it is the common denominator that can be applied to this overall activity.

Table B-10

OVERALL STORAGE MEASURES

Productivity	Utilization	Performance
1. Dollar value of inventory/ total storage cost		1. Actual storage cost/budgeted storage cost
2. Weight of inventory/ total storage cost		
3. Units of inventory/ total storage cost		2. Standard cost allowances earned/ actual cost incurred
4. Cube of inventory/ total storage cost		

(d) Measuring the Replenishment Activity

1. Replenishment Labor. Table B-11 presents potential measures for replenishment labor.

Table B-11

REPLENISHMENT LABOR MEASURES

Productivity	Utilization	Performance
1. Weight replenished/ labor hours 2. SKUs replenished/ labor hours 3. Units replenished/ labor hours	1. Labor hours replenishing/ hours worked	1. Actual weight replenished per labor hour/standard weight replenished per labor hour 2. Actual lines replenished per labor hour/standard lines replenished per labor hour 3. Actual units replenished per labor hour/standard units replenished per labor hour 4. Standard hours earned/actual labor hours

2. Replenishment Equipment. Potential measures for equipment used in replenishment are depicted in Table B-12.

The important factors of utilization are comparisons of time and weight capacity. These measures are of particular use when additional material handling equipment is being considered.

Table B-12

REPLENISHMENT EQUIPMENT MEASURES

Productivity	Utilization	Performance
1. Weight replenished/ equipment hours 2. Lines replenished/ equipment hours 3. Units replenished/ equipment hours	1. Equipment hours used in replenishment/ equipment hours available 2. Actual weight per movement/maximum weight capacity per movement	1. Actual equipment down time/standard equipment down time 2. Actual equipment cost/budgeted equipment cost

3. Overall Replenishment. Table B-13 indicates potential measures for the overall replenishment activity.

Delays in replenishment activity can impair order selection productivity by creating stock shortages in the primary inventory area. A measure of emergency replenishments can be an important management tool in pinpointing the cause of low order selection productivity.

Table B-13

OVERALL REPLENISHMENT MEASURES

Productivity	Utilization	Performance
1. Total weight replenished/ total replenishment cost		1. Actual replenishment cost/ budgeted cost
2. Total SKUs replenished/ total replenishment cost		2. Standard replenishment cost earned/actual cost
3. Total units replenished/ total replenishment cost		

(e) Measuring the Order Selection Activity

1. Order Selection Labor. Potential measures for order selection labor are presented in Table B-14.

Table B-14

ORDER SELECTION LABOR MEASURES

Productivity	Utilization	Performance
1. Dollar value selected/ labor hours	1. Labor hours selected/ labor hours worked	1. Actual weight selected per labor hour/standard weight selected per labor hour
2. Weight selected/ labor hours		
3. Orders selected/ labor hours		2. Actual orders selected per labor hour/standard orders selected per labor hour
4. Lines selected/ labor hours		3. Actual lines selected per labor hour/ standard lines selected per labor hour
5. Units selected/ labor hours		
		4. Actual units selected per labor hour/standard units selected per labor hour
		5. Standard hours earned/actual hours

2. Order Selection Equipment. Potential measures of order selection equipment are shown in Table B-15.

Also measured by many companies are order selection equipment operating costs per operating hour.

Table B-15

ORDER SELECTION EQUIPMENT MEASURES

Productivity	Utilization	Performance
1. Dollar value selected/ equipment hours	1. Equipment hours used in selection/ equipment hours available	1. Actual equipment down time/standard equipment down time
2. Weight selected/ equipment hours	2. Actual weight per movement/maximum weight capacity	2. Actual equipment cost/budgeted equipment cost
3. Orders selected/ equipment hours		
4. Lines selected/ equipment hours		

Units or weights handled per hour by order selecting equipment is a meaningful productivity measure. Equipment utilization is measured in terms of hours and weight capacity. Performance measures are based on down time and actual versus budgeted costs.

3. Overall Order Selection. Measures of the overall order selection activity are presented in Table B-16.

Table B-16

OVERALL ORDER SELECTION MEASURES

Productivity	Utilization	Performance
1. Total weight selected/ total order selection cost	1. Total volume selected per day/ total selection capacity per day	1. Actual selection cost/budgeted selection cost
2. Total lines selected/ total order selection cost		2. Standard order selection cost allowances earned/ actual cost incurred
3. Total units selected/ total order selection cost		

(f)   Measuring the Checking Activity

1. Checking Labor. Table B-17 shows potential measures for this activity/input.

It is also useful for management to measure the percent of errors found by the checking activity compared to total errors found by both customers and checkers.

Performance measures are in terms of physical output compared to a standard or standard hours to actual hours.

2. Checking Equipment. Measures for this activity/input are shown below in Table B-18.

3. Overall Checking. Table B-19 shows representative measures of the overall checking activity.

Table B-17

CHECKING LABOR MEASURES

Productivity	Utilization	Performance
1. Orders checked/labor hours 2. Line items checked/labor hours 3. Units checked/labor hours	1. Labor hours checking/labor hours worked	1. Actual orders checked per labor hour/standard orders checked per labor hour 2. Actual lines checked per labor hour/standard lines checked per labor hour 3. Actual units checked per labor hour/standard units checked per labor hour 4. Standard hours earned/actual hours

Table B-18

CHECKING EQUIPMENT MEASURES

Productivity	Utilization	Performance
1. Orders checked/equipment hours 2. Lines checked/equipment hours	1. Equipment hours used in checking/equipment hours available	1. Actual equipment down time/standard equipment down time 2. Actual equipment cost/budgeted equipment cost

Table B-19

OVERALL CHECKING MEASURES

Productivity	Utilization	Performance
1. Total orders checked/budgeted checking cost 2. Total lines checked/total checking cost		1. Actual checking total cost/checking cost 2. Standard checking cost allowances earned/actual cost incurred

Because the checking activity is an intermediate step between order selection and shipping, the cycle time required to perform this activity warrants careful observation and measurement. Imbalance in allotted time or even slight variations due to order size, product mix, etc., can cause deterioration of productivity in the activities preceding and following this activity.

(g) Measuring the Packing and Marking Activity

1. Packing and Marking Labor. Table B-20 presents suggested measures for labor in the packing and marking area.

Table B-20

PACKING AND MARKING LABOR MEASURES

Productivity	Utilization	Performance
1. Dollar value packed and marked/labor hours	1. Labor hours packing and marking/ labor hours worked	1. Actual orders packed and marked per labor hour/standard orders packed and marked per labor hour
2. Orders packed and marked/labor hours		
3. Lines packed and marked/labor hours		2. Actual lines packed and marked per labor hour/standard lines packed and marked per labor hour
4. Units packed and marked/labor hours		
5. Cases packed and marked/labor hours		3. Actual units packed and marked per labor hour/standard units packed and marked per labor hour
		4. Actual cases packed and marked per labor hour/standard cases packed and marked per labor hour
		5. Standard hours earned/actual hours

Productivity measures typically used are orders and/or lines per labor hour. Increasing importance is being given to units and cases as output. This is particularly true where the responsibility for packing is being shifted from the manufacturing to the logistics department. This shift is occurring in many companies that manufacture a variety of private label products where the only differences between these products and the standard products are those of product labeling, product literature, and carton labeling. In these cases, the product identification decision is usually deferred until an order is received. Thus, the final packaging activity is performed by warehouse personnel.

2. Packing and Marking Facility. Measures of this activity/input are illustrated in Table B-21.

Table B-21

PACKING AND MARKING FACILITY MEASURES

Productivity	Utilization	Performance
1. Dollar value packed and marked/square feet used 2. Orders packed and marked/square feet used 3. Lines packed and marked/square feet used	1. Square feet used/square feet available	1. Actual orders packed and marked per square foot/standard orders packed and marked per square feet 2. Actual lines packed and marked per square foot/standard lines packed and marked per square foot

The packing and marking facility may be measured in terms of cost. However, a more common and useful measurement base is square feet utilized.

In the packing and marking facility, utilization should not be pushed to the limit. High facility utilization could result in congestion and reduce overall packing and marking productivity.

3. Packing and Marking Equipment. Illustrated in Table B-22 are potential measures for packing and marking equipment.

Table B-22

PACKING AND MARKING EQUIPMENT MEASURES

Productivity	Utilization	Performance
1. Dollar value packed and marked/equipment hours 2. Orders packed and marked/equipment hours	1. Equipment hours used/equipment hours available	1. Actual equipment down time/standard equipment down time 2. Actual equipment cost/budgeted equipment cost

Another useful measure for packing and marking equipment is equipment operating costs per operating hour. This activity input is extremely important when a high degree of automation is involved.

4. Overall Packing and Marking. Potential measures for the overall packing and marking activity are presented in Table B-23.

Table B-23

OVERALL PACKING AND MARKING MEASURES

Productivity	Utilization	Performance
1. Dollar value packed and marked/total packing and marking cost		1. Actual packing and marking cost/ budgeted packing and marking cost
2. Orders packed and marked/ total packing and marking cost		2. Standard packing and marking cost allowances earned/ actual cost incurred
3. Lines packed and marked/ total packing and marking cost		
4. Units packed and marked/ total packing and marking cost		
5. Value added in packing and marking/total packing and marking cost		

In addition to the measures described elsewhere in this section, the output value-added appears. In companies where a significant difference between inbound value and outbound value exists, this difference may be the result of a packing operation. A typical example of this occurs when a bulk solid or liquid received in a distribution facility is repackaged into more readily salable package sizes and then distributed. Another example might be light final assembly and customer packing of manufactured goods. In packaged goods operations, value-added services might include special labeling and customer specific load building. In situations such as these, the value-added measure is of prime importance.

There may be a tendency to aggregate costs for performing these kinds of value-added services. However, it is important to measure the activities discretely to support profitability and analysis of the value-added service.

(h) Measuring the Staging and Order Consolidation Activity

1. Staging and Order Consolidation Labor. Table B-24 presents potential measures for this activity/input. There are two basic activities involved with order consolidation. The first is clerical in content, pertaining to the selection of orders to be consolidated and the transportation related decisions pertaining to this consolidation. The second is physical in content, pertaining to the actual sorting of specific orders to meet the requirements of the clerical activity. The measures presented in Table B-24 pertain to the second of these activities.

2. Staging and Order Consolidation Facility. Table B-25 presents potential measures for staging and order consolidation facilities.

Excessively high utilization of staging and order consolidation facilities may actually impair the overall productivity of the activity. Therefore, as in the packing and marking facility, utilization should not be pushed to the limit.

3. Staging and Order Consolidation Equipment. Table B-26 illustrates potential measures for equipment used in this activity.

Another commonly used measure for staging and order consolidation equipment is equipment operating costs per operating hour.

Table B-24

STAGING AND ORDER CONSOLIDATION LABOR MEASURES

Productivity	Utilization	Performance
1. Orders staged and consolidated/ labor hours 2. Lines staged and consolidated/ labor hours 3. Units staged and consolidated/ labor hours	1. Labor hours staging and consolidating/ labor hours worked	1. Actual orders staged and consolidated per labor hour/standard orders staged and consolidated per labor hour 2. Actual lines staged and consolidated per labor hour/standard lines staged and consolidated per labor hour 3. Actual units staged and consolidated per labor hour/standard units staged and consolidated per labor hour 4. Standard hours earned/ actual hours

Table B-25

STAGING AND ORDER CONSOLIDATION FACILITY MEASURES

Productivity	Utilization	Performance
1. Orders staged and consolidated/square feet used 2. Lines staged and consolidated/ square feet used 3. Units staged and consolidated/ square feet used	1. Square feet used/ square feet available	1. Actual orders staged and consolidated per square foot/ standard orders staged and consolidated per square foot 2. Actual lines staged and consolidated per square foot/ standard lines staged and consolidated per square foot 3. Actual units staged and consolidated per square foot/ standard units staged and consolidated per square foot

Table B-26

STAGING AND ORDER CONSOLIDATION EQUIPMENT MEASURES

Productivity	Utilization	Performance
1. Orders staged and consolidated/equipment hours 2. Units staged and consolidated/equipment hours	1. Equipment hours used/equipment hours available	1. Actual equipment down time/standard equipment down time 2. Actual equipment cost/budgeted equipment cost

4. Overall Staging and Order Consolidation. Suggested measures for the overall staging and order consolidation activity are provided in Table B-27.

Table B-27

OVERALL STAGING AND ORDER CONSOLIDATION MEASURES

Productivity	Utilization	Performance
1. Total orders staged and consolidated/total staging and consolidation cost 2. Total lines staged and consolidated/total staging and consolidation cost 3. Total units staged and consolidated/total staging and consolidation cost		1. Actual staging and consolidation cost/ budgeted staging and and consolidation cost 2. Standard staging and consolidation cost allowances earned/ actual cost incurred

Several companies perform the staging and consolidation activity along with the shipping activity. When this type of operation exists, the measures of the several activities should be reviewed and combined to provide a realistic representation of the particular operation.

(i)   Measuring the Shipping Activity

1. Shipping Labor. Table B-28 presents potential measures for shipping labor.

2. Shipping Facility. Table B-29 presents potential measures for the facility input to the shipping activity.

As with the measures used in Table B-2, other terms such as rail sidings or marine slips can be substituted for "dock doors" as appropriate.

3. Shipping Equipment. Table B-30 displays shipping equipment measures.

4. Overall Shipping. Measures for the overall shipping activity are presented in Table B-31.

Table B-28

SHIPPING LABOR MEASURES

Productivity	Utilization	Performance
1. Dollars shipped/ labor hours	1. Labor hours shipping/labor hours worked	1. Actual dollars shipped per labor hour/ standard dollars shipper per labor hour
2. Vehicles loaded/ labor hours		2. Actual equivalent vehicles loaded per labor hour/standard equivalent vehicles loaded per labor hour
3. Equivalent vehicles loaded/labor hours		3. Actual weight shipped per labor hour/ standard weight per labor hour
4. Weight shipped/ labor hours		4. Actual orders shipped per labor hour/ standard orders shipped per labor hour
5. Orders shipped/ labor hours		5. Actual lines shipped per labor hour/ standard lines shipped per labor hour
6. Cartons shipped/ labor hours		6. Actual units shipped per labor hour/ standard units shipped per labor hour
7. Lines shipped/ labor hours		7. Standard hours of work accomplished/ actual labor hours
8. Units shipped/ labor hours		

Table B-29

SHIPPING FACILITY MEASURES

Productivity	Utilization	Performance
1. Vehicles loaded per dock door/day	1. Dock doors used per day/ dock doors available	1. Actual vehicles loaded per dock door per day/standard vehicles loaded per dock door per day
2. Weight shipped per dock door/day		2. Actual weight shipped per dock door per day/standard orders shipped per dock door per day
3. Orders shipped per dock door/day	2. Hours dock doors used/ available hours	3. Actual orders shipped per dock door per day/standard orders shipped per dock door per day
4. Lines shipped per dock door/day		
5. Units shipped per dock door/day		4. Actual lines shipped per dock door per day/standard lines shipped per dock door per day
		5. Actual units shipped per dock door per day/standard units shipped per dock door per day

Table B-30

SHIPPING EQUIPMENT MEASURES

Productivity	Utilization	Performance
1. Dollar value shipped/ equipment hours	1. Equipment hours used in shipping/ equipment hours available	1. Actual equipment down time/standard equipment down time
2. Weight shipped/ equipment hours	2. Actual weight per movement/maximum weight capacity per movement	2. Actual equipment cost/budgeted equipment costs
3. Lines shipped/ equipment hours		
4. Units shipped/ equipment hours		

Table B-31

OVERALL SHIPPING MEASURES

Productivity	Utilization	Performance
1. Total dollars shipped/ total shipping cost	1. Total volume shipped per day/ total shipping capacity per day	1. Actual shipping costs/budgeted shipping costs
2. Total equivalent vehicles loaded/total shipping cost		2. Standard cost allowances earned/ total shipping costs incurred
3. Total weight shipped/ total shipping cost		
4. Total orders shipped/ total shipping cost		
5. Total cartons shipped/ total shipping cost		
6. Total lines shipped/ total shipping cost		
7. Total units shipped/ total shipping cost		

The transportation measure of weight/cube utilization of trucks and railcars is affected by the skill with which warehouse employees load these vehicles. Thus, while this is not strictly a warehousing measure, it is a measure that warehousing management should follow.

(j)   Measuring the Clerical Administrative Activity

1. Clerical/Administrative Labor. Table B-32 presents measures for clerical/administrative labor.

Table B-32

CLERICAL/ADMINISTRATIVE LABOR MEASURES

Productivity	Utilization	Performance
1. Dollar value processed/ labor hours		1. Actual dollar value processed per labor hour/ standard dollar value processed per labor hour
2. Orders processed/ labor hours		
3. Lines processed/ labor hours		2. Actual orders processed per labor hour/ standard orders processed per labor hour
4. Units processed/ labor hours		3. Actual lines processed per labor hour/standard lines processed per labor hour
		4. Actual units processed per labor hour/standard units processed per labor hour
		5. Standard hours earned/ actual hours

2. Clerical/Administrative Equipment. Table B-33 presents potential measures for equipment used in this activity.

Table B-33

CLERICAL/ADMINISTRATIVE EQUIPMENT MEASURES

Productivity	Utilization	Performance
1. Orders processed/ equipment hours	1. Equipment hours used/equipment hours available	1. Actual equipment up time/standard equipment up time
2. Lines processed/ equipment hours		2. Actual equipment cost/ budgeted equipment cost
3. Units processed/ equipment hours		3. Actual equipment response time/standard equipment response time

Equipment operating costs per operating hour is another potential measure to track.

3. Overall Clerical/Administrative. Table B-34 presents potential measures for warehouse operations to measure the overall clerical/administrative activity.

Table B-34

OVERALL CLERICAL/ADMINISTRATIVE MEASURES

Productivity	Utilization	Performance
1. Total dollar value processed/total clerical and administrative costs		1. Actual clerical and administrative cost/budgeted clerical and administrative cost
2. Total orders processed/ total clerical and administrative costs		2. Standard clerical and administrative cost allowances earned/actual cost incurred
3. Total lines processed/ total clerical and administrative costs		
4. Total units processed/ total clerical and administrative costs		

(k) Measuring the Overall Warehousing Inputs

1. Overall Warehouse Labor. Table B-35 presents overall warehouse labor measures.

Table B-35

OVERALL WAREHOUSE LABOR MEASURES

Productivity	Utilization	Performance
1. Dollar value throughput/ labor hours	1. Labor hours assigned/labor hours worked	1. Actual dollar value throughput per labor hour/standard dollar value throughput per labor hour
2. Weight throughput/ labor hours	2. Labor hours worked/labor hours paid	2. Actual weight throughput per labor hour/standard weight throughput per labor hour
3. Orders throughput/ labor hours		3. Actual orders throughput per labor hour/standard orders throughput per labor hour
4. Lines throughput/ labor hours		4. Actual lines throughput per labor hour/standard lines throughput per labor hour
5. Units throughput/ labor hours		5. Actual units throughput per labor hour/standard units throughput per labor hour
		6. Standard hours of work accomplished/actual labor hours

In most situations, the best overall measure of labor is standard hours of work accomplished/actual labor hours. This measure accounts for variation in warehouse layout, methods, equipment, and variations in product volumes and mix. Thus it allows for meaningful comparisons across time and among facilities.

2. Overall Warehouse Facility. Overall measures for the warehouse facility are presented in Table B-36.

Table B-36

OVERALL WAREHOUSE FACILITY MEASURES

Productivity	Utilization	Performance
1. Dollar value throughput/ total square feet	1. Square feet used/ square feet available	1. Actual dollar throughput per square foot/standard dollar value throughput per square foot
2. Weight throughput/ total square feet	2. Cubic feet used/ cubic feet available	
3. Orders throughput/ total square feet		2. Actual weight throughput per square foot/standard weight throughput per square foot
4. Lines throughput/ total square feet		
5. Units throughput/ total square feet		4. Actual lines throughput per square foot/standard lines throughput per square foot
		5. Actual units throughput per square foot/standard units throughput per square foot

Another measure commonly used by warehouse management is total facility cost/total warehousing costs. While facility input may be viewed in several ways, e.g., cubic feet, square feet, etc., the input of square feet is the most common for warehouse management. However, measuring the input in terms of cubic feet is more accurate, since the capacity of facilities with the same area, in terms of square feet, could be substantially different. All of the facility measures presented in Table B-36 can also be stated in terms of cubic feet.

3. Overall Warehouse Equipment. Potential measures for warehouse equipment are presented in Table B-37.

For most of these measures, it is necessary to calculate the total equipment hours used in the warehouse operation.

This practice does not seem to be widely used, but the measures are presented for consideration.

Table B-37

OVERALL WAREHOUSE EQUIPMENT MEASURES

Productivity	Utilization	Performance
1. Dollar value throughput/ equipment hours	1. Equipment hours used/equipment hours available	1. Actual equipment cost/budgeted equipment cost
2. Weight throughput/ equipment hours		
3. Orders throughput/ equipment hours		
4. Lines throughput/ equipment hours		
5. Units throughput/ equipment hours		

4. Overall Warehouse Energy. Table B-38 presents overall energy measures in the warehouse.

Table B-38

OVERALL WAREHOUSE ENERGY MEASURES

Productivity	Utilization	Performance
1. Dollar value throughput/ total energy cost		1. Actual energy cost/budgeted energy cost
2. Orders throughput/ total energy cost		
3. Lines throughput/ total energy cost		
4. Units throughput/ total energy cost		

Another measure of warehouse energy is total energy costs/total warehousing costs. Physical input is usually not measured in terms of energy units due to the difficulty typically encountered in converting different types of energy to consistent units. Therefore, energy cost is used, and caution is strongly suggested due to variability in energy costs that may make period to period comparisons suspect.

5. Overall Warehouse Financial. Overall warehouse financial measures are presented in Table B-39.

Another commonly used financial measure is the payback years for capital improvements.

Table B-39

OVERALL WAREHOUSE FINANCIAL MEASURES

Productivity	Utilization	Performance
1. Return on assets employed		1. Actual return on assets employed/ budgeted return on assets employed

(I) Measuring the Overall Warehouse

1. Overall Warehouse. Table B-40 presents overall measures for warehousing. Many warehouse operations are not measured by discrete activity (e.g., receiving, put-away, etc.) or by input category (e.g., labor, facility, etc.). Most companies, however, use one or more of the overall warehouse measures presented in Table B-40.

Table B-40

OVERALL WAREHOUSE EFFECTIVENESS MEASURES

Productivity	Utilization	Performance
1. Dollar value throughput/ total warehouse cost 2. Weight throughput/ total warehouse cost 3. Orders throughput/ total warehouse cost 4. Lines throughput/ total warehouse cost 5. Units throughput/ total warehouse cost	1. Actual weight throughput/ maximum weight throughput 2. Actual orders throughput/ maximum orders throughput 3. Actual lines throughput/ maximum lines throughput 4. Actual units throughput/ maximum units	1. Actual total warehouse cost/budgeted warehouse cost 2. Actual weight throughput/total warehouse cost 3. Actual orders throughput/total warehouse cost 4. Actual cost per lines throughput/ standard cost per lines throughput 5. Actual cost per units throughput/ standard cost per units throughput 6. Standard cost allowances earned/ actual costs incurred

PRODUCTIVITY MEASURES FOR PUBLIC WAREHOUSING

The specific resource inputs used by public warehouse operators are not under direct control of customers. Therefore, measures are meaningful only for overall activities. In selected instances, specific measures of inputs may be of concern to the company, e.g., during rate negotiations. In these cases, the measures presented are for company-operated warehousing. Likewise, *operators* of public warehouses can use the measures presented for company-operated warehousing to help manage their own facilities.

1. Overall Storage. Table B-41 presents potential overall storage measures. Also of interest to the company using public warehousing is a measure of inventory lost or damaged in storage/total inventory in storage (measured in terms of dollar value, cases, units, etc.).

Table B-41

PUBLIC WAREHOUSING: OVERALL STORAGE MEASURES

Productivity	Utilization	Performance
1. Dollar value of inventory/ total storage cost	1. Square feet of space used/square feet of space leased	1. Actual storage cost/budgeted storage cost
2. Weight of inventory/ total storage cost	2. Cubic feet of space used/cubic feet of space leased	
3. Cubic feet of inventory/ total storage cost		
4. Pallets of inventory/ total storage cost		
5. Cases of inventory/ total storage cost		
6. Units of inventory/ total storage cost		
7. Square feet of space/ total storage cost		
8. Cubic feet of space/ total storage cost		

2. Overall Handling. Table B-42 displays potential overall handling measures.

3. Overall Consolidation. Potential measures for overall consolidation are presented in Table B-43.

4. Overall Administration. A performance measure for overall administration is presented in Table B-44.

Table B-42

PUBLIC WAREHOUSING: OVERALL HANDLING MEASURES

Productivity	Utilization	Performance
1. Dollar value of throughput/ total handling cost		1. Actual handling cost/budgeted handling cost
2. Weight of product throughput/total handling cost		
3. Pallets of product throughput/total handling cost		
4. Cases of product throughput/total handling cost		
5. Units of product throughput/total handling cost		

Table B-43

PUBLIC WAREHOUSING: OVERALL CONSOLIDATION MEASURES

Productivity	Utilization	Performance
1. Weight consolidated/ total consolidation cost		1. Actual consolidation cost/budgeted consolidation cost
2. Pallets consolidated/ total consolidation cost		
3. Orders consolidated/ total consolidation cost		
4. Lines consolidated/ total consolidation cost		
5. Units consolidated/ total consolidation cost		

Table B-44

PUBLIC WAREHOUSING: OVERALL ADMINISTRATION MEASURES

Productivity	Utilization	Performance
		1. Actual administration cost/budgeted administration cost

5. Overall Public Warehousing. Table B-45 presents measures for overall public warehousing.

Table B-45

PUBLIC WAREHOUSING: OVERALL MEASURES

Productivity	Utilization	Performance
1. Dollar value of throughput/ total warehousing cost		1. Actual warehouse cost/ budgeted warehousing cost
2. Weight of throughput/ total warehousing cost		2. Actual cost per dollar value throughput/standard cost per dollar value throughput
3. Pallets of throughput/ total warehousing cost		
4. Cases of throughput/ total warehousing cost		3. Actual cost per weight throughput/standard cost per weight throughput
5. Orders throughput/ total warehousing cost		4. Actual cost per pallet (case) throughput/standard cost per pallet throughput
6. Lines throughput/total warehousing cost		5. Actual cost per orders (lines, units) throughput/ actual cost per orders throughput
7. Units of throughput/ total warehousing cost		6. Actual replenishment cycle time per receipt/ standard replenishment cycle time per receipt
		7. Actual loss or spoilage per time period/standard loss or spoilage per time period
		8. Actual unit throughput cost/budgeted unit throughput cost

OTHER KEY WAREHOUSING EFFECTIVENESS MEASURES

Several other key measures of the effectiveness of the warehousing process can be tracked. These measures generally indicate how well various components of the process are performing. They are indicators of good or poor practices and can be used as benchmarks.

(a) Company-Managed Warehousing

- Accuracy of inventory records (number of locations in error/gross number of units in error)
- Lines received in error/total lines received
- Equipment operating cost per operating hour
- Total cycle time from receipt of goods to put-away or to "ready for use" (e.g., loaded in a picking bay)
- Labor cost/total warehousing costs
- Nonlabor cost/total warehousing costs
- Demurrage cost/time period
- Capacity provided (in terms of square feet, cubic feet, or storage locations) per dollar of annual energy cost
- Total replenishment cycle time
- Number of unplanned/emergency replenishments per day
- Actual order selection cycle time/standard cycle time
- Total order throughput cycle time
- Value of product damaged/lost
- Value of inventory adjustments
- Total orders (lines, units) processed per day as a percent of total orders (lines, units) received per day
- Total warehouse costs/total logistics costs
- Total transactions processed per day/total transactions received for processing per day
- Total lines (orders) throughput without error per day/total lines (orders) throughput per day

(b) Public Warehousing

- Accuracy of inventory records (location/level)
- Order throughput cycle time
- Value of product damaged/lost
- Value of inventory adjustments
- Replenishment cycle time
- Transactions processed in error/total transactions processed
- Dollar value returned due to damage/dollar value shipped

CONCLUDING REMARKS ON MEASUREMENT

The measures presented in this appendix represent a broad cross section of potential measures. As stated earlier, no company can or should use all these measures. Instead, we recommend developing a tailored measurement system based on the concepts presented in Chapter 10 and using these potential measures as a starting point.

III. SURVEY RESPONDENTS' USE OF ACTIONS TO IMPROVE QUALITY AND PRODUCTIVITY IN WAREHOUSING MANAGEMENT

In this last section of Appendix B, we present the responses to our Logistics Management Survey that deal with quality and productivity-improvement actions in warehousing.

Figure B-3 presents responses to company-managed warehousing actions, and Figure B-4 presents responses for public warehousing actions.

Figure B-3

Company-Managed Warehousing Improvement Actions		
	Percent Of Respondents With Action In Place	
Action	**1983**	**1991**
■ Training of personnel in methods of handling	59%	73%
■ Adjustment of inventory storage area locations to reduce travel distances	71	69
■ Performance goals for: individuals, teams, shifts	49	68
■ Computerized warehouse operations (e.g., directing equipment/labor, improved documentation, location systems)	45	50
■ Elimination of mislocated or uneconomic warehouses	53	49
■ Labor standards for planning manpower and work load	50	46
■ Incentive schemes to encourage higher quality, productivity or safety	15	43
■ Mechanized storage and materials handling systems	14	42
■ Self-directed employee teams for warehouse operations	–	42
■ Improved package design to reduce product damage	–	42
■ Engineering analysis of warehousing methods and procedures	46	41
■ High-bay warehousing	–	35
■ Persuasion of customers to order in unit loads of full-pallet quantities	33	29
■ Minimization of orders with short lead times	23	19
■ Installation of automated storage and retrieval systems	–	17

Public Warehousing Improvement Actions

Action	Percent Of Respondents With Action In Place	
	1983	1991
• On-site audit	52%	62%
• Inventory audits to reduce loss, damage and shrinkage	59	57
• Elimination of mislocated or uneconomic warehouses	52	49
• On-line computerization of inventory and customer service functions	34	46
• More aggressive rate negotiations with public warehouse operators	64	44
• Strategic alliance with third-party providers	–	32
• Addition of specialized materials handling equipment to streamline product handling	12	17
• Converted public warehouses to transfer points by eliminating inventory	13	13

As Figure B-3 shows, there has been noticeable growth since 1983 in the number of respondents using training and motivational techniques with warehouse employees. These actions include materials handling training, incentive schemes, and performance goal setting.

The percent of respondents using mechanized storage and materials handling systems also represents a significant change over 1983.

For public warehouses (see Figure B-4), the action that represents the biggest gain in popularity is on-line computerization of inventory and customer service functions. The increased attention on partnerships between companies and their public warehousing service providers is in part a reason for the drop in the percent of respondents that conduct more aggressive rate negotiations.

The improvement actions presented in these tables may not be appropriate for every company. However, they provide a good starting point for developing a list of potential improvements to consider.

APPENDIX C:
MEASURING QUALITY AND
PRODUCTIVITY IN PURCHASING

INTRODUCTION

The purpose of this appendix is to help companies to develop and refine their quality and productivity measurement systems and to begin or expand their quality and productivity-improvement processes. Purchasing is the buying activity and includes sourcing, procurement, and cost control activities.

This appendix is a continuation of the main report. Thus, the concepts presented in the main report should be considered as a measurement system is developed for these functions.

Appendix C is organized into the following sections:

I.   Definition of Purchasing Activities Included in this Appendix

II. Potential Measures for the Management of Purchasing

   • Quality

   • Productivity

   • Other key measures

III. Survey Respondents' Use of Actions to Improve Quality and Productivity in Purchasing

Direct measurement of the activities associated with purchasing and sourcing management is often not possible nor desirable. Instead, measurement of these activities may be better accomplished by measuring the *result* of the activity. For example, the number of purchase orders processed per labor hour is not as important as vendor/supplier management or total purchased material cost management. Further complicating the measurement of purchasing management activities is the effect of interactions between purchasing and other activities. For example, the timing of purchases may be affected by sales forecasts and production plans, and so variances in either activity may have an effect on purchasing performance.

The next section provides definitions of activities described in this appendix, including definitions of procurement, sourcing, and cost control.

I.   DEFINITION OF PURCHASING ACTIVITIES

Purchasing is the activity associated with the outside acquisition of goods and services. This includes locating potential sources for goods and services; determining supplier qualifications in terms of quality, prices, lead time, and supply continuity; negotiating with vendors to establish the company-vendor relationship; and developing and maintaining systems for procuring the goods and services required. In addition, the purchasing activity is responsible for maintaining vendor relations necessary for good product service and cost. For purposes of the productivity sections of this appendix, purchasing has been divided into three categories:

1. Sourcing. Establishing the requirements and purchase specifications for the vendor's and company's consideration; locating, interviewing, and general negotiating with vendors; and qualifying those vendors who can reasonably meet the established requirements

2. Procurement. Buying the goods or services needed by the company from the approved vendor listing developed in the sourcing activity

3. Cost Control. Reviewing existing and future requirements in search of alternate sources of supply, alternate materials, potential standardization programs, and other types of value analysis in order to reduce the cost and increase the value of purchased products

II. POTENTIAL MEASURES FOR THE MANAGEMENT OF PURCHASING

In this section, measures of purchasing quality and productivity are discussed. Purchasing quality measures can be used to evaluate how *effectively* the purchasing process meets the requirements of its customers — typically inventory management or production management, who require timely receipt of high quality, low cost components and materials. Purchasing productivity measures can be used to determine how *efficiently* the purchasing process is able to meet these requirements.

This appendix includes a wide range of potential measures — far more than any one company can and should use. We recommend that this appendix be used in conjunction with the discussion in Chapter 10 on "Measurement System Design" as you tailor a measurement to meet your company's specific needs.

PURCHASING QUALITY MEASURES

This section discusses measures of the quality of the output of the purchasing process, i.e., how effectively the purchasing function is meeting requirements. As with most quality processes, improvements in effectiveness eventually translate into improved efficiency (i.e., productivity). For example, if the sourcing department certifies suppliers so they check their own quality, then the company will operate more efficiently by spending less time inspecting incoming shipments.

The following potential measures can be used to evaluate the quality of the purchasing management process, including measures of results (what is required), diagnostics (why requirements are not satisfied), and impact (effect of not meeting requirements):

- Incoming product quality/service measures
- Supplier quality measures
- Purchase order quality measures

(a) Incoming Product Quality/Service Measures

Results: Percent of products, orders, (units, dollar value) meeting quality/service specifications (by vendor)

Diagnostic: Number and percent of products not meeting specifications, with reasons, e.g.,

- Incorrect product
- Materials specifications not satisfied
- Incorrect quantity
- Late delivery
- Mislabeling
- Packaging problems
- Damage

  Impact: Cost of product not meeting specifications, e.g.,
- Cost of returns/reordering
- Production delays
- Substitution of alternate component/material
- Cost of increased quality inspections
- Increased inventory cost (safety stock)
- Lost sales

(b) Supplier Quality Measures

Results: Percent of suppliers meeting standards for certification or other measures of quality, e.g.,

- Percent of suppliers that are certified
- Percent of suppliers operating with the company in partnership relationships
- Percent of suppliers receiving training in procedures for doing business with the company
- Percent of business with highest quality rating suppliers (by commodity category)
- Percent of business covered by long-term (over one year) contracts or partnership commitments

  Diagnostic: Number and percent of orders/products requiring special attention, with reasons, e.g.,
- Noncontract order when item is available under contract
- Quality problems for noncertified suppliers
- Problems due to poor training of suppliers in procedures

  Impact: Cost impact of supplier quality-improvement efforts, e.g.,
- Cost savings resulting from elimination of incoming inspection
- Percent change in ordering costs resulting from change in contract vs. noncontract mix
- Percent of management time required to resolve quality or service problems

Supplier training, evaluation, partnerships, certification, and contracting can all have a direct impact on the effectiveness of the purchasing function's efforts. As responsibility for ensuring high quality is increasingly entrusted to the selected suppliers, purchasing management is able to focus on longer term improvement efforts such as the use of more cost effective alternative materials, supplier consolidation programs, and joint product design.

(c) Purchase Order Quality Measures

Results: Percent of purchase orders generated without delay or information problems

Diagnostic: Number and percent of orders requiring special attention or modification, with associated reasons, e.g.,

- Inaccurate/incomplete information on requisition
- Supplier unable to confirm delivery
- Processing errors in purchase order generation
- Change in internal requirements after requisition is issued
- Pricing errors or lack of information
- Wrong items specified on purchase orders

Impact: Cost of purchase order problems, e.g.,

- Cost to issue change orders
- Purchasing personnel time required to resolve problems
- Cost effects of delays in receiving required materials, e.g.,
  - Production line shut downs
  - Increased inventory

Generating purchase orders is a fundamental task of the purchasing department. Achieving high quality means minimizing the number of problems, i.e., ensuring that each purchase order is correct, timely, and requires no unusual attention.

PURCHASING PRODUCTIVITY MEASURES

Purchasing productivity measures track the efficiency with which purchasing activities are carried out. As stated earlier, efficiency is not the most appropriate measure of purchasing. Instead, effectiveness (e.g., results gained in supplier-customer management and cost containment) may be far more important. Still, measures of productivity, utilization, and performance can be useful supplemental guides.

Each of the tables presented in this section coincides with a cell in the matrix shown in Figure C-1. The purchasing resource inputs in this matrix are:

- Labor
- Equipment
- Overall cost

The relationship between these inputs and the purchasing activities described earlier leads to specific activity/input measures of purchasing productivity as indicated by the cells in which an "X" appears. For each activity/input that can be measured, potential measures of productivity, utilization, and performance are discussed in the following sections.

The following measures deal with the activities and inputs associated with purchasing.

Figure C-1

Purchasing Activity/Input Matrix			
Activities	**Labor**	**Equipment**	**Overall Cost**
■ Sourcing	X	–	X
■ Procurement	X	X	X
■ Cost control	X	–	X
■ Overall	–	–	X

(a) Measuring the Sourcing Activity

1. Sourcing Labor. Table C-1 presents potential measures for this activity/input.

Table C-1

SOURCING LABOR MEASURES

Productivity	Utilization	Performance
1. Qualified vendors added/ labor hours (days) in sourcing 2. Alternative vendors added/ labor hours (days) in sourcing 3. Number of price quotations received/labor hours (days) in sourcing	1. Labor hours in sourcing/total purchasing department labor hours	1. Actual price quotes received per labor hour/standard price quotes received per labor hour 2. Actual new vendors qualified per labor hour/ standard new vendors qualified per labor hour

The measures of sourcing labor productivity are in physical units of vendors added (qualified or alternative) and price quotations received compared to labor hours for sourcing activities. Qualifying vendors can be a time consuming task, many times taking up to several months. As a result, the time period over which these measures are used should be long enough to smooth out fluctuations. Many companies use a three-month time period for these measures.

The performance measures listed include actual price quotes received compared to a standard and new vendors qualified compared to a standard. Generally, these standards are part of an overall purchasing department plan to keep up to date on price developments and reduce overall purchased material costs.

2. Overall Sourcing. Potential measures for overall sourcing are listed in Table C-2.

A measure that tracks the number of local vendors used could be important to a company. If other factors (price, quality, stability, lead times, etc.) are equal, local vendors should be considered. The use of local vendors can reduce transportation costs and transit time for purchased goods.

Table C-2

OVERALL SOURCING MEASURES

Productivity	Utilization	Performance
1. Qualified vendors added/ total sourcing costs		1. Actual sourcing costs/budgeted sourcing costs
2. Alternative vendors added/ total sourcing costs		

(b) Measuring the Procurement Activity

1. Procurement Labor. Table C-3 presents measures of productivity, utilization, and performance for procurement labor.

Table C-3

PROCUREMENT LABOR MEASURES

Productivity	Utilization	Performance
1. Requisitions processed/ labor hours	1. Procurement labor hours/ total labor hours	1. Actual purchase price variance/budgeted purchase price variance
2. Purchase orders processed/ labor hours		2. Actual requisitions processed per labor hour/standard requisitions processed per labor hour
3. Change orders processed/ labor hours		3. Actual purchase orders processed per labor hour/ standard purchase orders processed per labor hour
4. Expedite requests processed/labor hours		4. Actual change orders processed per labor hour/ standard change orders processed per labor hour
5. Total dollar value purchased/labor hours		5. Actual expedite requests processed per labor hour/ standard expedite requests processed per labor hour
6. Total SKUs purchased/ labor hours		6. Actual dollar value purchased per labor hour/ standard dollar value purchased per labor hour
		7. Actual SKUs purchased per labor hour/standard SKUs purchased per labor hour

The productivity measures presented in Table C-3 are often not comparable across buyers because of differing responsibilities. A buyer of small parts, for example, may generate many more purchase orders than a buyer of bulk commodities. Thus, performance measures may be more appropriate in this case.

2. Procurement Equipment. Measures for procurement equipment (e.g., computers) are displayed in Table C-4.

Table C-4

PROCUREMENT EQUIPMENT MEASURES

Productivity	Utilization	Performance
1. Purchase orders generated/ total equipment hours	1. Equipment hours devoted to purchase order generation/ total equipment hours available	1. Actual equipment down time/standard equipment downtime 2. Actual equipment cost/budgeted equipment cost

3. Overall Procurement. Potential measures of the overall procurement activity are listed in Table C-5.

Table C-5

OVERALL PROCUREMENT MEASURES

Productivity	Utilization	Performance
1. Requisitions processed/ total procurement cost		1. Actual procurement cost/budgeted procurement cost
2. Purchase orders processed/ total procurement cost		2. Actual cost of purchased material/ standard cost of purchased material
3. Change orders processed/ total procurement cost		
4. Expedite requests processed/ total procurement cost		3. Actual number of parts standardized/ planned number of parts standardized
5. Total dollar value purchased/ total procurement cost		
6. Total SKUs purchased/ total procurement cost		

Two of the commonly used productivity measures listed in Table C-5 can vary greatly without any change in the underlying purchasing productivity. Thus, they should be used with caution. These measures are:

• Total dollar value purchased/total procurement cost

- Total SKUs purchased/total procurement cost

The two outputs (i.e., dollar value purchased and SKUs purchased) vary according to a company's daily requirements and, therefore, are not usually comparable across time or facilities.

The measures presented for the procurement activity are suggested as alternative approaches to measuring the procurement activity and its associated responsibilities. Each manager must select those measures that are best suited to the company's needs and resources.

(c) Measuring the Cost Control Activity

1. Cost Control Labor. Potential measures for cost control labor are presented in Table C-6.

Table C-6

COST CONTROL LABOR MEASURES

Productivity	Utilization	Performance
1. Cost savings/labor hours 2. Parts subjected to value analysis/labor hours	1. Labor hours on cost improvement/ total labor hours	1. Actual cost savings per labor hour/ standard cost savings per labor hour

2. Overall Cost Control. Measures for the overall cost control activity are displayed in Table C-7.

Table C-7

OVERALL COST CONTROL MEASURES

Productivity	Utilization	Performance
1. Cost savings/cost control activity costs		1. Actual material cost change/ planned material cost change

(d) Measuring the Overall Purchasing Function

1. Overall Purchasing. Suggested measures for the overall purchasing function are presented in Table C-8.

Table C-8

OVERALL PURCHASING MEASURES

Productivity	Utilization	Performance
1. Total purchase orders generated/total purchasing costs	1. Total volume of purchase orders generated/total purchase order generating capacity	1. Actual purchasing cost per purchase order generated/ standard purchasing cost per purchase order generated
2. Total dollar value purchased/total purchasing cost		
3. Total SKUs purchased/ total purchasing costs		2. Actual purchasing cost/budgeted purchasing cost

OTHER PURCHASING EFFECTIVENESS MEASURES

There are several other key measures of the *effectiveness* of the purchasing process. These measures generally indicate how well various components of the purchasing process are performing. They are indicators of good or poor practices and can be used as benchmarks. As appropriate, they may be used to measure by vendor and/or commodity.

(a) Sourcing Labor

- Number and percent of vendors' facilities visited per period
- Number and percent of vendors interviewed per period

(b) Overall Sourcing Activity

- Percent of total vendors qualified
- Percent of purchases from qualified vendors
- Percent of vendors located locally (other factors equal)
- Percent of old parts on which price quotes are received per period
- Percent of new parts on which price quotes are received per period
- Percent of vendors providing backup stock
- Percent of purchased parts that are single sourced
- Percent of newly qualified vendors qualified on price, lead times, and quality

(c) Procurement Labor

- Percent of advantageous price breaks taken
- Percent of purchase orders issued in error
- Percent of vendor acknowledgements received that match purchase order terms
- Percent of procurement labor hours devoted to the purchase of "A" items

(d) Overall Procurement Activity

- Percent of total purchase orders changed
- Percent of total purchase orders issued as blanket purchase orders
- Number of expedites processed as a percent of total purchase orders issued
- Number of receipts per purchase order
- Percent of orders received on time
- Percent of line items received completed
- Percent of purchase orders received complete
- Percent of receipts rejected
- Dollar value rejected as a percent of dollar value received
- Dollar value returned as a percent of dollar value received
- Expedites fulfilled as a percent of expedites processed
- Number of acknowledgements received with delivery date as requested as percent of acknowledgements received
- Dollar value reworked as a percent of dollar value received
- Part stockouts due to late delivery as a percent of total part stockouts
- Quotes received with both FOB vendor plant and FOB receiving location prices as a percent of total quotes received
- Percent of purchase orders issued with incomplete data

(e) Cost Control

- Material cost increases as a percent of competitor's or general inflation index material cost increases
- Percent of "A" items subject to value analysis
- Total cost savings as a percent of total dollar value purchased

(f) Overall Purchasing Management

- Material cost as a percent of total standard product cost
- Percent of vendors for whom capacity is known
- Percent of vendor shipments over or under quantity ordered
- Percent of vendor invoices containing errors
- Percent of purchases made without purchase orders

CONCLUDING REMARKS ON MEASUREMENT

The measures presented in this appendix represent a broad cross section of potential measures. As stated earlier, no company can or should use all these measures. Instead, we recommend developing a tailored measurement system based on the concepts presented in Chapter 10 and using these potential measures as a starting point.

III. SURVEY RESPONDENTS' USE OF ACTIONS TO IMPROVE QUALITY AND PRODUCTIVITY IN PURCHASING

In this last section of Appendix C, we present the responses to our Logistics Management Survey that deal with purchasing.

Figure C-2 presents responses to sourcing actions, and Figure C-3 presents responses to purchasing/buying actions.

Figure C-2

Sourcing Improvement Actions		
	Percent Of Respondents With Action In Place	
Action	1983	1991
• Establishing formalized partnership arrangements with key suppliers	–	78%
• Reducing the number of regular suppliers	–	75
• Negotiating long-term contracts for guaranteed supply/price	48%	68
• Developing strategic alliances with suppliers	–	66
• Entering into more single-source relationships	–	58
• Certifying suppliers	–	55
• Sourcing products globally	–	48
• Segmenting supplier base into strategic, value-added and commodity segments	–	34
• Developing tailored sourcing strategies for each segment	–	33
• Developing supplier database of potential suppliers	–	31
• Estimating standard purchase price through "should-cost" analysis	23	30
• Conducting formalized value analysis/engineering	16	29

There were relatively few sourcing actions identified in the 1991 survey for which we had comparable 1983 data. However, as Figure C-2 indicates, the percentage of companies negotiating long-term contracts grew sharply since 1983. Also, almost twice as many companies in 1991 use formalized value analysis/value engineering to reduce product cost.

Only limited data were available from our 1983 survey to compare with 1991 responses to purchasing improvement actions. Still, some trends are clear. There was a sharp increase in the percent of respondents that orders in small quantities to reduce raw materials inventories with a corresponding drop in the percent of companies that orders in larger quantities to obtain discounts or transportation savings.

Also, the percent of respondents that changed FOB terms to facilitate transportation savings grew sharply.

Surprisingly, in a time when supplier-customer partnerships are being touted, the percent of companies that asked suppliers to take across the board price reductions or hold back price increases grew from 27 percent to 48 percent.

The improvement actions presented in these tables may not be appropriate for every company. However, they provide a good starting point for developing a list of potential improvements to consider.

Figure C-3

	Purchasing/Buying Improvement Actions	
	Percent Of Respondents With Action In Place	
Action	**1983**	**1991**
• Meet with suppliers to define service requirements and measures	–	78%
• Develop supplier performance monitoring and feedback process	–	71
• Meet with suppliers to review their service performance and agree on improvement actions	–	71
• Involve suppliers early on in design and development process	–	65
• Order in smaller quantities to reduce raw materials/purchased goods inventories	39%	62
• Change FOB terms to facilitate transportation savings	36	62
• Provide suppliers with requirements planning information	–	62
• Negotiate with suppliers to store inventory on-site or in dedicated local facilities	–	58
• Draw on supplier's expertise to reduce internal development time and effort	–	54
• Establish joint teams with your unit and your suppliers to improve quality and productivity	–	49
• Ask suppliers to take "across the board" percentage price reductions or hold back price increases	27	48
• Implement continuous improvement processes with suppliers	–	44
• Establish quality awards for suppliers	–	36
• Capture "purchasing income" on deals and promotions through forward buying	31	34
• Order in larger quantities to obtain discounts or transportation savings	45	24

APPENDIX D:
MEASURING QUALITY AND
PRODUCTIVITY IN MATERIALS
PLANNING AND CONTROL

INTRODUCTION

The purpose of this appendix is to help companies develop or improve their quality and productivity measurement systems for materials planning and control and begin or expand their quality and productivity-improvement processes. Materials planning and control includes inventory management and production management, which are interrelated activities:

- Inventory management controls inventories through the forecasting, planning and budgeting, and execution and control activities.

- Production management, as used in this appendix, refers to those production activities that are most closely related to logistics. These activities are production planning, production scheduling and control, dispatching, and shop floor data collection.

This appendix is a continuation of the main report. Thus, the concepts presented in the main report should be considered while a measurement system is developed for these functions.

Appendix D is organized into the following sections:

I.   Definition of Materials Planning and Control Activities Included in this Appendix

II. Potential Measures for Materials Planning and Control

III. Survey Respondents' Use of Actions to Improve Quality and Productivity in Materials Planning and Control

Measurement of the inventory management and production management activities is complicated by the interactions between these and other activities. Sales forecasts and production plans are both inputs to the inventory planning activity. Therefore, variances in planned versus actual inventory levels may also result from either of these activities.

The next section provides definitions of the activities included in inventory management and production management, particularly those that are closely related to the logistics process.

I. DEFINITION OF MATERIALS PLANNING AND CONTROL ACTIVITIES

(a) Inventory Management

Inventory management is the activity concerned with the establishment and execution of inventory policies and plans needed to support marketing, sales, and customer service objectives. In many companies, this activity is the mechanism that drives the manufacturing and purchasing activities, using decision rules that reflect factors including lot sizes, lead times, purchasing economics, and inbound freight.

For purposes of this appendix, inventory management has been divided into three parts:

- Forecasting
- Planning and budgeting
- Execution and control

1. Forecasting. A systematic method of predicting the future sales demand based upon historical data and extrinsic market factors. Forecasting, as it usually applies to inventory management, is the conversion of a sales dollar forecast to a time-phased unit forecast by product group or SKU.

2. Planning and Budgeting. Establishing the inventory requirements in dollars and units by period in order to support the unit forecast, taking into consideration company constraints such as financial and manufacturing capacities and customer service requirements that require stocking levels. Establishing the inventory decision rules (e.g., review and reordering methodology) to support inventory planning.

3. Execution and Control. Maintaining the individual SKU inventories within the parameters established by the planning activity, recording daily transactions in order to track actual performance (i.e., stock status) versus budget, and executing replenishment ordering.

(b) Production Management

Production management is the activity associated with the manufacture of the company's products in the correct quantities and at the times required in order to support the inventory plan. A broader definition of production management includes activities such as methods analysis, plant layout, material handling, work measurement, wage incentives, manufacturing processes, and quality control. However, these activities have been excluded from this appendix since they are more closely associated with the manufacturing environment than the logistics environment.

The elements of production management that are addressed in this appendix include:

- Production planning
- Production control
- Scheduling and dispatching
- Shop floor data collection

1. Production Planning. Establishing the levels of manufacturing required to support the inventory plan. The output of this activity is a production plan, generally at a gross level, specifying manpower and machine requirements by period using departmental or machine (work) center capacities. Production planning includes decisions on production location for particular items where alternatives exist. In a retailing or wholesaling environment, a similar activity may be performed by the purchasing or buying function. Although the activities described here are more applicable to the manufacturing environment, the concepts may be adapted for use by a wholesaler or retailer.

2. Production Control. Regulating and monitoring the flow of material through the manufacturing process. In addition, production control has the responsibility for providing accurate production documents such as bills of material and routing sheets and for coordinating the efforts of the activities that correct and update these documents.

3. Scheduling and Dispatching. The development of detailed schedules by machine or work centers across a relatively short time frame and the release of actual job orders to manufacturing in accordance with the production schedule.

4. Shop Floor Data Collection. Monitoring the hourly or daily progress of jobs through machine or work centers by individual operation and the reporting of this progress back to production control.

II. POTENTIAL MEASURES FOR MATERIALS PLANNING AND CONTROL

In this section, measures of quality and productivity for inventory and production management are discussed. Quality measures can be used to evaluate how *effectively* the inventory/production management process meets the requirements of its customers — typically warehouse management, transportation management, or logistics management, who require timely receipt of the correct quantity of defect-free finished goods. Productivity measures can be used to determine how *efficiently* inventory management and production management are able to meet these requirements.

This appendix includes a wide range of potential measures — far more than any one company can and should use. We recommend that this appendix be used in conjunction with the discussion in Chapter 10 on "Measurement System Design" as you tailor a measurement to meet your company's specific needs.

QUALITY MEASURES FOR INVENTORY MANAGEMENT

Effective management of inventories requires an understanding of the tradeoffs between the cost of maintaining inventory levels and the benefits of meeting customer service requirements. The following potential measures can be used to evaluate the quality of the inventory management process, including measures of results (what is required), diagnostics (why requirements are not satisfied), and impact (effect of not meeting requirements):

- Service level measures
- Inventory accuracy measures
- Forecasting accuracy measures

(a) Service Level Measures

Results: Number and percent of line items filled when requested

Diagnostic: Number and percent of line items not filled when requested, with reasons, e.g.,

- Out of stock due to, e.g.,
  — Supplier failure
  — Manufacturing lead time failure
  — Out of sequence priority of production
  — Oversold
- Incorrect location
- Item damaged
- Communication delay
- Item in stock not meeting specifications
- Item past shelf life limits

   Impact: Cost of not meeting service level requirements, e.g.,
- Cost of lost sales
- Backorder cost

(b) Inventory Accuracy Measures

Results: Number and percent of line items with accurate inventory storage data

Diagnostic: Number and percent of line items with errors in inventory storage, with reasons, e.g.,
- Incorrect location
- Incorrect inventory count
- Mislabeled item
- Incorrect item specifications
- Obsolete inventory

   Impact: Cost of inventory errors, e.g.,
- Cost of lost sales
- Labor cost to correct errors

(c) Forecasting Accuracy Measures

Results: Number and percent of actual demand (sales) deviation versus forecast demand (sales)

Diagnostic: Percent deviation (up/down), along with causes of forecast inaccuracy, e.g.,
- Changes in customer demand not captured by revised forecast
- Forecast revisions
- Forecasting technique errors
- Communication deficiencies between forecasting and sales/marketing (e.g., promotions not planned for or unplanned price change)

   Impact: Cost of forecasting inaccuracy:
- Cost of excess inventory levels
- Lost revenue resulting from insufficient inventory levels

   Ideally, demand data should be used for forecasting inventory requirements.

However, demand data are typically not captured on a routine basis, and so the use of shipment data are usually a reasonable substitute. (Shipment data are preferable to sales data because sales may be booked well ahead of the required shipment date.) The sales forecast error (often expressed as the mean-average-deviation or MAD) is a critical determinant of safety stock requirements in statistical inventory control systems. The forecast error should be tracked routinely, by forecasting entity, to determine if the error is trending up or down. Upward trends may induce a deterioration in sales forecasting performance and should trigger investigation.

QUALITY MEASURES FOR PRODUCTION MANAGEMENT

Suggested measures for evaluating the quality of the production management process, including measures of results, diagnostics, and impact, are the following:
- Production planning accuracy measures
- Production scheduling quality measures

(a) Production Planning Accuracy Measures

Results: Number and percent of production plans that can be executed without errors or problems

Diagnostic: Number and percent of production plans that incur problems, including reasons, e.g.,
- Inaccurate labor requirements
- Capacity planning inaccuracy
- Poor capital equipment planning
- Inaccurate bills of material
- Inaccurate routing sheets

Impact: Cost of inaccurate production planning, e.g.,
- Idle equipment/labor
- Premium costs (e.g., overtime)

(b) Production Scheduling Quality Measures

Results: Percent of production jobs run complete with no unusual problems

Diagnostic: Percent of production jobs run with some problem, including reasons, e.g.,
- Incomplete job due to material shortage
- Schedule change due to material shortage
- Schedule change due to tooling unavailability
- Schedule change due to lack of dispatching orders
- Job order split in manufacturing
- Machine breakdown

Impact: Cost of production scheduling problems, e.g.,
- Setup time cost
- Run time cost

If a job is run incomplete due to material shortage, initial responsibility may rest with scheduling and dispatching for releasing a job to the shop floor for which there was no material. However, if the job was dispatched based on inaccurate information from a perpetual inventory system, then the responsibility lies within the activity responsible for that system's accuracy.

PRODUCTIVITY MEASURES

The inputs to the materials planning and control function are:
- Labor
- Equipment
- Financial investment
- Overall cost

The specific relationship between these inputs and the activities associated with inventory management and production management is shown in Figure D-1. Each cell of the matrix in which an "X" appears defines an activity/input relationship that can be measured.

Figure D-1

Materials Planning And Control Activity/Input Matrix				
	Inputs			
Functions/Activities	Labor	Equipment	Financial	Overall Cost
■ Inventory management				
• Forecasting	X	X	–	X
• Planning and budgeting	X	X	–	X
• Execution and control	X	X	–	X
• Overall	–	–	X	X
■ Production management				
• Production planning	X	–	–	X
• Production control	X	–	–	X
• Scheduling and dispatching	X	X	–	X
• Shop floor data collection	X	X	–	X
• Overall	–	–	–	X

INVENTORY MANAGEMENT PRODUCTIVITY MEASURES

The following tables present potential measures for inventory management activities and the associated inputs.

(a) Measuring the Forecasting Activity

1. Forecasting — Labor. Potential measures of forecasting labor are presented in Table D-1.

Table D-1

FORECASTING LABOR MEASURES

Productivity	Utilization	Performance
1. Product groups forecasted/ labor hours	1. Labor hours devoted to forecasting/total labor hours	1. Actual product groups forecast per labor hour/standard product groups fore- cast per labor hour
2. SKUs forecasted/ labor hours	2. Labor hours devoted to forecast revisions/ total labor hours	
3. Forecast revisions made/ labor hours		2. Actual SKUs fore- cast per labor hour/ standard SKUs fore- cast per labor hour

2. Forecasting — Equipment. Measures for forecasting equipment (e.g., computer systems) are displayed in Table D-2.

Table D-2

FORECASTING EQUIPMENT MEASURES

Productivity	Utilization	Performance
1. SKUs forecasted/ equipment hours	1. Equipment hours used in forecasting/ total equipment hours	1. Actual equipment down time/standard equipment down time
2. Product groups forecasted/ equipment hours		2. Actual equipment cost/budgeted equipment cost
3. Future periods forecasted/ equipment hours		

3. Overall Forecasting. Potential measures for the overall forecasting activity are presented in Table D-3.

Table D-3

OVERALL FORECASTING MEASURES

Productivity	Utilization	Performance
1. Product groups forecasted/ total forecasting costs		1. Actual forecasting costs/budgeted forecasting costs
2. SKUs forecasted/ total forecasting cost		

The forecasting of dependent SKUs (items that have their demand dependent upon a higher level assembly) is generally not recommended since there is no need to forecast that which may be calculated. Therefore, a measure designed to determine to what extent these dependent items are being forecasted is relevant to forecasting productivity.

However, some so-called dependent SKUs are features that can be varied across a mix of models (e.g., the size of a hard disk for a personal computer). In these cases, there can also be independent demand (from the aftermarket, for example) that needs to be forecasted.

(b) Measuring the Planning and Budgeting Activity

1. Planning and Budgeting — Labor. Potential measures for planning and budgeting labor are displayed in Table D-4.

Table D-4

PLANNING AND BUDGETING LABOR MEASURES

Productivity	Utilization	Performance
1. Product groups planned/ labor hours	1. Labor hours devoted to planning/total labor hours	1. Actual product groups planned per labor hour/standard product groups planned per labor hour
2. SKUs planned/ labor hours	2. Labor hours devoted to planning revisions/ total labor hours	2. Actual SKUs planned per labor hour/standard SKUs planned per labor hour

Inventory budgets are generally developed on a preliminary basis. Therefore, they must be revised periodically as external factors change or original assumptions are proved invalid. The utilization measure that tracks labor hours devoted to revising original budgets is an important measure, since the time devoted to revisions is generally much greater than the time needed to develop the initial budget.

2. Overall Planning and Budgeting. Measures for the overall planning and budgeting activity are presented in Table D-5.

(c) Measuring the Execution and Control Activity

1. Execution and Control — Labor. Potential measures for execution and control labor are provided in Table D-6.

2. Execution and Control — Equipment. Measures for the equipment used in the execution and control activity are presented in Table D-7.

3. Overall Execution and Control. Table D-8 displays potential measures for the overall execution and control activity.

Table D-5

OVERALL PLANNING AND BUDGETING MEASURES

Productivity	Utilization	Performance
1. Total plans generated per period/total planning cost period		1. Actual planning cost/budgeted planning cost

Table D-6

EXECUTION AND CONTROL LABOR MEASURES

Productivity	Utilization	Performance
1. Total SKUs controlled/ labor hours 2. Transactions processed/ labor hours	1. Labor hours devoted to control/labor hours	1. Actual SKUs controlled per labor hour/standard SKUs controlled per labor hour 2. Actual transactions processed per labor hour/standard transactions processed per labor hour

Table D-7

EXECUTION AND CONTROL EQUIPMENT MEASURES

Productivity	Utilization	Performance
1. Inventory control transactions/ equipment hours	1. Equipment hours devoted to control/ total equipment hours	1. Actual equipment cost/budgeted equipment cost

Table D-8

OVERALL EXECUTION AND CONTROL MEASURES

Productivity	Utilization	Performance
1. Total SKUs controlled/ total cost of control 2. Total transactions processed/total cost of control		1. Actual cost of control/budgeted cost of control

(d) Measuring the Overall Inventory Management Function

1. Overall Inventory Management — Financial. Inventory is viewed in several ways by a company. It may be considered capacity already utilized, a means used to stabilize production in the face of seasonal fluctuations, or a pool from which customer orders can be supplied without incurring purchase or factory lead times. Most importantly, inventory is an *asset* and, as such, represents an investment competing for a scarce resource — *capital*. As a result, the measurement of inventory investment is an important consideration for logistics management.

The measures included in this appendix are relatively standard throughout industry. There are, however, different methodologies for calculating these measures used by U.S. industry. The commonly used measures for the financial component of inventory management include:

- Return on inventory investment
- Inventory turns (past period sales)
- Inventory turns (forecasted shipments)
- Days of inventory onhand (past or forecasted shipment coverage)
- Percent of inventory increase (decrease) versus percent of sales increase (decrease)
- Percent of inventory increase (decrease) versus percent of cost of sales increase (decrease)

In some companies, inventory represents a sizable portion of total assets. Measures of financial assets that include inventory are important and include:

- Return on total assets
- Return on net assets employed
- Return on working capital

Since inventory comprises only a portion of each of these categories, it is also necessary to measure the percent of inventory included in each category. The financial impact of inventories upon each of these measures can then be determined.

Some companies have found that inventory levels can be better managed by breaking out each inventory category (i.e., raw material, work in progress, and finished goods) and measuring each according to its function in the operation. The measures that have been found useful are:

- Total factory throughput at standard cost/average raw material inventory at standard cost
- Total factory throughput at standard cost/average work in progress inventory at standard cost
- Cost of goods sold from finished goods inventory/average finished goods inventory

Caution is required when using financially based measures for inventory. Sometimes, financial requirements dictate inventory valuation techniques (e.g., "lowest of cost of market," FIFO, etc.) that can affect these measures without affecting the actual physical amount of inventory on hand. Thus, some companies use *unit* inventory levels to supplement financial measures. These unit measures track days (or even hours and minutes) of supply for major processing steps (e.g., a machine center or manufacturing cell).

Additionally, it should be recognized that finished goods inventory is not a single entity even though it physically is stated as such and financially reported as a single asset value. Finished goods average or period end inventories are the result of potentially many components such as safety, in-transit, cycle, production efficiency, seasonal build, and contingency stocks. Attempts to understand and measure these components will lead to a better control over the total inventory.

2. Overall Inventory Management. Potential measures for overall inventory management are presented in Table D-9.

Table D-9

OVERALL INVENTORY MANAGEMENT MEASURES

Productivity	Utilization	Performance
1. Total dollar value of inventory managed/ inventory management cost		1. Actual dollar value of inventory/planned dollar value of inventory
2. Total SKUs managed/ inventory management cost		2. Actual inventory management cost/ budgeted inventory management cost

PRODUCTION MANAGEMENT PRODUCTIVITY MEASURES

(a) Measuring the Production Planning Activity

1. Production Planning — Labor. Measures for production planning are presented in Table D-10.

Table D-10

PRODUCTION PLANNING LABOR MEASURES

Productivity	Utilization	Performance
1. SKUs planned/ labor hours	1. Labor hours devoted to production planning/total labor hours	1. Actual SKUs planned per labor hour/standard SKUs planned per labor hour
2. Machine (work) centers planned/ labor hours		2. Actual machine (work) centers planned per labor hour/standard machine (work) centers planned per labor hour

2. Overall Production Planning. Potential measures for the overall production planning activity are presented in Table D-11.

Table D-11

OVERALL PRODUCTION PLANNING MEASURES

Productivity	Utilization	Performance
1. Total plans generated per period/total planning cost per period		1. Actual planning cost/budgeted planning cost

(b) Measuring the Production Control Activity

1. Production Control — Labor. Measures of productivity, utilization, and performance for production control labor are provided in Table D-12.

Table D-12

PRODUCTION CONTROL LABOR MEASURES

Productivity	Utilization	Performance
1. Loading reports processed/ labor hours	1. Labor hours devoted to production control/ total labor hours	1. Actual loading reports processed per labor hour/ standard loading reports processed per labor hour
2. Transactions processed/ labor hours		
		2. Actual transactions processed per labor hour/standard transactions processed per labor hour

2. Overall Production Control. Measures for the overall production control activity are provided in Table D-13.

(c) Measuring the Scheduling and Dispatching Activity

1. Scheduling and Dispatching — Labor. Measures for this activity/input are displayed in Table D-14.

The large volume of paperwork normally associated with this activity has prompted the presentation of the many measures presented here.

If expediting exists as a separate activity, the measures presented in Table D-14 are applicable to that activity.

2. Scheduling and Dispatching — Equipment. Potential measures for scheduling and dispatching equipment are presented in Table D-15.

3. Scheduling and Dispatching — Overall. Potential measures for overall scheduling and dispatching are shown in Table D-16.

Table D-13

OVERALL PRODUCTION CONTROL MEASURES

Productivity	Utilization	Performance
1. Total transactions processed per period/total production control cost		1. Actual production control cost/budgeted production control cost
2. Total load reports processed per period/total production control cost		2. Actual transactions processed per production control cost/standard transactions processed per production control cost
		3. Actual load reports processed per production control cost/standard load reports processed per production control cost

Table D-14

SCHEDULING AND DISPATCHING LABOR MEASURES

Productivity	Utilization	Performance
1. Jobs scheduled/ labor hours	1. Labor hours devoted to job scheduling/total labor hours	1. Actual jobs scheduled per labor hour/standard jobs scheduled per labor hour
2. Schedules processed/ labor hours		
3. Machine (work) centers loaded/labor hours	2. Labor hours devoted to machine (work) center loading/ total labor hours	2. Actual machine centers loaded per labor hour/ standard machine (work) centers loaded per labor hour
4. Schedule changes processed/labor hours	3. Labor hours devoted to change order processing/ total labor hours	3. Actual machine hours loaded per labor hour/ standard machine hours loaded per labor hour
5. Machine (work) center loads changed/ labor hours		
6. Jobs changed/ labor hours	4. Labor hours devoted to dispatching/total labor hours	4. Actual direct labor hours loaded per labor hour/ standard direct labor hours loaded per labor hour
7. Machine hours loaded/ labor hours		
8. Direct labor hours loaded/labor hours		5. Actual jobs dispatched per labor hour/standard jobs dispatched per labor hour
9. Jobs dispatched/ labor hours		

Table D-15

SCHEDULING AND DISPATCHING EQUIPMENT MEASURES

Productivity	Utilization	Performance
1. Jobs processed/ equipment hours	1. Equipment hours devoted to scheduling and dispatching/ total equipment hours	1. Actual equipment down time/standard equipment down time
2. Schedules processed/ equipment hours		2. Actual equipment cost/budgeted equipment cost
3. Machine loads generated/ equipment hours		
4. Manpower loads generated/ equipment hours		

Table D-16

OVERALL SCHEDULING AND DISPATCHING MEASURES

Productivity	Utilization	Performance
1. Machine (work) centers scheduled per period/ total scheduling and dispatching cost per period		1. Actual machine (work) centers scheduled per scheduling and dispatching cost/ standard machine (work) centers scheduled per scheduling and dispatching cost
2. Jobs scheduled per period/total scheduling and dispatching cost per period		2. Actual jobs scheduled per scheduling and dispatching cost/ standard jobs scheduled per scheduling and dispatching cost
3. Jobs dispatched per period/total scheduling and dispatching cost per period		3. Actual jobs dispatched per scheduling and dispatching cost/ standard jobs dispatched per scheduling and dispatching cost
		4. Actual scheduling and dispatching cost/ budgeted scheduling and dispatching cost

(d) Measuring the Shop Floor Data Collection Activity

1. Shop Floor Data Collection — Labor. Shop floor data collection labor may be measured by using the measures presented in Table D-17.

Table D-17

SHOP FLOOR DATA COLLECTION LABOR MEASURES

Productivity	Utilization	Performance
1. Job tickets processed/ labor hours 2. Material move orders processed/ labor hours 3. Shop reports processed/ labor hours 4. Rework tickets processed/ labor hours	1. Labor hours in data collection/ total labor hours	1. Actual job tickets processed per labor hour/standard job tickets processed per labor hour 2. Actual material move orders processed per labor hour/ standard material move orders processed per labor hour 3. Actual shop reports processed per labor hour/standard shop reports processed per labor hour 4. Actual rework tickets processed per labor hour/standard rework tickets processed per labor hour

2. Shop Floor Data Collection Equipment. Potential measures for shop floor data collection equipment are displayed in Table D-18.

Table D-18

SHOP FLOOR DATA COLLECTION EQUIPMENT MEASURES

Productivity	Utilization	Performance
1. Job tickets processed/ equipment hours 2. Material move tickets processed/equipment hours 3. Shop reports processed/ equipment hours	1. Equipment hours in data collection/ total equipment hours	1. Actual equipment down time/standard equipment down time 2. Actual equipment cost/budgeted equipment cost

3. Overall Shop Floor Data Collection. Measures for the overall shop floor data collection are presented in Table D-19.

Table D-19

OVERALL SHOP FLOOR DATA COLLECTION MEASURES

Productivity	Utilization	Performance
1. Job tickets processed/ total data collection cost		1. Actual data collection cost/ budgeted data collection cost
2. Material move orders processed/total data collection cost		
3. Shop reports processed/ total data collection cost		

(e) Measuring the Overall Production Management Function

1. Overall Production Management. Measures for the overall production management function, as defined in this appendix, are depicted in Table D-20.

Table D-20

OVERALL PRODUCTION MANAGEMENT MEASURES

Productivity	Utilization	Performance
1. Total dollar value throughput/total production management cost		1. Actual dollar value throughput/ planned dollar value throughput
2. Total job orders processed per period/total production management cost		2. Actual job orders processed/planned job orders processed
3. Actual unit throughput/ total production management cost		3. Actual unit throughput/planned unit throughput
		4. Actual production management cost/ budgeted production management cost

OTHER INVENTORY/PRODUCTION MANAGEMENT EFFECTIVENESS MEASURES

Several other key measures of the effectiveness of the inventory management and production management process can be tracked. These measures generally indicate how well various components of the process are performing. They can be used as benchmarks of performance.

(a) Inventory Management — Forecasting

- Percent of forecasting labor hours devoted to forecasting "A" items
- Forecasted dollar sales as a percent of total actual dollar sales (total and by product line)
- Forecasted dollar sales by period as a percent of actual dollar sales by period
- Percent of SKUs forecasted by sophisticated techniques (e.g., exponential smoothing techniques or time series analysis)

(b) Inventory Management — Planning and Budgeting

- Percent of labor hours in planning devoted to planning "A" items
- Backorders as a percent of total dollars (or unit) sales
- Planned customer service level (line-item or case fill rate) based on planned inventories and forecasted demand versus customer service level goal
- Actual stock replenishment time by ABC category versus planned stock replenishment time

The sales or marketing department will often request a customer service level (by ABC class, customer class, order type, time period, etc.) that is found to be unattainable by the planning and budgeting activity due to financial or capacity constraints. The measure of planned customer service levels versus customer service goals is an indicator of the ability of the company to meet its desired line-item fill rates. A difference between the planned and actual replenishment times could indicate the need for additional capacity or a review of customer service objectives.

To further define customer service objectives, it is useful for planning and budgeting to specify a planned stock replenishment time by ABC class. This should be periodically checked against actual stock replenishment time to determine the accuracy of the plan. A large variance in this measure could indicate a need for additional capacity or a review of customer service objectives.

In addition to the difference between the planned and actual stock replenishment time, the variability of the actual time is also of significance and should be measured periodically and used in safety stock calculations. The greater the variance in lead time, the more safety stock is required to buffer the customer demand against unexpected delays in receipts. Automated tracking of lead time variance is now a part of many computerized inventory control systems that maintain the date the replenishment order is placed and the date the order is received.

(c) Inventory Management — Execution and Control

- Percent of labor hours devoted to the control of "A" items
- Actual versus planned inventory levels by SKU

- Actual customer service level (line-item fill rate) versus planned customer service level
- Percent of total inventory that is inactive or obsolete
- Number of SKUs added (deleted) versus total number of SKUs stocked
- Number and quantity of inventory adjustments
- Number of SKUs found not to be properly rotated
- Quantity of rejected material in inventory
- Accuracy of inventory locator system

The measures of stock rotation and shelf life deterioration and spoilage are important in certain industries such as food, brewing, and pharmaceuticals.

It is the responsibility of the execution and control activity to regularly purge obsolete and rejected material from stocks. Therefore, both of these measures will serve as motivating factors.

The direct responsibility for inventory receipts and disbursements may not be that of the execution and control activity. However, this activity is responsible for maintaining the accuracy of the inventory locator system (the accuracy of times an item is indicated to be in stock but is actually unavailable).

(d) Inventory Management — Overall

- Cycle count accuracy
- Customer orders canceled (lost) due to stockouts

A measure of customer orders canceled or lost can be compared with the costs that would have been incurred by stocking the inventory needed to meet the demand. If this is followed over a long period (to even out market fluctuations), it can indicate the need for an evaluation of inventory stocking policies.

(e) Production Management — Production Planning

- Percent of planning hours devoted to "A" items
- Planned machine (work) center utilization
- Planned labor utilization
- Actual versus planned capacity reserved for incoming orders

(f) Production Management — Production Control

- Actual manufacturing lead time per item versus standard lead time
- Actual machine (work) center utilization versus planned utilization
- Actual labor utilization versus planned utilization
- Actual overtime versus planned overtime
- Actual numbers of lots per period versus planned number of lots per period

(g) Production Management — Scheduling

- Actual production loaded into machine (work) centers versus actual production unloaded from machine (work) centers
- Actual lot size scheduled per period versus economic lot size per period
- Percent of machine (work) centers actually scheduled

- Actual jobs dispatched by machine or work center (standard hours) versus scheduled machine or work center plan (standard hours)
- Percent of jobs released that lack materials
- Percent of job orders run in issued sequence per period
- Percent of job orders run as scheduled per period
- Percent of job tickets completed as issued per period
- Setup time (cost) versus run time (cost)

(h) Production Management — Shop Floor

- Percent of total scrap quantity that is recorded
- Cycle time for job tickets, material move orders, direct labor tickets, etc.
- Percent of problems identified as they occur such as:
  — Machine problems
  — Tooling problems
  — Material quality problems
- On-time job completion status by period
- Job reject rate per period
- Accuracy of production counts between machine operations and between machine (work) centers

(i) Production Management — Overall

- Percent of total jobs expedited
- Open jobs in plant per period
- Percent of open jobs outstanding per period
- Percent of open jobs late per period
- Percent of total jobs completed by promised date
- Percent of labor variance (in hours) due to production management
- Percent of job orders ahead or behind schedule

The measurement of the percentage of jobs expedited could be an indication of problems in two areas. First, if many jobs are expedited, it is an indication that much time is consumed by this activity, leaving less time for the actual planning, scheduling, and dispatching activities. Second, if constant expediting is required, it may be an indication that the scheduling and dispatching activities are not addressing customer needs initially.

Labor variance due to the production management activity is a valid measurement of this function's ability to perform. However, in actual practice, the quantification of this portion of total labor variance is difficult to obtain.

CONCLUDING REMARKS ON MEASUREMENT

The measures presented in this appendix represent a broad cross section of potential measures. As stated earlier, no company can or should use all these measures. Instead, we recommend developing a tailored measurement system based on the concepts presented in Chapter 10 and using these potential measures as a starting point.

III. SURVEY RESPONDENTS' USE OF ACTIONS TO IMPROVE QUALITY AND PRODUCTIVITY IN MATERIALS PLANNING AND CONTROL

In this last section of Appendix D, we present the responses to our Logistics Management Survey that deal with quality and productivity-improvement actions in materials planning and control.

Figure D-2 shows responses to sales forecasting improvement actions. Only data for 1991 are shown, as comparable data do not exist for the 1983 survey. Figure D-3 presents responses to production planning/inventory management actions.

Comparable data for some production planning/inventory management actions are available. Since 1983, there was a significant increase in the percent of respondents that use MRP systems and ABC inventory planning approaches. Similarly, there has been a substantial increase in the use of formal EOQ techniques and in regular review of items for shift from make-to-order and make-to-stock.

The improvement actions presented in these tables may not be appropriate for every company. However, they provide a good starting point for developing a list of potential improvements to consider.

Figure D-2

Sales Forecasting Improvement Actions		
	Percent Of Respondents With Action In Place	
Action	**1983**	**1991**
• Improved basis for forecasting via capturing data from		
– Historical database	–	89%
– Sales organization input	–	86
– Market information	–	69
– Customers' input (for partnership relationships)	–	46
– Competitor information	–	38
• Improved sales forecasting system by		
– Increasing frequency of monitoring and correction cycle	–	48
– Installing sales forecasting package	–	42
• Improved historical data used for forecasting		
– Automation of data capture	–	43
– Refining/editing of raw input	–	35
– Links with EOS/POS (Electronic Order System/Point of Sale) systems of customers and suppliers	–	25

Figure D-3

Production Planning/Inventory Management Improvement Actions		
	Percent Of Respondents With Action In Place	
Action	**1983**	**1991**
• Separated A, B, C items for planning purposes	34%	62%
• Established formal economic order quantity levels	32	54
• Installed MRP computer package	32	51
• Regularly review item status for shifts from stock item to made-to-order or vice versa	18	41
• Reduced supplier/process lead time	–	41
• Improved production schedule stability by reducing changes/emergencies	36	40
• Reduced number of stockholding points	–	39
• Introduced "Zero Defects" concepts	–	35
• Installed Computer-Aided Design/ Manufacturing (CAD/CAM) tools	–	28
• Installed DRP computer package	–	25
• Installed Kanban/"just-in-time" techniques	–	25
• Introduced Computer-Integrated Manufacturing (CIM) concepts	–	24

APPENDIX E:
MEASURING QUALITY AND
PRODUCTIVITY IN CUSTOMER
SERVICE OPERATIONS

INTRODUCTION

The purpose of Appendix E is to help companies develop or improve their quality and productivity measurement systems for customer service operations and begin or expand their quality and productivity-improvement processes for the operation and administration of the customer service function.

The manner in which a company chooses to define and set goals for customer service has been discussed in detail in Section III of this book and, thus, is not covered in this appendix.

Appendix E is organized into the following sections:

I.   Definition of Customer Service Activities Included in this Appendix

II. Potential Measures for the Management of Customer Service Operations

   • Quality

   • Productivity

   • Other key measures

III. Survey Respondents' Use of Actions to Improve Quality and Productivity in Customer Service Operations

I. DEFINITION OF CUSTOMER SERVICE ACTIVITIES

Appendix E focuses on a discussion of measures that can be used specifically to evaluate customer service operations. Customer service operations include the following activities:

• Order processing
• Customer communications
• Credit and collections

Executing a customer service strategy, however, is the responsibility of many functions and departments. Thus, measures of how effectively customer service requirements are satisfied are also given in Appendixes A, B, C, D, and F. In developing a customer-focused *service* measurement system, readers are urged to review the quality measures in all six appendixes.

II. POTENTIAL MEASURES FOR THE MANAGEMENT OF CUSTOMER SERVICE OPERATIONS

In this section, potential measures of customer service operations quality and productivity are discussed. Customer service quality measures can be used to evaluate how *effectively* the customer service function meets the requirements of customers. Customer service productivity measures can be used to determine how *efficiently* customer service activities are administered.

This appendix includes a wide range of potential measures — far more than any one company can and should use. We recommend that this appendix be used in conjunction with the discussion in Chapter 10 on "Measurement System Design" as you tailor a measurement system to meet your company's specific needs.

CUSTOMER SERVICE QUALITY MEASURES

This section discusses measures for managing the quality of the output of the customer service function, i.e., how effectively customer requirements are being met. The following potential measures can be used to evaluate the quality of the customer service function, including measures of results (what is required), diagnostics (why requirements are not satisfied), and impact (effect of not meeting requirements) on four key service dimensions:

- Order cycle time
- On-time delivery
- Order accuracy and completeness
- Customer communication

(a) Order Cycle Time Measures

Results: Time from receipt of customer order to receipt of shipment by customer (average and statistical distribution)

Diagnostic: Number and percent of orders not received by customers within standard order cycle time specifications, along with reasons, e.g.,

- Order entry delay
- Order scheduling delay
- Inventory shortage
- Invoicing delay
- Customer change in order

Diagnostic: Number and percent of orders received by customers within standard order cycle time specifications but that required expedited handling

Impact: Cost of unacceptable order cycle time, e.g.,

- Cost of order expediting
- Value of lost orders
- Management/clerical time

Order cycle time is a measure of the total time during which the order is under the control of the supplier. This time should be measured from the receipt of the

Georgia-Pacific

intracompany memo

to   All Pulp and Paper Officers   location/facility code

from Logistics Task Force   location/facility code

subject Logistics Task Force Meeting   date January 24, 1992
        February 20, 1992

The Logistics Task Force is sponsored by Pete Correll to research and surface common logistical opportunities among the Pulp and Paper Group business units.

We have just begun our research of "cross-functional" logistics opportunities, but the improved communications among task force members has brought a keen awareness of common problems faced by all business units.

Enclosed is a copy of: <u>Improving Quality and Productivity in the Logistics Process</u>

This book is a research study performed for the Council of Logistics Management by A.T. Kearney. Over 400 U.S. companies were surveyed in the areas of transportation, materials handling, quality measurements, customer service, management information and many other areas key to logistical success.

The even better news is that we have many special
important area.

A.T. Kearney will be reviewing the results of the book with the Task Force
from 8:00am - 10:00am on February 20th in the Austrian Room of the Hyatt
Regency Hotel. If you are interested in attending this session, please notify
Brenda Barnes at 404-527-0286.

Please contact any of the Logistics Task Force members if you have any
questions or comments about the book.

Logistics Task Force

Mike Broecker
Jim Byrd
Joe Casatelli
Don Hedrick
Paul LaCroix
Norm Langberg
Peter Liberante
Chuck McElrea
Pete Mudar
John ODonnell
Lew Phillips
Eric Streed

Enclosure

cc: A. D. Correll - GA030 - 51st Floor

customer order until the shipment is received by the customer (not the shipment date, as is commonly measured).

(b) On-Time Delivery Measures

Results: Percent of orders received by the customer on-time, as defined by the customer

Diagnostic: Number and percent of orders not delivered on-time, including reasons for early or late deliveries, e.g.,

- Order entry delay
- Error in defining due date/time
- Order scheduling delay
- Customer change in order
- Invoicing delay

Impact: Cost delivery not on-time, e.g.,

- Value of lost orders
- Value of customer credits/allowances
- Unnecessary inventory or accounts receivable
- Cost of management/clerical time

This appendix deals specifically with customer service operations. Order handling delays may occur for other reasons than shown under the diagnostic measure, e.g., transportation delays. A robust measure of on-time performance would incorporate diagnostic measures for all functions involved in the logistics process.

Consistent on-time delivery is often more important than order cycle time. The effect on a customer of waiting a known, predictable, and reasonable number of days for an order is generally not as significant as the effect of missing a promised delivery date. Expected lead time requirements from a supplier can be incorporated into a customer's planning while an unexpected delay cannot.

(c) Order Accuracy and Completeness Measures

Results: Percent of orders delivered complete, as requested by the customer, and without errors

Diagnostic: Number and percent of orders not meeting customer requirements, along with reasons, e.g.,

- Error in defining item or quantity ordered
- Incomplete shipment (short items)
- Incorrect items shipped
- Damaged items

Diagnostic: Number and percent of invoices containing errors, along with reasons, e.g.,

- Incorrect price
- Incorrect terms
- Incorrect product description
- Other errors

Impact: Cost of incomplete or inaccurate orders, e.g.,

- Cost of backorder fulfillment
- Lost revenue
- Value of customer credits/allowances
- Administrative/clerical time

Incomplete or inaccurate orders can have a similar impact to that of late deliveries on total customer satisfaction, i.e., they result in an order being received that does not meet all customer specifications. When these measures are monitored by customer segment, by geographic region, or by key account, an effective customer service function will take actions to correct recurring problems after identifying sources of the problems.

Reducing the number of errors, company-caused emergency orders, and back-orders can lead to improved order processing productivity. Calling attention to these types of orders can help to minimize their frequency. Chapter 9 presents the various process analysis tools that can support investigation of problem causes and solutions.

(d) Customer Communication Measures

Results: Percent of orders delivered without unplanned communications or special attention

Results: Number and percent of customer inquiries answered to customer satisfaction

Diagnostic: Number and percent of orders that require unplanned communications, along with reasons, e.g.,

- Need to inform customer of order delays
- Need to inform customer of product unavailability
- Need to inform customer of changes (price, product substitution, etc.)

Diagnostic: Number and percent of orders requiring special communications that are not properly communicated to the customer

Diagnostic: Number and percent of customer inquiries not answered to customer satisfaction, along with reasons, e.g.,

- Call not answered within standard call pickup time (e.g., 20 seconds)
- Inaccurate response
- Late response
- Incomplete response

Impact: Cost of inadequate communication or inadequate response to inquiries, e.g.,

- Clerical/administrative time
- Lost revenue
- Expediting costs

Proactive communication of potential problems and timely response to inquiries are a means of providing value-added customer service. Effective customer communication, although more difficult to measure than traditional measures such as on-time delivery, can often provide a supplier with a distinct competitive advantage in the customer service area.

(e) Concluding Remarks on Quality Measures

The service quality measures included in this appendix form only a part of a robust service measurement system. Readers are directed to Appendixes A, B, C, D, and F for further discussion of service measurement in other areas of the logistics process.

CUSTOMER SERVICE PRODUCTIVITY MEASURES

Typical resource inputs to customer service activities include:
- Labor (direct and indirect)
- Facilities (e.g., office space) and equipment (e.g., telecommunications, computer, CRTs)
- Financial investment (e.g., inventories, accounts receivable)

Inventory investment productivity is also treated in Appendix D. Consequently, Appendix E will consider only the accounts receivable working capital aspect of financial investment.

The specific relationship between the above inputs and typical customer service activities is shown in Figure E-1. Each cell of the matrix in which an "X" appears defines an activity/input relationship that can be measured if the benefits of measurement justify the effort. See Chapter 10 for a discussion of "Desirable Characteristics of a Measurement System." Each of the tables presented in this section coincides with a cell in this matrix.

There are several aspects of order processing/customer communications that need to be considered in evaluating potential measures against the desirable characteristics of a measurement system. They include the following:

- Order processing methods may be different from one order center to another. If methods vary, the amount of time and effort required to process an order will vary, making it difficult to compare performance from center to center. The measurement system should take this into account.
- The mix of orders received by EDI, mail, phone, fax, or telex may vary from center to center, creating distinctly different order receipt work loads at each center. Productivity and performance measures should reflect these differences.
- The mix of order types (make-to-order versus to stock, regular, emergency, will call, etc.) may vary, creating different order processing work loads especially if emergency orders are processed manually and regular orders are processed via computer. The processing time allowances should reflect these differences.
- The order size (line items per order) mix may vary. Because of the fixed setup time per order and the variable time per line item, it is desirable to have a system that tracks and adjusts earned allowances for this factor.
- The mix of customer types may vary from center to center. Serving several smaller customers can represent an inherently different customer complaint, order status inquiry, and order modification request work load than serving fewer, larger customers.

These factors relate to physical differences. Additional difficulties are introduced when dealing with measures that include cost. Factors such as inflation and wage and benefit increases can directly affect cost based productivity measures when there has been no change in the physical ratios. Physical measures are generally better than economic measures.

Figure E-1

Customer Service Operations Activity/Input Matrix				
	Inputs			
Activity	Labor	Facilities/ Equipment	Working Capital	Overall
■ Order processing				
• Order entry/editing	X	X	X	X
• Scheduling	X	–	–	X
• Order/shipping set preparation	X	X	–	X
• Invoicing	X	X	–	X
■ Customer communication				
• Order modification	X	X	–	X
• Order status inquiries	X	X	–	X
• Tracing and expediting	X	X	–	X
• Error correction	X	–	–	X
• Product information requests	X	–	–	X
■ Credit and collection				
• Credit checking	X	X	–	X
• Account receivable processing/collecting	X	X	X	X

(a) Measuring The Order Processing Activity

Order processing generally includes order entry, order editing, scheduling, order/shipping set preparation, and invoicing. It may also include pricing and preparation of input to other systems such as inventory control or sales compensation. The key output is the number of transactions processed, a transaction being represented by any one of the many different types of orders, adjustments, credit memos, invoices, or other customer accounting documents.

1. Order Entry/Editing Labor. Table E-1 depicts various measures used for this activity/input.

Table E-1

ORDER ENTRY/EDITING LABOR MEASURES

Productivity	Utilization	Performance
1. Dollar value of orders entered/labor hours 2. Orders entered/ labor hours 3. Line items entered/ labor hours 4. Number of (other) transactions entered/ labor hours	1. Actual labor hours worked/ labor hours available for order entry and editing	1. Actual dollar value of orders entered per labor hour/ standard dollar value of orders entered per labor hour 2. Actual number of orders entered per labor hour/ standard number of orders entered per labor hour 3. Actual line items entered per labor hour/standard number of line items entered per labor hour 4. Actual number of (other) transactions entered per labor hour/standard number of (other) transactions entered per labor hour 5. Standard (earned) hours of work accomplished/actual labor hours expended 6. Actual labor cost/budgeted labor cost

Note: If warranted, figures in this table may be broken out by orders entered and orders edited, e.g.,
• Line items entered/entry labor hours
• Line items edited/edit labor hours

The measures presented in Table E-1 run the gamut from relatively simple, macro measures (e.g., dollar value of orders entered/labor hours) to relatively sophisticated measures (e.g., actual output versus engineered standards). In choosing measures for customer service operations, one must carefully consider how well each measure fits the "desirable" characteristics of measurement presented in Chapter 10. For instance, if the mix of orders is reasonably uniform and processing procedures do not vary from order center to order center, then orders per labor hour might be a good measure of productivity. If, however, the mix of order types and sizes is variable from center to center and methods are different, a more refined measurement system will be required to provide comparability across all centers and across time periods. This might require converting individual measures into the common denominator of standard processing time per line to aid comparability.

2. Order Entry/Editing Facilities and Equipment. Facility and equipment resource inputs include office space, telecommunications equipment, computer terminals, optical scanners, and all other types of equipment used to operate the order entry activity. Potential measures of productivity, utilization, and performance are shown in Table E-2.

Another useful measure for facilities and equipment is facility and equipment cost per operating hour. Productivity in this case is measured in terms of orders or lines entered (output) compared to facility and equipment cost per operating hour (input). This measure can be applied in total at each order center or tracked by individual piece of equipment, which facilitates comparison and evaluation between different types of equipment used for the same purpose.

Table E-2

ORDER ENTRY/EDITING FACILITIES AND EQUIPMENT MEASURES

Productivity	Utilization	Performance
1. Dollar value of orders entered per facility (or equipment unit)/ equipment hours	1. Number of equipment units used per day/units available for use (only for multiple unit equipment types)	1. Actual orders entered per facility (or equipment unit) per day/standard orders entered per facility (or equipment unit) per day
2. Orders entered per office/day		
3. Line items entered per office/day	2. Hours equipment units used/available hours	2. Actual line items entered per facility (or equipment unit) per day/ standard line items entered per facility (or equipment unit) per day
4. Orders entered per unit of equipment (e.g., per optical scanner)/ equipment hours		
5. Line items entered/ equipment hours		3. Actual equipment up time/standard up time
		4. Actual facility and equipment cost/ budgeted cost

Note: If warranted, figures may be broken out by orders entered and orders edited.

3. Overall Order Entry. Table E-3 presents measures that are of potential value either when specific nonlabor inputs (facilities and equipment) are not tracked independently or when it is desirable to measure the overall order entry activity.

The performance measures that compare actual units (orders or lines) entered per day to total units received represent a means of defining the true backlog of orders or order lag. The open order file may not represent the true order lag because of people or machine capacity constraints in order entry/editing that prevent all orders/lines received from being processed promptly.

Table E-3

OVERALL ORDER ENTRY MEASURES

Productivity	Utilization	Performance
1. Total orders entered/ total order entry costs	1. Total volume of orders entered/total order entry capacity	1. Actual order entry costs/budgeted order entry costs
2. Total lines entered/ total order entry costs	2. Total orders received/ total order capacity	2. Standard order entry cost allowances earned/total order entry costs incurred
3. Total dollar value of orders entered/ total order entry costs	3. Total actual transaction throughput/maximum transaction capacity	

Note: If warranted, total may be broken down by type of order, e.g., total regular orders entered/total regular order entry cost.

4. Order Scheduling Labor. Table E-4 displays potential measures for order scheduling labor.

Table E-4

ORDER SCHEDULING LABOR MEASURES

Productivity	Utilization	Performance
1. Orders scheduled/ labor hours	1. Actual labor hours worked in scheduling/ labor hours available for scheduling	1. Actual number of orders scheduled per labor hour/standard number of orders scheduled per labor hour
2. Line items scheduled/ labor hours		2. Standard (earned) hours of work accomplished/actual labor hours expended
		3. Actual labor cost/ budgeted labor cost

The order scheduling activity within the order processing function is usually associated with the planning and release of "make" (production) orders as opposed to orders to be filled from stock. However, it may also include the latter when orders from stock are scheduled to be picked and merged with make orders to consolidate both orders for more economical transportation. This measure is discussed in greater detail in Appendix D.

5. Overall Order Scheduling. The potential measures for overall order scheduling are the same as those for scheduling labor because there are seldom any significant discrete facility and equipment or working capital inputs required for the order scheduling activity.

6. Order/Shipping Set Preparation Labor. Order/shipping set preparation is the processing activity that creates hard copy orders and related shipping documentation. It also creates documentation for other transactions such as adjustments, credit memos, returned goods authorizations, and the like. It is sometimes broken out as activity separate from the other activities that comprise order/document processing.

Table E-5 shows several potential measures for the labor involved in preparing order sets or appropriate documentation for other types of transactions.

Table E-5

ORDER/SHIPPING SET PREPARATION LABOR MEASURES

Productivity	Utilization	Performance
1. Number of order sets prepared/labor hours	1. Actual labor hours worked/labor hours available for order set preparation	1. Actual number of order sets (or other transaction documents) prepared per labor hour/standard number of documents prepared per labor hour
2. Dollar value of order sets prepared/labor hours		
3. Number of other transaction documents prepared/labor hours		2. Standard (earned) hours of work accomplished/actual labor hours expended
		3. Actual labor cost/budgeted labor cost
		4. Actual dollar value of order sets prepared per labor hour/standard dollar value of orders sets prepared per labor hour

As indicated earlier, dollar value per labor hour is the *least* meaningful productivity measure. In addition to random variations in order size, dollar values are influenced greatly by price and/or cost changes and, therefore, may not accurately reflect real changes in physical productivity.

7. Order/Shipping Set Preparation Facilities and Equipment. Table E-6 contains potential measures for this activity/input.

Another measure for equipment is operating cost per day, week, or month. Although not a productivity measure (because of its input/input rather than output/output relationship), it is good information to have in evaluating alternative makes or types of equipment.

8. Overall Order/Shipping Set Preparation. Overall measures for this activity are presented in Table E-7.

Table E-6

ORDER/SHIPPING SET PREPARATION FACILITIES AND EQUIPMENT MEASURES

Productivity	Utilization	Performance
1. Order sets prepared per office/day	1. Hours equipment units used/available hours	1. Actual order sets prepared per facility (or equipment unit) per day/standard order sets prepared per facility (or equipment unit) per day
2. Order sets prepared per processing equipment unit/equipment hours		
3. Dollar value of order sets prepared per office/day		2. Actual equipment up time/standard equipment up time
4. Other transaction documents prepared per office/day		3. Actual facility and equipment cost/ budgeted cost
5. Other transaction documents prepared per equipment unit/ equipment hours		

Table E-7

OVERALL ORDER/SHIPPING SET PREPARATION MEASURES

Productivity	Utilization	Performance
1. Total number of order sets prepared/total order set preparation costs	1. Total volume of order sets prepared/total order set preparation capacity	1. Actual order set preparation cost/ budgeted order set preparation costs
2. Total number of other transaction documents prepared/ total cost of preparing other documents	2. Total volume of other transactions prepared/ total capacity for preparing other transactions	2. Actual "other document" preparation costs/budgeted "other document" preparation costs
3. Total dollar value of order sets prepared/ total order preparation costs	3. Total volume of orders received for preparation/ total order set preparation capacity	3. Standard order set preparation cost allowances earned/ actual order set preparation cost incurred
		4. Standard "other document" preparation cost allowances earned/actual "other document" preparation costs

9. Invoicing Labor. Invoicing may be an integral part of order set preparation, or it may be a separate activity. Table E-8 shows several potential measures for the labor involved in invoicing when it is large enough and specialized enough to be a separate activity for measurement.

Table E-8

INVOICING LABOR MEASURES

Productivity	Utilization	Performance
1. Number of invoices prepared/labor hours	1. Actual labor hours worked on invoicing/ labor hours available for invoicing	1. Standard (earned) hours of work accomplished/actual labor hours expended
2. Line items invoiced/ labor hours		2. Actual labor cost/ budgeted labor cost
3. Dollar value of orders invoiced/labor hours		3. Actual number of invoices prepared per labor hour/standard number of invoices prepared per labor hour
		4. Actual line items invoiced per labor hour/ standard number of line items invoiced per labor hour
		5. Actual dollar value of invoices processed per labor hour/standard dollar value of invoices processed per labor hour

10. Invoicing Facilities and Equipment. Table E-9 presents several potential measures to use in evaluating the productivity, utilization, and performance of invoicing facilities and equipment.

Another measure for equipment is operating cost per day, week, or month.

11. Overall Invoicing Measures. Table E-10 presents measures that may be useful in evaluating overall invoicing.

Table E-9

INVOICING FACILITIES AND EQUIPMENT MEASURES

Productivity	Utilization	Performance
1. Number of invoices prepared/day	1. Hours invoicing equipment used/ available hours	1. Actual invoices prepared per equipment hour/standard invoices prepared per equipment hours
2. Invoices prepared/ equipment hours		
3. Line items invoiced/ equipment hours		2. Actual line items invoiced per equipment hour/standard line items invoiced per equipment hour
4. Dollar value of invoices prepared/day		
		3. Actual equipment up time/standard equipment up time
		4. Actual facility and equipment cost/ budgeted cost

Table E-10

OVERALL INVOICING MEASURES

Productivity	Utilization	Performance
1. Total number of invoices prepared/total invoice preparation costs	1. Total volume of invoices processed/ total invoice processing capacity	1. Actual invoice processing costs/ budgeted invoice processing costs
2. Total dollar value invoiced/total invoice preparation costs		2. Standard invoice processing cost allowances earned/ total invoice processing costs incurred

Note: If warranted, totals may be broken down by type of invoice, e.g., total regular invoices/total cost of regular invoices.

(b) Measuring the Customer Communication Activity

Customer communication includes the following order and sales service activities:
- Order modification
- Order status inquiries
- Tracing and expediting
- Error correction
- Product information requests

This is by no means an all inclusive list, but it is representative of the type of activities typically carried out by customer service representatives. Because of the subjective nature of these activities and the wide variability in, for example, the amount of time required to respond to different types of inquiries as well as different inquiries of the same type, it is relatively more difficult to establish meaningful productivity measures for evaluation.

1. Customer Communication Labor. Table E-11 displays several labor measures that potentially are worth considering. Note that because of the similarity of the nature of the work, all customer communications activities have been grouped together under the general heading of customer inquiries.

Table E-11

CUSTOMER COMMUNICATION LABOR MEASURES

Productivity	Utilization	Performance
1. Customer inquiries handled/labor hours	1. Total labor hours devoted to handling customer inquiries/total labor hours available	1. Actual number of inquiries handled per labor hour/standard inquiries per labor hour
		2. Standard hours earned/actual labor hours

Note: If appropriate, these figures may be broken out by type of inquiry, e.g., order status inquiries/hours spent on order status inquiries.

It is important to define "customer inquiries handled" properly. In an attempt to improve productivity, some companies have placed limits on the amount of time that customer service representatives are allowed to "handle" an inquiry from the customer. They measure the total number of inquiries per labor hour rather than the total number of inquiries that were handled to the customer's satisfaction (i.e., the customer received the information sought or the customer's problem was resolved). Thus, these companies have overlooked a basic principle — a process is truly productive only when its output (e.g., "inquiries handled") has value to the customer.

2. Customer Communication Facilities and Equipment. Table E-12 presents several facility and equipment measures that could be used for customer communication.

As in other activities, this category of inputs includes all equipment and equipment associated operating costs, e.g., telecommunications expense.

3. Overall Customer Communication. Table E-13 presents potential measures to use in evaluating the overall customer communication activity.

Obviously, the ability to collect information on type of inquiry is critical in order to effectively improve a customer service communication process. Knowledge of the most frequent types of customer complaints, order information requested, or technical information sought will provide insight into those areas where assistance is most needed and the necessary staffing requirements to provide that assistance. Providing effective customer communication is a key step to improving the overall customer-company relationship.

Table E-12

CUSTOMER COMMUNICATION FACILITY AND EQUIPMENT MEASURES

Productivity	Utilization	Performance
1. Customer inquiries handled per center/day 2. Customer inquiries handled per equipment unit/equipment hours	1. Hours equipment unit used/hours available	1. Actual customer inquiries handled per equipment unit hour (or day)/standard inquiries handled per equipment hour (or day) 2. Actual equipment up time/standard equipment up time 3. Actual facility and equipment cost/ budgeted cost

Table E-13

OVERALL CUSTOMER COMMUNICATION MEASURES

Productivity	Utilization	Performance
1. Total number customer inquiries handled/ total customer communication costs	1. Total volume of inquiries handled/ total inquiry handling capacity	1. Actual customer communication cost/ budgeted communication cost 2. Standard customer communication cost allowances earned/ total actual costs incurred

Note: If appropriate, totals may be broken down by the type of customer inquiry.

(c) Measuring the Credit and Collection Activity

Credit and collection is not typically an activity that reports to the customer service department. However, it has been included with customer service in this appendix because it is an important element in the company-customer relationship.

Credit and collection has responsibility for monitoring and controlling the firm's accounts receivable balances. The reason that firms may choose to consider this function as part of the logistics process is that logistics activities such as shipping and order processing can have a significant impact on accounts receivable balances especially when there are problems in these areas. Past due invoices are frequently the result of some logistics related problem such as late or incorrect invoicing, late delivery, or incomplete shipment.

Working capital invested in accounts receivable can be viewed as one of the key resource inputs required to generate sales. For those companies employing sales promotions, deals, or extended payment terms (dating) to stimulate sales, this investment can become quite large at certain times.

Some of the measures employed for evaluating investment in accounts receivable include the following:

- Total accounts receivable dollars/total net sales dollars
- Total accounts receivable dollars/net daily sales
- Total sales on extended dating programs/total accounts receivable on extended dating
- Average age (in days) of accounts receivable
- Past due accounts receivable categorized by time period, e.g., 31-60 days, 61-90 days, over 90 days

The productivity of credit and collection department employees can be measured in a manner similar to other clerical functions, i.e., by comparing the number of credit checks made, customer payments processed, or other physical activities accomplished with actual labor hours.

OTHER CUSTOMER SERVICE EFFECTIVENESS MEASURES

Several other key measures of the effectiveness of the customer service function can be tracked. These measures generally indicate how well various components of the customer service function are performing. They are indicators of good or poor practices and can be used as benchmarks.

(a) Order Processing

- Lines (or transactions) entered in error/total lines (or transactions) entered
- Orders requiring edit change/total number of orders edited
- Lines requiring edit change/total number of lines edited
- Order entry labor cost/total order processing cost
- Order entry nonlabor cost/total order processing cost
- Total order entry cost/total logistics administrative cost
- Actual dollar value of orders entered per day/total dollar value of orders received per day
- Actual number of orders entered per day/total number of orders received per day
- Actual number of lines entered per day/total number of lines received per day
- Invoicing cost/total order processing cost

To track available backlog in invoicing work, or invoicing lag, the following measures may be helpful:

- Actual dollar value of invoices processed per day/actual dollar value of orders available for invoicing per day
- Actual number of invoices processed per day/actual number of orders available

for invoicing per day
- Actual number of line items invoiced per day/actual number of line items available for invoicing per day

The following measures may be useful in evaluating the complete order processing activity (including all subactivities):
- Actual order cycle time per order (by type)/standard cycle time
- Total order processing labor cost/total order processing cost
- Total order processing nonlabor cost/total order processing cost
- Total order processing cost/total logistics cost
- Number of transaction (order, invoice, etc.) errors/total number of transactions processed
- Number of (company-caused) emergency orders/total number of orders processed
- Number of backorders generated/total number of orders processed

(b) Customer Communication

- Elapsed time to complete the handling of customer inquiry
- Number of times the phone must ring per customer call before it is answered by a customer service representative
- Number of incoming customer calls going unanswered per day
- Number of busy signals registered per day/total number of incoming calls

CONCLUDING REMARKS ON MEASUREMENT

The measures presented in this appendix represent a broad cross section of potential measures. As stated earlier, no company can or should use all these measures. Instead, we recommend developing a tailored measurement system based on the concepts presented in Chapter 10 and using these potential measures as a starting point.

III. SURVEY RESPONDENTS' USE OF ACTIONS TO IMPROVE QUALITY AND PRODUCTIVITY IN CUSTOMER SERVICE OPERATIONS MANAGEMENT

In this last section of Appendix E, we present the responses to our Logistics Management Survey that deal with customer service operations.

Figure E-2 presents responses to service management actions, and Figure E-3 presents responses to order processing actions.

Several of these actions have already been discussed in Chapter 11 — "High-Impact Improvement Actions." In this appendix, we will just discuss briefly the major differences between the 1983 and 1991 responses.

The 1983 survey did not include a section on customer service improvement actions. Therefore, no comparisons are possible.

In the area of order processing improvements (see Figure E-3), there has been a

E

noticeable increase in the number of respondents who are using today's computer technology to improve quality, cycle time, and productivity. The greatest gain, in both percentage increase and absolute numbers, was for computer to computer ordering.

The improvement actions in Figures E-2 and E-3 may not be appropriate for every company. However, they provide a good starting point for developing a list of potential improvements to consider.

Figure E-2

Customer Service Improvement Actions		
	Percent Of Respondents With Action In Place	
Action	**1983**	**1991**
• Visit customer facilities to understand needs/constraints	–	80%
• Follow up on complaints/service breakdowns	–	78
• Meet with customers to review their perceptions of your service to them	–	75
• Reduce order cycle time by expediting transportation	–	69
• Reduce order cycle time by eliminating bottlenecks	–	66
• Reduce order cycle time by computer to computer ordering	–	63
• Differentiate service goals by market/product segment	–	51
• Establish joint teams between your unit and individual customer organizations to improve quality and productivity	–	50
• Provide feedback to customers on your unit's service performance to them	–	44
• Reduce order cycle time by decentralizing inventories	–	43
• Improve sales planning through exchange of requirements planning information with customers	–	43
• Integrate quality processes with customers	–	41
• Increase order frequency/reduce minimum order quantity	–	39
• Conduct profitability analysis on customer/product portfolio	–	36
• Implement hot line for expediting	–	36
• Differentiate pricing based on service levels	–	29
• Reduce order cycle time by staging subassemblies/assemblies to order	–	22
• Conduct "exit interviews" with lost customers as input to service improvement	–	14

Figure E-3

Order Processing Improvement Actions

Action	Percent Of Respondents With Action In Place	
	1983	**1991**
• Conversion from manual to computerized order processing	53%	75%
• Centralized order entry to improve productivity	52	74
• On-line confirmation of stock availability	–	67
• Systems analyses to improve effectiveness and efficiency of present order processing systems	44	64
• Use of computer to computer order entry	30	61
• Design and installation of new order processing system	49	54
• On-line reservation of inventory (on hand, in transit, or to be produced) for specific customer's orders	–	52
• Use of automated order entry systems such as hand-held computers	14	27
• Installation of proprietary order entry devices at customer's premises	–	20

E

APPENDIX F:
MEASURING QUALITY AND
PRODUCTIVITY IN LOGISTICS
MANAGEMENT

INTRODUCTION

The purpose of Appendix F is to help companies establish a quality and productivity measurement system for the management of the logistics process. Management of the logistics process means coordinating all of the activities discussed in the previous appendixes to effectively and efficiently meet the service requirements of customers.

The appendix is a continuation of the main report. Thus, the concepts presented in the main report should be considered as a measurement system is developed for these functions.

Appendix F is organized into the following sections:

I.   Definition of Logistics Management Activities Included in this Appendix

II. Potential Measures for Logistics Management

   • Quality

   • Productivity

III. Programs to Improve Quality and Productivity in Logistics Management

I. DEFINITION OF LOGISTICS
MANAGEMENT ACTIVITIES

Logistics management is that phase of administration responsible for the effective functioning of the overall logistics process. The scope of logistics management consists of:

• The senior logistics executive in the business unit.

• Line operations management personnel directly involved in the logistics process. This includes individuals responsible for purchasing, production planning, customer service operations, the distribution centers, transportation activities, and private fleet operations regardless of where these line organizations report in the corporation and their respective line and staff organizations.

• The corporate and divisional logistics staff groups, which may or may not fall under one of the previously mentioned support service groups. These may exist as separate staff groups within the logistics organization, or they may be made up of changing groups of line personnel who devote only a portion of their time to staff projects (e.g., planning a new distribution center, designing a new information system).

F

II. POTENTIAL MEASURES FOR LOGISTICS MANAGEMENT

Management outputs are less quantifiable than those of individual department employees assigned to specific tasks because management's inputs have only an indirect effect on output. Because of this somewhat diffused impact, it is often more important to evaluate management based on its ability to achieve results effectively rather than to evaluate management's *personal* productivity.

Logistics managers are evaluated primarily on the basis of:

1. Line management ability. This criterion considers the manager's ability to manage the department's day to day operations and meet goals that have been established for service quality, productivity, and all aspects of performance, including budget.

2. Problem solving ability. This deals with the ability to diagnose problems with the operation and to develop/apply innovative new ideas that result in cost savings, service improvement, or increased return on investment. Also included here is the logistics manager's ability to anticipate opportunities for improvement before they become problems that must be solved.

3. Project management ability. This refers to the ability to structure and manage projects designed to correct problems and improve the logistics process.

4. People management ability. Managers are generally evaluated to some extent on their ability to develop and motivate their employees' technical and management skills. Effectiveness in these areas might be measured by employee turnover, absenteeism, grievances, and other employee relations factors. This topic is not within the scope of this section, however, so a more detailed discussion is not included.

In the paragraphs that follow, we present potential quality and productivity measures for logistics management.

LOGISTICS MANAGEMENT QUALITY MEASURES

This section discusses measures for managing the quality of the logistics process, i.e., how effectively the logistics process is meeting customer requirements. The desired result of the logistics process is total customer satisfaction in all areas of logistics service. Thus, the customer service quality measures discussed in Appendix E are also suitable for measuring the effectiveness of the overall logistics process.

In addition to these customer service quality measures, logistics management can be evaluated through any ongoing measurement of total customer satisfaction with the logistics process. Customer satisfaction can be measured by means of a customer service audit administered annually to each key customer segment. Specific measures can be developed as follows:

Results: Percent of customers in each segment rating the company as an "excellent" supplier

Diagnostic: Percent of customers in each segment rating the company as an "average" or "poor" supplier, along with reasons, e.g.,

- Lead time requirements too long
- Poor on-time delivery performance
- Errors
- Product damage
- Poor communications
- Quality of service personnel
- Not responsive to problems

Impact: Cost of being rated lower than "excellent" by customers:
- Revenue decline in an account
- Lost customers
- Cost to provide additional service

LOGISTICS MANAGEMENT PRODUCTIVITY MEASURES

Logistics management productivity measures fall into the general categories of:
- Logistics cost as a percent of sales
    — Compared internally (e.g., among divisions)
    — Compared externally (between similar companies)
- Cost of specific logistics functions as a percent of sales or logistics cost
    — Compared internally (e.g., among divisions)
    — Compared externally (between similar companies)
- Performance
    — Budget versus actual expressed in terms of dollars, man-hours, headcount, or other appropriate measures
    — Productivity, output compared to input in appropriate terms

Often, year to year trend analysis of these measures is more meaningful than single year figures.

(a) Logistics Cost as a Percent of Sales

By far the most common measure to evaluate the top logistics executive is total logistics cost/dollar sales.

There are several problems with this measure:

- In most cases, sales dollars are not a direct driver of logistics costs. Instead, physical volume handled (weight, orders, miles) and service requirements (order completeness, cycle times) drive logistics cost regardless of the sales dollars the products represent.
- Measures that use dollars of cost of sales as elements of the equation are of questionable value due to the variability in the value of the dollar. Normalizing the measure to a base year through the use of appropriate deflation factors is one way to rectify the problem, but this practice is cumbersome and therefore not widespread.
- Macro measures of this type suffer from a definitional problem. Lines picked per

F

man-hour is fairly straightforward in this interpretation, but this is not the case with logistics cost as a percent of sales.

For instance:

— Were net or gross sales used?

— What logistics functions were included in the cost total?

— Were management salaries included?

— Was inventory carrying cost included?

— Has there been a change in order or customer mix or in service levels?

Despite the problems of definition, logistics cost as a percent of sales is a figure that is extensively used by many companies as a comparative measure. These problems of comparison will continue to exist whether the comparisons are made between companies or among business units within the same company.

Top logistics executives are also evaluated on the basis of their budget performance both with respect to dollars and headcount. Macro productivity measures such as "hundredweight units distributed per labor hour" and "cost of logistics per hundredweight" are in limited use. More frequently, actual performance against standards is used for evaluation purposes as is performance against service standards such as:

• Percent of orders delivered on-time

• Percent order fill rate

• Percent invoice errors

Top logistics executives are generally evaluated on the same basis as their subordinates except that:

• The measures used are generally macro level measures for the entire business unit.

• The measures are reported as performance indicators relating actual results to some predetermined objectives or standards.

• Their evaluations can be influenced to a greater extent by input from other senior functional managers with the extent of this influence dependent upon their reporting relationship to those individuals.

(b) Cost of Specific Logistics Functions

Managers of individual logistics activities such as warehousing or transportation are generally evaluated on the basis of the same criteria as the top logistics executive except that:

• Department or activity cost as a percent of sales (or cost of goods sold) is used as an evaluation criterion instead of total logistics cost.

• Department cost as a percent of total logistics cost is added to the evaluation criteria list.

• Evaluation of these managers tends to be more objective because they are usually working against a specific set of productivity, service level, and savings goals or objectives.

(c) Performance Measures

Managers of logistics support services (e.g., logistics planning, logistics engineering, logistics systems design) are generally evaluated on the basis of budget performance and (sometimes vaguely defined) service criteria. These managers and their staffs are viewed as resources to be used in supporting the functional managers and, as such, their service levels and productivity are not easily quantified. Typically, they are heavily involved in project type work, so that much of their evaluation occurs at project review or completion points.

Evaluation of project managers is based on three considerations:

- Performance relative to time constraints
- Budget performance relative to dollar limitations
- Actual benefits derived relative to goals such as:
  — Dollar savings or profit improvement
  — Service level improvements
  — Productivity improvements

Every organization must manage logistics projects but most find this a particularly difficult area in which to perform well. Some of the problems that cause difficulties include the following:

- Failure to start by establishing a "base case" against which to evaluate alternatives
- Failure to prepare realistic time and expense budgets for the project
- Failure to adequately specify project objectives and scope, including how to measure attainment of the objectives
- Failure to cancel or redirect projects when it becomes obvious that further work on the original plan will not be cost effective
- Failure to require and conduct post-project audits

(d) Final Comments on Measures

Ultimately, the true measure of logistics management and of the logistics process itself is the level of long-term customer satisfaction achieved for the total logistics costs incurred. Most companies have yet to develop such a measure because:

- They have not yet defined long-term customer satisfaction and, thus, cannot measure it.
- They do not accurately and completely identify total logistics costs because traditional accounting methods do not support activity and process costing requirements.

III. PROGRAMS TO IMPROVE QUALITY AND PRODUCTIVITY IN LOGISTICS MANAGEMENT

The actions discussed in Appendix E that are being used by survey companies to improve customer service quality are also effective in improving the quality of the overall logistics process, since the objective is similar. While these customer service improvement programs tend to deal with external actions to improve interactions with customers, the logistics management function is also concerned with internal improvement programs to enhance the effectiveness and productivity of the total process.

Programs that some companies in the survey are using to improve the quality and productivity of the overall logistics process are briefly described in the following paragraphs.

1. Formal Quality and Productivity Improvement Process. Developing and carrying out a formal process for improving quality and productivity throughout logistics is the central theme of this research report.

2. Integrated Operations Management. This approach was discussed at length in Chapter 11. In summary, it calls for integration of the major operational functions of the business at the strategic, tactical, and transaction processing levels. It also includes formal coordination with customers and suppliers at these three levels.

3. MBO Program. Another useful technique is that of MBO (Management by Objectives) and goal setting to establish performance standards for various activities as discussed in the previous section.

MBO-type programs are useful for two reasons:

- They give logistics management a target to shoot for with respect to the individual department's operations.
- Managers generally have a hand in establishing the goals, which forces them to plan their operation more carefully in order to ensure attainment of plans.

It is important that the MBO goals tie back to overall corporate goals and objectives. Thus, they should be developed as a part of an overall "policy deployment" approach as described in Chapter 2.

Detailing of objectives will vary depending upon the level within the organization. Figure F-1 lists an example of an annual action plan based on one developed by a logistics vice president in one of the companies interviewed. At the level of the logistics vice president, the goals are more general. They are more clearly defined with respect to the specific outputs required as they are "deployed" to lower levels within the logistics organization.

4. MBX Program. Once an operation is running relatively smoothly, a Management By Exception (MBX) program is often implemented. MBX reports exceptional performance to management, identifying only those areas that require attention. MBX suffers from the same problems as MBO, requiring that accurate cost and performance data be available and reported in a timely, understandable manner in order for the program to be effective.

5. Use of Analytical Tools. Many companies make use of computer based models to answer "what if" questions regarding possible logistics network alternatives, inventory level/service level tradeoffs, etc. Using such tools can provide a wealth of new, useful logistics service and cost information.

A major opportunity that is often overlooked is to use such tools as "checks" on actual decisions and results. For example, these tools can be used to look for a better approach or to help develop new logic for decision making in areas such as order consolidation, production scheduling, forecasting, and vehicle routing. When linked with expert system technology, such analytical capability can help improve the quality and consistency of decisions.

6. Capital Expenditure Management. Similarly, the development and use of a formal capital equipment justification system has helped ensure that funds are invested in projects that yield the highest return.

7. Employee Motivation Approaches. In order for an operation to be effective, employees and management must be motivated to excel. Employee motivation through the use of wage incentive systems and other gainsharing techniques was discussed in Chapter 13. Also, as a part of formal quality processes, firms are currently developing their managers into improved employee motivators by conducting training programs to improve this aspect of their managerial skills. This type of program, coupled with a feeling of identity and importance on the part of the employees, is a key to effectively motivating the work force.

Figure F-1

Corporate Logistics Department
Annual Plan Summary

Annual Action Plan Summary   **Prepared By:** _____

Planning Unit: **Approved By:** _____

Corporate Logistics

---

1. **Customer Service Survey**. Support Marketing Department project to survey top 100 accounts on customer service requirements. Develop and execute improvement plan based on study conclusions

2. **Quality Training Program**. Engage Corporate Quality staff to train logistics management and staff and Central Distribution Center management and staff in basic total quality principles and improvement techniques

3. **Dedicated Fleet Analysis** (Transportation). In conjunction with the Divisions, analyze potential use of a dedicated for-hire fleet within the corporation for selected primary and secondary traffic lanes to improve service reliability

4. **Computerized Freight Consolidation Program** (Transportation). Develop a system for automating the current manual Freight Consolidation Program. With the assistance of corporate MIS, organize data that are transmitted to shipping points sorted by destination location

5. **Hazardous Material Regulations Compliance Program**. In conjunction with the Divisions, develop a formal procedure to monitor and implement changes in requirements for transportation and materials handling based on new governmental regulations. This will be carried out through the efforts of a Hazardous Material Regulations Task Force

6. **Recognition Awards Program**. Develop and institute a formal awards program that will acknowledge the service improvement and reduction efforts at the Distribution Center

7. **Improve Warehouse Methods And Systems**. Evaluate various methods and systems changes for implementation at the Corporate Distribution Center to improve productivity

8. **New CDC Facilities Studies**. Determine feasibility of establishing new Corporation Distribution Centers

9. **Unitization**. Coordinate between CDCs and Divisions unitized handling, uniform pallet pattern and packaging design programs in an effort to reduce total distribution costs

F

APPENDIX G:
STUDY BACKGROUND

INTRODUCTION

This appendix discusses the background, approach, and demographics of the research supporting this book. In total, three different questionnaires were distributed, and 57 personal interviews were conducted.

The number of responses to each survey is shown in Figure G-1. Demographic data on respondents to each survey are presented later in this appendix.

Figure G-1

Types Of Questionnaire Surveys Conducted	
Survey	**Number Of Respondents**
■ Logistics Management Survey	308
■ Customer Expectations Survey	42
■ Logistics Service Provider Survey	68

The interviews were designed to identify the progress made by logistics innovators in quality and productivity improvement. The interviews covered:
- Background and major elements of their improvement processes
- Approaches to customer service goal setting
- Success stories in quality and productivity improvement
- Prerequisites for success
- Advice for others
  - Beginning an improvement process
  - Maintaining momentum

While some companies interviewed chose to remain anonymous, the companies listed in Figure G-2 allowed us to publicly recognize their participation and contribution to the research.

LOGISTICS MANAGEMENT SURVEY DEMOGRAPHICS

The Logistics Management Survey was the primary source of statistical data throughout the book. Its respondents are profiled in the paragraphs and figures that follow.

The industry breakdown of this survey is shown in Figure G-3. The food, pharmaceutical and drugs, chemical and plastics, and general merchandising industries are most strongly represented making up about 50 percent of the total. Eight percent of the respondents indicated "other industry" without specifying a particular industry.

Figure G-2

Interview Participants	
• American Airlines, Inc.	• Maytag Corporation
• Apple Computer, Inc.	• The Mead Corporation
• Bausch & Lomb	• Menlo Logistics
• Baxter Healthcare Corporation – Distribution Division	• Milliken and Company
• Burlington Motor Carriers	• Motorola, Inc.
• CF Motor Freight	• Nabisco Brands, Inc.
• Chesebrough-Pond's, Inc.	• Nalco Chemical Company
• Corn Products – A Unit of CPC International, Inc.	• National Starch & Chemical Company
• The Dannon Company, Inc.	• Pfizer, Inc.
• Dow Chemical USA	• PPG Industries, Inc.
• Dry Storage Corporation	• Procter & Gamble Company
• Eastman Kodak Company	• Preston Trucking Company, Inc.
• Esprit de Corp	• The Quaker Oats Company
• Exel Logistics – DCI	• Rohm & Haas Company
• Federal Express Corporation	• Sandoz Chemical Corporation
• Ford Motor Company	• Sara Lee Bakery – Sara Lee Corp.
• Fritz Companies Inc.	• Schneider National, Inc.
• W.W. Grainger, Inc.	• Scott Paper Company
• Hewlett-Packard Company	• The Stride Rite Corporation
• Hill's Pet Products, Inc.	• Sylvania Lighting – GTE Products Corp.
• J.B. Hunt Transport, Inc.	• Target Stores
• Johnson & Johnson, Hospital Services Division	• Texas Instruments, Inc.
• Keebler Company	• Trammell Crow Distribution Company
• Kraft General Foods U.S.A.	• United Parcel Service of America, Inc.
	• Wang Laboratories, Inc.
	• Westinghouse Electric Corporation
	• Xerox Corporation
	• Yellow Freight System, Inc.

Fifty-five percent of respondents reported their primary product type as consumer goods as shown in Figure G-4, while the others produce raw materials or components or distribute goods such as supplies or parts.

Forty-five percent of respondents were manufacturing business units, while 29 percent provided distribution services for their corporations (see Figure G-5). Wholesaling and retailing respondents made up the bulk of the remainder.

Forty-three percent of responses were from corporate logistics executives while 40 percent came from executives at the divisional level (see Figure G-6). The survey captures responses from a wide range of companies based on annual revenue (see Figure G-7). Business units in the $100-$500 million revenue were the most prevalent. Two-thirds of the businesses are publicly held, while one-third are privately held.

The organizational reporting structure for logistics activities in the respondent companies is displayed in Figure G-8.

As the figure indicates, traditional physical distribution activities most frequently report to the logistics department in the responding companies. These activities include transportation (inbound/outbound, intracompany, and private fleet), finished goods warehousing, finished goods inventory management, and the logistics management activities. Beyond these activities, however, other departments have line responsibility for logistics activities in many companies.

Figure G-3

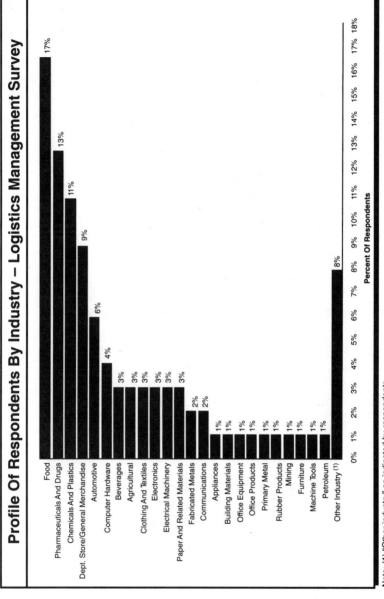

Profile Of Respondents By Industry – Logistics Management Survey

Note: (1) "Other industry" as indicated by respondents

Figure G-4

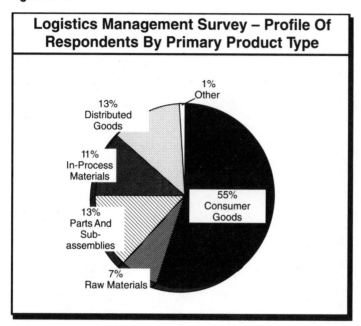

Logistics Management Survey – Profile Of Respondents By Primary Product Type

1% Other

13% Distributed Goods

11% In-Process Materials

13% Parts And Sub-assemblies

7% Raw Materials

55% Consumer Goods

Figure G-5

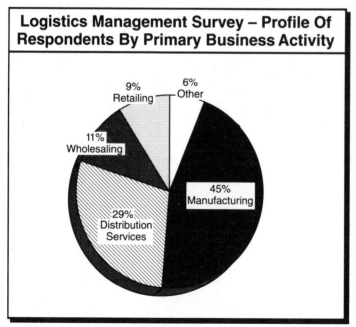

Logistics Management Survey – Profile Of Respondents By Primary Business Activity

9% Retailing

6% Other

11% Wholesaling

29% Distribution Services

45% Manufacturing

Figure G-6

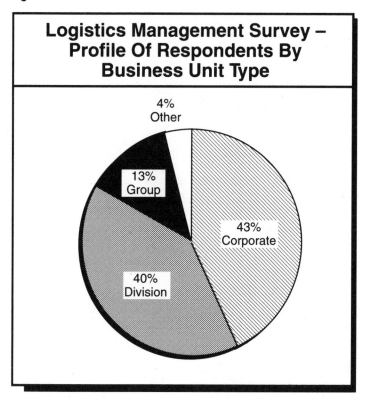

Logistics Management Survey – Profile Of Respondents By Business Unit Type

4% Other

13% Group

43% Corporate

40% Division

Figure G-7

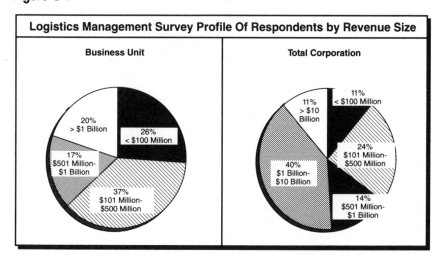

Logistics Management Survey Profile Of Respondents by Revenue Size

Business Unit

20% > $1 Billion

26% < $100 Million

17% $501 Million-$1 Billion

37% $101 Million-$500 Million

Total Corporation

11% > $10 Billion

11% < $100 Million

24% $101 Million-$500 Million

40% $1 Billion-$10 Billion

14% $501 Million-$1 Billion

Figure G-8

Logistics Management Survey – Profile Of Departments To Which Logistics Activities Report

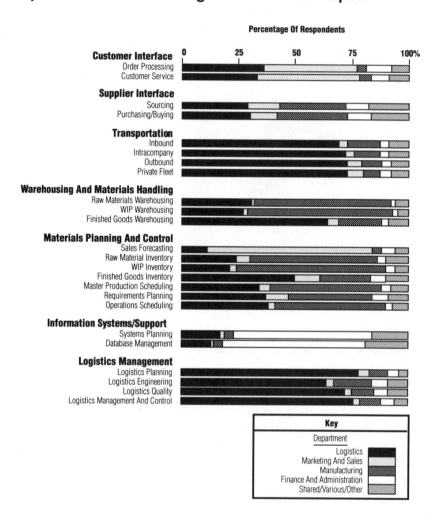

Percentage Of Respondents

Customer Interface
- Order Processing
- Customer Service

Supplier Interface
- Sourcing
- Purchasing/Buying

Transportation
- Inbound
- Intracompany
- Outbound
- Private Fleet

Warehousing And Materials Handling
- Raw Materials Warehousing
- WIP Warehousing
- Finished Goods Warehousing

Materials Planning And Control
- Sales Forecasting
- Raw Material Inventory
- WIP Inventory
- Finished Goods Inventory
- Master Production Scheduling
- Requirements Planning
- Operations Scheduling

Information Systems/Support
- Systems Planning
- Database Management

Logistics Management
- Logistics Planning
- Logistics Engineering
- Logistics Quality
- Logistics Management And Control

Key

Department
- Logistics
- Marketing And Sales
- Manufacturing
- Finance And Administration
- Shared/Various/Other

Responsibility for order processing and for customer service operations generally falls either to the logistics or the marketing and sales departments. Marketing and sales departments have responsibility for sales forecasting in most responding companies.

Purchasing activities are about as likely to report to the manufacturing department as to the logistics department. Manufacturing is the department most likely to have responsibility for warehousing and inventory management of raw materials and work in process inventories.

Companies in our survey are somewhat more likely to assign responsibility to manufacturing versus logistics for master production scheduling, requirements planning, and operations scheduling. Finally, logistics systems planning and database management reports in most cases to the finance and administration function.

Figure G-9 looks at the frequency with which each department was identified as having line responsibility for the 24 logistics activities in Figure G-8. In only 44 percent of the activity-department pairings in the entire database was a logistics activity assigned to the logistics department.

Figure G-9

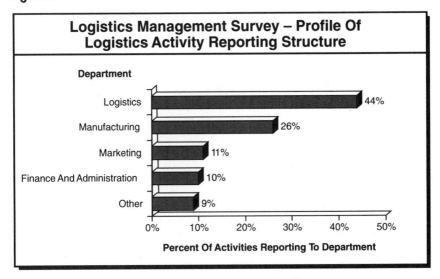

As these two figures indicate, responsibility for managing the entire set of logistics activities in a company very often is shared across two or more functional departments. This means that to operate logistics as a process in these companies will require either significant reassignment of responsibilities or close interfunctional planning and coordination.

CUSTOMER EXPECTATIONS SURVEY DEMOGRAPHICS

Forty-two companies participated in our Customer Expectations Survey. The profile by industry is shown in Figure G-10. Customers of the food, electronics, general merchandise, automotive, and chemicals/plastics industries were the most prevalent. A substantial number of respondents (10 percent) were customers of multiple industries.

For 71 percent of respondents, the primary activity of their business unit was wholesaling or retailing, as one might expect in a customer-oriented survey (see Figure G-11). However, 24 percent were manufacturers, who are customers of raw materials, parts, and component suppliers.

Two-thirds of responses came from corporate level executives, with 30 percent from divisional executives and the remainder from group executives.

Figure G-10

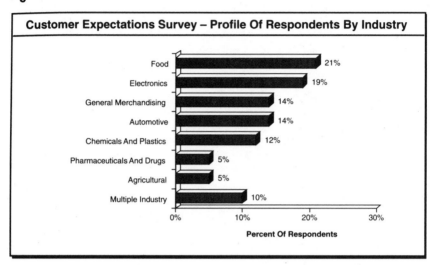

Customer Expectations Survey – Profile Of Respondents By Industry

Figure G-11

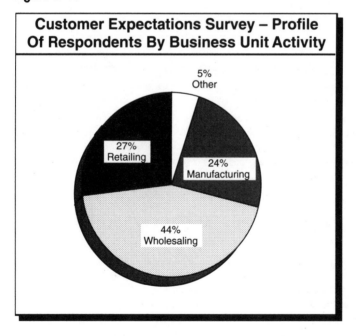

Customer Expectations Survey – Profile Of Respondents By Business Unit Activity

LOGISTICS SERVICE PROVIDER SURVEY

About half of the companies that responded to our Logistics Service Provider survey view themselves as primarily transportation carriers. Another 28 percent have warehouse/terminal operations as their primary focus (see Figure G-12). Twelve percent view themselves as service integrators.

Figure G-12

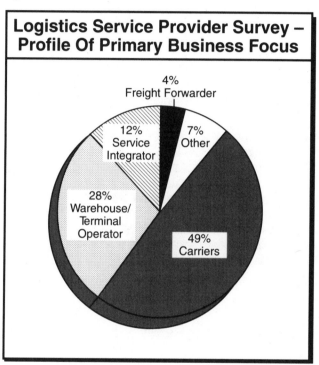

Logistics Service Provider Survey – Profile Of Primary Business Focus

4%
Freight Forwarder

12%
Service
Integrator

7%
Other

28%
Warehouse/
Terminal
Operator

49%
Carriers

Fifty-four percent own all primary distribution assets, while another 32 percent own at least part of their asset base. Figure G-13 profiles the range of services provided by respondents.

INTERPRETING THE DATA

In interpreting the data from this study, three factors should be considered:

1. The profiles of respondents reflect the general makeup of Council of Logistics Management membership and are not necessarily a true cross section of U.S. businesses in terms of company size and industry affiliation.

2. The respondents to the questionnaire are believed to be among the more progressive companies in their efforts to improve logistics quality and productivity. Thus, it is likely that there is a sample bias in favor of those companies that are

actively pursuing improvement opportunities in logistics. Thus, the questionnaire responses are likely to represent the views and experience of the *leaders* in logistics quality and productivity improvement and not the broad average of industry.

3. While every effort was made to standardize the responses to the questionnaires, some questions were subject to interpretation. An example of this is the section addressing productivity improvements. Respondents may have included cost avoidance in their responses to productivity improvement or may not have handled inflation uniformly. In any case, the overall methodology used to interpret productivity gains is similar to that of the 1978 and 1983 studies, so improvement estimates are comparable.

Figure G-13

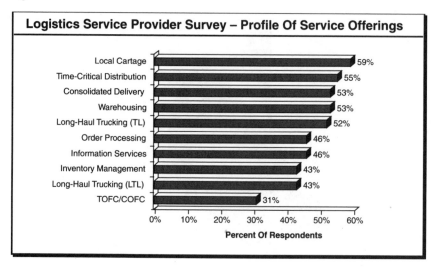

APPENDIX H:
GLOSSARY OF TERMS

ABC Classification: A method of categorizing inventory (purchased or manufactured) items into a descending order of annual dollar usage or sales. This listing is divided into "A," "B," and "C" categories based on the following accumulated percentage of annual dollar usage. Although the breakdown may vary, many companies find that:

- "A" line items represent the top 80 percent of the annual dollar usage or sales.
- "B" line items represent the next 15 percent of the annual dollar usage or sales.
- "C" line items represent the last 5 percent of the annual dollar usage or sales.

Most companies find that the "A" line items represent approximately 20 percent of the total items, "B" line items represent approximately 30 percent of the total items, and "C" line items represent approximately 50 percent of the total items.

"A" Items: Term pertaining to the "A" line items in an ABC classification. Considered to be the most important line items deserving most of the attention, since these line items account for 80 percent of the annual dollar usage or sales.

Attributes Data: Qualitative data that can be counted for recording and analysis. For example, the "on-time delivery" attribute can be counted for shipments using a simple yes/no attribute.

Average: Most commonly the arithmetic mean of a series of numbers (observations), which is calculated by totalling the values in the series and dividing by the number of observations.

Carton: A material handling related term usually referring to a cardboard container. May be similar to case, in the definition of "unit" (below), but generally used in industry when the size and/or weight is much more variable than that of a case. The term "crate" is also similarly used; however, crates are generally of wood or fiberboard construction.

Change Order: A document that amends or changes a purchase order in terms of quantity, date requested, or other pertinent data.

Common Cause: A source of variation that is part of the random variation inherent in the process itself. It can usually be traced to an element of the system that must be corrected by management. (See **Special Cause.**)

Control Chart: A graphic representation of a characteristic of a process. It shows values of some statistic gathered from that characteristic plotted on a scale, along with one or two control limits. Its uses are to determine if a process is in control and to help achieve and maintain statistical control.

Control Limits: Lines on a control chart that are used to judge the significance of variation in a process. Variation beyond a control limit indicates that special causes are affecting the process. Control limits are calculated from process data and should not be confused with specifications.

H

Cost Per Labor Hour: Total labor cost including basic wage or salary plus all fringe benefits and payroll costs. Cost per hour is usually calculated by dividing an employee's total annual costs by total working hours to obtain a total cost per hour worked.

Cost Savings: The dollar difference between the old price for a purchased item and the new, lower price for the item or its substitute, multiplied by the annual purchased quantity.

Cube: A measure of the cubic space available or cubic space used. Usually measured in cubic feet or meters.

Customer Inquiry: A customer's request (transmitted by mail, phone, telex, or fax) for information, expediting, order change, technical literature, or other help related to purchases from the company.

Cycle Time: Usually refers to the length of time between the start and the ultimate completion of an activity.

Deficit Weight: The difference between actual weight and "billed as" weight. "Billed as" weight is sometimes used to obtain a lower cost per hundredweight for transportation by qualifying for rates that apply to a higher weight break. Where deficit weight is large, it may represent an opportunity to change shipping volumes to "use up" the transportation capacity being paid for but not used.

Demand Coverage: The time period for which the expected demand for a product may be met by the existing inventory (i.e., the number of days of inventory on hand).

Demurrage Charge: The cost penalty charged by a carrier for demurrage time.

Demurrage Time: Length of time a carrier's equipment is detained beyond a specified free time for loading or unloading (also know as detention time).

Dock Door: A discrete shipping or receiving location designed for material access or egress.

Dollar Value: Usually refers to the purchased price, manufactured cost, or selling price, depending upon the activity utilizing this input for measurement.

Earned (Cost or Hour) Allowance: The amount of cost or labor time that is allowed to carry out an individual task, usually based on engineered standards.

Error: Wrong product, count, address, price, extension, terms, or any other physical or clerical aspect of a transaction.

Equipment Hours: Length of time a piece of equipment is in operation. Often specified as "run time" but could also apply to the time the piece of equipment is utilized for any function for which it was intended.

Equivalent Vehicle: Conversion on a weight or volume basis to equivalent full truckloads, carloads, bargeloads, etc.

Expedite Request: A document usually generated by inventory or production control and transmitted to purchasing requesting that a particular part or order be processed and delivered more quickly than planned.

Frequency Distribution: A statistical graph that presents a large volume of data in such a way that the mean and distribution (dispersion around the mean) are clearly displayed.

Freight Bill: A bill presented by a for-hire carrier to a shipper (or consignee) for transportation services rendered.

Inventory Locator System: System for determining the specific location of an SKU in the storage area in order to facilitate the order picking activity.

Invoice: An accounting document by which the seller charges the customer for products sold.

Job Order: A specific request for production of a part, assembly, or finished product indicating the quantity needed as well as the date required. This term could be used interchangeably with shop order, production order, or work order.

Labor Dollars: Labor hours multiplied by the actual or standard hourly labor rate. Usually does not include fringe benefits but may be so defined.

Labor Hours: Direct or indirect time spent on a task measured in hours worked. Typically, it does not include vacations, holidays, sick days, etc.

Line: An individual line item entry on an order or other customer transaction, usually involving a specific stock-keeping unit (SKU).

Line Item: A unique item from a product line on which inventory and other records are kept. Usually identified with a specific number for reference.

LTL (Less-Than-Truckload): Shipments of 10,000 pounds or less loaded on a truck.

Linehaul: The point to point movement of freight.

Load Factor: The amount of weight hauled by a vehicle.

Machine (Work) Center: A group of machines that because of similarities may be grouped together for loading considerations. In a nonmanufacturing environment, the term "work center" or "work station" can be substituted for any significant activity that is a part of the logistics process (e.g., warehouse receiving, warehouse order selection).

Make or Buy Decision: The determination of whether a product should be manufactured internally or purchased outside the company.

Nonconformities: Specific occurrences of a condition that do not conform to specifications or requirements. An individual nonconforming unit can have the potential for more than one nonconformity. For example, an order may be delivered late and be damaged. The nonconforming unit is an unacceptable order (from a service standpoint), while the nonconformities are late delivery and damage.

Order: A specific sales transaction generally defined by a sales or purchase order number. This term, when used as a measure of output, may refer to complete or partial orders processed.

Order/Shipping Set: A multipart business form creating a hard copy order and related documentation for input to attendant operating systems, including:

• Warehousing (order picking instructions)
• Transportation (bill of lading)

- Inventory control (stock status update)
- Financial accounting (invoicing)

Pareto's Law: Commonly accepted "rule" that the majority of a particular result comes from a small number of causes. It is often referred to as the "80-20" rule based on the observation that 80 percent of sales (for example) come from 20 percent of products in a product line. (See **ABC Classification.**)

Pallet: Material handling device for unitizing a number of individual cases to facilitate handling. Other unitizing devices include slip-sheets, film wrapping, etc.

P&D (Pickup and Delivery): The local or regional collection or distribution of goods by truck.

Piece: A single unit (case, carton, box, bundle) of a product for handling purposes.

Price Quote: A document received from a vendor indicating a specific price or various prices based upon the quantity of material desired by the customer.

Process: The combination of people, machines and equipment, information, raw materials, and methods that produces a given product or service.

Process Capability: The measured, built-in reproducibility (consistency) of the product or service created by the process. Process capability is determined by using statistical methods. Process capability may then be compared to specification limits to determine if a process can consistently deliver a result within specifications.

Purchase Order: A document that authorizes a vendor to supply a material or service in a specific quantity by a specific time.

Purchase Order Requisition: A document that authorizes the purchase of a material or service and specifies the particular type and quantity.

Purchase Price Variance: The difference between the standard purchase cost of a line item and the actual price paid for the line item, multiplied by the number of units of the line item purchased.

Range: A measure of the variation in a set of data. It is calculated by subtracting the lowest value in the data set from the highest value in the set.

Route: A defined set of pickup/delivery points to be visited by a P&D driver and vehicle.

Route Day: The activities of a P&D driver and vehicle for one day.

Safety Stock: The planned stock level carried to protect against stockouts due to unexpected demand and/or variations in lead time.

Service Time: The elapsed time between shipper's request for transportation service for a shipment and the shipment's delivery to the consignee.

Shipment: An individual release of product to a specific customer. A shipment may be comprised of only part of the customer's order, the entire order, or several orders consolidated into a single shipment.

Sigma: The Greek letter used to designate the estimated standard deviation of a set of data.

SKU: (See **Line Item.**)

Special Cause: A source of variation that is unpredictable, unstable; sometimes called an assignable cause. It is signalled by a point on a control chart that falls beyond the control limits. (See **Common Cause.**)

Specification: In manufacturing, usually an engineering requirement that is used to judge the acceptability of a certain characteristic of a process or product. In a service environment, it may refer to the formal customer service requirements that the company has defined as a part of its service strategy.

Standard Cost: Standard units of input (e.g., labor hours, equipment hours) multiplied by the cost per unit.

Standard Deviation: A measure of the spread of the process output or the spread of a sampling statistic from the process.

Standard Hours Earned: The standard time allotted for an activity cycle multiplied by the number of times the activity is repeated. For example, if unloading a pallet of product from a vehicle should take three minutes and the process is repeated twenty times, one standard hour is earned.

Standard Ton-Miles: A measure calculated by multiplying the number of tons of freight moved in a shipment by the standard origin-destination mileage for the shipment.

Statistical Control: The condition of describing a process from which all special causes have been removed. When a control chart for a process shows all points within control limits and shows no abnormal trends, the process is said to be in statistical control.

Statistical Process Control (SPC): Use of statistical techniques such as control charts to analyze a process or its output.

Stockout: An inventory condition that exists when the onhand quantity is zero or when the net available quantity is zero or negative (i.e., the orders already registered for the line item equal or exceed the available supply).

Stock Order: A production request for the manufacturing of a finished good for inventory.

Stock Rotation: Physically cycling inventory so that the oldest material is removed from stock first.

Stop: A pickup and/or delivery point served by a P&D route.

Storage Location: A geometrically definable position in a storage area, such as a bay, pallet space, bin, etc. Could be expressed in a numerical quantity such as pallet spaces in a rack or in terms of square or cubic feet.

Stratification: The process of classifying data into subgroups based on characteristics or categories.

TL (Truckload): Shipments of more than 10,000 pounds loaded on a truck.

Ton-Miles: A measure calculated by multiplying the number of tons transported by the number of miles they are carried. Hundredweight, barrels, or cubic feet may be substituted for tons if appropriate.

Unit: General term usually referring to the specific quantity of a line item.

Depending upon the specific product and industry characteristics, the term could be expressed in pieces (or multiple pieces), dozens, cases, gallons, cubic feet, barrels, etc. In addition, many companies have internally defined the term to represent a standard volume, weight, or density relationship in order to operationally define products with variable physical characteristics. For example, ten cubic feet of product may be defined as one "unit."

Variables: Those characteristics that can be measured. Examples are transit time (days), order completeness (cases or percent), invoice accuracy (dollars variation). (See **Attributes.**)

Variation: The difference among individual outputs of a process; the sources of variation can be grouped into two major classes: common causes and special causes.

Vehicles: Trucks, railcars, barges, etc.

Vendor: A company or individual that supplies goods or services.

Weight: Generally expressed in pounds, hundredweight (CWT), or tons. May be either actual physical weight or weight recorded on bill of lading, which may be higher than actual to obtain a more favorable rate. (See **Deficit Weight.**)

APPENDIX I:
BIBLIOGRAPHY AND REFERENCES

BOOKS

Akao, Yoji, Translation by Glenn H. Mazur, *Quality Function Deployment, Integrating Customer Requirements into Product Design*, Productivity Press, Cambridge, MA (1990)

Albrecht, Karl and Ron Zemke, *Service America!, Doing Business in the New Economy*, Warner Books, New York, NY (1985)

Asaka, Tetsuichi (General Editor) and Kazuo Ozeki (Editor), *Handbook of Quality Tools, The Japanese Approach*, Productivity Press, Cambridge, MA (1988)

Band, William A., *Creating Value for Customers, Designing and Implementing a Total Corporate Strategy*, John Wiley & Sons, Inc., New York, NY (1991)

Bowersox, Donald J., Ph.D., Patricia H. Dougherty, Ph.D., Cornelia L. Droge, Ph.D., Dale S. Rogers, Daniel L. Wardlow, *Leading Edge Logistics, Competitive Positioning for the 1990s,* for The Council of Logistics Management, Oak Brook, IL (1989)

Boyett, Joseph H., Ph.D., and Henry P. Conn, *Maximum Performance Management, How to Manage and Compensate People to Meet World Competition*, Glenbridge Publishing Ltd., Macomb, IL (1988)

Boyett, Joseph H., Ph.D., and Henry P. Conn, *Workplace 2000, The Revolution Reshaping American Business*, A Dutton Book, Penguin Books USA Inc., New York, NY (1991)

Buzzell, Robert D. and Bradley T. Gale, *The PIMS Principles, Linking Strategy to Performance*, The Free Press, Division of McMillan Inc., New York, NY (1987)

Byham, William C., Ph.D. with Jeff Cox, *Zapp! The Lightning of Empowerment, How to Improve Productivity, Quality, and Employee Satisfaction*, Harmony Books, New York, NY (1988)

Camp, Robert C., *Benchmarking, The Search for Industry Best Practices that Lead to Superior Performance*, Quality Press (American Society for Quality Control), Milwaukee, WI, and Quality Resources (A Div. of Kraus-Thomson Organization Ltd.), White Plains, NY (1989)

Crosby, Philip B., *Let's Talk Quality, 96 Questions You Always Wanted to Ask Phil Crosby*, A Plume Book, Penguin Books USA, Inc., New York, NY (1990)

Crosby, Philip B., *Quality is Free, The Art of Making Quality Certain*, A Mentor Book, McGraw Hill Book Co., New York, NY (1979)

Crosby, Philip B., *Quality Without Tears, The Art of Hassle-Free Management*, A Plume Book, McGraw Hill Book Co., New York, NY (1984)

Daniels, Aubrey C., Ph.D., *Performance Management, Improving Quality Productivity Through Positive Reinforcement,* Third Edition, Revised, Performance Management Publications, Tucker, GA (1989)

Davidow, William H. and Bro Uttal, *Total Customer Service, The Ultimate Weapon,* Harper & Row Publishers, New York, NY (1989)

Deming, W. Edwards, *Out of the Crisis,* Massachusetts Institute of Technology, Center for Advanced Engineering Study, Cambridge, MA (Eighth Printing 1989)

Denton, D. Keith, *Quality Service, How America's Top Companies are Competing in the Customer-Service Revolution ... and How You Can Too,* Gulf Publishing Co., Houston, TX (1989)

Drucker, Peter F., *Managing for Results, Economic Tasks and Risk-taking Decisions,* Perennial Library, Harper & Row Publishers, New York, NY (1986)

Ernst & Young Quality Improvement Consulting Group, *Total Quality, An Executive's Guide for the 1990s,* Dow Jones-Irwin, Homewood, IL (1990)

Feigenbaum, A.V., *Total Quality Control, Engineering and Management, The Technical and Managerial Field for Improving Product Quality, Including Its Reliability, and for Reducing Operating Costs and Losses,* McGraw-Hill Book Company, New York, NY (1983)

Gabor, Andrea, *The Man Who Discovered Quality, How W. Edwards Deming Brought the Quality Revolution to America,* Times Books, Random House, New York, NY (1990)

Garvin, David A., *Managing Quality, The Strategic and Competitive Edge,* The Free Press, New York, NY (1988)

Gitlow, Howard S., *Planning for Quality, Productivity, and Competitive Position,* Dow Jones-Irwin, Homewood, IL (1990)

Goldratt, Eliyahu M. and Jeff Cox, *The Goal, A Process of Ongoing Improvement,* Revised Edition, North River Press, Inc., Croton-on-Hudson, NY (1986)

Grieco, Peter L., Jr., Michael W. Gozzo, Jerry W. Claunch, *Supplier Certification: Achieving Excellence,* PT Publications, Inc., Plantsville, CT (1988)

Guaspari, John, *I Know It When I See It, A Modern Fable About Quality,* American Management Association, New York, NY (1985)

Guaspari, John, *The Customer Connection, Quality for the Rest of Us,* American Management Association, New York, NY (1988)

Hale, Roger L., Donald D. Carlton, Ronald E. Kowal, Tim K. Sehnert, *Made in the USA, How One Company Helps Satisfy Customer Needs Through Strategic Supplier Quality Management,* Tennant Company, Minneapolis, MN (1991)

Hall, Robert W. with American Production & Inventory Control Society, *Zero Inventories,* Dow Jones-Irwin, Homewood, IL (1983)

Harrington, Dr. H. J., *Business Process Improvement, The Breakthrough Strategy for Total Quality, Productivity, and Competitiveness,* Sponsored by the American Society for Quality Control, McGraw-Hill, Inc., New York, NY (1991)

Heskett, James L., W. Earl Sasser, Jr. and Christopher W.L. Hart, *Service Breakthroughs, Changing the Rules of the Game,* The Free Press, A Division of McMillan, Inc., New York, NY (1990)

Johnson, Perry L., *Keeping Score: Strategies and Tactics for Winning the Quality War,* Harper Business, Ballinger Publishing Co., New York, NY (1989)

Juran, J.M., *Juran on Planning for Quality,* The Free Press, A Division of McMillan, Inc., New York, NY (1988)

Juran, J.M. (Editor in Chief), Frank M. Gryna (Associate Editor), *Juran's Quality Control Handbook,* Fourth Edition, McGraw-Hill Book Company, New York, NY (1988)

Kearney, A.T., Inc., *Measuring and Improving Productivity in Physical Distribution,* for the National Council of Physical Distribution Management, Oak Brook, IL (1984)

LaLonde, Bernard J., Ph.D., Martha C. Cooper, Ph.D., Thomas G. Noordewier, Ph.D., of the College of Business, The Ohio State University, *Customer Service, A Management Perspective,* for the Council of Logistics Management, Oak Brook, IL (1988)

LaLonde, Bernard J., Ph.D. (Mason Professor of Transportation and Logistics) and Martha C. Cooper, Ph.D., (Associate Professor of Marketing and Logistics), *Partnerships in Providing Customer Service: A Third-Party Perspective,* for the Council of Logistics Management, Oak Brook, IL (1989)

LeBoeuf, Michael, Ph.D., *How to Win Customers and Keep Them for Life,* Berkley Books, New York, NY (1987)

Lele, Milind M. and Jagdish N. Sheth, *The Customer is Key: Gaining an Unbeatable Advantage Through Customer Satisfaction,* John Wiley & Sons, New York, NY (1987)

Olson, Ted, Craig Giffi, Aleda V. Roth, Gregory M. Seal, *Competing in World-Class Manufacturing: America's 21st Century Challenge,* National Center for Manufacturing Sciences, Business One Irwin, Homewood, IL (1990)

Peters, Tom and Nancy Austin, *A Passion for Excellence, The Leadership Difference,* Warner Books, New York, NY (1985)

Peters, Tom, *Thriving on Chaos, Handbook for a Management Revolution,* Harper & Row, New York, NY (1987)

Plossl, George W., *Managing in the New World of Manufacturing, How Companies Can Improve Operations to Compete Globally,* Prentice Hall, Englewood Cliffs, NJ (1991)

Porter, Michael E., *Competitive Advantage, Creating and Sustaining Superior Performance,* The Free Press, New York, NY (1985)

Schonberger, Richard J., *Building a Chain of Customers, Linking Business Functions to Create the World Class Company,* The Free Press, New York, NY (1990)

Sloma, Richard S., *How to Measure Managerial Performance,* MacMillan Publishing Co., Inc., New York, NY (1980)

Stalk, George, Jr., Thomas M. Hout, *Competing Against Time, How Time-based Competition is Reshaping Global Markets,* The Free Press, New York, NY (1990)

Talley, Dorsey J., *Total Quality Management, Performance and Cost Measures: The Strategy for Economic Survival,* ASQC Quality Press, Milwaukee, WI (1991)

Walton, Mary, *Deming Management at Work,* G.P. Putnam's Sons, New York, NY (1990)

Whiteley, Richard C., *The Customer-Driven Company, Moving from Talk to Action,* Addison-Wesley Publishing Co., Inc., Reading, MA (1991)

Zeithaml, Valarie A., A. Parasuraman, Leonard L. Berry, *Delivering Quality Service, Balancing Customer Perceptions and Expectations,* The Free Press, A Division of McMillan, Inc., New York, NY (1990)

Zemke, Ron with Dick Schaaf, *The Service Edge, 101 Companies that Profit from Customer Care,* New American Library, New York, NY (1989)

PERIODICALS/BULLETINS

Alster, Norm, "What Flexible Workers Can Do," *Fortune,* February 13, 1989

Bennett, Amanda, "Making the Grade with the Customer," *The Wall Street Journal,* November 12, 1990

Bower, Joseph L. and Thomas M. Hout, "Fast Cycle Capability for Competitive Power," *Harvard Business Review,* November-December 1988

Burt, David N., "Managing Suppliers up to Speed," *Harvard Business Review,* July-August 1989

Council of Logistics Management, "Tract Topic 1: Quality Issues in Logistics," 1990 Annual Conference Program

Dowst, Somerby, "Made in the USA Can Still Be a Quality Label," *Purchasing,* January 19, 1989

Dumaine, Brian, "How Managers Can Succeed Through Speed," *Fortune,* February 13, 1989

Dumaine, Brian, "P&G Rewrites the Marketing Rules," *Fortune,* November 6, 1989

Feare, Tom, "Quick Response: A Revolution Evolves," *Modern Materials Handling,* June 1991

Gill, Mark Stuart, "Stalking Six Sigma," *Business Month,* January 1990

Hart, Christopher W. L., "The Power of Unconditional Service Guarantees," *McKinsey Quarterly,* Summer 1989

Karr, Albert R., "Time is Elastic at Postal Service, Outside Test Finds," *The Wall Street Journal,* November 7, 1990

Kaufman, Steve, "Quest for Quality," *Business Month,* May 1989

Kearney, A.T., Inc., "U.S. Manufacturing Competitiveness," 1988

Kearns, David, "Xerox, Satisfying Customer Needs with a New Culture," *Management Review*, February 1989

Kurt Salmon Associates, "Quick Response Implementation, Action Steps for Retailers, Manufacturers and Suppliers"

Longo, Don, "Quick Response: Quickly Shaping Retail Business," *Discount Store News*, April 15, 1991

Main, Jeremy, "How to Win the Baldrige Award," *Fortune*, April 23, 1990

Martha, Joseph A., "Flexible Distribution Systems Needed; Logistics Technology for Manufacturer/Retail Partnerships," *Transportation and Distribution*, October 1990

McClenahan, John S., "So Long, Salespeople," *Industry Week*, February 18, 1991

Moore, Thomas L., "The Road to Quality," *Fleet Owner*, June 1991

Partch, Ken, "Partnering, A Win-Win Proposition or the Latest Hula-Hoop in Marketing?," *Supermarket Business*, May 1991

Perry, Nancy J., "The Education Crisis: What Business Can Do," *Fortune*, June 4, 1988

Peterson, Laurie, "Coping with the '90s; The Big Squeeze," *Adweek*, November 12, 1990

Quinn, Francis J., "Top 10 Logistics Ideas," *Traffic Management*, October 1990

Semick, J. William, "Accounting for Quality," *Purchasing*, January 19, 1989

Semick, J. William, "Tracking Quality Through the Supply Chain," *Purchasing*, January 18, 1990

Sheehy, Barry, "Hitting the Wall: How to Survive Your Quality Program's First Crisis," *National Productivity Review*, Summer 1990

Simmons, Ted, "Account Management; Food Manufacturers' Accounts with Supermarket Retailers," *Supermarket News*, December 17, 1990

Stundza, Tom, "Can Supplier Rating Be Standardized?," *Purchasing*, November 8, 1990

Taylor, Marianne, "Wal-Mart Prices Itself in the Market," *Chicago Tribune*, April 28, 1991

Tursi, Georgia, "To Improve Quality, Measure Performance," *Transportation and Distribution*, December 1989

United States General Accounting Office, "Management Practices - U.S. Companies Improve Performance Through Quality Efforts," GAO/NSIAD-91-190, May 1991

Walsh, Jr., Francis J., "Current Practices in Measuring Quality," Research Bulletin #234, *The Conference Board*, 1989

Woodruff, David, Karen Lowry Miller, Larry Armstrong, and Thane Peterson, "A New Era for Auto Quality," *Business Week*, October 22, 1990